Multivariate Analysis in Marketing: Theory and Application

Edited by

David A. Aaker
University of California, Berkeley

Wadsworth Publishing Company, Inc.
Belmont, California

To my parents

L. C. Cat. Card No. : 70-172073
ISBN-0-534-00016-9

Printed in the United States of America

1 2 3 4 5 6 7 8 9 10---75 74 73 72 71

Contents

Part Two
The Analysis of Interdependence

Preface

In view of the growing importance of multivariate analysis, it seems appropriate to expose marketing students in particular and business administration and social science students in general to these techniques. The problem is that students rarely get the opportunity to build upon their first course in statistics. There are, of course, multivariate analysis courses of various types given in statistics departments and also courses in econometrics and psychometrics. However, these courses normally have demanding prerequisites in terms of mathematics and statistics and thus are accessible mainly to those who want to be professional analysts.

This book is intended as a supplementary text for a market research course, a marketing models course, or a second statistics course. The objective is to provide some real understanding of the nature, the power, and the limitations of multivariate analysis for those whose only background is that acquired in a first course in statistics. Although the reader should be familiar with estimation and hypothesis testing, facility with matrix algebra and calculus is not assumed. However, those with a more advanced background should still find the book to be a useful overview and reference. The book is also designed for the professional researcher who wants to update his knowledge or to review these techniques in a systematic manner.

Marketing problems are inherently multidimensional. Customer types are described along a wide variety of dimensions. Stores and brands are perceived and evaluated with respect to many different attributes. To approach and understand multidimensional problems, researchers and managers are increasingly turning to multivariate analysis. The computer has made such techniques economical and accessible. Analysis now need not be inhibited because of practical considerations. At the same time, exciting new advances have been made in multidimensional scaling and preference mapping. Further, techniques such as simultaneous-equation regression analysis, canonical analysis, and cluster analysis are just beginning to be applied to marketing problems. The result has been fresh approaches to difficult marketing decision areas and a growing reliance upon multivariate analysis.

The rapid growth of multivariate analysis in marketing does not represent another technical fad which will soon burn out. Professor Jagdish Sheth, in an article entitled, "The Multivariate Revolution in Marketing Research," explains why.[1] First, he notes that many of the fads "presumed considerable knowledge about the response to marketing efforts at a time when no one actually understood how the marketing mix is related to market reactions." In contrast, "multivariate methods are largely empirical, deal with the market reality by working backward from reality to conceptualization." Second, they are based upon familiar univariate techniques so that they are less susceptible to being initially oversold. Third, they represent appropriate approaches to "the most pressing need of marketing research," which is to obtain "the ability to analyze complex data." Finally, multivariate analysis consists of a wide variety of flexible techniques whereas most fads involve highly specialized research tools.

Each section of the book contains both articles which set forth the theory and articles which illustrate the theory in a specific application. When one is learning the theory or when a practical problem is confronted, it is instructive and reassuring to see how others have applied it. Conversely, merely seeing applications, however well done, is inadequate. A knowledge of the underlying assumptions and an understanding of the proper interpretation of the results are critical to the use of the techniques.

M. G. Kendall, a British statistician, has suggested that multivariate analysis can be naturally divided into two areas: the analysis of dependence and the analysis of interdependence.[2] In the former, a variable or set of variables is to be predicted by or explained by other variables. Regression analysis is an example. In the latter, no one variable or group of variables is the focus of the analysis. The procedures operate on all variables in the set. Factor analysis is an example. This book has been similarly divided into two parts. Each part contains an introduction to the subject which relates the various sections. In addition, an introduction to each section highlights the contribution of each article to the section and attempts to supply any important concepts which were not covered adequately in the articles.

I owe a great debt of gratitude to those marketing researchers and practitioners who have over the years pioneered in the use of multivariate analysis in marketing. In this spirit a special acknowledgment is due Professors Ronald E. Frank, Paul E. Green, and William F. Massy for their contributions during the past decade.

I also wish to thank Andrew Mitchell, now Assistant Professor at Pennsylvania State University, who made many contributions to this book. Its quality would have been much lower were it not for his challenges to editorial decisions. The introductory sections were read by Professors James M. Carman and John G. Myers of the University of California at Berkeley, Donald G.

---

[1] Jagdish N. Sheth, "The Multivariate Revolution in Marketing Research," *Journal of Marketing*, 35 (January, 1971), 13–19.
[2] M. G. Kendall, "Factor Analysis as a Statistical Technique," *Journal of the Royal Statistical Society*, 121 (1950), 60–73.

Morrison of Columbia University, Lester A. Neidell of Georgia Tech., Ingram Olkin of Stanford University, and Leonard J. Parsons of Claremont Graduate School. Their helpful comments improved the material immeasurably. Occasionally, their advice was ignored. As a result, errors undoubtedly remain for which I assume full responsibility. Thanks are also due to my students, a constant source of stimulation, to my family, who cheerfully tolerates my literary efforts, and to my parents, who helped and encouraged me through the educational process.

The Analysis of Dependence

1

In the analysis of dependence a variable, or group of variables, is the focus of the analysis. This variable(s) is called the dependent variable and is explained or predicted by the remaining ones, which are termed independent or explanatory variables. The analysis of dependence is usually oriented toward prediction or toward obtaining information through structural analysis.

When prediction is the objective, the dependent variable(s) is to be predicted given a set of specific values for the independent variables. For example, a model might be desired that would predict sales, given expenditures on advertising, promotion, and direct sales (field salesmen). Such a model might form the basis for conditional sales forecasts—those conditional on marketing inputs. Nearly all management decisions depend upon accurate forecasts of key variables. Of course, if the market environment changes, the analyst must determine if model assumptions have been affected and modifications are needed.

In structural analysis, information is obtained from a knowledge of functional forms and parameter values. For example, we might identify diminishing returns to advertising by determining the relationship of advertising to sales. By studying the parameter values, the variables that are the most effective in predicting the dependent variable might be identified. If promotion seems unrelated to sales, whereas advertising is a significant explanatory variable, the market mix might deserve scrutiny. The objective in structural analysis is to gain understanding of the process being modeled—to test theoretical and conceptual hypotheses. Structural questions often imply a cause-effect relationship. As in correlation analysis, however, any causal judgments must be made very cautiously, for a statistical relationship—even though quite real with respect to a data set—can often have more than one causal explanation.

The different methods that constitute the analysis of dependence can be categorized by the number of dependent variables, the number of equations or relationships, and the type of measurement scale employed by the variables. There are four types of scales: nominal, ordinal, interval, and ratio.

In a nominal scale, the numbers merely label or identify objects. The number on a football jersey is an example. One type of nominal variable

1

frequently encountered in the analysis of dependence is the 0–1 binary variable, sometimes called a dummy variable. Suppose we wanted to identify a market group. Those families who are heavy users of a product could be assigned a 1, and all other families a 0. Ordinal scales are used to rank objects along certain dimensions. There is no implication, however, that the difference between objects ranked 8 and 9 is the same as that between objects ranked 1 and 2. In contrast, an interval scale has a constant unit of measurement. The difference between two numbers has the same meaning no matter where on the scale the difference is taken. Interval scales do not necessarily have a unique zero. A temperature scale is a good example. A five-degree difference, in an intuitive sense, has the same meaning throughout the scale. However, sixty degrees is not considered twice as cold as thirty degrees, since the zero point is arbitrary. Ratio scales are interval scales that have a unique zero. Length and weight are examples. Clearly, one foot is one third of three feet.

Variables used in the analysis of dependence are either nominally (usually 0–1 binary) scaled or interval (or ratio) scaled. In regression analysis, discriminant analysis, and canonical analysis, the independent variables are assumed to be interval scaled, although nominal scales are also used occasionally, as we shall see. In regression analysis, a single, interval-scaled, dependent variable appears, whereas in canonical analysis there is more than one. In contrast, discriminant analysis has a nominally scaled dependent variable. In simultaneous-equation regression analysis, a system of equations is considered simultaneously. In experimental design models, the independent variables are nominal and the dependent variable is interval scaled. It is, in this respect, the reverse of discriminant analysis. The analysis of covariance is an exception to experimental design models in that one or more interval variables are added to the nominal independent variables. These distinctions will become clearer as we proceed.

It should be noted that all techniques for the analysis of dependence are closely related, as the classification system sketched above suggests. Thus, particular problems that are discussed in one section will often apply to the others.

A. Regression Analysis

For analyzing dependence, regression analysis is the most commonly used technique. Its underlying theory is also the most developed. In regression analysis, a single, interval-scaled, dependent variable is to be predicted or explained by a set of independent variables which are assumed to be interval scaled.

In the first article in this section, Massy provides a solid theoretical foundation for the analysis of dependence in general and regression analysis in particular. He presents a lucid discussion of such issues as bias, efficiency, and multicollinearity, all of which pervade the analysis of dependence. Bias in a parameter estimate can be caused by several problems, but one of the most serious is that of model misspecification—for example, the omission of an independent variable that should be included. If the omitted variable is related to or correlated with an included variable, the coefficient of the included one will, in part, represent the indirect impact of the omitted one and thus be biased. When constructing the model, the analyst must include all relevant variables, or, if that is not possible, must recognize that their impact can appear indirectly through the included variables. An efficient estimate is one that has a small sampling error or variance relative to other estimators. The object of statistical parameter estimation is usually to obtain estimates that are unbiased and have small variances. Multicollinearity arises when independent variables are correlated and it becomes difficult to separate the individual effects of the variables involved. If sales are to be explained by advertising and dollar promotion and the two are highly correlated (both are increased and decreased together), then it is difficult to determine which of the two is causing the changes in sales.

Massy also sets forth the assumptions of the regression model. It is not enough to learn how to interpret a model. The underlying assumptions must be understood so their validity in a given situation may be evaluated. The sensitivity of the model's interpretations to the assumptions (the robustness of the model), is, of course, also important, as is a knowledge of how to adjust the model to overcome the failure of critical assumptions to hold.

Palda discusses the evaluation of regression results. He presents the R^2 statistic, which represents the percent of the original dependent variable variation that has been explained by the model. This statistic is a descriptive and widely used measure of a regression model. However, Palda correctly notes that a test demanding that the model predict is much superior. This issue will again emerge in the discussion of discriminant analysis.

A fortuitous property of the assumptions of the regression model is that if one fails, there is a good chance that others will, too. Further, it is often possible to correct matters by making a transformation, such as logarithmic, on all or some of the variables involved. For example, if sales were not a linear function of advertising, we might consider the relationship between sales and the logarithm of advertising. Frank suggests some transformations that are often effective and notes what assumptions they will affect.

Although the independent variables are assumed to be interval scaled in regression analysis, nominal variables are sometimes also inserted. For many applications, the analyst can proceed with the normal interpretation of the results. Claycamp presents a model that uses 0–1 binary variables—termed, in this context, dummy variables.

The Claycamp model is a time-series model, which means that the data represent successive time periods. In such a model the analyst must be concerned with serial correlation—the error terms are not independent; a large positive error in one period is likely to be followed by another positive error in the next period. Serial correlation was not a problem in the Claycamp study, but when it exists, it can cause inefficient parameter (coefficient) estimates and biased (understated) estimates of parameter (coefficient) variances. The Durbin-Watson test for serial correlation is often used in time-series studies when this problem is suspected. The problem can usually be reduced by using the change in the variable value—that is, the change in sales from one period to another—instead of the variable value itself. The Aaker-Day paper presents another example of a time-series model in which the Durbin-Watson test was employed. It also presents a distributed-lag model, a model that handles carry-over effects—the effects that carry over from one time period to the next. For example, advertising is thought to have both an effect on immediate sales and a carry-over effect on future sales.

Hughes presents a cross-section model for which data were gathered across people instead of through time. Thus, serial correlation and carry-over effects are not a problem. He uses one of the transformations suggested by Frank.

A central tool of structural analysis is the hypothesis test that a regression coefficient is actually zero, and that a non-zero coefficient appeared only by chance. The test uses the t value, which is the estimated regression coefficient divided by its standard error. For example, if the normal distribution was used to approximate the t distribution and the (real) coefficient was actually zero, there would be only one chance in twenty that a t value would exceed 1.96. If a t value of such magnitude occurred, the analyst would be reasonably confident that the coefficient was not zero. Claycamp reports the t values, and Hughes reports the standard deviations of the coefficients from which the t values are easily obtained.

1

William F. Massy: Statistical Analysis of Relations between Variables

Knowledge of a cause and effect link implies that we understand a relationship between two or more variables. We must search for independent or explanatory variables that (1) account for a substantial fraction of the behavior of the dependent variable under study, and (2) appear reasonable in terms of our subjective understanding of the problem. This chapter is devoted to the study of statistical techniques that can help to determine the form and extent of the relationship between a dependent and one or more independent variables.

Introduction to the Analysis of Relationships

The procedures to be discussed below are designed to provide measures of *statistical association*, that is, the extent to which two or more variables tend to change together. Association alone, however, can never be sufficient to establish a causal link between different variables, since statistical measures of association are very sensitive to the effects of extraneous variables. An analyst who obtains a high correlation (a measure of statistical association to be discussed below) between the birth rate in India and the United States gross national product, for example, had best think twice before concluding that one *causes* the other. Statistical association is only half the story; few reasonable men would agree that there is a causal link between the two. In this case, both births and GNP are growing through time as the result of their own (independent) causal mechanisms; since both are highly correlated with time, they are correlated with each other. This effect is known as spurious correlation, which might better be called *spurious causal association*. We emphasize that there is nothing wrong with the correlation measure. It shows a real statistical association, but the conclusion of causality is spurious because of the extraneous factor, time.

The validity of causal interpretations based on statistical association depend upon the effects of variables that have not been specifically included in the analysis. Real art is required in order to assess the effects of uncontrolled (and usually unmeasured) variables. Much of the discussion presented

---

Reprinted with deletions from Frank, Kuehn, Massy, *Quantitative Techniques in Marketing Analysis*, "Statistical Analysis of Relations between Variables" by Massy (Homewood, Ill.: Richard D. Irwin, Inc.), pp. 56–95.

below will be aimed at developing criteria for deciding whether the effects of an excluded variable are likely to spoil the causal interpretation of a statistical analysis.

Many of these criteria can only be evaluated in terms of the analyst's subjective judgment: there are few statistical tests which can provide "scientific" assurance that the data's meaning is really what it appears. Unfortunately, many people believe that data speak for themselves. They do not, and any analyst who looks *only* to his tables and charts is in for some rude surprises. In the sections that follow we will see that the same set of data can be interpreted in many different ways. Only by thinking over what he already knows about the particular problem in question can the analyst decide which of the alternative conclusions is the most reasonable.

It does not make sense to throw away knowledge obtained from previous experience when we begin the analysis of a particular set of statistical data. Besides its critical role in the interpretation of causal relations, prior knowledge can be put to work in the following ways:

1. We can choose the *statistical procedure* which best fits our problem and the type of data which is available.
2. We can choose a *structural model* to provide a framework in which to apply the statistical procedures and interpret their results.
3. We can assess the *amount of information* contributed by our statistical analysis in terms of our needs and what we already know.

Problems (2) and (3) will be discussed briefly here; (1) will be an independent part of each of the following sections.

Models

A model can be viewed as an hypothesis about the way the world operates. In the most general sense, it is a *collection of statements about the way in which certain variables are causally related to one another.*

All of us make use of models in carrying on our everyday lives. Business decisions are no exception to this rule. A marketing executive might say to himself:

> If I cut my price to customer X in Kansas City, my largest competitor will cut his everywhere. I believe this for two reasons: (1) the competitor's general pricing policy, as publicly stated on numerous occasions, implies this kind of retaliation; and (2) when we tried to shave a price in Cincinnati a few months ago, he *did* cut across the board. A national price cut on this product would be disastrous; therefore, I will hold the line in Kansas City.

The foregoing is an example of a simple model of competitive behavior. The executive probably has a high degree of confidence about the truth of his hypothesis, since it is based on both a priori and empirical evidence: the competitor has said he would cut price if challenged in any one market, and he did. The forecast of the competitor's behavior, which was based on this model, is highly believable.

If, on the other hand, our hypothetical executive knew only about his competitor's reaction to the price cut in Cincinnati, it would be very dangerous to infer that the action was part of a consistent long-run policy and would be repeated under similar circumstances; many other equally plausible reasons are possible. By supplementing this observation with subjective knowledge about the competitor's general policy, acquired gradually over a period of time, the behavior actually observed takes on new meaning. We will see that many statistical techniques derive their power from the ability of the user to specify the kind of relationship he expects to obtain.

Models must be rich enough to take account of the relevant and important variables. Nevertheless, complication is not desirable per se. The temperament of the secretary to the president of the competing company would not normally be included in the model given above (although that of her boss might). One of a model's advantages is that it is an *abstraction* from the real process being described. Only the variables that are relevant and important are included, allowing attention to be focused upon them and not diverted along blind alleys. This view is compatible with the principle of *parsimony of variables,* from the philosophy of science: the simplest model that can adequately describe the phenomenon under study should be adopted. On the other hand, too much abstraction reduces the model's usefulness in the solution of real problems.

Verbal models are often inefficient tools for the interpretation of empirical data. If the data are quantitative, it is usually best to describe the model in terms of mathematical equations. The mathematical model implies no more than the word model and can be constructed using similar information. Its advantage is that it is unambiguous and lends itself to algebraic manipulation and statistical analysis. The "relationships" discussed in this paper are usually posed in mathematical terms. They are nothing more nor less than simple models of the behavior under study.

Information

It is easy to see that an analysis of empirical data will contribute some information (however small in amount) to the problem under study. The amount of information so contributed can be measured in many kinds of problems. In turn, this provides the basis for appraising the *efficiency* of alternative statistical procedures.

The concept of information is closely related to a well-known measure of statistical dispersion, the *variance* (the square of the standard deviation). Denoted by the symbol σ^2, the variance of any statistical quantity is defined as the average of the squared deviations of that quantity from its mean or expected value. While the variance may serve merely as a summary of the degree of dispersion present in a particular set of known numbers, it usually is used as a measure of the amount of random fluctuation associated with the estimate of a statistical parameter, of the kinds discussed in later sections. The theory of random errors and the calculation of variances and standard deviations are covered in almost all basic statistics texts.[1]

A statistical estimate of the value of any quantity is subject to errors of estimation; their source will be discussed in connection with the various statistical procedures covered below. For now, it is enough to understand that the *precision* of any estimate is a function of the likely size of these errors. Providing that no bias is present, precision is measured by the variance of the estimate. The smaller the variance, the more precise is the estimate on average.

Bias can occur for one of two reasons:

1. The methods by which the original data were collected were incorrect. If the data are obtained by sample survey, for example, bias may be introduced by: (*a*) improper procedure in selecting the sample, leading to a sample that was not representative of the underlying population (for example, through failure to follow up on the nonrespondents); or (*b*) errors in the measuring process itself, such as faulty interviewing methods or questionnaire design, leading to answers that do not mean what was intended (for example, through inadvertently asking "leading" questions). These problems are extremely important for marketing analysts, but they are beyond the scope of this paper.
2. The statistical procedures used to analyze the data were improperly specified. Later in this paper we shall see that some statistical techniques will, if improperly used, yield biased estimates of the effects of particular variables, even though the original data are unbiased.

The ideas about information developed below are based on the assumption that both the data and the statistical procedures utilized are unbiased. The latter assumption will be relaxed in the subsequent sections, but we will continue to assume that our data are "good" throughout the chapter.

While the variance of an estimate may be used to test hypotheses or to establish confidence intervals according to the standard techniques of statistical inference,[2] we will consider only its role as a measure of the amount

---

[1] Cf. William A. Spurr, Lester S. Kellogg, and John H. Smith, *Business and Economic Statistics* (rev. ed.; Homewood Ill.: Richard D. Irwin, Inc., 1961), chaps. ix-xiii.

[2] *Ibid.*, chaps. xiii and xiv.

of information which the estimate contributes to our knowledge about the true state of the world.

For unbiased estimates with normally distributed errors, for which the variance is known, the amount of information contained is defined as the reciprocal of the variance.[3] If we are trying to estimate the average income of families in the United States, for example, we would define the amount of information contained in a given sample of families as

$$I_s = \frac{1}{\sigma_{\overline{X}_s}{}^2}$$

where $\overline{X}_s$ is the average income for families in the sample (s), and I_s is the amount of information in (s). If the sample median (the income of the middle family, where all families have been listed in order of income level) had been used as an estimate of the average income of the population, the amount of information available would have been smaller: other things being equal it can be shown that the variance of the sample median is larger than that of the sample mean. The sample median is said to be a less *efficient* estimator of the population average than is the sample mean.[4]

It is obvious that if two statistical procedures measure the same thing and cost about the same, we would do better to use the one that was more efficient, that is, the one that contained the most information. When we speak of reducing the variance of an estimate, increasing the amount of information contained in it, or improving its efficiency, we will be talking about the same thing. We will want to use statistical procedures that are as efficient as possible, given the level of accuracy required in the final results and the amount of money we are able to spend.

The simplest way to learn about relations between variables is to form the data into an array. If done graphically, the array is called a *scatter diagram*, or, if graphical analysis is not desired, the data can be arranged in a *cross-classification table*. This technique will be discussed in the next section.

While arrays offer a quick and relatively easy method for evaluating gross relationships in data, a more objective form of analysis is required if subtle and partially hidden relationships are to be uncovered. A number of statistical procedures have been developed for measuring various types of relationships which may be found in empirical data. Two of the most important ones, correlation and regression, will be discussed below.

---

[3] Robert Schlaifer, *Probability and Statistics for Business Decisions* (New York: McGraw-Hill Book Co., Inc., 1959), p. 443.

[4] For large samples the sample median provides unbiased estimates of the population mean with 64 percent of the efficiency of the sample mean: R. L. Anderson and T. A. Bancroft, *Statistical Theory in Research* (New York, McGraw-Hill Book Co., Inc., 1952), p. 95.

Cross-Classification

Arrays are designed to allow the visual interpretation of the relation between two or more variables. The idea can be illustrated in terms of some hypothetical data on an "apparel" firm's sales. Let us assume that the company has prepared data on its sale of dog sweaters for a sample of 18 metropolitan areas in the United States. These data, together with that for consumers' effective buying income and an index of minimum winter temperatures in each of the areas, are presented in Table 1.

Table 1.   *Warm* Brand Canine Coats: Yearly Sales by Metropolitan Area and Effective Buying Income and Average January Temperature

Area*	Warm Brand Sales (per Licensed Dog)† (Units × 10⁻³)	Effective Buying Income‡ per Family ($ × 10³)	Average January Temperature§ (°F)
Atlanta	2.9	7.15	44.0
Baltimore	4.5	7.31	35.5
Chattanooga	1.6	5.54	42.5
Chicago	5.1	8.17	25.7
Cincinnati	2.6	6.74	32.6
Dallas	3.5	6.79	45.8
Detroit	4.5	8.10	25.5
Fort Lauderdale	1.9	5.79	68.0
Houston	4.1	6.86	54.2
Macon	1.1	5.76	46.8
Miami	3.4	7.13	68.0
Milwaukee	5.3	7.69	20.6
Minneapolis-St. Paul	3.7	7.13	13.1
Mobile	2.6	5.92	52.8
New Orleans	4.2	6.46	53.5
New York	5.5	8.36	32.1
Oklahoma City	1.3	6.23	37.6
Philadelphia	5.4	7.97	34.4

* Standard metropolitan areas as defined by the U.S. Department of Commerce.
† Hypothetical.
‡ *Survey of Buying Power (Sales Management,* 1961).
§ *Rand McNally Commercial Atlas and Marketing Guide,* 1958.

We begin by looking at sales and income. While Table 1 presents the data for inspection, it is not an *array* because no effort has been made to throw the assumed relationship into prominence. In contrast, Figure 1 gives the *scatter* of sales values upon income. Each point on the diagram refers to a particular metropolitan area, with its Y and X coordinates being that area's sales and income values, respectively. High income areas tend to have high sales, and vice versa, although the relationship is not perfect.

Two other kinds of arrays can be based upon Table 1. Both are cross-classification tables but each focuses on a different attribute of the data. Table 2-A is a tabular summary of the scatter diagram. The values of sales and income are divided into ranges, and the number of points falling into each cell are counted. The resulting table, often called an *enumeration table*, thus gives the number of geographic areas having the specified magnitudes of

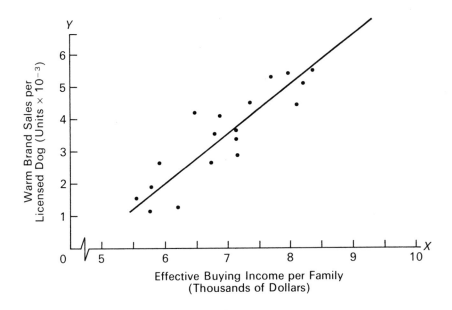

Figure 1. Scatter of Sales on Income for *Warm* Brand Canine Coats, based on the Data in Table 1

Table 2. Cross-Classification of Sales and Income for *Warm* Brand Canine Coats.

A. Number of Areas Having Specified Values for Sales and Income

Income ($1,000)

Y \ X	5.5–5.99	6.0–6.49	6.5–6.99	7.0–7.49	7.5–7.99	8.0–8.49	Row Totals
Sales ($\times 10^{-3}$) 5–5.9	0	0	0	0	2	2	4
4–4.9	0	1	1	1	0	1	4
3–3.9	0	0	1	2	0	0	3
2–2.9	1	0	1	1	0	0	3
1–1.9	3	1	0	0	0	0	4
Column totals	4	2	3	4	2	3	18

B. Average Sales for Areas Having Specified Values for Income

Income ($1,000)

Y \ X	5.5–5.99	6.0–6.49	6.5–6.99	7.0–7.49	7.5–7.99	8.0–8.49	Grand Average
Average sales ($\times 10^{-3}$)	1.8	2.9	3.4	3.6	5.3	5.0	3.5

* Based on the scatter diagram in Figure 1.

sales and income. Table 2-B presents another kind of summary: the average value of sales for all the areas having the specified levels of income. It focuses attention directly upon the assumed dependent variable, sales, and is sometimes called an *attributes table*.

Correlation Analysis

Two variables are said to be highly correlated if the degree of *linear dependence* between them is large. The correlation coefficient, denoted by the symbol r_{XY}, is a summary measure of the association between two variables, X and Y, that is present in a particular set of data. It is a quantitative measure of the extent to which the points in a scatter like that presented in Figure 1 tend to lie on a straight line. If their trend is upward and to the right, as is the case for the sales-income array, $r_{(Sales\text{-}Income)}$ will be positive. If the reverse had been true, it would have been negative. The coefficient is defined so that its value must always lie between $+1$ and -1: it is $+1$ if all the points in the scatter lie on an upward sloping straight line, and -1 if all of them lie on a line that slopes downward. If X and Y are not linearly related at all, r_{XY} will be equal to zero.

Simple Correlation

The simple correlation coefficient between X and Y is defined:

$$r_{XY} = \frac{\sum_{i=1}^{n} (X_i - \bar{X})(Y_i - \bar{Y})}{\sqrt{[\sum_{i=1}^{n} (X_i - \bar{X})^2][\sum_{i=1}^{n} (Y_i - \bar{Y})^2]}}$$

The capital Greek letter sigma (Σ) is the symbol for addition: the numerator signifies that the quantity $(X_i - \bar{X})(Y_i - \bar{Y})$ for each of the n observations in the scatter ($i = 1, \ldots, n$) should be added together. The symbols $\bar{X}$ and $\bar{Y}$ refer to the sample averages of X and Y, respectively.[5]

---

[5] For actual computations it is more convenient to use the formula:

$$r_{XY} = \frac{\Sigma XY - \dfrac{(\Sigma X)(\Sigma Y)}{n}}{\sqrt{\left[\Sigma X^2 - \dfrac{(\Sigma X)^2}{n}\right]\left[\Sigma Y^2 - \dfrac{(\Sigma Y)^2}{n}\right]}}$$

where all the necessary quantities may be accumulated on the dials of a desk calculator. Cf. Wilfred J. Dixon and Frank J. Massey, Jr., *Introduction to Statistical Analysis* (New York: McGraw-Hill Book Co., Inc., 1951), pp. 20–21, and 165–69.

The formula given above is equivalent to the following expression:

$$r_{XY} = \frac{\sigma_{XY}}{\sqrt{\sigma_X^2 \sigma_Y^2}}$$

where σ_X^2 and σ_Y^2 are the variances of X and Y. The quantity in the numerator is a measure of the amount of *covariation* that is present in the sample; it is defined in a manner similar to the variance:

$$\sigma_{XY} = \sum_{i=1}^{n} \frac{(X_i - \bar{X})(Y_i - \bar{Y})}{n}$$

Covariance is highly positive if X_i and Y_i values that deviate from their means in the same direction (that is, both positive or both negative) are associated with one another. It is negative if X_i and Y_i for the same observation tend to deviate in opposite directions. In addition, covariance will increase (either in a positive or negative direction) as the variance of X and Y increases.

The correlation coefficient is really a standardized measure of covariation: covariance, σ_{XY}, is divided by the square root of the variance for the particular sample. Standardization allows two correlations to be compared without regard to the amount of variation exhibited by each variable separately.

A number of scatter diagrams and correlation coefficients are presented in Figure 2. Study of these diagrams will develop some feel for the magnitude of the correlation coefficient, given a visual assessment of the degree of association in a particular scatter. Two other facts can be seen as well. (1) the value of r is not affected by the average values of X and Y—only deviations from means enter the correlation formula; and (2) scatters that differ in their direction of trend, but are identical in degree of association (for example, diagrams C and F) yield correlation coefficients that differ only in sign.

Diagrams G through I demonstrate the fact that r_{XY} is a measure of linear association only. While anyone would agree that no relationship between X and Y exists for Diagram G, this can hardly be the case for H and I. The points in H all fall between two concentric circles—hardly a random layout. In I the points lie exactly on the parabola

$$Y = 1.3 + 1.2(X - \bar{X})^2$$

The relationship is exact, but the correlation coefficient is zero because there is no linear term in the parabola! Correlation coefficients measure only the degree of *linear* association that is present in a set of data. If the equation had been:

$$Y = a + b(X - \bar{X}) + c(X - \bar{X})^2$$

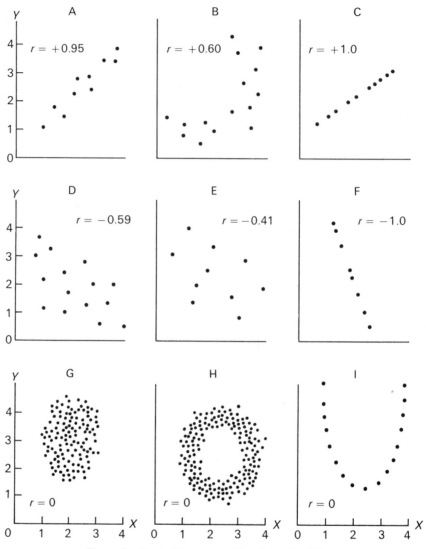

Figure 2.   Scatter Diagrams and Correlation Coefficients

r would have been nonzero because of the linear term, $b(X - \bar{X})$. The correlation would not be perfect; even though the relationship is exact and a linear term is present, the deviations from a linear trend caused by the squared term will have their effect.

The square of r_{XY} is equal to the proportion of the variation of Y and X that is accounted for by the linear relationship between them. In Figure 2-A, the scatter tends along an imaginary line moving upward and to the right. We would say that the line accounts for r^2, or 90 percent of the variation of X

and Y. In diagram C, where all the points lie exactly on the line, 100 percent of their variation is accounted for by the linear relationship.

Correlation coefficients are useful because they summarize the covariation of variables in large bodies of data. All the information about the amount of linear association between sales and income that is contained in the 18 points of Figure 1, for example, is also contained in the single number r. Such "boiling down" of data into a more concise and easily usable form usually pays dividends in the success of later analysis.

Partial Correlation

We now wish to explore the concept of the correlation between two variables when the effects of other variables have been removed. The addition of the third hypothetical variable given in Table 1, winter temperature, to

Table 3. Simple Correlation Matrix for Market Analysis of *Warm* Brand Canine Coats*

	Sales Y	Income X	Temperature Z
Sales Y	r_{YY} 1.0	r_{YX} +0.89	r_{YZ} −0.45
Income X		r_{XX} 1.0	r_{XZ} −0.57
Temperature Z			r_{ZZ} 1.0

* Based on the data in Table 1.

our analysis of the relation between canine coat sales and income in urban areas will illustrate the point.

Table 3 presents the simple correlation matrix for sales (Y), income (X), and January average temperature (Z)—a measure of the winter climate for each metropolitan area. The value of r_{YX} summarizes the linear association between sales and income; it is large and positive, as would be expected from the scatter diagram in Figure 1. The value of r_{YZ} (-0.45) suggests that canine coats are not as eagerly sought in areas having warmer winters, while r_{XZ} (-0.57) shows that the cities in the sample with high income levels tend to have relatively cold winters.

We now ask ourselves whether the combined effect of income and temperature upon sales is really as large as would seem to be implied by the simple correlations r_{YX} and r_{YZ}. If this were the case, the two independent variables should explain $r_{YX}^2 + r_{YZ}^2$ or: $(0.89)^2 + (-0.45)^2 = 0.995$, or $99\frac{1}{2}$ percent of the total variation in sales. But this conclusion would be overly optimistic. Our data for income and temperature are, in part, measures of the same thing: to be precise, exactly r_{XZ}^2 or 32 percent of the information contained in one is also contained in the other. To claim that 99½ percent of the variation in sales among metropolitan areas can be attributed to the combined effects of income and temperature would require that the effect common to both be counted twice. Since claiming the same result twice would be cheating, some other method for assessing the combined contribution of the two independent variables must be found.

The proper approach is to find a measure of the relationship between income and sales, with the effect of variations in temperature taken out, and vice versa. The measures we seek are called *partial correlation coefficients*. The first is designated by $r_{YX.Z}$, which is read "correlation between Y (sales) and X (income) with Z (temperature) held constant;" and the second by "$r_{YX.Z}$," where income is held constant. Their values are shown in Table 4 (the method of computation is discussed below).

Table 4.
Partial Correlation Matrix for Market
Analysis of *Warm* Brand Canine Coats*

	Income X	Temperature Z
Sales Y	$r_{YX.Z}$ +0.85	$r_{YZ.X}$ +0.16
Income X	—	$r_{XZ.Y}$ −0.41

* Computed from the simple correlation
coefficients in Table 3.

Since partial correlation coefficients measure the relationship between the pair of variables listed ahead of the "dot," as it would appear if the third variable had been held constant, $r_{YX.Z}^2$ may be regarded as an approximation of the *net* contribution of X to an explanation of Y. Therefore, the combined effects of income and temperature account for approximately $(0.85)^2 + (0.16)^2 = 0.748$, or 75 percent of the total variation in sales. The sum of the squares of the partial correlations does not exactly give the proportion of the variance of Y explained by X, even though such would seem to be the case on heuristic grounds. The precise value of the statistic is given by the square of the multiple correlation coefficient, which will be discussed presently.

The two partial correlations allow us to disentangle the separate effects of the independent variables. For canine coats, the figures show that, taken by themselves, milder winters are associated with more demand—perhaps because more delicate breeds of dogs reside in the warmer climates. (We re-emphasize that these data are purely hypothetical!) The value of $r_{YZ.X}$ is +0.16, which accounts for only about 2½ percent of the variation in sales, but is positive. The negative simple correlation between Y and Z was really due to the effect of income, which completely swamped that of temperature. On the other hand, r_{YX} is almost equal to $r_{YX.Z}$: Z is a relatively unimportant cause of variation in Y and so did not affect the other simple correlations very much.

Geometric interpretations of simple and partial correlation coefficients are presented in Figure 3. The points ($\cdot$) in the three dimensional space are projected horizontally to form scatters ($\times$) on each of the three vertical planes. The scatter on plane "0," at the right, includes the projections of *all* the points and so represents the simple correlation between Y and X. Planes 1 and 2 differ from plane 0 because each of them contain the projections of only those points which lie in a specified range of Z, whereas plane 0 embraces all

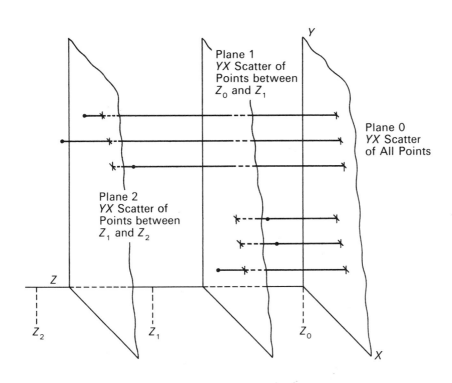

Figure 3. Partial Correlation Scatter Diagram (Hypothetical Data)

the points without regard to the value of Z. The scatters on planes 1 and 2 also represent simple correlation coefficients; they might be described as follows:

Plane 1: $r_{YX.}$ (with Z held between Z_0 and Z_1)

Plane 2: $r_{YX.}$ (with Z held between Z_1 and Z_2)

A crude measure of the relationship between Y and X with the effect of Z removed could be obtained by averaging these two values of r_{YX}. (There is no reason why the two values should be equal.) The reader may note that in this particular example the correlations represented on both planes 1 and 2 are exactly -1, whereas the simple correlation on plane 0 is relatively small because the perfect negative relationship between Y and X has been obscured by the effect of Z.

Now let us imagine that more and more planes are added to Figure 3, with the ranges of Z from which points are projected onto each becoming smaller and smaller. As the number of planes becomes very large, the influence of Z upon the value of $\bar{r}_{YX}$ obtained by averaging over the planes becomes negligible, and $\bar{r}_{YX}$ converges to the partial correlation coefficient $r_{YX.Z}$.

The partial correlation of Y and X can be computed directly from the simple correlation matrix by the formula:[6]

$$r_{YX.Z} = \frac{r_{YX} - r_{XZ} r_{YZ}}{\sqrt{(1 - r_{XZ}^2)(1 - r_{YZ}^2)}}$$

The reader should be able to write similar formulas for computing $r_{YZ.X}$ and $r_{XZ.Y}$.

Multiple Correlation

The idea of a multiple correlation between three or more variables has already been discussed indirectly. Designated by the symbol $R_{Y.XZ}$, it is a measure of the degree of linear association between a dependent variable (Y) and two (or more) explanatory variables (X and Z). Its square is exactly equal to the proportion of the variation of Y that is explained by the linear relationship—which in this case involves the two other variables simultaneously.

The multiple correlation coefficient may be computed from the following formula:

$$R_{Y.XZ} = \sqrt{\frac{r_{YX}^2 + r_{YZ}^2 - 2r_{YX} r_{YZ} r_{YZ}}{1 - r_{XZ}^2}}$$

For the values of the simple correlation coefficients given in the example, the multiple correlation between sales and its two explanatory variables is about 0.89; its square shows that 80 percent of the variance of sales is accounted for by the linear association with X and Z. (Compare this figure with the approximate estimate of 75 percent obtained by squaring the partial correlation coefficients.)

---

[6] George W. Snedecor, *Statistical Methods* (5th ed.; Ames, Iowa: The Iowa State University Press, 1956), p. 430.

The multiple correlation coefficient can be viewed in a slightly different way, as well. Let us define a new variable, W, as the *linear combination* of our two independent variables, X and Z. (A linear combination of two or more variables is merely their weighted sum.) For each observation ($i = 1, \ldots, n$) in the sample we have:

$$W_i = aX_i + bZ_i$$

We have chosen a *linear* combination rather than some other way of combining X and Z (for example, a quadratic or logarithmic equation) because, as the reader will recall, the whole concept of correlation analysis is based upon linear relationships.

Now we will compute the simple correlation coefficient between Y and W in the usual manner. Clearly, the value of r_{YW} will depend upon the particular weighting factors chosen in computing W in the first place: if a is zero, for example, we would have $r_{YW} = r_{YZ}$, and similarly for b. If we were to calculate r_{YW} for a great many different values of a and b, we would find that one pair yields a larger correlation between Y and W than does any other; *this maximum value for r_{YW} is equal exactly to $R_{Y.XZ}$*, as computed from the simple correlations of Y with the original independent variables.

The idea that the effects of a number of independent variables can be summed up in a new variable, W, is of key importance. It will be pursued in the next section, under the heading of multiple regression analysis.

Partial and multiple correlation analysis can be extended to include any number of variables. For partial correlations, the symbol $r_{YX.ZQRL}$ would be read "correlation between Y and X, with the variables Z, Q, R, and L held constant." The formula for its calculation is analogous to that for $r_{YX.Z}$: it explicitly involves all of the possible simple correlation coefficients. Likewise, the multiple correlation coefficient $R_{Y.XZQRL}$ is a measure of the relationship between Y and all of the independent variables taken together. It might be rewritten as r_{YW}, where W is the linear combination of X, Z, Q, R, and L that yields the greatest possible association with Y.

Regression Analysis

Suppose that our hypothetical canine coat firm wanted to estimate the number of sales that could be obtained from a metropolitan area that was not in its original sample. Such an estimate would be required if the firm was considering an expansion of operations into a new market area, for example, Kansas City.

If we had no statistical information whatsoever about Kansas City but believed that conditions there were about like those in our existing markets, our best forecast would be the average level of sales that had been obtained elsewhere. If we designate sales in Kansas City by Y_*, we have

$$\hat{Y}_* = \bar{Y}$$

where the caret ($\wedge$) over Y_* indicates an *estimated* rather than an *observed* value.

This simple estimate of Y_* would be efficient if we really had no information about the new area, but it is inappropriate if Kansas City's income level is known. Since we have already shown that there is a relationship between sales and income in our existing markets, we should surely take advantage of this knowledge when preparing sales estimates for new areas.

Introduction to Univariate Regression: Forecasting

How should information on income be incorporated into the forecast of sales in Kansas City? The correlation coefficient between the two gives the *magnitude* of linear relationship, but that is all. We need to know the average change in Y that has been associated with a change in the value of X. This figure is the slope of the linear relationship, and is sometimes called the *regression of Y on X*, or more simply the *slope parameter* of the regression equation.

The forecast value for sales in Kansas City, or for any metropolitan area, can be written as the linear combination of the mean of Y (that is, the simple forecast value discussed above) and the difference between the area's X value and the mean of all the X's:

$$\hat{Y}_* = \bar{Y} + b(X_* - \bar{X})$$

The goal in making a forecast is to make the difference between the forecast estimate and what eventually turns out to be the actual value be as small as possible. This criterion provides the key for obtaining a value for b. Write the forecast error as:

$$u_* = \hat{Y}_* - Y_*$$

If forecasts were prepared for many metropolitan areas, one would hope that the values of u would all be small, clustered around zero, and devoid of any regular pattern. The characteristics of the u's are so important for the validity of regression procedures that a whole section will be devoted to them.

It will be recalled that the amount of information contained in an unbiased statistical measure is inversely proportional to its variance: therefore the information contributed by $\hat{Y}_*$ will go up as the variance of u_* goes down. Consequently, we must find the value of b that minimizes $\sigma_{u_*}^2$. While u cannot be calculated for Kansas City because actual sales there are not yet known, observed sales figures *are* available for the original group of areas. Various values of b can be used to prepare hypothetical sales estimates for existing market areas and the value of u calculated for each of them. Since the value that yields the smallest sum of squares for u is chosen as the regression slope parameter, the method has become known as *least squares analysis*.

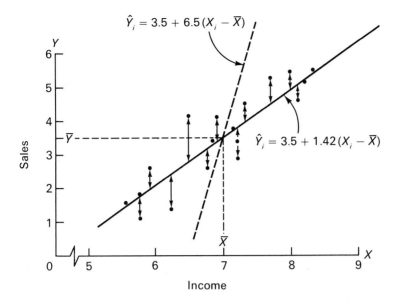

Figure 4. Regression of Sales (Y) on Income (X)

The procedure is shown graphically in Figure 4. The value of b must be chosen in a way such that the sum of the squares of the vertical distances between the raw data points and the regression line is as small as possible. It is apparent, for example, that the sum of squared deviations is larger for the dashed regression line that for the solid one, thus making the value 1.42 a better estimate of b than is 6.5. Note also that the regression line passes through the point $(\bar{X}, \bar{Y})$; this condition results automatically from the least squares procedure.

It is not necessary actually to compute the squared deviations from a large number of alternative regression lines. The problem has been solved mathematically and the following formula obtained:[7]

$$b = \frac{\sum_{i=1}^{n}(Y_i - \bar{Y})(X_i - \bar{X})}{\sum_{i=1}^{n}(X_i - \bar{X}_i)^2} = \frac{\sigma_{XY}}{\sigma_X^2}$$

It can be read as "covariance (XY) over variance (X)." Recalling the formula for the simple correlation coefficient between X and Y, we can write:

$$b = \frac{r_{XY}\,\sigma_X\,\sigma_Y}{\sigma_X^2} = r_{XY}\frac{\sigma_Y}{\sigma_X}$$

---

[7] Anderson and Bancroft, *op. cit.*, chap. xiii.

The regression parameter b represents the value of the correlation coefficient with information on the relative variability of X and Y put back in. Understanding the regression slope parameter allows a clearer interpretation of the correlation coefficient; it is nothing less than the slope of the regression line expressed in standardized units!

The nature of linear relationships as discussed in connection with correlation coefficients can now be made clear. *Two variables stand in a relationship to one another if knowledge of the value of one will improve the prediction of the other, in the sense of reducing the variance of the forecast error.* For the linear case, this requires that the value of the regression slope parameter be nonzero: if it were zero, the independent variable would drop out of the forecasting equation.

One final point must be considered: *the slope parameter of the regression of Y on X is not the same as that for the regression of X on Y.* The regression equation is not statistically reversible. To estimate the value of income from the number of sales made in a given metropolitan area would require knowledge of b' in the following equation:

$$\hat{X}_i = \bar{X} + b'(Y_i - \bar{Y})$$

A value of b' is optimal if and only if the variance of the forecast error

$$v_i = \hat{X}_i - X_i$$

is as small as possible. Since we are concerned with differences between the X's, rather than the Y's, as was previously the case, the sum of the squared horizontal deviations between the regression line and the raw data points must be minimized. The model is shown in Figure 5.

The formula for computing b' is similar to that for b. It reduces to:

$$b' = r_{XY} \frac{\sigma_X}{\sigma_Y}$$

In order for the regression relation to be reversible, the condition

$$b' = \frac{1}{b}$$

would have to be satisfied. Substituting the expressions for each coefficient, we would have

$$r_{XY} = \frac{1}{r_{XY}}$$

The equality holds only for the case where $r_{XY} = \pm 1$: all of the points lie on the (single) regression line, and both X and Y could be predicted without any error at all.

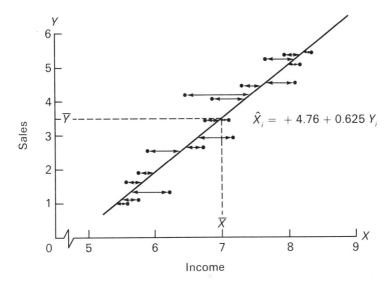

Figure 5.   Regression of Income (X) on Sales (Y)

Minimizing the sums of squared deviations in the Y direction, as indicated above, yields the *best unbiased forecasts of the dependent variable* that are available from any procedure utilizing linear relationships. This powerful result follows from a fundamental theorem on least squares due to Markov, a Russian mathematician.[8] He has shown that for linear models least squares forecasts are (*a*) unbiased, and (*b*) more efficient than those obtained by any other unbiased forecasting procedure.

Univariate Regression: Structural Analysis

Regression was introduced as a technique for the prediction of Y given a particular value of X, but perhaps its major role lies in helping us to understand causal links between variables. In causal analysis, attention focuses on the value of b, which in the example is a measure of the response of sales to changes in income, rather than on the prediction for Y (sales) as in forecasting problems. We might wish to compare the observed sales response to changes in income against our previous beliefs—which may have resulted either from a carefully worked out theory or from a hunch—in order to test our understanding of the environment in which the firm operates. Or, if the effect of income upon sales is itself undergoing change, we may be able to

---

[8] Discussed in Gerhard Tintner, *Econometrics* (New York: John Wiley & Sons, Inc., 1952), pp. 83–84.

make rough adjustments in the regression slope parameters on the basis of our subjective understanding of the problem area, without waiting for actual data on which to base additional statistical analysis to become available. This can be done only if the effects of income upon sales have been disentangled from those of other variables.[9]

The regression technique discussed above yields the best possible forecast for Y, but may at the same time fail to give a good estimate of b. Regression can produce good forecasts on the basis of very biased estimates of response coefficients for the independent variables (that is, the b's).

One of the reasons is already familiar; we considered it . . . in connection with partial correlation. Recall the effect of a third variable, temperature, on the net relationship between sales and income. Since income and temperature are negatively correlated, the partial correlation between sales and income as shown in Table 4 is smaller than the simple correlation given in Table 3. Regression coefficients behave in the same way. The value of b computed from the formula given above includes some of the effect of temperature; the true sensitivity of sales to changes in income is somewhat smaller.

To anticipate the section on multiple regression for a moment, we can designate our original value of b as a *simple regression coefficient*, denoted by b_{YX}, and define a *partial regression coefficient*, for which the effects of temperature are excluded, as $b_{YX.Z}$. The latter is analogous to the partial correlation concept, and is read "coefficient of regression Y on X, with Z held constant." For the correlations given in Table 3, we have:

$$b_{YX.Z} = 0.94 b_{YX}$$

We would say that the statistic b_{YX} is a *biased* estimator of $b_{YX.Z}$ (although here the bias is small because the effect of temperature on sales is small). A biased estimator is one that, on the average, will give wrong values for the population value of the coefficient under study.

Given the effects of the temperature variable, the value of b_{YX} should not be used as an estimate of the importance of income as a cause of variations in sales among areas. While the error in the example is only in the order of 6 percent, errors of twice or even 10 times as much are not at all uncommon in actual cases. Where more than one variable is believed to exert an effect upon sales, or any other dependent variable, the best course of action is to proceed immediately to the multivariate procedure discussed below.

The *source* of the regression error term, or difference between forecast and actual values of Y, is a second determinant of bias in the estimate of b_{YX}. The error term comes into being through one or both of the following two mechanisms:

---

[9] Cf. William C. Hood and Tjalling C. Koopmans (eds.), *Studies in Econometric Methods* (New York: John Wiley & Sons, Inc., 1953), chap. i.

1. Not all of the variables that cause fluctuations in the dependent variable have been explicitly included in the regression equation. The combined effects of all the excluded variables can be summed up in the error term, u_i.
2. The measuring process for Y and/or X is subject to random error. The discrepancies between actual and reported values of the regression variables can also be summed up in the error term, u_i.

These are called *errors in equation* and *errors in variables* models, respectively.

The regression procedure described above was derived under the assumption that either (1) or a special case of (2) holds. The error term, u, can arise from the effects of excluded variables, in which case the regression could be written:

$$Y_i \text{ (actual)} = \overline{Y} + b(X_i - \overline{X}) + u_i \text{ (effects of excluded variables)}$$

The u might also be an error of measurement for the *dependent variable*, Y:

$$Y_i \text{ (as measured)} = Y_i \text{ (actual)} - u_i \text{ (measurement error)} = \overline{Y} + b(X_i - \overline{X})$$

Both models yield the same regression equation, since the quantity u_i can be moved from one side of the equality to the other by simple addition or subtraction.

If the measurement of X is subject to error, on the other hand, the regression equation should be written:

$$Y_i \text{ (actual)} = \overline{Y} + b\{[X_i \text{ (as measured)} + v_i \text{ (measurement error)}] - \overline{X}\}$$

where the error term v_i is multiplied by the parameter b. This result can be recast into the form

$$X_i = \overline{X} - \frac{1}{b}(Y_i - \overline{Y}) + v_i$$

It is the same as an "ordinary" regression with X rather than Y taken as the dependent variable. The parameter $\frac{1}{b}$ is equal to b', obtained by minimizing the sum of squares of the horizontal deviations in Figure 5. On the other hand, regression of Y and X where the X's are subject to error will yield an estimate of b that is too small in absolute value; we say that such estimates of b are biased toward zero. Unbiased parameter estimates can be obtained only if the sum of squares of the error component of the regression equation is minimized: if the measurement of Y contains error we must minimize the Y direction, or if X contains error the squares of the X deviations must be minimized.

If both Y and X are subject to measurement errors, the sums of *diagonal* deviations from the regression line must be minimized if unbiased estimates of b_{YX} are to be obtained. The direction of the proper diagonal is defined by the ratio of the variances of the measurement errors for X and Y.[10]

Errors due to excluded variables and measurement errors for the dependent variable can occur at the same time without invalidating the normal regression procedure. The analyst can also take comfort from the fact that errors of measurement for X that have small variance relative to σ_u^2 will lead to only a small bias in the estimate of b. In addition, the reader will recall that forecasts of the dependent variable are not affected by the source of the regression error term.

Review of Bias and Efficiency in Regression

Questions of *bias* refer to the average or *expected value* of an estimate: will $\hat{Y}$ be right on the average, in the sense that overestimates will be canceled out by underestimates? Questions of *efficiency*, on the other hand, are based upon the inherent variability of an estimate.[11] One forecast is more efficient than another if it has a smaller *variance*, and it is quite possible for one unbiased estimate to be more efficient than another. Since we are looking for forecasts that have errors which are small and distributed irregularly, it is clear that estimates that are both unbiased *and* efficient are desired.

The coefficient b_{YX} is a biased estimator for $b_{YX.Z}$, the true response of sales to income. Nevertheless, the regression equation:

$$\hat{Y}_i = \overline{Y}_i + b_{YX}(X_i - \overline{X})$$

will yield an unbiased estimate of Y_i regardless of whether or not the additional variable Z should have been included. Bias in our estimate of the effect of income will not affect the forecast of Y *as long as the relationship between X and Z remains unchanged*. This can be demonstrated in the following way: Z is not included in the regression, but X can be used as an estimator of Z, as well as a measure of itself; therefore, the estimated value of Y is based on information on X, which is available directly, and upon Z, which is introduced via X and the underlying relationship between X and Z. Only a part of the effect of Z upon Y can be determined as long as the correlation between X and Z is not perfect. Consequently, the efficiency of the forecast of Y can be improved by adding Z to the regression equation.

---

[10] Laurence R. Klein, *A Textbook of Econometrics* (Evanston, Ill.: Row, Peterson & Co., 1953), pp. 282–305.

[11] For an elementary discussion of bias and efficiency in the context of sampling theory, see Spurr, Kellogg, and Smith, *op. cit.*, pp. 232–33. A more advanced treatment can be found in Anderson and Bancroft, *op. cit.*, chap. viii.

Assumptions Underlying the Use of Regression

We are now in a position to systematically state the assumptions that underlie the use of regression methods for forecasting and structural analysis.[12] Five assumptions will be given. Assumption (4) is a key factor in structural analysis, but does not apply to forecasting. All the others apply to both.

1. The most basic assumption for all kinds of regression is that the regression error term must be *randomly distributed*. Measurement errors due to sampling for the dependent variable are usually distributed randomly. (The independent variables must be measured exactly if the assumptions underlying ordinary regression analysis are to be valid.) In errors in equations models, on the other hand, the assumption will normally be justified only if all the variables whose *individual* effect on Y is large are included as independent variables in the regression.

If we were to discover that one of the metropolitan areas in our canine coats sample charged a $100 annual dog licensing fee, for example, the validity of the regressions calculated above would be open to serious question. Since such a high fee would limit dog registration to upper income families, we could easily predict that sales *per licensed dog* would be much higher for that area than for others with similar income characteristics: the value of u_i would be large because the regression of sales per dog on income would underestimate the true sales figure. Given this situation, we should not regard the error as being randomly distributed.[13]

We also proceed as if the errors have *zero expected value* (for example, the measurement of Y was unbiased), although the failure of this assumption will affect only the estimate of the mean of Y, and not that of the regression slope parameter.

2. The second assumption deals with the variance of the error term. We must postulate that the range of variation between actual and forecast values of Y is no more likely to be large for one metropolitan area than for another. If we think that the people of Boston have the same average characteristics as do those in Philadelphia, but are much more variable in their day-to-day behavior, we should not assume that forecast errors for the two cities will have the same variance. In technical terms, we say that the u's must be *homoscedastic*.

Heteroscedasticity does not imply that our structural estimates or forecasts will be biased; on the contrary, uniform error variances are required only if highly efficient estimates are desired. The reason can be seen easily for

---

[12] An excellent and highly readable summary of assumptions underlying regression and similar statistical methods can be found in Stefan Valavanis, *Econometrics—An Introduction to Maximum Likelihood Methods* (New York: McGraw-Hill Book Co., Inc., 1959), pp. 8–17.

[13] In the context of experimental design, this u could be considered as randomly distributed if the metropolitan areas in the sample had been randomly selected in the first place. Random selection is unlikely for observational data of the kind considered in this example, however.

models where the u's occur because of errors in the measurement of Y, although the result holds for error in equation models as well. Suppose (a) the number of sales for Philadelphia was known exactly (without error), (b) sales for Boston were known only approximately, and (c) sales for all the other cities were known with an accuracy between that of Philadelphia and Boston. It would make sense to give Philadelphia, for which accurate information is available, more weight in estimating the regression equation. Likewise, Boston should have a smaller influence on the estimates than cities whose Y measurements have smaller variances. By using the ordinary least squares method we ignore these differences, and hence throw away information about the relative accuracy of the observed Y's; this loss of information results in forecasts and estimates of the regression slope parameter that are less than fully efficient.

3. The u's must be statistically independent of one another, in the sense that knowing the value for any u_i will add no information about the value of u_j (where $i \neq j$). Measurement errors for different Y's in errors in variables models, and excluded variables in errors in equations models, must not be correlated with one another.

This assumption is closely related to (1), since randomly distributed errors are the most likely to be statistically independent. We must recognize, however, that two truly random variables may be highly correlated: for example, the total number of "heads" obtained in a coin tossing experiment after trial t will be highly correlated with that after trial $t + 1$, although both are random variables. Regressions on time series data often have error terms that exhibit exactly the same characteristics as demonstrated in the coin tossing experiment; we would say that these errors are *autocorrelated*.[14] For survey data, the assumption of independent errors may be seriously questioned in cases where the observations are obtained by sampling clusters of respondents: for example, errors in equations which attempt to explain the behavior of next-door neighbors are quite likely to be correlated.

Failure of the independence assumption does not affect the expected values of forecasts or regression parameters, so that we can be assured that no bias will be introduced by autocorrelation of the error terms. Efficiency does suffer, and what is potentially more serious is the fact that estimates of the *forecast variance* and the *variance of the regression slope parameter* (denoted σ_b^2) will in general be biased downward. If the regression errors are highly correlated among themselves, the computed variances will indicate more information on b than we actually have. This misleading statement is often more dangerous than the loss of efficiency itself, and especially so since no adequate means of correction exist.

4. Structural analysis (but not forecasting) requires that the u's be uncorrelated with the independent variable, X, in the regression equation. While this assumption usually holds for errors in variables models, it must

---

[14] Cf. Tintner, *op. cit.*, chap. x.

always be challenged and considered carefully when dealing with errors in equations.

By requiring that r_{uX} be equal to zero, we are doing nothing more than formalizing the conditions we discussed with respect to structural estimation and bias in regression. There we found that $b_{YX} \neq b_{YX.Z}$ for $r_{XZ} \neq 0$. Since Z was lumped into the error term in the single variable regression equation, a nonzero r_{XY} violated assumption (4) and produced a biased estimate of the slope parameter.

Failure of this assumption can lead to serious bias in the estimate of b, and the analyst must be constantly on the lookout for variables that may: (a) affect the dependent variable, (b) be correlated with an independent variable, and (c) are not included in the regression equation. But one never knows when another significant variable may be lurking unseen in the shadows, and the bias introduced will never show up in the variance of the parameter estimate $(\hat{\sigma}_b^2)$.

While the statistician has no assurance that his results are not biased and misleading, the *proximity theorem* of regression offers considerable comfort. It states:[15] (a) *if the correlation between u and X is small, the bias of the slope parameter estimate will be small*; (b) *if the variance of u is small, the bias will be small*; and (c) *if both r_{uX} and σ_u^2 are small, the bias will be negligible.* If one makes an honest and informed attempt to include all of the relevant variables in the regression equation, the parameter estimates are likely to be relatively unbiased.

5. Our final assumption refers to the *linearity of the model* upon which regression forecasts or structural estimates are based. Do we believe that the true relationship between Y and X is strictly linear (or can be made so by a suitable transformation of variables),[16] or are we approximating some other form of relationship with a linear regression equation? Such approximations are probably more the rule than the exception in regression analysis, but it is important to recognize that departure from a strictly linear model requires a restriction on the distribution of the *independent* variable.

The theory of regression discussed in most textbooks is based upon strictly linear models.[17] Given a linear relationship, the values of the independent variables can be selected arbitrarily, and the value of Y measured for each. While often applied to observational data, this approach is particularly well suited to the analysis of experimental results, where the behavior of the independent variables has been specified by the experimenter.

---

[15] Herman Wold, *Demand Analysis* (New York: John Wiley & Sons, Inc., 1953), pp. 37–38.

[16] The concept of regression linearity refers to the way in which the coefficients enter the equation. For example, $\log Y = a + b \log X$ is considered to be a linear regression, while the algebraically equivalent $Y = A \cdot X^b$ is not. Likewise, $Y = a + bX + cX^2$ is linear as far as the mechanics of regression are concerned, because the variables (X) and (X^2) enter in linear combination.

[17] Wold provides a notable exception. *Ibid.*, chap. xii.

Arbitrary selection of the X values can lead to difficulties in the comparison of different regression lines where the linear regression equation is only an approximation to a more complicated relationship. Figure 6 shows how different linear approximations to the same relation will be obtained, depending upon the particular set of X's appearing in the sample. Parameters of regression "A" were estimated using X's that were uniformly distributed

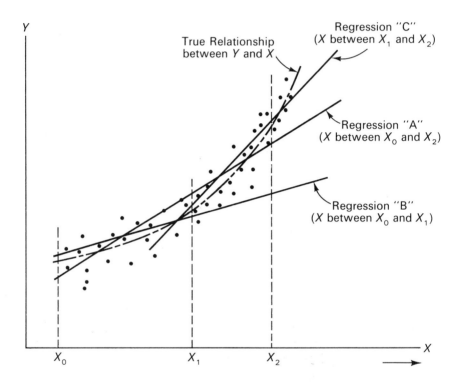

Figure 6.   Linear Regression Equations as Approximations to an
Underlying Curvilinear Relationship

within the interval X_0 to X_2, while lines "B" and "C" are based on X's in the subintervals X_0 to X_1, and X_1 to X_2 respectively. While all of the lines are good approximations to the true curve over the irrespective X-intervals, it would be a mistake to consider all of them as merely regressions of Y on X.

In other words, we must assume that the relationship between Y and X is strictly linear if different sets of arbitrary values of X are to yield comparable regression parameters. If the regression is regarded as being only a linear approximation, the distribution of the independent variable, X, in the sample must be carefully controlled in order for the regression parameters to be interpreted properly.

Consider the following example. Our company has prepared regressions of sales on income, by metropolitan area, during two successive years, and we wish to determine whether the relationship has changed during the period. If we find that the regression slope parameter is much larger for the second year than for the first, but the second sample contained many more areas with high incomes, what should we conclude? If we are very sure that the relationship between sales and income is strictly linear we would disregard the differences between the X distributions for the two years and conclude, on the basis of the two b's alone, that sales sensitivity to income had increased during the year. If we cannot be sure of the underlying relationship, however, we had better allow for the possibility that the difference between the b's occurred because of a situation like that shown in Figure 6, that is, that the regressions for the two years approximate different portions of a stable but curvilinear relation. In this case, two samples having the same X's would allow us to determine whether a change had occurred. A transformation of variables, or the addition of higher order terms in X to the regression (for example, X^2 or X^3) might restore our powers of comparison, but only if a wide range of income variation were available in both samples.

Summary of Regression Assumptions

The five assumptions underlying the use of regression methods for making forecasts and estimating structural parameters are re-stated below:

1. The error must be randomly distributed, with zero expected value.
2. The error variance must be the same for all values of X (homoscedasticity).
3. The individual errors, u_i, must be statistically independent of one another ($r_{u_i u_j} = 0$, for $i \neq j$).
4. The errors must be uncorrelated with the independent variable in the regression equation ($r_{ux} = 0$). Applies to problems of estimating structural parameters only.
5. The underlying relationship between Y and X must be strictly linear if the regression slope parameter and forecasts based upon it are to be independent of the distribution of the X's in the sample.

Analysis of the Regression Residuals

Let us focus on the differences between the actual and forecast values of Y, as defined by the vertical distances between the points in the scatter diagram of Figure 4 and the regression line. They are written as r_i, and result from the application of the regression method to a given set of data points; *they are not necessarily the same as the theoretical* u_i which are specified as part of the underlying model. Frequency distributions of the r_i and u_i may differ for one of two reasons: (1) the assumptions upon which the regression method is based were violated; or (2) the regression assumptions were valid,

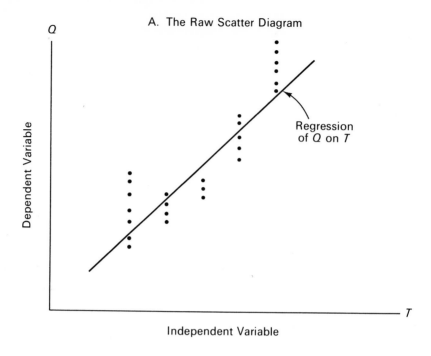

A. The Raw Scatter Diagram

Regression of Q on T

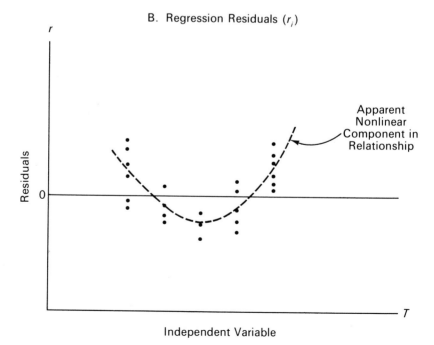

B. Regression Residuals (r_i)

Apparent Nonlinear Component in Relationship

Figure 7. Effects of a Curvilinear Relationship on Regression Residuals

but not enough observations on the r_i were available to produce a good estimate of the u_i distribution. In the latter case, the observed values of r_i can be regarded as a sample from the underlying u_i population.

Figure 7 presents a scatter diagram, regression line, and a graph of regression residuals for two new hypothetical variables, Q and T. Inspection of the residuals plot suggests that at least two of the assumptions about the underlying error process were not justified: (1) the residuals exhibit a definite nonlinear pattern (violation of assumption 5) and (2) the variances of the residuals are not the same for the various values of X (violation of assumption 2). The analyst might therefore consider adding a nonlinear term in X (perhaps X^2) and working with the multiple regression model discussed below; and/or using a *weighted regression*[18] method to compensate for the differing variances in order to improve estimating efficiency. Both moves should be considered carefully, since aberrations in the r_i are often caused only by fluctuations of sampling, and neither of the more complicated techniques can be used without incurring additional costs.

The independence of errors assumption (3) can be roughly evaluated in a similar manner. For time series, one can look at the residuals for adjacent periods, while if the data were obtained from a sample survey, residuals for neighbors, adjacent blocks, cities, and so on can be examined. If a marked degree of clustering of r_i values can be discerned, the validity of assumption (3) is in doubt.

Assumption (4) can never be evaluated using information on the observed residuals, since the regression method insures that the r_i will be uncorrelated with the independent variable whether u_i is or not. While higher order relationships are possible, as is demonstrated by Figure 7, one will always get a correlation coefficient of precisely zero. (Recall Figure 2-I for a demonstration that $r_{rT} = 0$.)

Analysis of the regression residuals often provides a great deal of information for the analyst. Without it there is no way of checking his intuitive assumptions about the nature of the error term. While the available tests are inexact and incomplete, their use is a great deal better than no testing at all. Residuals should be computed, plotted, and analyzed wherever possible.

Multiple Regression Analysis

Multiple regression is an extension of the univariate regression principles to allow the effects of more than one independent variable to be taken into account at the same time. The multiple regression of sales on income and temperature is written:

$$Y_i = \bar{Y} + b_{YX.Z}(X_i - \bar{X}) + b_{YZ.X}(Z_i - \bar{Z}) + u_i$$

---

[18] Klein, *op cit.*, pp. 305–13.

This equation has exactly the same interpretation as those in the preceding sections. All of the same conditions and assumptions apply for both structural estimation and forecasting.

The partial regression parameters ($b_{YX.Z}$ and $b_{YZ.X}$) are closely related to the equivalent partial correlation coefficients discussed above. Their values can be computed from the simple correlation matrix and the variances of Y, X, and Z by using the following formulas:

$$b_{YX.Z} = \frac{\sigma_Y}{\sigma_X}\left[\frac{r_{YX} - r_{ZX}r_{YZ}}{1 - r_{ZX}^2}\right]$$

$$b_{YZ.X} = \frac{\sigma_Y}{\sigma_Z}\left[\frac{r_{YZ} - r_{ZX}r_{YX}}{1 - r_{ZX}^2}\right]$$

Note that the simple correlations between all of the pairs of variables appear in both equations.

Table 5.   Multiple Regression of *Warm* Brand Canine Coats on Income and Temperature*

Calculation of the multiple regression coefficients:

$$b_{YX.Z} = \frac{\sigma_Y}{\sigma_X}\left[\frac{r_{YX} - r_{ZX}r_{YZ}}{1 - r_{ZX}^2}\right] = \frac{1.39}{0.87}\left[\frac{0.89 - (-0.57)(-0.45)}{1 - (-0.57)^2}\right] = +1.51$$

$$b_{YZ.X} = \frac{\sigma_Y}{\sigma_Z}\left[\frac{r_{YZ} - r_{ZX}r_{YX}}{1 - r_{ZX}^2}\right] = \frac{1.39}{14.7}\left[\frac{-0.45 - (-0.57)(+0.89)}{1 - (-0.57)^2}\right] = +0.0086$$

Forecast of sales for Kansas City:

(Income (X) = 7.05; temperature (Z) = 26.7)

$$\hat{Y} = 3.52 + 1.51(7.05 - 6.96) + 0.0086(26.7 - 40.9) = 5.06$$

* Computed from the simple correlation coefficients in Table 3.

Multicollinearity is said to be present in a multiple regression computation if the independent variables are highly correlated among themselves. This condition reduces the efficiency of the estimates for the regression parameters because for given values of r_{YX} and r_{YZ} the amount of information about the effect of each independent variable, taken separately, declines as r_{XZ} increases.

The reduction in efficiency can easily be seen in the limiting case, as r_{XZ} approaches one. If r_{XZ} equals one, we know, for the sample at least, that both independent variables varied in perfect proportion to one another. But if X and Z vary together for all observations in the sample, how can we hope to separate their influence on Y? X and Z can have distinctly different effects in the underlying population, but our particular sample does not contain enough information to separate them. In terms of the regression coefficients, we see that the formulas given above break down when $r_{XZ} = 1$; no calculation is possible when the denominator $(1 - r_{XZ}^2)$ is equal to zero.

It can be shown that the variance of the estimates for both $b_{YX.Z}$ and $b_{YZ.X}$ is directly proportional to the quantity $(1 - r_{XZ}^2)$: their variance is infinite (estimating efficiency is zero) when $r_{XZ} = 1$, and decreases steadily as r_{XZ} declines. Thus, correlation between X and Z reduces the efficiency of estimates of the regression slope parameters. Consequently, it is desirable to design experiments or to use observations whose values of X and Z exhibit as low a correlation among themselves as is possible. Observational data often exhibits high multicollinearity, but sometimes a careful selection of variables or observations can minimize the damage. At other times it may be possible to combine two or more independent variables into a new variable and use that for computing the regression line.

The efficiency of *forecasts of* Y, on the other hand, is unaffected by the correlation between the independent variables (unless $r_{XZ} = 1$, where the multiple regression technique breaks down and the univariate method must be adopted). Forecasts depend only upon the total amount of information about Y contributed by X and Z, not on their effects taken separately. While it is desirable to use independent variables that together contribute a maximum of information, the correlation between them does not matter, per se.

2

Kristian S. Palda: The Evaluation of
Regression Results

Criteria

There are three groups of criteria with which to judge least-squares regression results: *theoretical, statistical,* and *predictive.*

Theoretical Criteria

The results should be in accord with theoretical expectations or well-known empirical facts. Thus, a regression coefficient indicating a negative advertising elasticity of demand would automatically be suspect. The theo-

---

Abridged from *Proceedings of the AMA Winter Conference*, published by the American Marketing Association. Kristian S. Palda, "The Evaluation of Regression Results," *Proceedings of the AMA Winter Conference*, December 1963, pp. 282–287. The author has benefited from comments by William F. Massy and Harry V. Roberts.

retical implications of regression results need not, however, be as trivially obvious as that.

In the writer's study of cumulative advertising effects, two models were fitted with the same set of data.[1] One model provided for the operation of long-run advertising effects, the other did not.

Dorfman and Steiner have shown the validity of the following rule for profit maximization:[2]

> A firm should set the advertising appropriation and the price for its product in such a way that the increase in revenue which will result from a one-dollar increase in advertising (the marginal sales effect of advertising) should equal the (absolute) price elasticity of the demand for the product: Δ sales revenue/Δ advertising expenditure = | price elasticity |.

The marginal sales effect of advertising estimated from the fitting of the "non-cumulative" model was less than 1, implying that the firm operated on the price-inelastic portion of its demand curve, a manifestly non-maximizing behavior. At the same time, estimates from the "cumulative effects" model led to price elasticities larger than 1. This became additional evidence in favor of that regression model's results.

Statistical Criteria

There is also a group of predominantly statistical criteria. Among the most important are those which enable the investigator to pass judgment on the amount of autocorrelation among successive disturbances. Correlation among disturbances signals the presence of an unexplained, systematic influence over the phenomenon studied and thus a basic weakness in the model. Autocorrelation, as already mentioned, will also bias downward the estimate of the standard deviation of regression residuals and lead to inefficient parameter estimates.

The Durbin-Watson statistic, d, is commonly used to test for the presence of autocorrelated disturbances.[3] Less powerful but often satisfactory is a chi-square test based on a two-by-two table of positive or negative successive residuals.[4] More personal judgments about the presence of autocorrelation are formulated on the basis of the estimated autocorrelation coefficient, $\hat{\rho}$

---

[1] Palda, *The Measurement of Cumulative Advertising Effects* (Prentice-Hall, forthcoming).

[2] R. Dorfman and P. O. Steiner, "Optimal Advertising and Optimal Quality." *American Economic Review*, XLIV (1954), pp. 826–36.

[3] H. Theil and A. L. Nagar, "Testing the Independence of Regression Disturbances," *Journal of the American Statistical Association*, LVI (December, 1961), pp. 793–807.

[4] Griliches, Maddala, Lucas, and Wallace, "Notes on Estimated Aggregate Quarterly Consumption Functions," *Econometrica*, XXX (July, 1962), pp. 497–98.

(related to the Durbin-Watson statistic by the formula $\hat{\rho} = -\frac{1}{2}d$) or of scatter diagrams. In the latter, either residuals are plotted over time or calculated values are plotted against observed values of the dependent variables. The resulting graphs are then examined for non-randomness.

The standard deviation of regression residuals, also called the standard error of estimate, is another very important yardstick in evaluating regression results. It describes, in a way that is analogous to the standard deviation of the sample, the dispersion of the residuals around the fitted regression line. The smaller it is, the tighter the regression fit; regressions with a smaller standard error are thus to be preferred to those having a larger one, other things being equal. The comparison can be made directly between different equations without the mental reservations necessary when coefficients of multiple determination (R^2's) are compared.

Most computers do nowadays stepwise calculations which give the standard deviation of residuals after the inclusion of each successive exogenous variable. This statistic can therefore be employed in judging whether the added variable has reduced dispersion (i.e., contributed information). A judgment based on it does not depend—as does the t-test commonly employed to disclose whether the estimated coefficient of the added variable differs "significantly" from zero—upon normality of disturbances.[5]

Finally, and perhaps most importantly, the standard deviation of residuals is the only regression measure which is directly related to the predictive ability of the regression equation, because it enters the formula for the standard error of forecast.[6]

As a consequence, a rough judgment about the potential forecasting performance of various regression models can be made by comparing their standard deviations of residuals.

The most venerable and in some ways least satisfactory of regression criteria is R^2, the coefficient of multiple determination. Its formula is

$$\frac{\hat{\sigma}_Y^{\,2} - \hat{\sigma}_u^{\,2}}{\hat{\sigma}_Y^{\,2}}$$

or, in words,

$$\frac{\text{Variance in } Y \text{ associated with the predetermined variables}}{\text{Variance of } Y}$$

Since it measures the proportion of the variation in the dependent variable

---

[5] See J. Johnston, *Econometric Methods* (New York: McGraw-Hill, 1963), pp. 115–19.

[6] For the formula of the standard error of individual forecast see M. Ezekiel and K. Fox, *Methods of Correlation and Regression Analysis* (New York: Wiley, 1959), pp. 320–21. The standard error of individual forecast will differ for each combination of values of the predetermined variables. If these all fall near their means, this statistic will be only slightly larger than the standard deviation of regression residuals. If one or more fall far from it, the standard error of forecast will be correspondingly large.

which is associated with the variation in the "explanatory" variables, it is frequently used to judge how much more is "explained" by one regression than by another. Often it is forgotten that a high value of R^2 may have been obtained at the cost of a high degree of autocorrelation among residuals or of other undesirable features.[7] It is also forgotten that, because the sample variance of the dependent variable enters its formula, only regressions based on samples that have identical variances in the dependent variable can be directly compared. Put differently, the coefficient of determination is a relative measure, depending not only on how well the regression line fits the observations (on $\hat{\sigma}_u{}^2$), but also on the amount of the dispersion in the sample observations of the dependent variable (on $\hat{\sigma}_Y{}^2$).

It is also desirable that the partial regression coefficients be large compared to their own standard errors. When relatively large standard errors of partials are observed, some statisticians worry because they may be an indication of collinearity among the predetermined variables or of heteroscedasticity in residuals. Others will chiefly worry about the resultant low values of the t-statistic which is used to test the partial's "significance."

Predictive Criteria

From the foregoing discussion it appears that there is no single statistical criterion which will leave the investigator certain of the quality of the fitted regression or enable him to choose one in preference to another without trepidation. Clearly, the best way, especially from a decision-making perspective, is to look at the predictive performance of the regressions.[8] This is done less often than might be expected. A recent devastating experiment conducted by Shupack on Stone's demand regressions shows why forecasting performances should be given the heaviest emphasis as indicator of regression quality.[9]

It is even conceivable that judicious use of the predominantly statistical criteria will lead to the selection of a regression model which gives less accurate forecasts than its rejected "rivals." Thus, in the writer's study[10] of advertising effects a pre-forecast confrontation of two regressions left $R1$ a clear winner:

---

[7] "...it must be noted that 76.3% of the best predictors were *not* the regressions with the highest correlation coefficients. This is a highly significant difference." Mark B. Shupack, "The Predictive Accuracy of Empirical Demand Analyses," *Economic Journal*, LXXII (September, 1962), p. 559.

[8] A good forecasting performance does not necessarily mean that estimates of individual coefficients are reliable (i.e., that they are efficient and consistent). But obviously a good forecast will instill more confidence in point estimates of coefficients than a poor one.

[9] M. B. Shupack, *op. cit.*

[10] Palda, *op. cit.*

$R1 \quad S_t = -3649 + .67\, S_{t-1} + 1180 \log A_t + 774 D + 32 T - 2.83\, Y$
$$\qquad\qquad (.06) \qquad\quad (243) \qquad\quad (107) \quad (6) \quad (.67)$$

629   153

$$N = 53 \qquad R^2 = .94 \qquad d = 1.59 \qquad \hat{\rho} = .20$$

$R2 \quad S_t = -3663 + .66\, S_{t-1} + 1314 \log A_t + 482 D + 9.8 T$
$$\qquad\qquad (.07) \qquad\quad (280) \qquad\quad (95) \quad (2.9)$$

629   180

$$N = 53 \qquad R^2 = .92 \qquad d = 1.16 \qquad \hat{\rho} = .42$$

(S stands for yearly sales in thousands of dollars, A for yearly advertising expenditure in thousands, D for a dummy, T for trend and Y for disposable income; the second line gives standard errors of coefficients in parentheses; the third line shows the standard deviation of the dependent variable and of residuals; d is the Durbin-Watson statistic, and $\hat{\rho}$ the estimated autocorrelation coefficient.)

However, the forecast of 1961 sales by $R2$ was only $27,000 off the mark, while $R1$ underpredicted by $170,000. The first regression had, in this instance, a much better fit (compare the standard deviations of residuals, the d's, even the R^2's), which did not protect it from predictive failure. Upon reflection it appeared that the poor forecast was due to the fact that Y, disposable income (not included in $R2$), at $365 billion in the forecast period, was at a considerable distance from its mean of $110 billion over the 53-year period. It is possible that computation of the standard error of individual forecast would have given a preliminary warning; *the point is that the commonly used statistical criteria of fit may be in conflict with the forecasting criterion.*

3

Ronald E. Frank: Use of Transformations

Introduction

Modern multivariate statistical techniques, combined with the existing state of computer technology, provide the marketing model builder with a powerful set of tools with which to gain increased *structural insights* (in

Abridged from *Journal of Marketing Research*, published by the American Marketing Association. Ronald E. Frank, "Use of Transformations," *Journal of Marketing Research*, Vol. III, August 1966, pp. 247–53.

determining, for example, the effect of changing a brand's price level or advertising activity on its market share) and *predictive power* (e.g., forecasting market share). The adequacy of a statistical technique aimed at characterizing a given dimension of human behavior depends, in large part, on the validity of the assumptions underlying the technique. Often the methods used to measure or accumulate raw data for the estimation process violate one or more of the assumptions on which the statistical technique is based. These violations can result in errors in structural interpretation and prediction.

For example, suppose the following linear regression model was used to characterize the structural relationship between expected household consumption of a given product and income:

$$Y = a + bX + cZ$$

Y is the expected consumption rate, a is a constant, and b and c are the changes in Y that are associated with a unit change in income (X), and any other variable (Z), respectively. This statistical model implicitly assumes that the structural relationship between consumption and income is linear, as shown in Figure 1, Function C. Suppose that this assumption is erroneous,

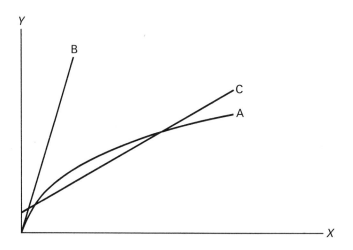

Figure 1. Square Root Transformation

and that the actual structural relationship looks more like that depicted by Function A in the same figure. The actual response (b) of Y to a unit change in X is not a constant, as assumed in the above equation. It decreases as income increases. (It is assumed in this illustration and throughout that the relationship between Y and X is conditional on the values of whatever other variables are included in the equation. In addition, subscripts have been suppressed throughout.)

Most standard statistical techniques assume that b is constant throughout the range of the observed values of X. In many marketing investigations this is suspected of being an erroneous assumption. Must one use a more complex statistical technique to be able to handle these investigations, or can something be done with the data inputs to make their form closer to assumptions underlying more readily available and easily interpreted statistical techniques? Fortunately for the model builder, a number of the departures from the underlying assumptions of the more common statistical techniques can, at least in part, be adjusted for by transforming Y and/or X, depending on the circumstances.

For example, in the preceding illustration, taking the square root of X will result in a new relationship between Y and $X^{1/2}$ (or equivalently $\sqrt{X}$) that will be linear and can therefore be handled by a standard regression model:

$$Y = a + bX^{1/2} + cZ$$

In the example shown in Figure 1 this amounts to transforming function A into function B, which now has a linear form.

The inclusion of routines for handling transformations in a number of the available standard statistical programs has made many of them more easily accomplished. (Often one simply fills out an appropriate control card.) The programs developed by the Health Sciences Computing Facility, School of Medicine, University of California, Los Angeles, are good examples [1]. The programs contained in this series cover virtually every major statistical technique, including analysis of variance, regression, correlation, N-way discriminant analysis, factor analysis and canonical analysis.

These transformations help expand the range of real world problems that a given technique can usefully characterize beyond what its underlying assumptions would at first seem to permit. They constitute an important adjunct to the model builder's tool kit.

The purpose of this article is to illustrate the use of the principal types of transformations applied to model building in marketing. To understand the importance of transformations it is necessary to understand the nature of the assumptions they are designed to meet.

Assumptions

Changing the scale in terms of which a given variable is expressed primarily serves to relax the constraints imposed by two assumptions, both of which are common to a broad range of statistical techniques:

1. That the relation between the expected value of the dependent variable (Y) and an independent variable (X) is *additive and linear*.

2. That the range of variations between actual and expected values is the same for all levels of X (i.e., that the errors are *homoscedastic*).

These assumptions are important in the application of virtually every multivariate statistical technique in use. While they are not the only assumptions made when using a given technique, they are the ones that most transformations are designed to help overcome. Overcoming the additivity and linearity constraints is of particular importance in that many of the relationships of interest in marketing are suspected of being nonlinear or nonadditive.

Additivity and Linearity

Some nonlinear statistical models are available. However, *given the scale of measurement chosen by the researcher*, if a problem can be adequately characterized by a linear model, the appropriate analytical techniques are usually better documented, more easily interpreted, and more readily available in the form of a packaged statistical program, such as the BMD series. This is true of analysis of variance, regression, correlation, discriminant analysis, factor analysis and canonical analysis.

The regression equation

$$Y = a + bX + cZ + u$$

embodies the assumption of additivity and linearity. In the equation, Y represents the value of the dependent variable . . . , a is a constant, b and c are the coefficients that serve as measures of response of Y to each of the variables as represented by X and Z, and u is the error term [now explicitly introduced].

Additivity implies that the effect (b) on Y of any variable (X) is independent of the level of any other variable (say Z). Suppose, for example, that Y is the market share for Brand M at time t, X is a price index for Brand M's price relative to those of competitors at time t, and Z is an index of the degree of dealing (coupons, cents-off on cans, etc.) for Brand M relative to competitors at t. If the above equation is an adequate characterization of the relationship, it states that a cut in price will have an effect (b) on Y, the magnitude of which will be the same regardless of the leveling of dealing (Z) being engaged in by the brand.

If in reality the effect of a cut in price is related to the degree of dealing or the level of some other promotional variable, then the assumption of additivity is being violated. The importance of the violation depends on the relationship among the price response and the levels of the other promotional variables, as well as on the economics of the decision problem to which the analysis is related.

The assumption of linearity not only embraces the additivity assumption, but also goes further since it assumes that the response of Y to X is the same for all levels of X. Or put another way, it assumes that there is a straight line relationship between Y and X.

Homoscedasticity

If a linear function were fitted to the relationship between Y and X pictured in Figure 2a, the amount of variation (as defined by the variance

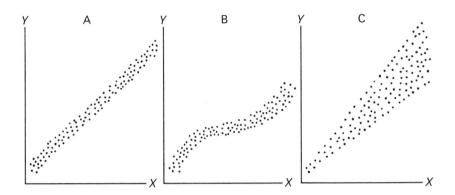

Figure 2.   Nonlinearity and Heteroscedasticity Illustrations

σ_u^2) between the actual and expected values of Y would be the same for all levels of X; that is, the errors would be homoscedastic. In the case of Figure 2b or 2c, the fitting of a linear function would result in errors between the actual and forecasted value of Y that vary from one level of X to another. In these two cases the assumption of homoscedasticity would be violated.

The violation of this assumption often has the effect of increasing the uncertainty (or, alternatively, of decreasing the amount of information) associated with the estimate of the effect (b) of X on Y. Transformations that increase the degree of homoscedasticity help increase the amount of information gained about the effect of X on Y.

Often a transformation that helps to overcome one of these two assumptions (additivity-linearity and homoscedasticity) will also contribute to overcoming the other. In Figure 1b, for example, if the scale of X could be changed in a way that would help to linearize the relationship between Y and X, that relationship would be more homoscedastic than one in which a linear function is fitted without the transformation. Such a transformation would yield a greater degree of both linearity and homoscedasticity at the same time.

The lack of homoscedasticity is not always associated with nonlinearity. For example, in Figure 2c the assumption of linearity is adequate; however, there is a marked departure from the condition of homoscedasticity. What is needed is a transformation that will not disturb the linearity, but will nonetheless increase the degree of homoscedasticity. Transformations designed to deal with homoscedasticity but not linearity are performed on the dependent variable (Y), whereas those dealing with both types of departures can involve the dependent variable or the independent variables (X and Z).

The assumption that the differences between actual and expected share (the u's) are normally distributed is also important, especially with respect to the validity of the standard procedures for determining confidence limits and doing statistical tests. The discussion to follow, however, is not focused on this assumption because there is typically little information on the distribution of ε that is not bound up in the questions of linearity and homoscedasticity. If departures from these latter assumptions can be handled adequately, the chances are reasonably good that departures from normality will not be serious.

Transformations

Exponential

Exponential transformations take the the general form of $(X - d)^c$, where X is a generic observation for the variable in question, and c and d are constants whose value is determined by the purpose the transform is meant to serve. Transformations of this type can be conveniently grouped into three categories depending on the value of c, namely: (1) c greater than 1; (2) c between, but not equal to, 1 and 0; and (3) c less than 0. The most commonly used transforms in the first category are squares $(X - d)^2$ and cubes $(X - d)^3$. The second category involves taking the roots of numbers, of which the square root $\sqrt{X - d}$ (or equivalently $(X - d)^{1/2}$) is the most common. The third category consists of reciprocals of which $1/X$ (or equivalently X^{-1}) is the most often used.

c Equals 2.   In a recent study of household buying behavior for three frequently purchased food products (beer, coffee and tea), [4] it was hypothesized that age differences among older wives would have a greater effect on the expected degree of brand loyalty (Y) than age differences among younger wives. The functional form envisioned by the hypothesis is shown by the plot of function A in Figure 3. If the underlying functional form is suspected of being similar to that pictured by function A, then squaring the X's will tend to linearize the relationship. Function B in Figure 3 is a plot of A after transforming the X's by replacing each of them with X^2.

For the transformation to result in as great a degree of linearization as possible, the minimum value of X should be positive and either equal to zero or as close to zero as possible. If there are negative values of X, d should

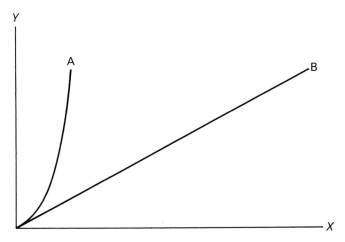

Figure 3. Square Transformation

be positive and equal in absolute value to the minimum value of X. If the minimum value is unknown, d should be set so that all the resulting $(X - d)$'s will be positive. Otherwise squaring the term $(X - d)^2$ will change the signs and reorder the observations along the X continuum. If the minimum value of X is positive, d should be set to equal it.

As is often the case, the violation of one regression assumption is apt to be associated with the violation of others. For example, if the actual relationship between Y and X corresponds to that pictured by function A in Figure 3, then fitting a linear function without transforming the variable will also result in departures from homoscedasticity. The transformation will not only increase the validity of the linearity assumption, but will also increase the validity of this assumption as well.

c **Equals 1/2.**   If the relationship between X and Y is suspected of having a shape similar to that of Function A in Figure 1, then taking the square root of the X's will tend to linearize it. The value of d should be chosen so that the minimum value of $(X - d)$ is a positive number as close to zero as possible. Obviously, the square roots of negative numbers cannot be taken. The farther the lower end of the scale is from zero the less the linearizing effect of the transformation. Function B in Figure 1 shows the relationship between X and Y after transformation.

In the buying behavior and personality study, it was hypothesized that changes in family size might be more closely related to changes in brand and store loyalty for small families than for large, the notion being that at some point the effect of changes in family size on store and brand shopping habits would tend to decline. A square root transformation was performed and the results contrasted to the relationship before transformation.

In the examples shown, heteroscedasticity existed largely because of a nonlinear relationship. The appropriate transformation took into account the nonlinearity and at the same time decreased the degree of heteroscedasticity. While nonlinearity, if it is not considered, implies heteroscedasticity, such heteroscedasticity can occur without regard to the problem of linearity.

For example, suppose there is an experiment where the experimental variable (X) occurs at three levels. Suppose further that the results are like those in Figure 4. The higher the average resulting value of Y, the dependent

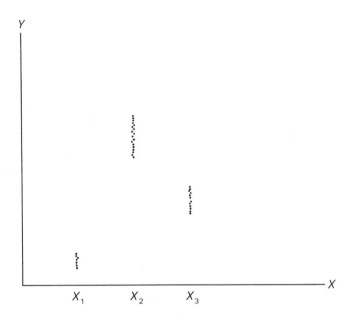

Figure 4.   Transforming the Dependent Variable: Heteroscedasticity

variable, the greater the variance of Y. Where the relationship of the variance of Y is a linear function of the level of Y, a square root transformation of Y will increase the degree of homoscedasticity. The higher values of Y will be cut more in value than lower values will be. This will tend to reduce the variation in each of the three X categories. However, the extent of reduced variation will be greater for X_2, which involves high levels of Y, than for X_1. The same will also be true of X_3. Thus the variance of Y, given X, will be more homoscedastic after the transformation. As previously, the transformation will often be more effective if d is set so that the minimum value of $(Y - d)$ is positive but as close to zero as possible.

Logarithmic

The principal rationale for transforming a variable into logs is that the rate of change in the variable is of greater interest or is better behaved in connection with the model being used than the absolute amount of change. Equal changes on a logarithmic scale represent equal percentage changes in the variable, as opposed to the equal changes in absolute amounts on an arithmetic scale. Logarithmic transformations can be usefully divided into two categories: (1) semi-log transformations, which involve one or more of the independent variables in an equation, and (2) double-log transformations, which involve one or more of the independent variables as well as the dependent variable.

Semi-Log

If the relationship between X and Y is such that the rate of growth in X is more apt to bear a linear relationship to Y than are changes in its absolute magnitude (Figure 5, for example), transforming the X variable into logs will

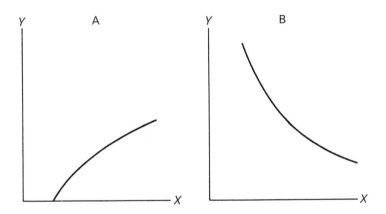

Figure 5.   Logarithmic Transformations

tend to linearize the relationship.

For example, in a two-way multiple discriminant analysis intended to discriminate between households that would become loyal to a new brand of regular coffee and those that would not, a logarithmic transformation of income was found to do a slightly better job of discrimination than was simply leaving income stated in absolute value. A given percentage change in income tended to result in the same change in a household's discriminant score, regardless of the level of income involved.

Double-Log

The double-log is one of the most commonly used transformations, especially in analyses of the economic consequences of trends or company policies. The equation for the double-log transform has the following general form: $\log Y = a + b \log X + c \log Z$. Given that the dependent variable is transformed to logs, the coefficient (b) for any variable (say X) has a natural and useful interpretation: it equals the percentage of change in the dependent variable associated with a 1 percent change in the independent variable. These coefficients are in effect estimates of the *elasticity* of response of a given variable with respect to Y. The underlying relationship between X and Y that is implicit in a linear log-log function is presented in Figure 5b. The double-log transformation corresponds to the assumption of a constant elasticity between X and Y.

One study, for example, focused on determining the response of weekly market share for a given brand to changes in the brand's relative price and dealing activity [3]. By transforming both the dependent variable and the terms used to measure the three policy inputs into logarithms, the coefficients provided direct estimates of the brand's price and dealing elasticities.

These elasticities are, in effect, dimensionless numbers. This means that the elasticities that are associated with different inputs in the same equation, or with the same input in different equations, can be compared without reference to the level of original units in which the variables were expressed. This is useful when wanting to compare the elasticities associated with different markets, or segments of the same market, when the average level of variables such as market share and price are quite different. In the study mentioned before, estimates were developed for the price and dealing elasticities pertaining to different chain stores. Time series information on market share, price and dealing conditions on a weekly basis was available not only for the entire market but also separately for several of the major chains. The brand being studied had quite different market shares among different categories of retail stores. Using a double-log transformation meant that these differences in level no longer influenced the magnitude of the response elasticities as they would have, had the data remained untransformed. This permitted direct comparison of the economic consequences of cutting price or modifying dealing policies for one group of stores with consequences to another group.

Similar types of log transforms are quite common in demand analysis for many types of nondurable, durable, and capital goods. For example, the relationship between beer sales, measured in millions of barrels annually in the United States, to real disposable income is better expressed in terms of a double-log transform [6, 7].

Conclusion

The original scale of a variable is often easier to understand than is its transformation (e.g., What does the cube of a housewife's age mean, anyway?). This fact is occasionally used to argue against transformations. However, as has been shown, transformations make it possible to include a broader class of structural relations (with regard to additivity-linearity and homoscedasticity) than can be handled by most statistical models. In addition, a given value can always be transformed back to its original scale. For the types of nonlinear structure illustrated in this article, this procedure will usually result in a better estimate, either of the responses (*b*) of *Y* to *X* or of *Y* given *X*, than would result from using estimation procedures based on the original scale without transformation.

While some transformations have the undesirable side effect of constricting the normal distribution of differences between actual and forecasted values, for most problems this is a small price for the improved insight transformations give into the nature of the underlying structural relationships.

References

1. W. J. Dixon, ed., *BMD: Biomedical Computer Programs*, Los Angeles, Calif: School of Medicine, University of California, January 1, 1964.
2. Ronald E. Frank, "Store Location and Characteristic Analysis: A Progress Report," Mimeographed, June 1963.
3. ———— and William F. Massy, "Market Segmentation and the Effectiveness of a Brand's Price and Dealing Policies," Working Paper No. 3, Graduate School of Business, Stanford University, March 1964.
4. William F. Massy, Ronald E. Frank, and Thomas M. Lodahl, "Purchasing Behavior and Personality," Working paper, forthcoming, Graduate School of Business, Stanford University, 1966.
5. George W. Snedecor, *Statistical Methods*, Ames, Iowa: Iowa State College Press, 1956, 316–9.
6. Milton H. Spencer, Colin G. Clark, and Peter W. Houget, *Business and Economic Forecasting*, Homewood, Ill.: Richard D. Irwin, Inc., 1961.
7. J. R. N. Stone, "The Measurement of Consumers' Expenditure and Behavior in the United Kingdom, 1920–1938," Cambridge, London, 1954.

4

H. J. Claycamp: Dynamic Effects of
Short Duration Price Differentials on
Retail Gasoline Sales

Introduction

Knowledge of the dynamic pattern of sales responses to short duration differentials between prices of competing products is important to price leaders and price followers alike. Price leaders must determine whether the sales response is adequate to justify continuing the price at the new level, while price followers must decide if and when the new price should be countered. Since the rate of information diffusion and the extent of information seeking by consumers at the time of purchase may cause the sales effect to lag, vary with item or carry over after prices have been returned to former levels or equalized by competitors, dynamic rather than static estimates of price elasticities are required for informed decision making.

This study was designed:

1. Show how regression analysis can be used to obtain statistical estimates of the dynamic sales effect of short-term price differentials on competing products.
2. Provide some first approximations of the magnitude of the sales effect of unusual[1] price differentials on the sales of gasoline at retail outlets.

In retail distribution of gasoline, operators who do not follow a policy of price leadership must frequently decide whether to ignore or react to lower prices of competition.[2] The operator who is not a price leader and who wishes to maximize his revenue can choose the optimal strategy if he has accurate estimates of the daily cross elasticity of demand and the carry-over effect. For example, as long as the cross-elasticity coefficient of daily sales is alge-

Reprinted from *Journal of Marketing Research*, published by the American Marketing Association. H. J. Claycamp, "Dynamic Effects of Short Duration Price Differentials on Retail Gasoline Sales," *Journal of Marketing Research*, Vol. III, May 1968, pp. 175–178. The author owes a special acknowledgment to Phares Risser III, whose efforts made the data available for this study.

[1] Price differentials other than those usually present between major nationally advertised brands and independent or regional brands.

[2] The occurrence of differentials at competing outlets is more frequent than most observers believe. See: S. Morris Livingstone and Theodore Levitt, "Competition and Retail Gasoline Prices," *Review of Economics and Statistics*, XLI (May 1959), 119–32.

braically greater than -1.0 and the carry-over effect is insignificant, the operator should ignore the lower prices of competitors. However, when the coefficient becomes less than -1.0, he should react to the competitive price. Note that the latter strategy may be appropriate even if the elasticity coefficients indicate otherwise. If enough consumers make purchase decisions based on price differentials no longer in existence, the carry-over effect would be large enough to cause a net loss in revenue for entire period.

The model used in this study permits estimation of:

1. The cross-elasticity coefficient for the first day of a price differential.
2. The cross-elasticity coefficient for subsequent days of a price differential.
3. A coefficient for the short run carry-over effect.
4. And a coefficient for the effect of serial correlation.

The Data

Operators of five retail service stations selling a nationally advertised brand of gasoline in a metropolitan area of the Southeastern United States were asked to provide the following data for a 90-day period:

1. Gallons sold each day.
2. Price per gallon each day.
3. Price per gallon for the same grade posted at the outlet which the operator considered as his primary competitor.
4. Incidents which would result in an unusual increase or decrease in sales.

All operators chose competitors selling nationally advertised brands, and no sample outlet chose another sample outlet as its primary competitor. The normal price condition was one of equality on like grades of gasoline. All stations used large uniform signs posted on the premises to advertise the current price.

Stations 1, 2 and 3 were neighborhood stations which presumably drew most of their business from residents of the area. Stations 4 and 5 were located close to major traffic arteries and presumably sold to customers from a wider area.

Weather and business conditions were highly stable over the period, and none of the stations showed a significant upward or downward trend in sales. In approximately 10 percent of the 450 station-days, the competitive price was less than the price at the sample station. Although none of the sample stations lowered its price before its competitor, on several occasions sample stations attempted to lead prices to higher levels. If the major competitor failed to follow, the price was returned to its former level. Most differentials were less than three cents per gallon and lasted for one or two days. There was only one occurrence of a four-cent differential and only one instance where a differential lasted as long as four days.

The Model

The following model was specified and tested on each of the five stations:

$$\frac{X_{i,t} - \overline{X}_{i,dt}}{\overline{X}_{i,dt}} = a_0 + b_1 \left[\frac{X_{i,t-1} - \overline{X}_{i,dt-1}}{\overline{X}_{i,dt}}\right] + b_2 \left[D_1 \frac{P_{i,t} - P_{c,t}}{P_{c,t}}\right]$$

$$+ b_3 \left[D_2 \frac{P_{i,t} - P_{c,t}}{P_{c,t}}\right] + b_4 D_3 + U_t, \quad (1)$$

where

$a_0 =$ intercept
$X_{i,t} =$ gallons sold by station i on day t
$\overline{X}_{i,dt} =$ average gallons sold by station i on the day of week corresponding to t
$P_{i,t} =$ price per gallon at station i on day t
$P_{c,t} =$ price per gallon at primary competitor on day t
$D_1 =$ dummy variable
$\quad = 1.0$ for first day in which $P_{i,t} \neq P_{c,t}$
$\quad = 0.0$ for all other days
$D_2 =$ dummy variable
$\quad = 1.0$ for second day or subsequent days in which $P_{i,t} \neq P_{c,t}$
$\quad = 0.0$ for all other days
$D_3 =$ dummy variable
$\quad = 1.0$ for first day after a price differential in which $P_{i,t} = P_{c,t}$
$\quad = 0.0$ for all other days
$U_t =$ error term

The dependent variable was specified in terms of the relative deviation from the station's normal gallonage for each day of the week to eliminate variance attributable to the day-of-week cycle and to permit comparisons of stations of different sizes.

The serial correlation term (the first variable on the right side of Equation 1) was included to account for the suspected interdependence between daily sales at a specific station. Because of the wide range of day-of-week normal gallonages, deviations on day t-1 were related to normal gallonages on day t. Although this formulation deviates from the usual formulation in a distributed lag model, the regression coefficient for the serial correlation term can be interpreted as a summary of residual effects of past price variations and the effect of deviations from normal sales on day t-1.

To obtain separate estimates for first and subsequent day effects of a price differential, two price terms involving dummy variables were specified. The first price term, involving dummy variable D_1, was non-zero only on the first day of a price differential, while the second price term, involving dummy variable D_2, was non-zero only on subsequent days of a differential.[3] Since the price variables were specified in terms of the relative change of the primary competitor's price, and the dependent variable for sales at the sample station was also specified in relative terms, the partial regression coefficients b_2 and b_3 in Equation (1) can be interpreted as coefficients of the cross-elasticity of price.

It is important to note that the existence of only positive price differentials, i.e., sample station price greater than competitor price, during the data collection period simplified the model. If negative differentials had occurred, additional price terms involving two new dummy variables (say D_4 and D_5) would have been required. Under this condition D_1 and D_2 would be used to represent first and subsequent days of positive differentials, while D_4 and D_5 would designate first and subsequent days of negative differentials. Note that the partial regression coefficients for terms involving D_4 and D_5 would then be interpreted as ordinary price elasticity coefficients rather than cross-elasticity coefficients, and there would be an implicit assumption that the increment in gallonage comes from the primary competitor whose price is used as a proxy for the market price.

Two assumptions were made when specifying a variable for the carry-over effect. First, it was assumed that if such an effect were present it would have its maximum value immediately after prices were brought into equality and would become less important as information about the parity of prices became common knowledge. Second, since there was no downward trend in gallonage for any of the stations during the period, it was assumed that frequent existence of a positive price differential produced no long term carry-over effect. Hence the dummy variable D_3 was specified as nonzero only on the first day of price equality after a price differential.

In order to test the reliability of the findings, the model was replicated on data for each station independently and on the combined data for all stations.

Results

Analysis of results presented in Table 1 reveals the following:

1. There is little serial correlation between deviations from day-of-week normal gallonages.
2. In spite of low values for R^2, a high degree of consistency exists in estimates of the first day effect of price differentials in four of the five replications.

---

[3] Inclusion of the observations for days in which sample station prices equalled competitive prices circumvented the problem of perfect negative correlation between $D_1 + D_2$.

3. Only one station failed to show a higher subsequent day effect than the first day effect.
4. There is little or no short term carry-over effect of price differentials.

The first finding is contrary to *a priori* expectations. Although the combined analysis indicates a slight negative serial correlation, estimates of this effect for individual stations show little consistency. Only Station 1, the smallest of the neighborhood stations, shows a strong relationship between

Table 1.   Regression Results

Station	Serial Correlation	First Day Price Elasticity	Subsequent Day Price Elasticity	Carry-Over Effect	R^2	N
1	−0.193 (1.810)*	−2.971 (1.068)	1.473 (0.344)	0.056 (0.432)	.062	87
2	0.870 (0.679)	−1.708 (1.196)	−4.624 (1.040)	0.034 (0.348)	.045	73
3	−0.043 (0.468)	−1.409 (0.545)	−1.927 (0.563)	0.136 (1.073)	.032	75
4	0.052 (0.463)	−1.860 (0.853)	−4.919 (1.745)	−0.061 (0.597)	.058	77
5	−0.014 (0.121)	−1.743 (1.421)	−3.720 (1.766)	0.033 (0.308)	.072	72
Combined	−0.053 (1.114)	−1.843 (2.227)	−2.916 (2.037)	0.031 (0.622)	.027	384

* *T* values.

deviations from normal on Day t-1 and Day t. The absence of a strong serial correlation term, particularly for the neighborhood Stations 1, 2, and 3, is surprising since purchases of gasoline can be, in most cases, accelerated or deferred by one day, and all the stations make sales to customers using credit cards.

Since little serial correlation appears in the data, and price differentials existed on only 10 percent of the sample days, the low values of R^2 are to be expected. Given that the model accounts for less than ten percent of the variance in sales of each station, the similarity of estimates of the first day cross-elasticity coefficients is surprising. Obtaining four of five separate estimates of the coefficient within a range of −1.409 to −1.860 seems more important than individual tests of significance of the regression or determination coefficients.

Although the range of estimates of subsequent day elasticity coefficients is greater than that of the first day effect, in all cases except Station 1 the subsequent day coefficients have negative signs and indicate a greater effect on sales than do first day coefficients. The greater variability of subsequent day estimates is undoubtedly due in part to the fact that data were too sparse to permit separate estimation of second, third, and fourth day coefficients. Hence, the estimates actually represent an average daily effect for price differential days after the first day.

Price changes at stations other than the primary competitor could also cause the variability of the estimates. However, given the available data, there was no way to estimate the extent of this influence.

The absence of important negative coefficients for D_3 indicates that the carry-over effect of price differentials is negligible. Apparently information about differentials which existed at an earlier date has little effect on consumer's choice of outlets at the time of purchase.

This result could reflect the following behavior:

1. Consumers who are likely to switch outlets in response to price do not perceive price differentials when they do not need to make a purchase.
2. If consumers are aware of price differentials as they occur, they verify the fact before switching outlets.

Additional information from a consumer survey would be required to verify whether consumers perceive gasoline price information when the purchase is not needed.

The results of this study clearly indicate that operators of the sample stations should counter lower competitive prices immediately if they wish to maximize revenue. For example, the expected loss for the operator of Station 5 is .743 percent of his normal daily revenue for each percentage point of the price differential. On subsequent days the expected daily revenue loss is 2.72 percent for each percentage point of the unmatched price differential.

Summary and Limitations

Results of this study indicate that short term price differentials between competing retail outlets produce greater than proportional losses in the normal gallonages of price followers. Although the effect increases with the duration of the differential, there does not appear to be a measurable carry-over effect. Contrary to *a priori* expectations there does not appear to be a significant amount of interdependence between daily deviations from normal gallonages—even for neighborhood stations.

Several limitations which may influence generalizations of these results should be noted. First, the sample was taken in one geographic location and represents interactions between stations selling only major brands of gasoline.

Second, since the data did not include observations of price differentials greater than ten percent, and most differentials existed for less than four days, no conclusions can be drawn about larger differentials and longer time periods.

Third, all stations in the sample were price followers. Hence it would be improper to infer that the same effects would be present if they attempted a policy of price leadership.

Fourth, this analysis has not attempted to measure possible "halo" effects on other products sold by the outlet. To the extent that sales of other products are affected, the impact of the price differential on total station revenue may be understated.

5

G. David Hughes: Developing Marketing Strategy through Multiple Regression

---

This study focuses on a retailer's problem of increasing sales to his present customers, in this instance college coeds. A solution to this problem was sought by using cross-sectional multiple regression that related the size of dollar purchases of the present customers to their appropriate attitudinal, economic, and sociological variables.

Method

The variables selected after an extensive preliminary investigation included: (1) monthly allowance, in dollars; (2) the number of years in college; (3) attitudes toward the store's price levels, quality, style, selection, and sales service; (4) sorority membership; and (5) the coed's purchases, in dollars, at Willards,[1] a women's clothing store in upstate New York. To disguise the identity of Willards to the respondents, data were collected for four additional stores, but only data for Willards are reported here.

The respondents were a random sample of 70 coeds receiving a monthly allowance who had purchased at Willards during the six months prior to receiving the questionnaire. Thus, the problem investigated was: "How can Willards increase its average sales to its coed customers?"

Reprinted from *Journal of Marketing Research*, published by the American Marketing Association. G. David Hughes, "Developing Marketing Strategy through Multiple Regression," *Journal of Marketing Research*, Vol. III, November 1966, pp. 412–415. The author gratefully acknowledges the fieldwork done by graduate students, D. A. Doyle, P. J. McCarthy, M. S. Oh, P. D. Wheeler, and P. M. Worthing.

[1] Store names are disguised.

Measuring the Variables

Data for all variables were collected by mail questionnaire. Although the independence of attitudes and sales reported this way may be questioned, it was the only feasible method for collecting information about cash sales over a six-month period.

The number of years in college (1 through 4) provided a proxy measure of the freedom to purchase that increased with the years away from home. As will be noted below, this variable failed to explain a significant amount of purchase behavior. We do not know, therefore, if the amount of freedom is unimportant, or if the years in college were a poor proxy.

Sorority membership was measured as an attribute, yes or no. A better measurement would have been an estimate of the number of hours per week spent in formal and informal contact with other sorority members. This measurement would enable an estimate of the degree of group influence on buying behavior.

The respective attitudes toward price, quality, style, selection, and sales service of each store were measured on a six-point semantic differential scale, as is illustrated by the following:

	Price				
	High			*Low*	
Willards	6 5	4	3	2	1
Straights	6 5	4	3	2	1

A scale with only six items has both advantages and disadvantages. Respondent cooperation tends to increase as the number of items (and therefore decisions) decreases. But this fewness of items produces coarse measurements, which in turn lead to estimates of parameters that are extremely sensitive to unit changes in attitude.

Selecting the Form of Regression

Ideally, the structure of the regression should be determined by the theories underlying the relationships among the observable phenomena, but marketing, still in the inductive stage of development, lacks theories and possesses few empirical constants. For precedents we must turn to complementary disciplines.

The linear form was selected first because it was used extensively by economists who have examined the relationship between buying intentions and buying behavior. Much of the work reported by the Survey Research Center, University of Michigan, has included linear regressions.

Regressions of Coed Sportswear Purchases on Interdisciplinary Variables

Equation (Standard Error)	Percentage of Variance Explained	Sample Size

---

Linear Equations

Sorority and nonsorority members

(1) $P = -8.341 + 5.082^* X_{sl} + .156^* X_a + 3.199 X_q$
$\qquad\quad\;\;(2.500)\qquad\;(.079)\qquad(3.496)$

$\qquad - 2.480 X_{st} + 1.448 X_{sv} - 1.198 X_y$
$\qquad\quad(3.421)\qquad(2.333)\qquad(2.122)$

$R^2 = .171$†   70

Sorority members

(2) $P = -48.678 + 12.608\ddagger X_{sv} \; .196 \; X_a + 3.933 \; X_{sl}$
$\qquad\qquad\;\;(5.358)\qquad\;(.117)\qquad(4.366)$

$\qquad + 3.494 \; X_y - 2.355 \; X_q$
$\qquad\quad(3.559)\qquad(4.247)$

$R^2 = .395$†   29

Nonsorority members

(3) $P = 6.512 + 5.122^* X_{sl} - 1.867 \; X_y + .066 \; X_a + 3.286 \; X_q$
$\qquad\qquad\;(2.965)\qquad(2.808)\qquad(.115)\qquad(3.926)$

$\qquad - 1.894 \; X_{sv} - 1.464 \; X_p$
$\qquad\quad(2.662)\qquad(3.858)$

$R^2 = .161$ 41

Nonlinear Equations

Sorority members

(4) $P = 80.559 + 43.258\ddagger \log_e X_{sv} + 13.360 \log_e X_a$
$\qquad\qquad\;\;(22.003)\qquad\qquad(8.052)$

$\qquad - 14.285 \log_e X_p + 3.534 \log_e X_{sl} + 23.108 \log_e X_{st}$
$\qquad\quad(15.410)\qquad\qquad(18.894)\qquad\qquad(29.231)$

$\qquad - 17.621 \log_e X_q + 3.524 \log_e X_y$
$\qquad\quad(27.401)\qquad\qquad(7.901)$

$R^2 = .379$†   29

(5) $\text{Log}_e \, P = -1.986 + 1.834\ddagger \log_e X_{sv} + .538 \log_e X_a$
$\qquad\qquad\qquad\;\;(.794)\qquad\qquad(.276)$

$\qquad + .291 \log_e X_{sl} - 1.271 \log_e X_q + 1.146 \log_e X_{st}$
$\qquad\quad(.647)\qquad\qquad(.923)\qquad\qquad(.989)$

$\qquad + .097 \log_e X_y$
$\qquad\quad(.265)$

$R^2 = .476$†   29

---

* Significant at the .05 level.

† The correlation coefficient standard was at least three times its own standard error.

‡ Significant at the .01 level.

P = Purchases of sportswear, in dollars.

X_{sv} (service), X_{sl} (selection) X_q (quality), X_{st} (style), X_p (price) = Dimensions of store image measured on six-point semantic differential scale with 3.5 equal to the point of indifference.

X_a = Monthly allowance, in dollars.

X_y = Years in college.

Note: Variables are shown in rank order of the amount of variance explained; variables that failed to explain any variance are not shown.

The second form, the logarithm of the independent variable, was borrowed from psychophysics, the study of the relationships between physical stimuli and human responses. One of the early laws in this field was expressed by Fechner as:

$$R = C \log S$$

where R is the response, C is a constant, and S is an absolute-threshold stimulus, such as weights measured in grams.[2]

Empirical investigators frequently are interested in the percentage change in the dependent variable associated with a one percent change in the independent variable. To an economist this relationship is the coefficient of elasticity.[3] Guilford [1] suggests that this relationship is the general form for psychophysics:

$$Y = aX^b$$

By transforming the independent and the dependent variables into logarithms, the parameters can be estimated by least-squares linear regression. This transformation yields the third and last of the functions to be considered here. This function was used by Steele [5] when he examined the relationship between attitudes and milk consumption, and by Reilly [3] when he estimated the squared relationship in his now famous law.

The foregoing brief examination of relevant precedents does not indicate a clear choice of form to apply to the problem of developing marketing strategy. Yet, Shupack's research suggests that results are sensitive to the form of the model. He has concluded that there should be further "investigation of the predictive accuracies of a large number of different models under various circumstances."[4] Because this note is concerned primarily with methodology, and at the risk of appearing to be on a "fishing expedition," we will explore empirically each of the functions noted above.

Findings

The equations, estimated by the least-squares method, are presented in the rank order of the amount of variance explained by each. When a variable failed to explain any variance, it was excluded and is therefore not reported.

Initially the coed market was treated as a single, homogeneous segment and a linear equation was fitted to the entire 70 respondents (Equation 1).

---

[2] Guilford [1, p. 37].

[3] For a discussion of direct estimation elasticity see Johnston [2, pp. 48–9].

[4] Shupack [4, p. 575].

The results were not impressive ($R^2 = .171$). After the respondents were divided into sorority members and nonsorority members, a linear equation was fitted to each of these subgroups. The result of the further segmentation were most revealing. The percentage of variance explained by the sorority equation increased to 39.5 percent (Equation 2) while the percentage of variance explained among nonsorority members declined to 16.1 percent (Equation 3). These findings suggest that sorority members tend to be more homogeneous with regard to the variables examined.

Equations (2) and (3) suggest that the merchandising strategy for the sorority group should differ from the strategy for the nonsorority group. In Equation (2), service (X_{sv}) was the most important variable to the sorority members and in Equation (3), selection (X_{sl}) was the most important variable to the nonsorority members. Thus, service should be improved and promoted to the sorority segment and selection should be widened and promoted to the nonsorority segment.

Equation (4) regresses the dollar value of purchases reported by the sorority members on the logarithm of the independent variables. In percentage of variance explained, this function was slightly less desirable because it explained less variance than Equation (2).

Equation (5), the regression of the natural logarithm of purchases on the natural logarithm of the independent variables, explained 47.6 percent of the variance, more than any of the previous equations. This form relates proportional increases in purchases to proportional increases in the independent variables. In this equation, for example, the service parameter (X_{sv}) indicates that a one percent change in respondents' attitudes toward Willards' sales service is associated with a 1.8 percent increase in the same respondents' purchases, an elastic relationship.[5] In the same way, the relationship between purchases at Willards and monthly allowance (.54) is inelastic.

Conclusions

The small experiment described in this note leads to three conclusions about the use of cross-sectional multiple regression. First, the results are encouraging. Marketing strategists should consider the technique as a means of identifying those attitudinal, economic, and sociological variables that are most closely associated with the purchase of particular goods or services. Second, the technique provides a way to identify market segments and those variables within each segment that are closely associated with buying behavior. These variables then become the basis for promotion for each segment.

---

[5] The term income *sensitivity* is generally used to describe the relationship between *dollar* purchases and income, while income *elasticity* is used to describe the relationship between the *quantity* purchased and income. This distinction is important to long-run analyses because of price changes. The term elasticity was used throughout this article because it is more widely understood and because the analysis examined purchases in the short run.

Finally, the recommendations to management were insensitive to the form of the equation. Equations (2), (4), and (5) yielded the same recommendation: stress service to those coeds who are sorority members. Because of the limited nature of this study we cannot conclude that the recommendations will always be insensitive to the form. Therefore, several forms will usually have to be explored. The availability of computers makes this a rather simple task.

References

1. Joy P. Guilford, *Psychometric Methods*, New York: McGraw-Hill Book Co., Inc., 1954.
2. J. Johnston, *Econometric Methods*, New York: McGraw-Hill Book Co., Inc., 1963.
3. William J. Reilly, *The Law of Retail Gravitation*, New York: Pilsbury Publishers, Inc., 1953.
4. Mark B. Shupack, "The Predictive Accuracy of Empirical Demand Analysis," *Economic Journal*, 72 (September 1962), 550–75.
5. Howard L. Steele, "On the Validity of Projective Questions," *Journal of Marketing Research*, 1 (August 1964), 46–9.

B. Simultaneous-Equation Regression Analysis

In a single-equation model, the direction of influence is assumed to flow from the independent variables to the dependent variable. However, there are situations where the reverse flow can also exist. For instance, advertising is usually assumed to influence sales. However, a common mechanism for establishing an advertising budget is to assign automatically to advertising a fixed percentage of sales. Under such a policy, if sales increase or decrease due to exogenous market factors, a change in the advertising budget would soon follow. In this case, the assumption that advertising effort affects sales, and not the reverse, is suspect. To disentangle the two-way flow of influence, one or more additional equations are introduced into the model. The second equation would have advertising as its dependent variable and sales among its independent variables. The analyst then considers the equations simultaneously. If the two-way flow of influence existed, and a single-equation model was used, the analyst could easily be misled by the results.

It is worth noting that in such a model a variable like sales could appear as a dependent variable in one equation and as an independent variable in another. A variable that appears somewhere in the model as a dependent variable is called an endogenous variable. Those whose values are given from outside the equation system are termed exogenous variables. Lagged, endogenous variables have some of the same statistical properties as exogenous variables and are correspondingly grouped with the latter as predetermined variables.

The use of simultaneous-equation models introduces two complications: identifiability and bias. An equation that is underidentified cannot be estimated. Let us assume that the two relationships between sales and advertising were as shown in Figure 1. The demand curve reflects the market response to advertising input. The advertising budget curve reflects the firm's response in terms of advertising input to an anticipated sales level.

If neither curve shifted over time, and the effects of other external marketing factors were minimal, then the data points would lie near the intersection of the two curves, providing no information about the two curves. Each equation or relationship would be underidentified. Suppose, however, that the demand curve shifts over time due to the impact of an external or

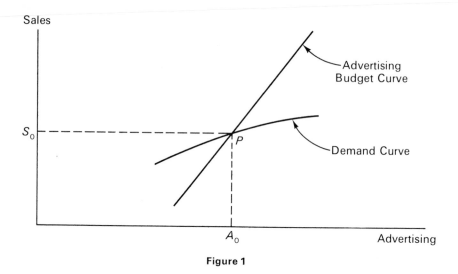

Figure 1

exogenous "shift variable" such as income. In this case, the data points, as shown in Figure 2, will indeed provide information about the shape of the advertising budget curve. The advertising budget curve is now identified, but the demand curve is still underidentified. If the demand curve is to become identified, a shift variable or exogenous variable, which operates on the budget curve (and not on the demand curve), must be available.

When building a simultaneous-equation model, each equation must be tested for identifiability. A simple rule provides such a test for most applications. To identify an equation in a model consisting of G equations, a minimum of $G-1$ of the variables contained in the model must be excluded from that equation. Thus, in a two-equation model, the advertising budget equation is identifiable, since one (2-1) variable (the income variable) was excluded

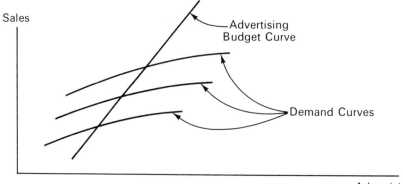

Figure 2

from it.[1] Foote provides additional insight by discussing the identifiability problem from a different perspective.

The second problem introduced by the use of simultaneous-equation models is bias of the variable coefficient estimates. If the normal regression parameter estimation procedures are applied to each equation separately, the estimation procedure is called ordinary least squares (OLS) and will generate biased estimates. Foote discusses the sources and possible extent of this bias. He also mentions several alternative estimation techniques designed to eliminate the bias. One technique, called two-stage least squares (2SLS), has been developed since the Foote article was written and is relatively economical to use.

Farley and Leavitt present a six-equation model of the distribution of branded personal products in Jamaica. The reader can check the conclusion that all equations are identified. The rows in their matrices are the coefficients of the equations. Thus, the first equation is

$$-y_1 + \beta_{12} y_2 + \beta_{13} y_3 + \beta_{14} y_4 + 0y_5 + 0x_1 + 0x_2 + 0x_3 + 0x_4 + \gamma_{15} x_5 = u_1$$

There are five variables excluded (those with zero coefficients), which exceeds the number required ($G - 1 = 5 - 1 = 4$). They use three estimation techniques, including OLS and 2SLS, and compare the results.

Bass presents a four-equation system which studies the sales and advertising relationship. He uses a somewhat unusual technique to test the model. A set of premises about the parameter values is developed and defended on theoretical grounds. The model is then estimated and the resulting estimates are contrasted with the hypothesized ranges.

There is a type of multiple-equation system, termed a recursive model, to which OLS can be applied without fear of resulting bias. A recursive model also has an advantage in discovering cause-effect relationships, since it naturally considers a time lag between variables. Since an effect rarely occurs instantaneously with the causal event, such lags are quite appropriate in causal time-series relationships. Aaker and Day describe a recursive model in the context of a test of several communication hypotheses.

---

[1] For a further conceptual discussion of the identifiability problem, the reader is referred to Baumol, from which these comments were drawn: William J. Baumol, *Economic Theory and Operations Analysis* (Englewood Cliffs, N.J.: Prentice-Hall, Inc., 1965), pp. 221–228. For a more complete, though more advanced, discussion, see Carl F. Christ, *Econometric Models and Methods* (New York: John Wiley & Sons, Inc., 1966), Ch. 8.

6

Richard J. Foote: A Comparison of
Single and Simultaneous Equation
Techniques

In my opinion, much needless confusion exists in the minds of economists
and statisticians when they think about least squares versus simultaneous
equation techniques. Some analysts believe that the method of least squares
now is completely outmoded; others feel that simultaneous equation methods
are so complex and computationally expensive that they should be avoided
whenever possible. Each of these viewpoints is wrong. Simultaneous equation
techniques are a useful addition to our kit of tools for use in problems that
deal with the obtaining of structural coefficients. When they are needed, they
should be used, just as a hacksaw is used to cut metal, whereas various wood-
saws can be used to cut wood. In systems of equations, one, several, or perhaps all frequently can be fitted by least squares. Moreover, least squares
equations are useful now, just as they always have been, in showing normal
or average *relationships* that exist between sets of variables. Many problems
that relate to analyses of this kind, such as choice of variables, location of
data, choice of functional forms, and the testing and interpretation of results,
are almost identical regardless of whether the equations are to be fitted by
least squares or by simultaneous equation techniques.

Because of the confusion that exists, I propose to start with some extremely elementary concepts with which I am sure you are all familiar. We
shall then proceed step by step in such a way as to show precisely when and
why simultaneous equation techniques are needed. In later sections, I shall
discuss some computational aspects and some considerations relating to the
degree of complexity that may be desirable in formulating a system of
economic relationships.

Some Economic Considerations

In 1927, Elmer Working gave an excellent discussion of what now is
called the *identification* problem in his classic paper "What Do Statistical

Abridged from Richard J. Foote, "A Comparison of Single and Simultaneous Equation
Techniques," *Journal of Farm Economics*, December, 1955, pp. 975–990. Reprinted by
permission of the author. The author wishes to thank Glenn Burrows of the Agricultural
Marketing Service for a number of helpful suggestions on the statistical aspects of this
paper.

'Demand Curves' Show?"[1] He pointed out that when a research worker begins a demand study, he is confronted with a set of dots like that shown in section A of [Figure 1]. He knows that each can be thought of as the intersection of a demand and a supply curve, as in section B, but, without further information, neither curve can be determined from the data. Working then noted that if the demand curve has shifted over time but the supply curve has remained relatively stable, as in section C, the dots trace out a supply curve; conversely, if the supply curve has shifted but the demand curve has remained stable, as in section D, the dots trace out a demand curve. If correlated shifts for each curve have taken place, as in section E, the dots trace out what may look like a structural demand or supply curve, but the slope will be too flat or too steep.

In many analyses of the demand for agricultural products, factors that cause the demand curve to shift over time are included as separate variables in a multiple regression equation. In effect, we are then able to derive from our estimating equation an average demand curve. This is indicated in a rough way in section F. In some analyses, we can assume that the quantity supplied is essentially unaffected by current price. When price is plotted on the vertical scale, the supply curve in such cases is a vertical line, and year-to-year shifts in the supply curve trace out a demand curve, just as they did in section D. Under these circumstances, we may be able to obtain valid estimates of the elasticity of demand by use of a least squares multiple regression analysis for which price is the dependent variable and supply and some demand shifters are used as independent variables. This point was noted by Working in his 1927 paper,[2] emphasized by Ezekiel in a paper published in 1928,[3] and reconsidered in 1953 by Fox[4] in the light of modern simultaneous equations theory. For many agricultural products, this set of circumstances permits us to estimate elasticities of demand with respect to price by use of single equation methods. Two points however, should be kept in mind: (1) Price must be used as the dependent variable in order to obtain elasticity estimates that are statistically consistent, since, to use the least squares technique, the supply curve must be a vertical line; and (2) an algebraic transformation must be made after the equation has been fitted to derive the appropriate coefficient of elasticity, since the definition is in terms of the percentage change in quantity associated with a given percentage change in price. Other

---

[1] *Quart. Jour. Econ.*, 41:212–235, February 1927. A similar line of reasoning is followed by Tjalling C. Koopmans in his "Identification Problems in Economic Model Construction," pp. 27–35. This is given as Chap. II of *Studies on Econometric Method*, Cowles Commission for Research in Economics Monogr. 14, 1953.

[2] *Op. cit.*, p. 223.

[3] Mordecai Ezekiel, "Statistical Analyses and the 'Laws' of Price," *Quart. Jour. Econ.*, 42:199–225, February 1928.

[4] Karl A. Fox, "The Analysis of Demand for Farm Products," U.S. Dept. Agr. Tech. Bul. 1081, September 1953.

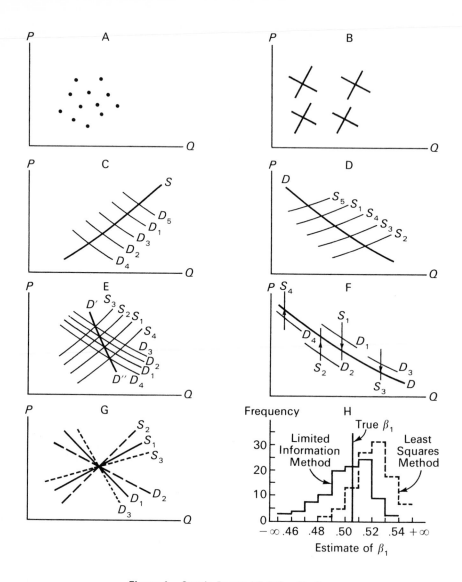

Figure 1. Supply-Demand Relationships*

* U.S. Department of Agriculture. Neg. 1695-55(6), Agricultural Marketing Service.

circumstances under which least squares equations can be used to derive co-efficients of elasticity are discussed in a later section.

What happens if we have a supply curve that is not a vertical line? If we consider any single point, as in section G, we have no way of knowing on which demand and supply curve of a whole family of curves it lies. The basic problem of indeterminateness is similar to that in which correlated shifts in the demand and supply curves take place. What is needed is some hypothesis, adequately tested and proven to be sound, as to the nature of the joint relationships between supply and demand. We should then be able to untangle the two and to obtain a reliable estimate of the slope of each curve. This is essentially what is involved in the simultaneous equations approach. This concept was set forth by Haavelmo in 1948.[5] Staff members of the Cowles Commission spent a considerable part of the next 10 years in showing how to implement it when working with actual data.

Suppose, however, that the analyst has no interest in the true demand and supply curves but only wants a method that will assist him in studying probable future trends in prices. Working had some suggestions on this point, too. He said, "It does not follow from the foregoing analysis that, when conditions are such that shifts of the supply and demand curves are correlated, an attempt to construct a demand curve will give a result that will be useless. Even though shifts of the supply and demand curves are correlated, a curve which is fitted to the points of intersection will be useful for purposes of price forecasting, provided no new factors are introduced which did not affect the price during the period of study. Thus, so long as the shifts of the supply and demand curves remain correlated in the same way, and so long as they shift through approximately the same range, the curve of regression of price upon quantity can be used as a means of estimating price from quantity."[6]

The problem here is that the shifts almost never "remain correlated in the same way" over a sufficiently long period to generate enough data to fit our equation. In some circumstances, changes in structure are so frequent that multiple regression equations almost always yield low correlations and frequently even "wrong" signs on the coefficients. This is particularly apparent when we attempt, by the single equation approach, to study factors that affect volume of exports. In other cases, changes in structure are of minor importance and least squares equations may yield completely satisfactory results in terms of showing relationships that have prevailed between simultaneously-determined economic variables over a considerable period of time. This is frequently true when we study relationships between prices at specified locations or at local market, wholesale, or retail levels. Even here, however, the analyst should examine his results closely, perhaps by plotting the data in scatter diagrams, to determine whether changes in structure have affected the relationship. The in-between case is the one that can be dangerous. Here the coefficients may suggest that the analysis is satisfactory; it may, in fact, be of little value for the study of future trends.

---

[5] Trygve Haavelmo, "The Statistical Implications of a System of Simultaneous Equations," *Econometrica*, 11:1–12, January 1943. A more complete discussion by the same author is given in "The Probability Approach to Econometrics," *Econometrica*, v. 12, Supplement, 1944.

[6] *Op. cit.*, p. 227.

Marschak[7] gives an interesting example of the importance of changes in structure on the need for using a complete system of equations. He considers the old problem of taxation of a monopoly. He points out, "Knowledge is useful if it helps to make the best decisions." He considers, among other things, the kinds of knowledge that are useful to guide the firm in its choice of the most profitable output level. If the tax rate has not changed in the past and is not expected to change, the firm can fit an empirical curve to observed data on output and profits and immediately derive the point of maximum revenue. If the tax rate has not changed in the past but is expected to change in the future, the firm could, if it so desired, vary its output and profits under the new tax structure and derive a new empirical relation. But this takes time, and substantial losses might occur during the experimental period. If the firm had taken the trouble to derive the structural demand and net revenue curves, it could determine immediately its most profitable output under the new tax structure. If the tax rate had varied during the initial period, an empirical regression of net revenue on output and the tax rate could have been fitted and used to find the most profitable output under the new tax structure. In many real-life situations, changes in structure are frequent. Hence Marschak concludes: "A theory may appear unnecessary for policy decisions (or forecasting) until a certain structural change is expected or intended. It becomes necessary then. Since it is difficult to specify in advance what structural changes may be visualized later, it is almost certain that a broad analysis of economic structure, later to be filled out in detail according to needs, is not a wasted effort."

This argument in no way invalidates the use of a single equation to estimate elasticities of demand in those cases in which the supply can be considered as unaffected by current price. In such cases, we may obtain estimates of the structural parameters that can be used in the same way as any other statistically valid estimates. Instead, Marschak is arguing that only rarely should the economic analyst be satisfied with a purely empirical fit if he can obtain structural relationships with some additional work.

Some Statistical Considerations

We now turn to some statistical considerations that have a bearing on the extent to which we can use least squares to estimate the coefficients in a given equation. In the relationships discussed in the preceding section, we have assumed, more or less implicitly, that the points lie exactly on the demand or supply curve. In actual statistical analyses, this is never true, since some variables that cause the curves to shift always are omitted and the precise

---

[7] Jacob Marschak, "Economic Measurements for Policy and Prediction," Chap. I, in *Studies in Econometric Method*, Cowles Commission for Research in Economics Monogr. 14, 1953.

shape of the curves to be fitted are not known. Thus we assume that we are dealing with *stochastic* rather than *functional* relations. A stochastic relation basically is one that includes a set of unexplained residuals or error terms whose direction and magnitude are usually not known exactly for any particular set of calculations, but whose behavior on the average over repeated samples can be described or assumed.

In order to have a concrete example about which to talk, let us consider the following equation:

$$Y = a + b_1 Z_1 + b_2 Z_2 + u \tag{1}$$

Here Y is the variable for which an estimate is desired, the Z's are 2 variables which are known to affect Y, and u is an error term. We assume that for a number of periods we know the value of Y and the Z's and we wish to estimate a, b_1, and b_2. We do not know the value of u but can estimate it in a rough way for any given period as the difference between the value of Y computed from the equation and its actual value.

We know that estimates of the regression coefficients will differ for different sets of observations. However, we would like to estimate them in such a way that the *average* value for a large number of periods or samples equals the value that would be obtained from a similar calculation based on the combined evidence of all possible samples. Estimates of this sort are known statistically as *unbiased* estimates. We also would like the variation of the estimates about their average or true value to be as small as possible, since under this circumstance we would have more confidence in any single estimate than if we had a large amount of variation. Estimating procedures that give the smallest possible variance are known as *best* estimates. Despite their name, such estimates possess no more desirable properties than many alternative estimates. So the choice of terminology is unfortunate, but it has become firmly established. In certain circumstances, we may be unable to obtain best unbiased estimates, but may be able to obtain estimates that are *consistent* and *efficient*. A consistent estimate is one that is unbiased when we work with all the possible data; it may or may not be biased in small samples. In actual practice, of course, we never have all possible data, but estimation procedures that give consistent estimates presumably are better even with small samples than are those that are known to be biased even with an infinitely large sample. Efficient estimates are similar to "best" estimates, except that they are known to give the smallest possible variance only when we work with all possible data.

If we use the method of least squares to estimate the coefficients in equation (1), we obtain best unbiased estimates if the u's and Z's meet certain rather rigid specifications. Some of the specifications that relate to the u's are difficult to state precisely in nonmathematical terms, but essentially they require that the u's follow *some* (not necessarily a normal) probability distribution, that their average or expected value be zero, that their variance be finite and independent of the Z's (the latter is the property of homoscedasticity, for those of you who remember your elementary statistics), and, finally, they must be serially independent. When working with economic data, we usually assume that these assumptions hold; but we may test at least the one regarding serial independence of the residuals after we have run the analysis. In some cases, we transform the data to (1) logarithms, which frequently helps to render the variance of u less dependent upon the Z's, or (2) first differences, which when working with economic data frequently tends to reduce the serial correlation in the u's. As an alternative we may, of course, use first differences of logarithms.

In addition there is a specification regarding the Z's that is easily stated but frequently disregarded by economists. To be certain that the least squares approach will give best unbiased estimates, each Z must be a *set of known numbers*, in contrast to a random variable. When attempting to obtain elasticities of demand, this is true only in rare instances. The only case of which I can think is the one for which prices are arbitrarily set at certain levels, as in a retail store experiment, and the quantity bought by consumers at these prices are recorded. I know of only one experiment that has been conducted in this way—that for oranges by Godwin.[8] The least squares method was developed for use in connection with experiments in the physical sciences, where the independent variables frequently are sets of known numbers, or to study relationships between variables, such as heights of fathers and heights of sons, where no "structural" coefficients are involved.

Econometricians have shown that the least squares approach will give estimates of the structural coefficients that are statistically consistent and efficient, provided the u's meet approximately the same requirements as for the previous case, if the Z's are predetermined variables. A simplified proof of this is given by Klein,[9] although a fairly advanced knowledge of calculus and of the principles of probability given in chapter 2 of his book are required to follow his development. Just as the term "best" as used by statisticians is an unfortunate one, the term "predetermined" as used by econometricians is unfortunate. But as it now is commonly used in the literature, it seems advisable to learn what it means so that we can continue to use it. *Predetermined* variables include those that the analyst takes as given, while *endogenous* variables are those that are determined simultaneously by the same set of economic forces and, therefore, are to be estimated from the model. The predetermined variables commonly are divided into *exogenous* variables and lagged values of endogenous variables. Lagged values of the endogenous variables, naturally, are values of these variables for a previous time period. Exogenous variables include all other variables that might enter into an

[8] Marshall R. Godwin, "Customer Response to Varying Prices for Florida Oranges," Fla. Agr. Expt. Sta. Bul. 508, 1952.

[9] Lawrence R. Klein, *A Textbook of Econometrics*, Row, Peterson and Co., 1953, pp. 80–85.

analysis. Weather is a commonly cited exogenous variable. For many variables, the exact economic structure of the segment of the economy being studied must be carefully considered to determine whether they should be classified as endogenous or exogenous, and frequently different analysts will classify them in different ways.

We now can reconsider an example cited earlier. In section F we showed a diagrammatic representation of a situation for which the least squares method could be used to estimate the slope of the demand curve. We now know that this estimate will be statistically consistent and efficient only if the quantity consumed and the demand shifters each can be classified as an exogenous or lagged endogenous variable. Fox[10] has argued that this is approximately true for a considerable number of agricultural products, including meat, poultry and eggs, feed grains, and a number of fresh fruits and vegetables. Under the assumptions of Fox, market price is used as the dependent variable and the independent variables are supply (which is assumed to be highly correlated with consumption) and some relevant demand shifters, including usually disposable income. Another situation under which we can use the method of least squares to estimate elasticities of demand is that for which data are available on purchases or consumption of individual consumers, as prices that confront consumers are determined chiefly by factors other than those that affect their purchases. In this case, consumption is taken as the dependent variable and retail prices of the various items, family income and perhaps other household characteristics, are taken as independent variables.

One further problem needs to be considered before leaving the statistical aspects of this subject. In all cases given previously, we have assumed implicitly that the variables are known without error. Any analyst who has been connected with the compilation of data from original sources knows that errors of one sort or another always creep in. These can result from memory bias on the part of respondents, inability to find all of the people in a complete census, errors of sampling, and a host of other reasons beyond the control of the most careful investigator. Whenever we work with economic series, nonnegligible errors in the data are known to exist.

Some Econometric Considerations

Discussion in the preceding section suggests, and econometricians have shown that if we use the least squares approach to estimate the structural coefficients in an equation that contains current values of 2 or more endogenous variables, we obtain estimates that are statistically biased. The mathematical nature of the bias has been shown by a number of authors in a

[10] *Op. cit.*

supposedly popular way,[11] but I have yet to find an explanation that is completely satisfactory for a nonmathematician. We do, however, have some experimental evidence of the kind of bias that results when the method of least squares is applied in such cases. Methods which have been developed to handle equations that contain 2 or more endogenous variables are known to give estimates that are statistically consistent, but methods are not now available that are known to be statistically unbiased. Thus, we cannot say for sure what happens when we work with the small samples that usually are involved in economic research. An experiment was designed to measure the kind of bias that arises when we apply these methods to small samples[12] and, as a byproduct of this experiment, we have some concrete evidence of the kind of bias that may arise when we use the method of least squares instead.

In this experiment, a simple 3-equation model was formulated with known coefficients. Variables generated by the model were obtained and random error terms added to them. Two thousand observations were obtained in this way, and they were then divided into 100 samples of 20 observations each. The first equation contains 2 endogenous variables. Structural coefficients were obtained for this equation for each sample by the limited information approach, which I will discuss later, and by the method of least squares. Since there were 100 samples, 100 separate estimates of the single coefficient involved was obtained by each approach. Frequency distributions of these estimates are shown in section II of the chart, together with the true value of the coefficient. Each method gives estimates that are biased, but the 3 highest frequencies for the limited information approach are grouped about the true value, whereas the 3 highest frequencies for the least squares approach each are to the right of the true value. The *average* bias of the least squares estimates was almost 3 times as large as that for the limited information approach. This study was carried out at Stanford University by making use of a large-scale electronic computor. It is to be hoped that further experiments of similar character, with different sorts of models, will be undertaken.

In discussing methods that are used to handle equations that involve more than 1 endogenous variable, it is convenient to introduce a mathematical concept that deals with the *degree of identification*. We saw earlier that it is sometimes impossible to estimate the coefficients in certain structural equations with the kind of statistical data available to do the job. Such equations are said to lack identifiability or to be *underidentified*. Identifiable equa-

---

[11] See, for example, Jean Bronfenbrenner, "Sources and Size of Least-Squares Bias in a Two-Equation Model," Chap. IX in *Studies in Econometric Method*, Cowles Commission for Research in Economics Monogr. 14, 1953; E. G. Bennion, "The Cowles Commission's 'Simultaneous-Equation Approach': A Simplified Explanation," *Review Econ. and Statis.*, 34:49–56, February 1952; and John R. Meyer and Henry Lawrence Miller, Jr., "Some Comments on the 'Simultaneous-Equations Approach'," *Review Econ. and Statis.*, 36:88–92, February 1954.

[12] Harvey M. Wagner, "A Monte Carlo Study of Estimates of Simultaneous Linear Structural Equations," Tech. Rpt. 12, Dept. of Econ., Stanford Univ., 1954.

tions, however, may be *just identified* or *overidentified*. In the discussion that follows, we deal only with identifiable equations. The degree of identification relates to individual equations in a system, not to the entire system.

By algebraic manipulation, we always can write down the equations in a complete system so that the number of equations equals the number of endogenous variables. We then can think of these as n equations in n unknown endogenous variables, and we can always solve the equations so that each endogenous variable is expressed as a function of all of the predetermined variables in the system. These are called *reduced form* equations. Since each reduced form equation contains only a single endogenous variable, we can obtain estimates of the coefficient in these equations that are statistically consistent and efficient by use of the method of least squares.

If each equation in the system is just identified, there is always a unique transformation by which we can go from the coefficients in the reduced form equations to the coefficients in the structural equations. I am sure that many of you have seen this transformation for simple systems of equations, but perhaps it is worthwhile to run through an example to make sure that its nature is clear to everyone. Suppose that we have the following structural demand and supply equations, where q and p have their usual meaning, y is consumer income, w represents important weather factors that affect supply, and each variable is expressed in terms of deviations from its respective mean:

$$p = b_{11}q + b_{12}y \tag{2}$$

$$q = b_{21}p + b_{22}w \tag{3}$$

We have 4 variables in the system and 3 variables in each equation; since $4 - 3$ equals the number of endogenous variables in the system minus one, we can assume that each equation is just identified. Several rules of thumb like this are available to determine the degree of identification; more exact rules depend on the rank of certain matrices.

If we substitute the right-hand side of equation (3) for q in equation (2) and the right-hand side of equation (2) for p in equation (3) and simplify terms, we obtain the following:

$$p = \frac{b_{11}b_{22}}{1 - b_{11}b_{21}}w + \frac{b_{12}}{1 - b_{11}b_{21}}y \tag{4}$$

$$q = \frac{b_{22}}{1 - b_{11}b_{21}}w + \frac{b_{12}b_{21}}{1 - b_{11}b_{21}}y \tag{5}$$

Since the denominator of each term on the right of the equality sign is identical, we can ignore these denominators for the moment. If we divide the coefficient of w in equation (4) by the coefficient of w in equation (5) we obtain an estimate of b_{11}. If we divide the coefficient of y in equation (5) by the coefficient of y in equation (4), we obtain an estimate of b_{21}. Given an estimate of b_{11} and b_{21}, we can estimate b_{12} from the coefficient of y in equation (4) and b_{22} from the coefficient of w in equation (5). This gives the 4 regression coefficients needed for our structural equations. Estimates that are uniquely equivalent are obtained by any alternative algebraic manipulation. Since the b's are known to be statistically consistent estimates, the estimates of the structural coefficients obtained in this way are statistically consistent.

Computationally, we may wish to estimate the coefficients in another way, but the answers obtained are identical to those that would have been gotten by an algebraic manipulation of the regression coefficients from the reduced form equations.

Let us now consider an equation that is overidentified. Suppose that our supply equation contains a second predetermined variable, z, that represents lagged values of prices. We now have 5 variables in the system. The supply equation still is just identified, since $5 - 4$ equals the number of endogenous variables in the system minus one. However, the demand equation is overidentified, since $5 - 3$ is greater than $2 - 1$. The new reduced form equations can be obtained by the same general approach as used previously, but the result now looks like this:

$$p = \frac{b_{11}b_{22}}{1 - b_{11}b_{21}} w + \frac{b_{11}b_{23}}{1 - b_{11}b_{21}} z + \frac{b_{12}}{1 - b_{11}b_{21}} y \qquad (6)$$

$$q = \frac{b_{22}}{1 - b_{11}b_{21}} w + \frac{b_{23}}{1 - b_{11}b_{21}} z + \frac{b_{12}b_{21}}{1 - b_{11}b_{21}} y \qquad (7)$$

With this set of equations, b_{11} could be estimated either by dividing the coefficient of w in equation (6) by the coefficient of w in equation (7) *or by* dividing the coefficient of z in equation (6) by the coefficient of z in equation (7). Different answers are obtained from the 2 estimates. It is in this way that overidentified equations differ from just identified ones; for overidentified equations, we have an oversufficiency of information and no direct way to decide which answer to use. In fact, neither answer obtained by the use of reduced form equations is statistically consistent.

It would be possible to solve the 2 structural equations directly for the several coefficients involved by making use of a *maximum likelihood* approach. Maximum likelihood estimates are known to be statistically consistent and efficient. They are used widely in statistical work because the necessary equations always can be derived by performing certain mathematical operations that involve the maximization of the so-called likelihood function. The general approach is the same as for any maximization process by use of calculus and it is not difficult. For complex systems of equations, however, the mathematics involved in solving the resulting equations is generally complex. That part of Klein referred to in footnote 9 involved the derivation of maximum likelihood estimates. Methods for obtaining maximum likelihood estimates based on a simultaneous solution for all of the structural equations are discussed by Klein and in Cowles Commission Monograph 14 and are called *full-information* maximum likelihood estimates but, to quote Klein, the computations involved in general are "formidable." Hence this method is seldom used.

Another method, developed by staff members of the Cowles Commission, is called the single-equation *limited-information* maximum-likelihood method. In this approach, equations are fitted one at a time and information regarding variables that appear in *each* of the other equations of the system is disregarded. Use is made, however, of all endogenous and predetermined variables that appear in the equation and of all other predetermined variables that appear in the system. This method is known to give estimates of the structural coefficients that are statistically consistent and as efficient as any other method that utilizes the same amount of information. . . . Most of the systems of simultaneous equations that have been fitted and that involve overidentified equations have been based on the single-equation limited information approach. This is the approach that generally is meant when reference is made to the use of the limited information method.

7

John U. Farley and Harold J. Leavitt:
A Model of the Distribution of
Branded Personal Products in Jamaica

Introduction

A behavioral model of a developing economy's distribution system might be useful to governments and private businesses. Governments sometimes channel little public capital into the distribution sector; therefore, balanced development depends on response of this private distribution structure to external change. Similarly, private industry interested in tapping substantial and growing markets of developing countries must understand how the

Reprinted from *Journal of Marketing Research*, published by the American Marketing Association. John U. Farley and Harold J. Leavitt, "A Model of the Distribution of Branded Personal Products in Jamaica," *Journal of Marketing Research*, V, November 1968, pp. 362–368. Mr. and Mrs. C. W. Wilson of Caribbean Research, Ltd., aided all aspects of the study, and computations were facilitated by the Northern European University Computation Center, Danish Technical University, Lyngby. The Ford Foundation Research Grant in Operations Management to GSIA partially supported the study.

merchandising structure functions and how it responds to various elements inside and outside the structure.

Such a model has been developed for Jamaica. This Caribbean island nation, an independent member of the British Commonwealth since 1961, is representative of a group of relatively poor countries experiencing rapid economic development. Encouraged by government support and trade protection, a growing manufacturing sector complements the economic mix including agriculture, bauxite production, and tourism. In 1964, the population of 1.8 million had a per capita income of $441 and ranked among nations in the fourth quintile of the world's income distribution, near such nations as Malta, Mexico, and Chile [18]. The 1950–64 estimated growth rate in GNP per capita was a substantial 5.43 percent—comparable to the stellar growth rate for Puerto Rico during the same period [7].

Description of the Model

The model involves key decisions for each member of the three-level structure:

1. Manufacturers and importers who sell either through wholesalers or directly to retail outlets. A single firm may manufacture or package part of its line and import another part.
2. Wholesalers, located in various parts of the island, who often retail and wholesale. They are supplied by manufacturers and importers.
3. Retailers, including several general merchandisers and fewer other kinds of outlets. For reasons discussed in the appendix, this analysis focuses on general merchandisers.

The model's structure is based on pilot interviews and analysis of data collected at various stages of a cross-sectional field study but not used in the testing phase. The key decisions for retailers are whether to stock a product and whether to stock more than one brand of the product; for manufacturers and importers, to call directly on retailers or to deal through wholesalers; and for wholesalers, to compete with wholesalers of related products that might otherwise be supplied by a single wholesaler. These decisions depend on each other and on sales through feedback on other decisions.

The model has five dependent variables that are influenced by several other elements in the system:

1. Distribution is f_1 (sales, manufacturer-importer merchandising, wholesaler merchandising).
2. Sales is f_2 (distribution multiple brand stocking, income, population).
3. Manufacturer-importer merchandising activity is f_3 (sales, distance from Kingston).

4. Wholesaler merchandising activity is f_4 (sales, distance from nearest wholesaling center).
5. Multiple brand stocking is f_5 (sales, manufacturer-importer merchandising, wholesale merchandising).

The definitions of these elements and of the dependent variables follow.

Distribution

Measured distribution of a product is the proportion of all interviewed retailers who stock the product. Retailers' short-run decisions to stock are based on perceived sales potential for the product; current sales are used as a proxy for short-run expected sales. The product can be supplied and promoted either directly by importers or manufacturers who are aggressive merchandisers, or less directly through repeated contact with more than one wholesaler. Intensity of direct contact is defined as the percentage of all retailers stocking the product who are supplied directly by manufacturers and importers. The index is product specific. An index of wholesale merchandising activity is the number of wholesalers identified by retailers as suppliers for a set of products (discussed later) by all those retailers stocking these products. This measure is area specific. Both indexes of merchandising intensity are, themselves, dependent variables in other relationships.

Sales

Monthly sales rates depend on basic demand determinants of population and income and on certain aspects of merchandising activities. The data indicated that retailers generally adopt fixed markup rules and that suppliers' prices are quite homogeneous; hence there is negligible average retail price variation in Jamaica. Real prices vary, of course, but are affected much more by consumers' income than by nominal price differentials. Population is defined for each product by a supplier-defined target group; men over 15 years old for shaving cream, women 15 to 65 years old for skin cream and sanitary napkins, and the total population for toothpaste. Merchandising practices that affect sales are the availability of product and of alternative brands, that is, ease of access to supply.

Manufacturer-Importer Merchandising Activity

Importers and manufacturers perform similar merchandising activities. They maintain sales forces that put special effort where sales potential exists. As with retailers' stocking decisions, current sales are used as a proxy for short-run expectations. All such firms are located in the capital, Kingston, and their cost of reaching other parts of Jamaica is approximated by distance from the center of Kingston to the approximate population center of gravity of these areas.

Wholesaler Merchandising Activity

As with manufacturers and importers, wholesalers' activities seem to depend on sales potential described earlier and on the distance from customers. Distance is measured from the approximate population center of gravity of a sample area to the nearest wholesaling center. A wholesaling center is a location where more than one retailer identified a wholesaler whose address could be determined independently.

Brand Stocking Practices

As with distribution, retailers will stock more than one brand of any product that has substantial local sales. They also respond to sales contacts with distributors and wholesalers. The depth index of brand stocking is the average number of brands of the product stocked by stores carrying the product.

Distribution and multiple brand stocking are complementary and correspond to the extensive and intensive margins of the distribution system [4]. These margins are analogous to economic concepts, i.e., the extensive margin marks the limit where new land can economically be brought into use, and the intensive margin marks where output can be economically increased on land already in use. Here, the extensive margin (distribution) determines whether the product is stocked at all, and the intensive margin (the brand stocking index) indicates how much the line is stocked by retailers who stock the product. External influences affect the margins similarly, but they are nonetheless separable empirically.

The sales feedback relationship, strong in the empirical results, discussed later, enters all aspects of the model. Using current sales as a proxy for short-term expected sales in the relationships can be justified in two ways. First current sales volume is, in fact, an excellent predictor of short-run future sales volume [17]; models of rational [12] and static [10] expectations are often formulated in this way. Interview results determine the second rationale. For example, the reason for stocking a new product or brand usually cited by retailers [5] and almost universally cited by wholesalers was that they had been asked for the item. Since stocking decisions can be implemented quickly, they rapidly feed back through the sales equation and into the other relationships. This is the behavioral kind of decision making discussed by Cyert and March in connection with behavioral theory of the firm [1]. Interviews revealed that behavior patterns, particularly those connected with decisions to introduce new items, include pervasive elements of problem-oriented and localized search for alternatives and feedback response to request rather than planned response to the environment. Although the sales feedback formulation in the model is a reasonable approximation of the situation, more detailed fieldwork on expectation formation is required.

Identification

The interactions of sales and the marketing decision rules imply an interdependent system of relationships. The variables can be divided into two sets—those determined within the system (endogenous) and those determined outside (exogenous or predetermined). Four endogenous variables cover the merchandising activities of the distribution system's three levels. The fifth endogenous variable, sales, is the key link to the exogenous variables related to basic demand.

Endogenous	*Exogenous*
Y_1 is percent of stores stocking the product	X_1 is target population for the product
Y_2 is sales in units per month	X_2 is income per capita in the parish where the area is
Y_3 is index of direct contact with importer and manufacturer for the product	X_3 is distance from population center of gravity to Kingston
Y_4 is index of wholesale activity in the area	X_4 is distance from population center of gravity to nearest wholesale town
Y_5 is index of depth of brand stocking for the product	

Since scatter diagrams revealed no obvious nonlinearities, the model was formulated as a set of linear relationships. Define y' as a column vector of observations of endogenous variables, [x' as a column vector of observations of exogenous variables] augmented by unity in the last position, u' as a vector of errors, and B and Γ as the matrices of coefficients of the endogenous and exogenous variables, respectively [8][1]. The well-known matrix equation expression for the model is:

$$By' + \Gamma x' = u'$$

---

[1] Editor's Note. The matrix equation represents five equations. The coefficients for the ith equation are given by the ith rows in the matrixes. For example, the third equation is: $0\,Y_1 + \beta_{32}\,Y_2 - 1\,Y_3 + 0\,Y_4 + 0\,Y_5 + 0\,X_1 + 0\,X_2 + \gamma_{33}\,X_3 + 0\,X_4 + \gamma_{35}\,X_5 = u_3$ which can be rewritten as: $Y_3 = +\beta_{32}\,Y_2 + \gamma_{33}\,X_3 + \gamma_{35}\,X_5 - u_3$ where now the endogenous variable in the third equation, y_3, appears alone on the left side. The term x_5 is defined to be 1.

The actual matrices are:

$$
B = \begin{bmatrix}
-1 & \beta_{12} & \beta_{13} & \beta_{14} & 0 \\
\beta_{21} & -1 & 0 & 0 & \beta_{25} \\
0 & \beta_{32} & -1 & 0 & 0 \\
0 & \beta_{42} & 0 & -1 & 0 \\
0 & \beta_{52} & \beta_{53} & \beta_{54} & -1
\end{bmatrix}
$$

$$
\Gamma = \begin{bmatrix}
0 & 0 & 0 & 0 & \gamma_{15} \\
\gamma_{21} & \gamma_{22} & 0 & 0 & \gamma_{25} \\
0 & 0 & \gamma_{33} & 0 & \gamma_{35} \\
0 & 0 & 0 & \gamma_{44} & \gamma_{45} \\
0 & 0 & 0 & 0 & \gamma_{55}
\end{bmatrix}
$$

The last column in the Γ matrix contains the constant term, unrestricted in value, in each equation. The second column in B shows how greatly all the decision rules are oriented toward sales, (Y_2), a variable that shows up in every equation. Similarly, the link of sales to the basic determinants (X_1 and X_2) of demand through the second equation is shown in the second row of Γ. The first and fifth rows in the B matrix, both involving decisions by retailers, are unusual because the corresponding rows in Γ are all zero, except for the constant. The first and fifth equations thus involve no exogenous variables. Despite this, necessary and sufficient conditions for identification are met, and estimation of the structural parameters is feasible [18]. Equation 2 is exactly identified and the others are overidentified.

Normalization of the diagonal elements of B to -1 means that the hypothesized signs of the coefficients correspond to their natural influence on the dependent variables. All coefficients are, by hypothesis, positive except γ_{33} and γ_{44}, the coefficients of the two distance variables approximating travel costs for wholesalers and retailers.

The Data

This article reports the results of fitting the model to data on shaving cream, skin cream, sanitary napkins, and toothpaste. These products were chosen for several reasons. First, preliminary inquiries and coincident pretests showed that markets for these products are in various stages of development throughout the island. Second, because the product classes are narrowly defined and have relatively few brands, suppliers and manufacturers are easy to identify. Third, there are no special public policy or excise problems associated with the products' internal distribution, though there are some tax incentives that encourage domestic production. Domestic production has apparently had little impact on the brand structure. Fourth, the products are in the same expenditure class in previous Jamaican budget analyses [16], personal and medical care. This makes analysis of the four products replicative to some extent. Fifth, marketing strategy for each product has been similar—heavy emphasis on distribution and negligible advertising at this point of market development.

The model is fit to cross-sectional data from 30 of the 32 constituencies into which Jamaica is divided for census and administrative purposes. The sampling plan and sources of subsidiary data are described in the appendix. This formulation assumes implicitly that various parts of Jamaica are in different stages of a homogeneous process of each product's market development [11], although the pattern may be different for different products. This is a palatable assumption, given the geographic, climatic, and cultural homogeneity of the relatively small island.

Ordinary Least-Squares Estimates

The coefficients' signs are generally consistent with those hypothesized since 46 of 56 coefficients, excluding constants, have the expected signs and 23 of these are statistically significant at $\alpha = .05$ or better (Table 1). The coefficients of determination for 18 of the 20 equations are significant at the .05 level and most at much higher levels, although the fits vary substantially over products.

The most apparent particular effect is the impact of sales on the structure at all levels. The sales variable occurs as an independent variable 16 times; 15 coefficients are positive and 12 are significant at $\alpha = .05$ or higher. It thus appears that all members of the structure—retailer, wholesaler, manufacturer, and importer—are indeed responding with decision rules geared to sales or near-run expected sales.

All eight coefficients for manufacturer-importer merchandising activities are positive and four are significant at least at $\alpha = .05$. This influence is therefore felt both through distribution (the extensive margin in Equation 1) and through brand stocking (the intensive margin in Equation 5). These results suggest that any group, public or private, interested in stimulating activity in the private retailing sector should look to the community of manufacturers and importers. This group is small, geographically concentrated, and highly influential on the remainder of the structure. Interviews also indicated that all firms in this group have ties—corporate, personal for the managers, or both—to agents of change, both at home and abroad. For stimulating these firms, subsidies for wider coverage are particularly appropriate since distribution appears sensitive to any such contact. In turn, manufacturers and importers appear to be sensitive to distances they must travel to reach customers. (The distance coefficient in Equation 3 is always negative and highly significant in three cases.) A subsidy would reduce costs associated with traveling these distances.

However, interviews with wholesalers showed that they are rather passive

Table 1. Ordinary Least-Squares Estimates of Parameters
in Five Equation Model

Dependent Variable	Independent Variable	Shaving Cream	Sanitary Napkins	Skin Cream	Toothpaste
Distribution (Y_1)	Sales (Y_2)	20.67*	.0314†	.0737†	.0128
	Importer-manu- facturer activity (Y_3)	3.29†	30.89‡	16.60	35.58*
	Wholesale activity (Y_4)	7.61‡	−26.765	−10.69	−28.96
	Constant	−3.18	33.124	30.08	69.34
	R^2 (unadjusted)	.797*	.491*	.270†	.401*
Sales (Y_2)	Distribution (Y_1)	.0275*	3.040‡	2.148*	5.023‡
	Multiple brand stocking (Y_5)	.0284	133.37‡	−34.642	553.7‡
	Income (X_1)	.0317	1.167‡	.5467†	.779
	Population (X_2)	.0599	.9839†	−.0021	.130
	Constant	.1209	.1736	.1139	.1470
	R^2 (unadjusted)	.897*	.675*	.352*	.548*
Importer-manu- facturer activity (Y_3)	Sales	1.069*	.6829*	1.074*	4.164*
	Distance from Kingston	−.0502	−.2044*	−1.682*	.0218*
	Constant	.1209	.1736	.1139	.1470
	R^2 (unadjusted)	.365*	.6825*	.5391*	.6364*
Wholesale activity (Y_4)	Sales (Y_2)	.2775*	.3010*	.3767†	.2649*
	Distance from nearest wholesale center (X_4)	−.0409	−.2347	−.2139	.0636
	Constant	.6851	.4437	.6810	.4067
	R^2 (unadjusted)	.409*	.407*	.156	.3686*
Multiple brand stock- ing index (Y_5)	Sales (Y_2)	2.231*	.6578*	−.0861	.0735
	Importer-manu- facturer activity (Y_3)	.6354*	.5780‡	.1127	.5671*
	Wholesale activity (Y_4)	−.3546	−1.501†	.1235	.0559
	Constant	.4379	1.963	.992	.9385
	R^2 (unadjusted)	.749*	.314†	.0624	.7436*

* Significant at 1 percent level.
† Significant at 5 percent level.
‡ Significant at 10 percent level.

order takers and that they do very little active soliciting for business. This is supported by the eight coefficients of the wholesale contact index distributed about zero. The wholesalers thus appear inert, for both securing distribution and actively encouraging retailers to stock new brands. The distance variable appears to have only a weak negative effect, probably because the wholesalers are spread over the island instead of concentrated in Kingston as the manufacturers are. It is possible that, despite clustering of wholesalers in market towns, individual wholesalers hold considerable monopolistic power over retailers because of institutional factors such as credit arrangements. This can be especially true outside main metropolitan areas where multiple wholesaler arrangements are fairly rare and where credit arrangements may be crucial to small-scale retailers. Field work is planned to examine these issues more deeply.

The exogenous demand variables in the sales equation are population and income. All income coefficients are positive, and one is significant at $\alpha = .05$. Three population coefficients are positive and one is significant at $\alpha = .05$. Collinearity problems between these variables, discussed later, are probably related to the apparent weak effects of the two variables.

Simultaneous Estimation Procedures

The discussion has, thus far, skirted an important set of methodological issues related to the model's involving a set of interdependent equations rather than a single relationship. Ordinary least-squares estimates of parameters are biased for small samples and are inconsistent when used to estimate the structural parameters of such a system. Even an infinite sample size will not remove the bias [8]. Lack of bias and consistency are not necessarily attractive properties for an estimator but, other things being equal, consistency is more desirable than inconsistency. Various adjustments that take into account interdependencies among the equations produce consistent estimates. Three such procedures were used to fit the equations of the model simultaneously. Two techniques estimate the equations one at a time—two-stage least squares and limited information maximum likelihood. Each is a linear procedure in which certain matrices are adjusted before the normal equations are solved. The third technique, full information maximum likelihood, involves solution by iteration of a system of nonlinear equations to estimate all coefficients simultaneously. The three methods appear to break down because of a problem plaguing many single-equation analyses—multicollinearity.

These three multiple-equation methods will generally yield estimates which for small samples are biased but consistent—approach the true value asymptotically in probability as the sample size increases. Asymptotic properties, especially consistency, offer little relief for dealing with small bodies of data, but they are desirable, other things being equal. Knowledge of the small sample properties of these methods comes chiefly from Monte Carlo studies of known systems of equations subjected to known errors—usually specification errors [8]. Ordinary least squares generally performs somewhat worse than the other methods for squared error, mainly because of greater bias. Recently, however, studies of nonnormal errors and collinearity indicate ordinary least squares is more capable than the other methods in overcoming these difficulties [13]. This robustness appears important in estimating structural parameters of this model. For example, the behavior of the four methods for the shaving cream distribution equation (Table 2) is typical of the results of procedures for all the products and for all equations.

Table 2 shows that, for all three multiple-equation methods, standard errors increase and some signs change. None of the coefficients is significant. Nearly collinear variables in single equations often produce similar estimation problems. The negative estimated variances of the full information coefficients

Table 2. Structural Parameters for Equation 1, Estimated by Alternative Methods for Shaving Cream

| Coefficients Estimated by | Independent Variable | | | |
	Sales	Importer-Manufacturer Activity	Wholesale Activity	Constant
Ordinary least squares	20.67 (4.11)*	3.29 (1.89)*	7.61 (5.91)*	−3.18
Two-stage least squares	58.76 (42.2)*	−4.45 (9.68)*	−31.11 (68.2)*	14.33
Limited information maximum likelihood	65.48 (52.34)*	−4.47 (11.1)*	−41.38 (83.38)*	18.91
Full information maximum likelihood	67.86†	−7.37 (7.81)*	−33.94†	15.4

* Standard errors.
† Estimated variances negative

provide more evidence of near singularity of at least one of the many matrices that must be inverted in this procedure. Of course, there is no such thing as a negative variance. The variances were approximated by an iterative procedure that involves matrices of derivatives, which may be singular up to, perhaps, computer rounding error.

Table 3. Simple Correlation Coefficients of Nine Variables for Shaving Cream

Variable	Sales	Importer-Manufacturer Activity	Wholesale Activity	Multiple Brand Stocking	Income	Population	Distance to Kingston	Distance to Nearest Market Town
Endogenous variables								
Distribution	.867	.655	.684	.745	.596	.183	−.600	−.371
Sales		.587	.666	.703	.657	.304	−.570	−.356
Importer-manufacturer activity			.493	.675	.631	.493	−.392	−.463
Wholesale activity				.483	.668	.398	−.602	−.329
Multiple brand stocking					.488	.313	−.604	−.327
Exogenous variables								
Income						.603	−.531	−.385
Population							−.407	−.498
Distance to Kingston								.454

The matrix of simple correlation coefficients (Table 3)—again for shaving cream—provides additional insight. The simple correlations between pairs of variables that appear in each equation are high, but many others are also large enough to warn of potential difficulty even in single-equation estimation. Wide disparity of the eigenvalues of the covariance matrix for the exogenous variables—one of many submatrices to be inverted in the multiple-equation methods—provides further evidence of potential matrix arithmetic problems [3]. (The largest eigenvalue is 10^6 times the smallest.) Collinearity between income and population (both exogenous) may also partially explain why these variables had such weak effects in the sales equation.

A final matter related to collinearity involves the full information procedure that did not converge in 25 minutes of 7,090 computations for two products and converged in 15 and 19 minutes, respectively, for the other two. This enormous amount of computation time for a small system of equations [15] is another symptom of the near-singularity of some submatrices.

Similar estimation dilemmas are reported elsewhere, and multiple-equation methods are generally considered more sensitive to multicollinearity than are ordinary least squares [9]. Here the choice of estimation procedures lies between biased results and consistent results that are not interpretable because of an external problem. The decision favored the more flexible ordinary least-squares procedure, noting of course the salient characteristics of the alternative procedures.

Summary

A five equation model of the Jamaican distribution structure was developed. The structural parameters were estimated with ordinary least squares for four branded personal product markets in various stages of development—shaving cream, skin cream, sanitary napkins, and toothpaste. Some difficulties apparently caused by multicollinearity in connection with methods of simultaneous estimation of the structural parameters led to the choice of ordinary least squares as the primary estimation technique.

The signs of the estimated parameters generally corresponded to those hypothesized, and the fits were generally satisfactory. For the products studied, it appears that all parties in the structure—manufacturers and importers, wholesalers and retailers—respond sensitively to decision rules based on sales or short-run expected sales. It also appears that wholesalers are relatively inactive merchandisers and that the entire structure is sensitive to manufacturer-importer sales effort. The structure's characteristics indicate that aggressive introduction or demand stimulation programs should include incentives for manufacturers and importers to increase the number of retailers to which their sales forces sell directly.

These four products are, of course, not necessarily representative of branded goods or of branded personal products. Nevertheless, although the numerical estimates of the parameters range widely, the general structure appears similar over products.

Appendix

Sampling

The sampling was carried out in three stages.

1. *Interviews with importers and manufacturers.* All identifiable large im-
    porters and manufacturers were interviewed in 1965 on the basis of
    business registration directories, conversations with other suppliers,
    and the advice of an independent research agency. There were 13 such
    firms dealing in these products.
2. *Interviews with retailers.* Jamaica is divided for census purposes into
    small areas called enumeration districts, each with from 200 to 900
    inhabitants. Sets of three contiguous enumeration districts were drawn
    from the detailed Jamaican census of 1960 [2]. Of the 2,661 enumera-
    tion districts, 234 were drawn; these were supplemented by 37 districts
    from a random sample drawn in connection with another study, plus
    two districts contiguous to each. The latter were included for special
    reasons outside the scope of the present report [14]. In all, 345 districts
    were included. Within each district, all retailers of food, drug, and
    grocery products were interviewed in 1964. The refusal rate in this group
    was zero.
3. *Interviews with wholesalers.* As part of the interviews, retailers were asked
    to identify suppliers of the products that they stocked. (The business
    registers are much less complete and reliable in their listing of whole-
    salers than of importers and manufacturers.) From the list of 137 dif-
    ferent suppliers identified in the retailer interviews, a sample of 21 was
    drawn randomly for interviews in the wholesale sector. One wholesaler
    refused to participate. Always, the wholesalers identified importers or
    manufacturers as their suppliers, giving evidence of a three-level
    distribution system.

The sampling plan, which represented retailers randomly by area, led to
underweighting of large retail outlets. This could have been remedied by
using a sampling frame of outlets weighted by sales; unfortunately, no list of
outlets was available for Jamaica. It also could have been remedied by a
two-stage sampling plan, the first stage an area sample to verify strata, and
the second a stratified sample with probabilites proportionate to outlet size
[6]; it was infeasible to follow this procedure after the initial sample was
drawn and the problem discovered. A disparity of some 20 percent exists
between total industry volumes estimated by the importers and manufacturers
and projections of retailer's sales to total sales in each product class. (The
importers and manufacturers may also err, of course.) The underrepresented
large outlets are chiefly modern drug stores and supermarkets, and the actual
sample mainly covers more traditional, general merchandise retailers.

The enumeration districts are aggregated into 32 constituencies that
became the study's basic sampling units and that also meshed conveniently
with census demographic data. Reliable income data are available only for the
14 parishes, each of which contains two or three constituencies with no overlap; constituency income was approximated by the parish income. Thirty of

the 32 constituencies are included in the sample. Evident interviewer errors in one constituency in the skin cream data could not be corrected with follow up, so the sample for that product contains 29 not 30 points.

References

1. Richard M. Cyert and James G. March, *A Behavioral Theory of the Firm*, Englewood Cliffs, N.J.: Prentice-Hall, Inc., 1963, 114–28.

2. Department of Statistics, *Census of Jamaica*, Kingston, Jamaica, 1960.

3. Harry Eisenpress, *Forecasting by Econometric Systems*, White Plains, N.Y.: IBM Data Processing Division, Share General Program Library, 1963.

4. John U. Farley, "Intensive and Extensive Margins as Summary Measures of Consumer Brand Choice Patterns," in L. G. Smith, ed., *Reflections on Progress in Marketing*, American Marketing Association, 1964, 258–66.

5. ———— and Harold J. Leavitt, "Private Sector Logistics and Population Control: A Case in Jamaica," Working paper, GSIA, Carnegie-Mellon University, 1968.

6. Robert Ferber, *Market Research*, New York: McGraw-Hill Book Co., 1949, 69–76.

7. International Bank for Reconstruction and Development, *World Bank Atlas of Per Capita Product and Population*, Washington: IBRD, 1966.

8. J. Johnston, *Econometric Methods*, New York: McGraw-Hill Book Co., 1963, 246–57.

9. Lawrence Klein and M. Nakamura, "Singularity in the Equation Systems and the Problem of Multicollinearity," *International Economic Review*, 3 (September 1962), 274–99.

10. Robert E. Lucas, "Adjustment Costs and The Theory of Supply," *Journal of Political Economy*, 75 (August, 1967), 321–34.

11. William F. Massy, "Television Ownership in 1950: Results of a Factor Analytic Study," in Ronald E. Frank, Alfred A. Kuehn, and William F. Massy, ed., *Quantitative Techniques in Marketing Analysis*, Homewood Ill.: Richard D. Irwin, Inc., 1962, 440–61.

12. John F. Muth, "Rational Expectations and the Theory of Price Movements," *Econometrica*, 29 (July 1961), 315–35.

13. Thomas Sargent, "Simultaneous Equation Systems with Non-Normal Disturbances: A Pilot Study," Unpublished working paper, GSIA, Carnegie-Mellon University, 1967.

14. J. Mayone Stycos and Kurt W. Back, *The Control of Human Fertility in Jamaica*, Ithaca, N.Y.: Cornell University Press, 1964.

15. Richard Summers, "A Capital Intensive Approach to the Small Sample Properties of Various Simultaneous Equation Estimators," *Econometrica*, 33 (January 1965), 1–41.

16. LeRoy Taylor, *Consumers Expenditure in Jamaica*, University of the West Indies, 1964.

17. Lester G. Telser, "The Demand For Branded Goods as Estimated from Consumer Panel Data," *Review of Economics and Statistics*, 44 (August 1962), 300–24.

18. J. H. Weaver and L. P. Jones, "International Distribution of Income: 1950–1964," Unpublished manuscript, American University, Washington, 1967.

8

Frank M. Bass: A Simultaneous
Equation Regression Study of
Advertising and Sales of Cigarettes

Introduction

There is no more difficult, complex, or controversial problem in marketing than measuring the influence of advertising on sales. There is also probably no more interesting or potentially profitable measurement problem than this one. The difficulties involved in measuring the influence of advertising may generally be separated into three major categories:

1. Isolating advertising effects from the many other variables that affect sales.
2. Measuring the quantity of advertising, considering that advertising dollar expenditures reflect alternative choices of media, psychological appeals, and copy.
3. Identifying the relationship that reflects the influence of sales on advertising, as well as that which reflects advertising's influence on sales—the so-called identification problem.

Quandt [17] has analyzed these and other difficulties at length. Kuehn and Rohloff [12] have argued that because of the severity of these measurement difficulties, greater progress in studying advertising effectiveness can be made by analyzing household or individual consumer behavior than aggregative data. Simple regression studies are particularly susceptible to criticism because of the serial correlation in sales and advertising [5].

There have been several interesting brand-switching studies [7, 9, 10]. However, only a few of these studies have attempted to relate changes in brand-switching activity to marketing decision variables [11, 14, 15, 24]. Furthermore, no known published work deals with the identification problem in advertising. Telser [18, 19], Palda [16], Weinberg [23], and Vidale and Wolfe [22] have applied single-equation regression models to macro sales and advertising data. Besides failing to solve the identification problem, these

Reprinted from *Journal of Marketing Research*, published by the American Marketing Association. Frank M. Bass, "A Simultaneous Equation Regression Study of Advertising and Sales of Cigarettes," *Journal of Marketing Research*, Vol. VI, August 1969, pp. 291–300. The author is indebted to Robert L. Basmann for his advice, criticism, and contribution of ideas. Thomas H. Bruhn, Gordon Constable, and Marvin Margolis provided computational assistance. The author assumes full responsibility for this article.

single-equation regression studies permit only a weak or ambiguous test of the model.

This article suggests that progress can be made in studying advertising effectiveness by: (a) trying various approaches and models, (b) devising models that must pass an unambiguous test, in a scientific sense, to be found to agree with the data and, (c) publishing enough detail to permit and foster debate and criticism.

The study presented in this article is not without limitations. The scarcity of data not only hinders model formulation but also poses unknown dangers associated with errors in the equations. Because data are only available annually, the number of observations is restricted, and short-term variations are concealed.

This study deals with aggregative sales and advertising data, the form in which data are commonly available to management. The model must pass a severe test to be acceptable. Furthermore, it takes into account the simultaneous nature of the relationship between sales and advertising, a serious omission in previous studies. Not only is sales influenced by advertising, but advertising is also influenced by sales. Advertising decision rules, whether rigid or flexible, certainly account for sales. Therefore, single-equation regression models cannot adequately identify advertising-sales and sales-advertising relationships. The multiple-equation regression model explored here deals explicitly with these simultaneous relationships.

Organization

The organization of this study closely follows that suggested by Basmann [3]. The model is formulated in terms of a system of equations including endogenous and exogenous variables—the structural relations. Besides the set of structural equations, the model comprises restrictions on the parameters of structural relations which are determined theoretically and provide the basis for testing the model. As indicated by Basmann [3] "...the testing of theoretical premises about an economic parameter is logically prior to its estimation."

The system of structural equations is uniquely related to a set of reduced-form equations in which each endogenous variable is separately related to the exogenous variables. Assumptions that restrict the structural parameters necessarily imply limits on the parameters in the reduced-form equations. Estimates of the reduced-form parameters taken in conjunction with the implied boundaries on these parameters constitute the test of the model.

This model was constructed to explain recent sales levels of groups of competitive cigarette brands for which given initial conditions and background assumptions are met. The initial conditions for this explanatory model are described by sequences of two exogenous variables, disposable personal income and prices. The background conditions imply the absence of external perturbations.

Each structural equation explains a part of the system of relations being studied when that part is isolated from the rest of the system. We shall construct the model by building the parts and then assembling the components to derive the system.

System and Assumptions

The model consists of two demand equations for two competing groups of cigarette brands and two equations that describe the advertising relations for these groups of brands. The sales of the major filter cigarette brands have been aggregated to give one demand equation for this group. Similarly, there is one demand equation for the major nonfilter brands. The system's two remaining equations describe the behavior of advertising for the two competing groups of cigarette brands. The filter brands are: Winston, Kent, Marlboro, Herbert Tareyton, Viceroy, L & M, and Parliament; the nonfilter brands are: Pall Mall, Camel, Lucky Strike, Chesterfield, Old Gold, and Philip Morris. Sales and advertising data for 1953–1965 were obtained from *Advertising Age* [1, 2].

Since the prices of filter brands are identical as are the prices of nonfilter brands, the aggregation of brand sales in each class is justified theoretically. The Leontieff-Hicks theorem [8, 13, 25] establishes that if the prices of a group of goods change in equal proportion, that group can then be treated as a single commodity. Basmann [4] has shown that this theorem applies when the parameters of the consumer's utility function depend on advertising of competitive commodities. Since the Leontieff-Hicks theorem justifies aggregation in this study, concepts of complementarity, substitutability, price-elasticity, income elasticity, etc., apply to the grouped commodities just as the corresponding concepts and measures apply to single goods.

In developing a test of the model we shall require specification of the structural equations as well as hypothesized limits on the values of the struc-

Table 1. Endogenous and Exogenous Variables

Year	Y_1	Y_2	Y_3	Y_4	X_1	X_2
1953	2.39851	3.50465	−1.26117	−0.28369	3.41653	−0.60906
1954	2.60060	3.45582	−0.90035	−0.37119	3.41876	−0.60906
1955	2.83890	3.42632	−0.62703	−0.43061	3.44491	−0.60206
1956	2.97883	3.38979	−0.43572	−0.44389	3.46147	−0.60033
1957	3.09065	3.33810	−0.34364	−0.55378	3.46451	−0.59176
1958	3.15067	3.30278	−0.34605	−0.53839	3.46304	−0.59860
1959	3.18361	3.30251	−0.30510	−0.54141	3.47986	−0.57349
1960	3.19626	3.29920	−0.33548	−0.53467	3.48502	−0.57675
1961	3.20779	3.29484	−0.34157	−0.54432	3.49358	−0.57675
1962	3.21945	3.27891	−0.36206	−0.54872	3.50804	−0.57840
1963	3.23843	3.25720	−0.28542	−0.54580	3.51834	−0.56543
1964	3.22329	3.20154	−0.29571	−0.54809	3.54063	−0.55596
1965	3.23099	3.21304	−0.31297	−0.49872	3.56335	−0.53910

Sources: See [1, 2, 20, 21, 26].

tural parameters. Although the estimates of parameters are not restricted by the hypotheses, we shall test the hypothesis that the structural parameters lie within certain intervals by making predictions about the reduced-form parameters. We shall therefore give the hypothesized limits on each structural parameter and discuss the reasons for establishing these limits.

Demand for Major Brands of Filter and Nonfilter Cigarettes

Demand Equation for Filter Brands

For every year t, if the demand for filter brands is considered in isolation from the rest of the system,

$$y_{1t} = \beta_1 y_{3t} + \beta_2 y_{4t} + \gamma_1 x_{1t} + \gamma_2 x_{2t} + \gamma_3 + \mu_{1t} \tag{1}$$

where

y_{1t} is logarithm of sales of filter cigarettes (number of cigarettes) divided by population over age 20

y_{3t} is logarithm of advertising dollars for filter cigarettes divided by population over age 20 divided by advertising price index

y_{4t} is logarithm of advertising dollars for nonfilter cigarettes divided by population over age 20 divided by advertising price index

x_{1t} is logarithm of disposable personal income divided by population over age 20 divided by consumer price index

x_{2t} is logarithm of price per package of nonfilter cigarettes divided by consumer price index

$E(\mu_{1t}) = 0$, and

$$\mathrm{Var}(\mu_{1t}) = E(\mu_{1t}^2) = \omega_{\mu_1}^2$$

We therefore postulate that the per capita sales of filter cigarettes is a nonlinear function of the ratio of per capita advertising for the two competitive types of cigarettes and the two exogenous variables. Advertising dollars have been deflated by an advertising price index developed by Yang [26]. Although it might have been desirable to include prices of the filter and nonfilter cigarettes as variables, the nonfilter price is available as a component of the consumer price index, but the filter price is not.

Premises about Equation 1 Parameters $\beta_1 + \beta_2 = 0$. This premise implies that the ratio of filter advertising to nonfilter advertising governs the influence of advertising on the demand for filter cigarettes. Since Equation 1 is expressed in logarithms of the quantities, it may be written in terms of the original quantities as:

$$Y_{1t} = Y_{3t}{}^{\beta_1} Y_{4t}{}^{\beta_2} X_{1t}{}^{\gamma_1} X_{3t}{}^{\gamma_2} 10^{\gamma_3 + \mu_{1t}}$$

If $\beta_1 = -\beta_2$, this equation is then:

$$Y_{1t} = (Y_{3t} \mid Y_{4t})^{\beta_1} X_{1t}{}^{\gamma_1} X_{3t}{}^{\gamma_2} 10^{\gamma_3 + \mu_{1t}}$$

The premise that $\beta_1 + \beta_2 = 0$ is therefore consistent with the idea that the demand for filter cigarettes is influenced by the ratio of advertising for the two different types of cigarettes. This premise and the others which follow were derived from theory and judgment. Regardless of the origins of the premises, they are explicit and testable.

$.5 \leq \beta_1 \leq .6$. The assumptions that demand elasticity with respect to advertising is inelastic and that advertising has a positive effect on sales imply that β_1 is between zero and one. This range has been substantially narrowed to test rigidly the premises.

$1.0 \leq \gamma_1 \leq 1.3$. Filter and nonfilter cigarette brands are clearly highly substitutable commodities, the filter brand being favored. The income elasticity of filter brands is assumed to reflect the income effect over the historical period analyzed.

$0 < \gamma_2 \leq .8$. Consistent with the previous premise, it is logical to assume that the cross-elasticity of demand for filter brands with respect to the price of nonfilter brands should be nonnegative and possibly high.

$-1.25 \leq \gamma_3 \leq -.75$. The intercept term is the most difficult parameter to interpret economically. The restrictions on this parameter have therefore been established residually, using the other restrictions and typical values of the other variables.

Demand Equation for Nonfilter Brands

For every year t, if the demand for nonfilter brands is considered in isolation from the rest of the system,

$$y_{2t} = \beta_3 y_{3t} + \beta_4 y_{4t} + \gamma_4 x_{1t} + \gamma_5 x_{2t} + \gamma_6 + \mu_{2t} \tag{2}$$

where

y_{2t} is logarithm of sales of nonfilter cigarettes (number of cigarettes) divided by population over age 20

$y_{3t}, y_{4t}, x_{1t}, x_{2t}$ are as defined previously

$E(\mu_{2t}) = 0$, and

$$\mathrm{Var}(\mu_{2t}) = E(\mu_{2t}{}^2) = \omega_{\mu_2}{}^2$$

Premises about Equation 2 Parameters $\beta_3 + \beta_4 = 0$. This premise implies, as in Equation 1, the ratio of the advertising hypothesis.

$.2 \leq \beta_4 \leq .3$. In keeping with the premise that nonfilter cigarettes are inferior, we shall test the hypothesis that the advertising elasticity for this group of brands is approximately one-half that of filter brands.

$0 \leq \gamma_4 \leq .8$. The income elasticity of nonfilter brands is assumed to be less than unity (less than the corresponding elasticity for filter brands) and possibly near zero. This restriction is consistent with the premise that income effects differentially favor filter brands.

$-3.0 \leq \gamma_5 \leq -1.0$. The demand for nonfilter cigarettes is assumed to be price elastic and possibly high. This premise is consistent with the assertion that nonfilters are inferior to filters. An increase in the price of nonfilters therefore induces a more than proportionate decline in demand.

$-1.25 \leq \gamma_6 \leq -.75$. The limits on the intercept term are deduced residually.

Advertising Relationships for Major Brands of Filter and Nonfilter Cigarettes

Equation Describing Advertising Behavior of Filter Brands

For every year t, if the advertising of filter cigarettes is considered in isolation from the rest of the system,

$$y_{1t} = \beta_5 y_{2t} + \beta_6 y_{3t} + \gamma_7 + \mu_{3t} \tag{3}$$

or

$$y_{3t} = \frac{1}{\beta_6} y_{1t} - \frac{\beta_5}{\beta_5} y_{2t} - \frac{\gamma_7}{\beta_6} - \frac{1}{\beta_6} \mu_{3t}$$

$E(\mu_{3t}) = 0$, and

$$\text{Var}(\mu_{3t}) = E(\mu_{3t}^2) = \omega_{\mu_3}^2$$

Premises about Equation 3 Parameters $.6 \leq \beta_6 \leq .7$.

$-1.0 \leq \beta_5 \leq -.9$. Equation 3 postulates that advertisers consider the sales of both types of cigarettes in determining the advertising budget for filter cigarettes. The restriction on β_5 implies that the advertising of filter cigarettes responds positively to increases in filter cigarette sales. The advertising response is assumed to be more than proportionate to the increase in filter cigarette sales and possibly smaller for nonfilter cigarettes.

$5.0 \leq \gamma_7 \leq 7.0$. The limits on the intercept term are deduced residually.

Equation Describing Advertising Behavior of Nonfilter Brands

For every year t, if the advertising of nonfilter cigarettes is considered in isolation from the rest of the system,

$$y_{2t} = \beta_7 y_{1t} + \beta_8 y_{4t} - \gamma_8 - \mu_{4t} \tag{4}$$

or

$$y_{4t} = \frac{1}{\beta_8} y_{2t} - \frac{\beta_7}{\beta_8} y_{1t} - \frac{\gamma_8}{\beta_8} - \frac{1}{\beta_8} \mu_{4t}$$

where

$$E(\mu_{4t}) = 0 \text{ and}$$

$$\text{Var}(\mu_{4t}) = E(\mu_{4t}^2) = \omega_{\mu_{4t}}^2$$

Premises about Equation 4 Parameters $-1.0 \le \beta_7 \le -1.5$.
$-3.0 \le \beta_8 \le -3.5$. The advertising of nonfilter cigarettes is assumed to respond negatively to higher levels of sales of both filter and nonfilter cigarettes, but the response is possibly slightly greater to the sales of filter than to nonfilter cigarettes.
$5.0 \le \gamma_8 \le 7.0$. The limits on the intercept term are deduced residually.

Model of Sales and Advertising of Filter and Nonfilter Cigarettes

The model's parts produce the system of structural equations that describe the sales and advertising of the two competing products:

$$-y_{1t} + 0y_{2t} + \beta_1 y_{3t} + \beta_2 y_{4t} + \gamma_1 x_{1t} + \gamma_2 x_{2t} + \gamma_3 + \mu_{1t} = 0$$

$$0y_{1t} - y_{2t} + \beta_3 y_{3t} + \beta_4 y_{4t} + \gamma_4 x_{1t} + \gamma_5 x_{2t} + \gamma_6 + \mu_{2t} = 0$$

$$-y_{1t} + \beta_5 y_{2t} + \beta_6 y_{3t} + 0y_{4t} + 0x_{1t} + 0x_{2t} + \gamma_7 + \mu_{3t} = 0$$

$$\beta_7 y_{1t} - y_{2t} + 0y_{3t} + \beta_8 y_{4t} + 0x_{1t} + 0x_{2t} + \gamma_8 + \mu_{4t} = 0$$

or

$$\boldsymbol{\beta} y_t + \boldsymbol{\Gamma} x_t + u_t = 0$$

Reduced-Form Equations

The system of structural equations

$$\beta y_t + \Gamma x_t + \mu_t = 0$$

is equivalent to the system of equations

$$y_t = -(\beta)^{-1} \Gamma x_t - (\beta)^{-1} \mu_t$$

if β is nonsingular. This set of reduced-form equations is:

$$y_{1t} = \alpha_1 x_{1t} + \alpha_2 x_{2t} + \alpha_3 + \eta_{1t}$$

$$y_{2t} = \alpha_4 x_{1t} + \alpha_5 x_{2t} + \alpha_6 + \eta_{2t}$$

$$y_{3t} = \alpha_7 x_{1t} + \alpha_8 x_{2t} + \alpha_9 + \eta_{3t}$$

$$y_{4t} = \alpha_{10} x_{1t} + \alpha_{11} x_{2t} + \alpha_{12} + \eta_{4t}$$

The parameters α_i, $i = 1, 2, \ldots, 12$ and η_{it}, $i = 1, \ldots, 4$ are functions of the structural parameters. Therefore the premises about the structural equations may be used to make predictions about the reduced-form parameters. Unless all the reduced-form parameter estimates lie within the acceptable limits of their predicted values as implied by the structural premises, at least one of the premises is discredited. For this predictive test to be valid, the determinant of β, Δ, must not be zero. Therefore it is necessary to show that the structural premises exclude the possibility of a zero Δ.

No empirical test can prove conclusively that a theory is true, but it can disprove a theory. Under certain circumstances structural parameters may be estimated without testing the model; however, if the structural equations are unidentified or over-identified, estimation procedures are debatable. In any case the predictive test shows whether a theory agrees with the empirical evidence.

Test of the Model

To test the model, the implied maximum and minimum values of the reduced-form coefficients were calculated[1] and appear with the estimated values in Table 2.

A more complete test of the model could have been conducted by making explicit assumptions about the covariance terms of the structural equations

---

[1] These calculations were made using the gradient projection method with the computer program Share Distribution #1399 SDGP 90.

and solving for maxima and minima of the reduced-form covariance terms. This was not done for this study. The results in Table 2 clearly show that the model satisfies the conditions implied by the structural premises. All 12 reduced-form coefficient estimates lie within the acceptable region. For this test, the model is in good agreement with the data.

Table 2. Maxima and Minima of Regression Parameters Admissible under Structural Premises and Estimates of Regression Parameters

Minimum Value	Coefficient Estimate	Maximum Value
2.30	α_1 (8.75)	39.85
−49.50	α_2 (−7.82)	−0.32
−148.25	α_3 (−31.96)	−7.92
−12.05	α_4 (−2.34)	−0.47
−1.24	α_5 (0.78)	13.50
3.69	α_6 (11.94)	55.75
2.17	α_7 (10.11)	48.34
−62.25	α_8 (−10.90)	−1.19
−215.12	α_9 (−42.01)	−14.13
−15.91	α_{10} (−2.64)	−0.43
0.25	α_{11} (2.77)	20.25
2.83	α_{12} (10.33)	69.87
−1.61	Δ	−0.12

Identifiability and Structural Parameter Estimation

Since the model satisfies the test conditions associated with the reduced-form equations, we may proceed to structural estimation and further testing, if necessary.

In this study, the structural parameters β_5, β_6, β_7, β_8, γ_7, and γ_8 are uniquely identified, i.e., estimates of these parameters are implied by estimates of the reduced-form parameters. Estimates of the remaining structural parameters were developed by two-stage least squares regression, but the significance of this estimation was not determined. The unidentified parameters remain unidentified except for the limits of restrictions placed on them. The estimated parameter values are:

$$\hat{\beta}_1 = .594 \qquad \hat{\gamma}_1 = 1.173$$
$$\hat{\beta}_4 = .247 \qquad \hat{\gamma}_2 = .305$$
$$\hat{\beta}_5 = -.924 \qquad \hat{\gamma}_3 = -.874$$
$$\hat{\beta}_6 = .651 \qquad \hat{\gamma}_4 = .815$$
$$\hat{\beta}_7 = -1.222 \qquad \hat{\gamma}_5 = -2.607$$
$$\hat{\beta}_8 = -3.158 \qquad \hat{\gamma}_6 = -1.027$$
$$\hat{\gamma}_7 = -6.425$$
$$\hat{\gamma}_8 = 5.496$$

Comparisons of the fitted equations with actual observations of sales of both types of cigarette brands are shown in Figure 1.

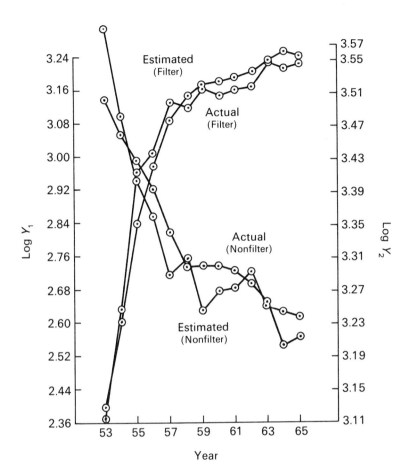

Figure 1. Comparison of Actual and Estimated Sales, Filter Cigarettes and
Nonfilter Cigarettes

References

1. Advertising Publications, Inc., "Costs of Cigarette Advertising: 1952–1959," *Advertising Age*, 31 (September 19, 1960), 126–7.

2. ———, "Costs of Cigarette Advertising: 1957–1965," *Advertising Age*, 37 (July 25, 1966), 56–8.

3. Robert L. Basmann, "On the Application of the Identifiability Test Statistic in Predictive Testing of Explanatory Economic Models," *Econometric Annual, Indian Economic Journal*, 13, No. 3 (1965), 387–423.

4. ———, "A Theory of Demand with Variable Consumer Preferences," *Econometrica*, 24 (January), 1956, 47–58.

5. Frank M. Bass, "A Dynamic Model of Market Share and Sales Behavior," *Toward Scientific Marketing*, in Stephen A. Greyser, ed., Chicago: American Marketing Association, 1963, 263–76.

6. Robert Dorfman and Peter O. Steiner, "Optimal Advertising and Optimal Quality," *The American Economic Review*, 44 (December 1954), 826–36.

7. Ronald E. Frank, "Brand Choice as a Probability Process," *Journal of Business*, 35 (January 1962), 43–56.

8. John R. Hicks, *Value and Capital*, Oxford: Clarendon Press, 1946, 312–3.

9. Ronald A. Howard, "Stochastic Models of Consumer Behavior," in Frank M. Bass *et al.*, eds., *Application of the Sciences in Marketing Management*, New York: John Wiley & Sons, Inc., 1967.

10. Alfred E. Kuehn, "Consumer Brand Choice—A Learning Process?" in Ronald E. Frank *et al.*, eds., *Quantitative Techniques in Marketing Analysis*, Homewood, Ill.: Richard D. Irwin, 1962.

11. ———, "A Model for Budgeting Advertising," in Frank M. Bass *et al.*, ed., *Mathematical Models and Methods in Marketing*, Homewood, Ill.: Richard D. Irwin, 1961.

12. ——— and Albert C. Rohloff, "On Methods: Fitting Models to Aggregate Data," *Journal of Advertising Research* (March 1967), 43–7.

13. Wassily Leontieff, "Composite Commodities and the Problem of Index Numbers," *Econometrica*, 4 (January 1936), 39–59.

14. Richard Maffei, "Advertising Effectiveness, Brand Switching, and Market Dynamics," *Journal of Industrial Economics*, 9 (April 1961), 119–31.

15. William F. Massy and Ronald E. Frank, "Short Term Price and Dealing Effects in Selected Market Segments," *Journal of Marketing Research*, 2 (May 1965), 171–85.

16. Kristian S. Palda, *The Measurement of Cumulative Advertising Effects*, New York: Prentice-Hall, 1964.

17. Richard E. Quandt, "Estimating Advertising Effectiveness: Some Pitfalls in Econometric Methods," *Journal of Marketing Research*, 1 (May 1964), 51–60.

18. Lester G. Telser, "The Demand for Branded Goods as Estimated from Consumer Panel Data," *The Review of Economics and Statistics*, 44 (August 1962), 300–42.

19. ———, "Advertising and Cigarettes," *The Journal of Political Economy*, 70 (October 1962), 471–99.

20. U.S. Census Bureau, *Statistical Abstract of United States*, Washington, D.C.: Government Printing Office, 1965, 327; 360–1.

21. U.S. Department of Agriculture, *Agricultural Statistics*, Washington, D.C.: Government Printing Office, 1965, 111–2.

22. M. L. Vidale and H. B. Wolfe, "An Operation-Research Study of Sales Response to Advertising," *Operations Research*, 5 (June 1957).

23. Robert S. Weinberg, "The Uses and Limitations of Mathematical Models for Market Planning," in Frank N. Bass *et al.*, eds., *Mathematical Models and Methods in Marketing*, Homewood, Ill.: Richard D. Irwin, 1961.

24. Doyle Weiss, Alfred A. Kuehn, and T. McGuire, "Measuring the Effectiveness of Advertising," in Ray Haas, ed., *Science, Technology and Marketing*, Chicago: American Marketing Association, 1966.

25. Herman Wold, *Demand Analysis: A Study in Econometrics*, New York: John Wiley & Sons, Inc., 1953, 108–9.

26. Charles Yang, "A Theoretical and Empirical Investigation of Advertising Cycles," unpublished Ph.D. thesis, New York University, 1962.

9

David A. Aaker and George S. Day:
A Recursive Model of Communication
Processes

A durable model of the communication process is based upon the hierarchy-of-effects hypothesis. According to this hypothesis, the effect of a perceived advertisement is to move an individual from unawareness to awareness and then to knowledge, preference, and, finally, purchase (Lavidge and Steiner, 1961). The simplicity and intuitive reasonableness of the resulting communication process model has led to its wide acceptance in marketing circles. At the same time, it has been sharply criticized (Palda, 1966), mainly on the grounds that the progression is not necessarily a one-way sequence from unawareness to purchase and not all individuals will proceed through each step in the hierarchy. Further, the ability of advertising to influence movement through the hierarchy will depend upon many variables, including the appeals, the brand, and the hierarchy level involved. This paper will examine the communication process, with emphasis on the applicability of the hierarchy process and on the role of advertising.

An earlier paper (Assael and Day, 1968) showed that aggregate brand attitude change tended to lead to changes in brand sales. This current paper extends that analysis by using a recursive model that includes the contributions of price and advertising. In addition, a different model formulation and an improved data base substantially increase the scope and reliability of the results.

Hypotheses about Communication Effects

In this study we will consider market behavior (market share), two intervening variables (awareness and attitude), and two external or exogenous variables (price and advertising). In developing alternate hypotheses, we will first focus upon the hierarchy variables—awareness, attitude, and market share.

This is the first publication of this article. All rights reserved. Permission to reprint must be obtained from the publisher. An abridged version of this article appeared in Neil Borden, Jr., (Editor) proceeding of the 1971 Fall Conference of the American Marketing Association. The authors are grateful to Mr. C. E. Wilson, formerly of The Nestle Co., for contributing the data and assisting in the analysis, and to Arif Waqif for his many contributions to the research. Clerical assistance was provided by the Institute of Business and Economic Research, University of California, Berkeley.

Attitude and Behavior

The hierarchy-of-effects model in Figure 1 makes explicit the assumption that awareness (change) is a precursor of attitude (change), which, in turn, leads to sales (as a change in market share). In other words, attitude is assumed to predict behavior.

A major competing hypothesis (shown in Figure 2) is that attitude (change) may follow a behavior (change). Since this hypothesis is somewhat counter-intuitive, it is useful to look at the various theoretical and method-ological reasons advanced for this possibility.

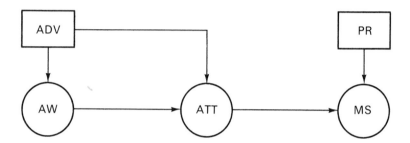

Figure 1.   The Hierarchy-of-Effects Hypothesis, Hypothesis (1)

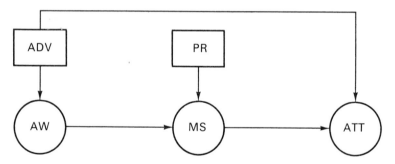

Figure 2.   A Competing Hypothesis of the Communication Process, Hypothesis (2)

Cognitive Dissonance Theory   One view is that attitude change gives meaning to prior behavior change—as in the case of the buyer who has to justify a prior choice or usage experience to himself. For example, "imagine a purchasing situation in which advertising, effective as a reminder of a particular brand name, caused the consumer to select this rather than another brand. Satisfaction with the consequences of the purchase evoked a favorable attitude where none existed before, or strengthened a weak preference" (Palda, 1966). Without attitude change, the beliefs of favorable use experience and weak or nonexistent brand preference are inconsistent, a condition that most people cannot tolerate. Wherever behavior is induced by environmental situations—such as a coupon, or a free sample, or an out-of-stock of a favorite brand—we can expect attitude change to follow behavior change.

Learning without Involvement   A second conceptual argument for a reverse flow of influence follows from Krugman's (1965) observation that television messages are usually received under conditions of low involvement when perceptual defenses are absent or reduced. The consequence is a shift in the cognitive structure but no corresponding attitude change. The acts of shopping, purchase, or subsequent use release new attitudes that support the prior cognitive change.

Methodological Problems   The attitude change triggered by pre-purchase shopping is likely to appear to follow the behavior change for yet another reason (Ramond, 1965). The problem is one of interview timing. No matter how closely spaced the successive surveys, there will always be a significant proportion who change both their attitude and their behavior between surveys. An aggregate time-series analysis of this group would show a change in market share in the period between surveys, and a later change in attitude.

The Effect of Product and Brand Differences   Lipstein (1968: p. 14) argues that the hierarchy model is particularly inappropriate for products where (1) the attitude structure is well defined as a consequence of recent prior purchasing and usage experience, (2) there is relatively little economic or psychological risk in a single purchase, and, consequently, (3) there is little pressure to acquire information prior to purchase. This is an apt description of the instant coffee market to be studied in this paper, which suggests that relatively little attitude change should be expected prior to purchase.

Even within a single product category, the applicability of the hierarchy hypothesis may vary with the positioning and promotion strategies of the individual brands. Little research has been reported on the extent of these differences between brands.

The Awareness Variable

In the hierarchy model, the awareness increase achieved by advertising is assumed to influence attitude, which, in turn, is expected to affect market position. The idea that learning represented by awareness or by brand comprehension precedes and "causes" attitude change was challenged by Haskins (1964). He suggested that the importance of fact learning is overrated by both advertisers and fourth-grade teachers. More important, he surveyed advertising and psychological journals covering a ten-year period noting research projects that reported changes in knowledge and in attitudes or behavior. The results were illuminating. Out of 21 studies in communication research, mostly in controlled laboratory settings with small samples, two showed a positive relationship between changes in knowledge or factual recall and changes in attitudes or behavior, two showed a negative relationship, and the rest showed little or no relationship. Haskins found seven relevant studies conducted by advertising people, but in all cases the expected positive relationship was found to be absent. Thus, there is some question whether awareness is a relevant variable on which advertising should operate. Further, if awareness is relevant, does it operate through an attitude construct or does it operate directly upon market behavior?

The Dynamics of the Process

There is another set of relevant questions about the process that will be considered in this research. How lasting is the impact of advertising on the hierarchy variables? Does any impact tend to dissipate rapidly or does it decay rather slowly instead?

The Role of Exogenous Variables

The expected impacts of the exogenous variables are included in Figures 1 and 2. Price is assumed to affect mainly the market share—reflecting the brand-switching of price-sensitive buyers. It may have some effect upon attitude—particularly in Hypothesis (2)—in that price is an important product attribute for some segments. Price should not have much impact upon awareness.

Theoretically, advertising can operate on awareness, attitude, or directly upon market behavior. However, it is often assumed that advertising is more effective in creating awareness than in affecting attitudes, and that it is least effective in directly affecting market behavior. It will be of interest to explore this assumption and to determine what differences emerge with the different brands. It should be noted that advertising, in this case, is primarily directed at attitude and behavior, since the brands are well established.

Description of the Data

Two data sources were used in this study of the instant coffee market. A national store audit was used to provide estimates of average retail price and dollar market share during 19 successive bi-monthly periods. The estimates of aggregate attitude, awareness, and advertising exposure were obtained from 19 independent cross-section telephone surveys, timed to coincide with the beginning of an audit period. The variable descriptions are summarized in Table 1. Each survey was based upon a national probability sample of approximately 1,200 households prequalified as users of the product class within the preceding 60 days. The 19 data points used in this study compare to 14 used in the earlier study.

During the three-year period of this study, the total dollar and unit sales were relatively stable; thus any increase in the sales of one brand came primarily at the expense of other brands. This study is confined to the top five nationally distributed and promoted brands; none had less than a 5 percent share at any time during the study.

Table 1. Variable Definition

Variable Type	Variable	Abbreviation	Description
Endogenous	Awareness	AW(t)	% of households aware of brand at t (unaided recall)
Endogenous	Attitude	ATT(t)	Weighted average of % saying brand is best at t and % saying brand is one of several better brands at t*
Endogenous	Market share	MS($t, t+1$)	Average dollar market share during period t to $t+1$
Exogenous	Price	PR($t, t+1$)	Price (in cents) that brand is above or below the average price for all brands in the market during the period t to $t+1$
Exogenous	Advertising	ADV(t)	% of households who correctly recalled specific copy claims at t

* The attitude score ATT$(t)_t$, for each brand m, is based on the following weighted sum of responses:

$$\frac{\text{Proportion of total sample saying brand } m \text{ is better than the rest of the brands in the market}}{2.00} + \frac{\text{Proportion saying brand } m \text{ is one of several better brands}}{3.86}$$

The weights are based on the judgments of an independent sample of housewives of the degree of favorableness or unfavorableness of the item on an 11-point scale, using Thurstone's scaling procedures 5. Theoretically, this score can range from zero, if no users of the product thought the brand had any merit, to 50.0, if everyone agreed the brand was the best.

The hypotheses suggested above were developed primarily from a consideration of the behavior of individuals. Clearly, people differ, and the same ones do not behave identically in all situations. Since aggregate data are used in this study, we are asking which hypotheses have enough general application to emerge in the face of the aggregation. It should be emphasized that conflicting hypotheses can indeed be simultaneously operating in the market.

Model Specification

The three hierarchy variables of awareness, attitude, and market share are considered *endogenous*—they are explained by the model. Each appears as a dependent variable in the system of equations which defines the recursive model. In contrast, advertising and price are treated as *exogenous*;[1] they are

---

[1] The use of change in all-commodity distribution as a third exogenous variable was considered. Independent examination showed so little variability over time for any of the brands that it was decided to limit it entirely.

determined by forces outside the process being modeled and are not influenced by the other model variables. Lagged endogenous variables (i.e., those from previous time periods), together with exogenous variables, form the *predetermined* variables. These latter variables are not determined by the model in the time period under study.

The general model for exploring the various hypotheses is defined by the following three equations:

$$
\begin{aligned}
\mathrm{AW}(t) = {} & a_0 + a_1 \mathrm{AW}(t-1) + a_2 \mathrm{ATT}(t-1) + a_3 \mathrm{MS}(t-1, t) \\
& + a_4 \mathrm{ADV}(t) + a_5 \mathrm{PR}(t, t+1) + u_a(t)
\end{aligned}
\tag{1}
$$

$$
\begin{aligned}
\mathrm{ATT}(t) = {} & b_0 + b_1 \mathrm{AW}(t-1) + b_2 \mathrm{ATT}(t-1) + b_3 \mathrm{MS}(t-1, t) \\
& + b_4 \mathrm{ADV}(t) + b_5 \mathrm{PR}(t, t+1) + u_b(t)
\end{aligned}
\tag{2}
$$

$$
\begin{aligned}
\mathrm{MS}(t, t+1) = {} & c_0 + c_1 \mathrm{AW}(t) + c_2 \mathrm{ATT}(t) + c_3 \mathrm{MS}(t-1, t) \\
& + c_4 \mathrm{ADV}(t) + c_5 \mathrm{PR}(t+1) + u_c(t)
\end{aligned}
\tag{3}
$$

This model overcomes many of the deficiencies of past research in this area by considering lagged variables and a system of equations. Further, this model has several characteristics distinguishing it from most other applications of simultaneous equation analysis in marketing—it is a recursive model and it avoids an a priori specification of the model structure.

A model is defined by Malinvaud (1966: p. 60) to be recursive "if there exists an ordering of the endogenous variables and an ordering of the equations such that the ith equation can be considered to describe the determination of the value of the ith endogenous variable during period t as a function of the predetermined variables and of the endogenous variables of index less than i. A model is said to be 'interdependent' if it is not recursive."[2] Clearly, the model defined by the three equations satisfies this definition.

Recursive models have an important statistical property that interdependent models lack. The parameters can be estimated by applying ordinary least squares to each equation, and the resulting estimates are unbiased (Malinvaud, 1966: p. 514). Thus, we need not consider alternate estimation techniques—a convenient circumstance considering the difficulty that other researchers have had in applying and interpreting alternate estimation methods (e.g., Farley and Leavitt, 1968).

Perhaps more important, recursive models using lagged endogenous variables permit direction-of-influence interpretations to emerge. Malinvaud has summarized the position of Wold (1954), who contributed in the mid-fifties to the development of the theory of recursive models, as follows: " Herman Wold supported the thesis that a good model should describe causal chains and therefore be recursive, since in reality one quantity cannot be at the same time cause and effect of another" (Malinvaud, 1966: p. 60).

---

[2] This definition is sufficient for a deterministic model. With the error terms included, we must also assume that the covariance matrix of the error terms is a diagonal.

A second characteristic of the model defined by Equations (1), (2), and (3) is that any one of several behavioral hypotheses is permitted to emerge. In contrast, most researchers, in using simultaneous equation models (e.g., Bass, 1969; Farley and Leavitt, 1968; and Farley and Ring, n.d.), specify a structure compatible with some "model" or hypothesis and deduce parameter values which are then compared with resulting parameter estimates. The underlying model is deemed supported if a suitable number of estimates are "reasonable." In this research, we avoid the a priori specification of a structure. Rather, the parameter estimates are permitted to suggest a posteriori the structure-defining constraints. The objective is to avoid inhibiting the empirical phase wherever possible.

The model is also in a distributed-lag format, since in each equation the dependent variable, lagged one period, is included among the independent variables. Distributed-lag models have been applied in marketing by Palda (1964), Massy and Frank (1965), and others. The assumption of the most common single-equation version of this model is that the independent variables have an immediate impact, and also a carry-over (or "distribution" over time) effect, that decays geometrically. In the case of two variables, the model would appear as:

$$\begin{aligned} \text{MS}(t, t+1) = a &+ b_1\text{ATT}(t) + b_2\lambda\text{ATT}(t-1) + b_3\lambda^2\text{ATT}(t-2) \\ &+ \cdots + c_1\text{AW}(t) + c_2\lambda\text{AW}(t-1) + c_3\lambda^2\text{AW}(t-2) \\ &+ \cdots \end{aligned} \tag{4}$$

If we multiply Equation (4), lagged one period, by λ and subtract it from Equation (4), we get:

$$\text{MS}(t, t+1) = a + \lambda\text{MS}(t-1, t) + b_1\text{ATT}(t) + c_1\text{AW}(t) \tag{5}$$

Thus, the coefficient, λ, of the lagged endogenous variable becomes a measure of the extent to which the influence of the independent variables are dissipated quickly. If it is large, then their influence is distributed over many time periods.

In summary, the model is conceived to contain the types of evidence relevant to causation studies (Green and Tull, 1966: pp. 96–98), associative variation, sequence of events (the lagged endogenous variables), and the absence of other possible causal factors (via the inclusion of relevant exogenous variables and the lack of an a priori imposed structure).

Results

The Quality of the Results

Scatter diagrams of a sample of the data did not suggest any nonlinearities, so no transformations were performed. The price variable was available only for Brands 3, 4, and 5. Consequently, the model with the price variable

Table 2. Regression Results, Price Excluded* (t Values in Parentheses)

Brand	Dependent Variable	AW($t-1$)	ATT($t-1$)	MS($t-1, t$)	ADV(t)	a_0	R^2†	Standard Error	Durbin-Watson	Sample Size
1	AW(t)	0.39 (1.80)	3.30 (1.20)	-2.01 (1.40)	2.85 (2.42)	21.8 (3.65)	0.50	3.96	1.84	19
2	AW(t)	0.01 (0.06)	-0.18 (0.11)	2.13 (1.44)	2.6 (3.82)	11.2 (1.6)	0.62	1.42	1.52	19
3	AW(t)	0.30 (1.06)	0.75 (0.47)	-0.33 (0.26)	0.16 (0.81)	23.2 (2.41)	0.42	1.81	1.98	19
4	AW(t)	0.26 (0.96)	-4.13 (1.30)	0.95 (0.57)	1.2 (2.6)	33.61 (1.97)	0.38	4.67	2.10	19
5	AW(t)	0.61 (2.56)	-0.08 (1.52)	0.08 (0.24)	0.42 (2.67)	24.5 (1.5)	0.57	1.42	1.52	19
All	AW(t)	0.37 (3.60)	-0.09 (0.86)	0.33 (0.71)	0.46 (3.01)	—	0.977	3.20	1.90	95

Brand	Dependent Variable	AW($t-1$)	ATT($t-1$)	MS($t-1, t$)	ADV(t)	b_0	R^2†	Standard Error	Durbin-Watson	Sample Size
1	ATT(t)	-0.01 (0.68)	0.45 (1.84)	0.07 (0.57)	0.13 (0.92)	0.88 (1.70)	0.30	0.35	1.84	19
2	ATT(t)	-0.01 (0.15)	-0.18 (0.53)	0.68 (2.07)	0.10 (0.68)	0.48 (0.32)	0.30	0.39	1.77	19
3	ATT(t)	0.11 (1.89)	-0.08 (0.26)	0.09 (0.34)	0.03 (0.85)	-0.21 (0.11)	0.55	0.37	1.55	19
4	ATT(t)	0.01 (0.67)	0.16 (0.70)	-0.03 (0.27)	0.11 (3.37)	2.51 (2.02)	0.54	0.34	1.98	19
5	ATT(t)	0.23 (1.28)	0.02 (0.49)	0.13 (0.51)	0.27 (2.3)	-13.5 (1.09)	0.51	1.07	2.70	19
All	ATT(t)	0.01 (0.36)	0.03 (1.70)	0.26 (3.00)	0.10 (3.60)	—	0.986	0.60	2.20	95

Brand	Dependent Variable	AW($t-1$)	ATT($t-1$)	MS($t-1, t$)	ADV(t)	c_0	R^2†	Standard Error	Durbin-Watson	Sample Size
1	MS($t, t+1$)	0.05 (1.23)	0.70 (1.40)	0.03 (0.18)	0.01 (0.04)	2.45 (1.80)	0.40	0.65	1.03	19
2	MS($t, t+1$)	-0.05 (1.26)	0.35 (2.20)	0.76 (5.20)	-0.76 (0.07)	1.27 (1.86)	0.79	0.20	1.98	19
3	MS($t, t+1$)	0.06 (1.12)	0.03 (0.14)	0.70 (3.30)	0.02 (0.68)	-0.31 (0.16)	0.80	0.32	1.68	19
4	MS($t, t+1$)	0.05 (1.27)	0.71 (1.27)	0.23 (1.05)	-0.08 (0.80)	-4.34 (1.38)	0.34	0.72	2.36	19
5	MS($t, t+1$)	0.23 (1.77)	0.66 (3.35)	0.34 (2.07)	-0.12 (1.37)	-4.33 (0.46)	0.78	0.83	2.40	19
All	MS($t, t+1$)	0.05 (6.05)	0.40 (5.77)	0.51 (6.92)	0.06 (1.63)	—	0.998	0.52	2.34	95

* Dummy variables for each brand were inserted in the aggregate equations.   † R^2 is unadjusted.

Table 3. Regression Results, Price Included,* Brands 3–5 (t Values in Parentheses)

Brand	Dependent Variable	AW$(t-1)$	ATT$(t-1)$	MS$(t-1,t)$	ADV(t)	PR(t)	a_0	R^2†	Standard Error	Durbin-Watson	Sample Size
3	AW(t)	0.28 (0.85)	0.79 (0.47)	−0.40 (0.29)	0.16 (0.79)	0.06 (0.15)	24.10 (2.05)	0.42	1.90	2.00	19
4	AW(t)	0.22 (0.80)	−3.24 (0.92)	0.42 (0.23)	1.15 (2.50)	−0.21 (0.30)	38.8 (2.05)	0.41	4.7	2.13	19
5	AW(t)	0.61 (2.50)	−0.07 (1.43)	0.14 (0.39)	4.6 (2.5)	−0.15 (0.47)	21.8 (1.23)	0.58	1.5	1.5	19
All	AW(t)	0.17 (1.33)	−0.04 (0.40)	0.16 (0.33)	0.44 (3.27)	−0.26 (1.72)	—	0.982	3.06	2.08	57
		AW$(t-1)$	ATT$(t-1)$	MS$(t-1,t)$	ADV(t)	PR(t)	b_0				
3	ATT(t)	0.13 (1.96)	−0.12 (0.37)	0.15 (0.53)	0.03 (0.82)	−0.05 (0.66)	−1.04 (0.44)	0.57	0.37	1.62	19
4	ATT(t)	0.02 (0.91)	0.05 (0.20)	0.04 (0.29)	0.12 (3.60)	0.03 (1.30)	1.83 (1.41)	0.59	0.33	2.31	19
5	ATT(t)	0.23 (1.40)	0.01 (0.33)	−0.06 (0.26)	0.16 (1.40)	0.46 (2.15)	−5.4 (0.46)	0.64	0.96	2.80	19
All	ATT(t)	0.02 (0.58)	0.03 (1.33)	0.24 (2.25)	0.09 (2.70)	0.06 (1.82)	—	0.985	0.70	2.10	57
		AW$(t-1)$	ATT$(t-1)$	MS$(t-1,t)$	ADV(t)	PR(t)	c_0				
3	MS$(t,t+1)$	0.06 (1.05)	0.03 (0.14)	0.68 (2.96)	0.02 (0.65)	0.07 (0.11)	−0.22 (0.10)	0.80	0.33	1.66	19
4	MS$(t,t+1)$	0.03 (0.69)	1.05 (1.69)	0.12 (0.49)	−0.10 (1.00)	−0.06 (1.16)	5.68 (1.72)	0.40	0.72	2.43	19
5	MS$(t,t+1)$	0.28 (2.13)	0.49 (2.16)	0.25 (1.43)	−0.17 (1.80)	0.29 (1.37)	−2.36 (0.25)	0.81	0.81	2.47	19
All	MS$(t,t+1)$	0.05 (1.64)	0.62 (4.46)	0.41 (3.95)	−0.24 (0.67)	−0.45 (0.12)	—	0.997	0.67	2.39	57

Independent Variables span the AW$(t-1)$ through constant columns.

* Dummy variables for each brand were inserted in the aggregate equations.   † R^2 is unadjusted.

deleted was first estimated using ordinary least squares (OLS) for each of the five brands individually, and for all five brands combined. The results are shown in Table 2. The model with the price variable included was then run on Brands 3, 4, and 5 individually, and on the three brands combined. These results are presented in Table 3.

When the brands were aggregated, dummy variables were inserted to compensate for the different variable levels at which the brands operate. An assumption of the model when applied to this aggregate data is that each coefficient is the same for all brands. A gross comparison of the individual brand coefficients and their standard deviations indicates that this assumption is not extremely unreasonable.[3]

The R^2 values for the individual brands are certainly respectable. The lowest R^2 is 0.30, and in two thirds of the equations it is over 0.50. Further, in over half of the equations the lagged endogenous variable is not significant, so the remaining variables are explaining most of the variance. The R^2 for the equations with aggregated data are deceptively high. The three brands had relatively small variation around different levels, reflecting the fact that they had very different average market shares. Thus, the total variance went up enormously when the brands were combined. The standard error of regression is the more appropriate indicator of the performance with the aggregated set.

A common problem in time series studies is serial correlation, which leads to inefficient coefficient estimates and understated estimates of coefficient variances. The Durbin-Watson statistics shown in the tables indicate that this statistical problem is not troublesome in this research. Over half of the values are above the upper limit of the Durbin-Watson test, and none are close to the lower limit at which the hypothesis of serial independence is rejected. However, this test is biased when lagged dependent variables are used. This bias, of course, is small when the lagged dependent variables are insignificant, as they often were in this research, especially in the awareness and attitude equations. Further, several of the equations were run with the dependent variable omitted. The results suggest that if the bias were removed from the test, the hypothesis of serial independence would still not be rejected at the 0.05 level.

Testing Specific Hypotheses

First, consider Table 2. The influence of AW upon ATT seems extremely low. In the aggregate, the t value is only 0.36. Only Brand 3 has a positive coefficient significant at the 0.10 level, and Brands 1 and 2 have negative

---

[3] The model was also run with the data divided by the appropriate mean for each brand. The results were not affected significantly. Thus, we have reported the results using the original data so that the results will have more meaning.

coefficients. In contrast, AW seems to be much more significant in the MS equation. In the aggregate, the t value is 6.05, and all the coefficients except that of Brand 2 are positive, with t values exceeding 1.0. This result casts some doubt upon the hierarchy concept as portrayed in Hypothesis 1. However, it is undoubtedly also reflecting the fact that there is a longer time lag between AW$(t-1)$ and ATT(t) than between AW(t) and MS$(t, t+1)$. It may be that a shorter time lag between AW$(t-1)$ and ATT(t) would show a greater relationship. Nevertheless, the minimal impact of lagged AW on ATT and the strong link between AW and MS are surprising.

As expected, neither the ATT nor the MS variable seemed to influence the AW variable to any significant degree. The relevant t values in the aggregate case were both below 1.0. It should be noted that Brand 2 has a relatively high positive MS coefficient in the AW equation. Thus, there is some suggestion in the Brand 2 case, especially noting the negative AW coefficient in the MS equation, that usage is preceding and perhaps "causing" changes in the awareness level. There are at least two possible explanations for this finding. First, impulse buying may be particularly important for this brand. Second, it might indicate that for this brand the link between AW and MS influences purchase behavior very quickly. If AW and MS were affected in the same time period, the AW would appear to follow the MS change, since it was measured at the end of the time period. Brand 2 differed from the others in that it had a higher emphasis upon quality. It was also available as a regular coffee. Further, it was the smallest brand studied and did grow slightly during the time periods involved.

We now consider the ATT and MS terms which are at the heart of the two major competing hypotheses summarized in Figures 1 and 2. Does an attitude change precede and cause a behavioral change, or does the reverse occur? It seems clear that ATT is a significant influence on MS in this study. In the aggregate, the t value of the ATT coefficient in the MS equation was 5.77, and the t values for Brands 2 and 5 were over 2.2. Only for Brand 3 was the t value low. In the ATT equation, the conclusion is not so clear. The coefficients and t values are lower. Only Brand 2 had a significantly positive coefficient. These results thus offer some support to the hierarchy-of-effects hypothesis. However, there is certainly evidence of some influence moving in the opposite direction. In the aggregate, the MS t value in the ATT equation was 3.0, and for Brand 2 it was 2.07. Also, the effect of MS on ATT seems higher than that of AW. However, there is a methodological bias, as mentioned before, which tends to emphasize the MS to ATT flow of influence. It is caused by the fact that an MS and ATT change in the same time period will appear as an MS to ATT flow of influence. With this in mind, the ATT to MS flow of influence predicted by the hierarchy model does seem to appear more dominant in this study.

These conclusions do not seem to be affected by the addition of the price variable in Table 3. For example, the AW coefficients in the ATT equation are slightly higher, but still only those of Brand 3 are significantly positive.

The *advertising* variable was expected to influence AW, and to a lesser extent ATT, but to have little direct impact upon MS. These hypotheses seem to be supported. In Table 2, the impact of ADV upon MS seems small. It is negative, in fact, for three of the five brands. When price is added in Table 3, the negative coefficient for Brand 5 becomes significant. In contrast, ADV is a strong influence upon AW and ATT. In the AW equation there is only one case where the ADV variable is not significantly positive. In the ATT equation the results for the individual brands are less significant, but the overall results are still strong. ADV for Brands 1 and 2 seemed to have more impact on AW than on ATT. We have already noted that Brand 2 was the smallest studied, Brand 1 was similar in market size to Brand 2, and Brands 4 and 5 were the largest. Here, ADV seemed to have an equal impact upon AW and ATT. Again it should be noted that these results could partially be reflecting the nature of the time lags actually operating.

The *price* variable was expected to primarily influence MS. Since a price decline should create a positive MS change, the coefficients should be negative. The empirical results are somewhat puzzling. Price seemed to have little influence upon market share—a *t* value of 0.12 in the aggregate. There was an apparent impact of price upon AW and ATT. It seemed to have a slight positive impact upon AW (represented by a negative coefficient). Perhaps price reductions accompanying promotions attract sufficient attention to influence AW. Conversely, the impact of price upon ATT tended to be negative (a positive coefficient). Perhaps these same promotions had an image-tarnishing effect upon the brand which canceled the increase in awareness. The net result on MS was, consequently, very small. There is a competing explanation. It is possible that price declines follow and thus are associated with weak demand instead of preceding and being associated with strong demand. In the tradition of simultaneous-equation analysis, this suggests considering price as an endogenous variable.

The coefficients of the lagged endogenous variables in the recursive equations are also of interest. In general, lagged effects were more important in the MS equations. Thus, the effect of the independent variables on awareness and attitude seems to dissipate rather rapidly, whereas their impact on behavior is of a longer-run nature. This conclusion, where confirmed, suggests that advertising campaigns addressed solely to awareness and attitude may not have the long-term impact they desire unless the campaign's impact is felt fairly soon in market behavior.

It should be noted that this study was conducted under the handicap of significant multicollinearity. Thus, the regression coefficients tend to have higher variances and covariances than would be desirable. Fortunately, the *t*-test is still appropriate, and conclusions based upon it are still valid. However, one must realize that misspecification could distort these findings. Two further qualifications concern the generally crude nature of the attitude and advertising effects variables, which tend to mask subtle changes in the market, and the mature but highly competitive character of the instant coffee market.

Other measures and markets may yield different communication processes when subjected to this type of time series analysis. Nonetheless, the consistency of the effects across five brands enhances the validity of the conclusions.

Summary and Conclusions

It appears that neither of the basic hypotheses of communication effects is an accurate representation of the empirical results of this study. A more appropriate description would be the model suggested by Figure 3. We have omitted price, since the results in this area were inconsistent.

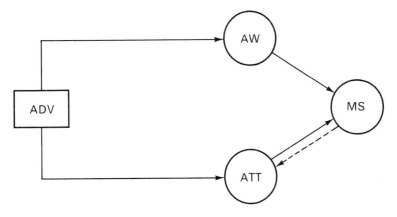

Figure 3. A Revised Model of Communication Effects

The first conclusion is that advertising can influence behavior (market share) by working through awareness. There are undoubtedly those to whom brand awareness is an important determinant of purchase for this product class. But advertising can also affect behavior through its influence upon attitude—probably by reaching a different type of buyer. These observations held across the five brands studied here. Thus, it appeared that all brands had advertising campaigns that affected both awareness and attitude simultaneously. One surprising result was that the influence of advertising seems to go from awareness directly to behavior and does not operate through the attitude construct. Relatively strong support for the hypothesis that attitude change precedes behavior change was found in this study. Not surprisingly, the reverse effect also emerged, although it was relatively less significant.

References

Assael, Henry, and George S. Day. "Attitudes and Awareness as Predictors of Market Share," *Journal of Advertising Research*, 8 (December 1968), 3–12.

Bass, Frank M. "A Simultaneous Regression Study of Advertising and Sales of Cigarettes," *Journal of Marketing Research*, 6 (August 1969), 291–300.

Claycamp, Henry J., and Lucien E. Liddy. "Prediction of New Product Performance: An Analytical Approach," *Journal of Marketing Research*, 6 (November 1969), 414–420.

Edwards, Allen L. *Techniques of Attitude Scale Construction*. New York: Appleton-Century-Crofts, 1957.

Farley, John U., and Harold J. Leavitt. "A Model of the Distribution of Branded Personal Products in Jamaica," *Journal of Marketing Research*, 5 (November 1968), 362–369.

Farley, John U., and L. Winston Ring. "An Empirical Test of the Howard-Sheth Model of Buying Behavior," unpublished Working Paper. New York: Columbia University, n.d.

Green, Paul E., and Donald S. Tull. *Research for Marketing Decisions*. Englewood Cliffs, N.J.: Prentice-Hall, 1966.

Haskins, Jack B. "Factual Recall as a Measure of Advertising Effectiveness," *Journal of Advertising Research*, 4 (1964), 2–8.

Krugman, Herbert E. "The Impact of Television Advertising: Learning without Involvement," *The Public Opinion Quarterly*, 29 (Fall 1965), 349–356.

Lavidge, Robert, J., and Gary A. Steiner. "A Model for Predictive Measurements of Advertising Effectiveness," *Journal of Marketing*, 25 (October 1961), 59–62.

Lipstein, Benjamin. "Anxiety, Risk, and Uncertainty in Advertising Effectiveness Measurements," in L. Adler and I. Crespi (eds.), *Attitude Research on the Rocks*. Chicago: American Marketing Association, 1968.

Malinvaud, E. *Statistical Methods of Econometrics*. Chicago: Rand McNally & Co., 1966.

Massy, William F., and R. E. Frank. "Short-Term Price and Dealing Effects in Selected Market Segments," *Journal of Marketing Research*, 2 (May 1965), 171–185.

Maloney, John C. "Attitude Measurement and Formation," paper presented at the Test Market Design and Measurement Workshop, American Marketing Association, Chicago, April 21, 1966.

Palda, Kristian S. *The Measurement of Cumulative Advertising Effects*. Englewood Cliffs, N.J.: Prentice-Hall, 1964.

———. "The Hypothesis of a Hierarchy of Effects: A Partial Evaluation," *Journal of Marketing Research*, 3 (February 1966), 13–25.

Ramond, Charles K. "Must Advertising Communicate to Sell?" *Harvard Business Review*, 43 (September-October 1965), 148–161.

Wold, H. "Causality and Econometrics," *Econometrica* (April 1954).

C. Discriminant Analysis

We now return to single-equation models. In discriminant analysis, the dependent variable is nominal. For example, a subject might be classified as a user of one of five brands that dominate a market. In this case, the subjects would fall into five groups or classifications. The predictive problem in discriminant analysis is to predict to which group a subject will belong on the basis of a set of independent variables. In a structural sense, the analyst may want to identify those variables that are effective in predicting group membership or what variables discriminate well between groups.

Massy provides a good introduction to discriminant analysis. He describes the confusion matrix, one that summarizes the number of correct and incorrect classifications that were obtained by the discriminant analysis. The confusion matrix, as Massy illustrates, can be used to test the discriminant model and to interpret the relationships between the groups. In the context of an example, the discriminant coefficients are used to characterize the different groups in terms of the variables.

Morrison presents some comments on the interpretation of discriminant analysis. His suggestion on normalizing the independent variables by dividing by the variable standard deviation is applicable to other multivariate techniques as well. If the dependent variable is also normalized, the resulting coefficients are called beta coefficients and are often used to report results. In either case, the resulting coefficients indicate the relative contribution made by the corresponding variables in predicting the dependent variable, whether the independent variables are measured in yards, ounces, or months.

When the analysis uses data on n observations to calculate the discriminant functions (the set of discriminant coefficients), and then classifies these same n observations with this function, the confusion matrix will be biased. There will tend to be more correct classifications than the discriminant function is capable of delivering under more realistic conditions. It is worthwhile to explain this bias, since Morrison only briefly refers to it and it highlights an important issue of all multivariate analysis.

There are two sources of the bias. The first is a bias that might be created by the model-building process. Suppose an analyst starts out with 50 variables. No matter how unrelated these are to the dependent variable, some will be correlated with it simply by accident. If five or six of those variables that are correlated are selected for the discriminant model, the model will be bound to look good as long as it is applied to the original data. The second bias is caused by sampling error. Even if variables were not culled from a larger group, there are still likely to be some that have some correlation with the dependent variable just by chance. This last bias is "compensated for" in regression analysis when the R^2 statistic is replaced by an adjusted R^2 that reflects the number of dependent variables involved. However, there is no such adjustment routinely available to discriminant analysts.

The latter bias can sometimes be measured by generating an artificial data set with similar properties—the same number of objects and variables, for example—and performing a discriminant analysis on it. A better method, which attacks both sources of bias, is to split the sample, using one part for analysis and the other part for validation. The confusion matrix obtained from applying the discriminant function estimated from the analysis sample to the validation sample would then fairly reflect its ability to discriminate.[1]

Robertson and Kennedy apply discriminant analysis to the problem of predicting whether consumers are innovative in their buying habits. They present a manual technique to calculate discriminant weights or coefficients, which provides additional insight into their meaning. Their paper also presents an example of the use of a split-example approach to eliminate the biases discussed above.

---

[1] For a more complete discussion, see Ronald E. Frank, William F. Massy, and Donald G. Morrison, "Bias in Multiple Discriminant Analysis," *Journal of Marketing Research*, 2 (August 1965), 250–258.

10

William F. Massy: Discriminant
Analysis of Audience Characteristics

How similar are the audiences of two or more advertising vehicles? While most would agree, for example, that *Life* and *Look* readers are more nearly alike than those of *Life* and *New Yorker*, methods for quantifying these differences are rather unwieldy. The usual procedure is to collect data for each audience group on several interesting variables, compute the means of the variables, and then compare them among the audience groups. Thus, it might be found that "*Life* readers show more preference for Brand X than do those of *New Yorker*," or "*Life* readers tend to be drawn from the Y socio-economic class, whereas *New Yorker* readers tend to be in the Z class."

While statements like these are very useful for sorting out gross differences in audience characteristics, they do not readily combine into a compact index of overall audience similarity. It is difficult to look at two columns of means and decide how different, on balance, they really are. The problem becomes much more complicated when comparing three or more audiences.

The method of *N*-way multiple discriminant analysis discussed in this paper can provide a set of aggregate similarity indices for a given number of audiences. Basically, the procedure attempts to "predict" which audience group an individual belongs to, based on the sets of group means discussed above, together with the set of sample variances and co-variances of the variables. That is, the individual is assigned to the audience group whose characteristics are most like his own. Since it is known beforehand which group the person actually belongs to, we can prepare a table of correct and incorrect classifications. This "score sheet" of correct and incorrect classifications, or *confusion matrix*, then provides the basis for the desired similarity indices. That is, the fewer the misclassifications of individuals to audience groups, the more distinct or dissimilar the audience groups.

Reprinted from the *Journal of Advertising Research.* © Copyrighted 1965 by the Advertising Research Foundation. This study was supported, in part, by funds made available by the Ford Foundation to the Graduate School of Business, Stanford University. Conclusions, opinions, and other statements are those of the author and do not necessarily represent those of the Ford Foundation. Computations were subsidized by and performed at the Western Data Processing Center, University of California at Los Angeles.

The author also expresses his appreciation to Herbert Taylor, who collected the data upon which this study is based in the Spring of 1962, as part of the requirements for the degree of Master of Science in Industrial Management at the Massachusetts Institute of Technology, and to Professor Thomas Lodahl of the Graduate School of Business and Public Administration, Cornell University, for making the information available. The data also are discussed in a previous paper by the author (Massy, 1963).

This paper describes an application of the confusion matrix method in measuring the similarity of audiences for five Boston FM radio stations. But first let us examine the statistical underpinnings of N-way multiple discriminant analysis, starting with two-way analysis.

Two-Way Discriminant Analysis

Two-way discriminant analysis, which deals with an arbitrary number of variables but only two populations, is becoming more common in marketing (see, for example, Banks, 1958; Evans, 1959; and Frank and Massy, 1963). The first step in this form of analysis is to estimate the coefficients in a linear discriminant function. Here is an example of this type of function, in terms of two hypothetical variables, X and Y.

$$f_i = c_X X_i + c_Y Y_i$$

The subscript i runs over the individuals included in the analysis.

A critical value of f is determined such that if an individual's f value is above the break-point he is classified in one group and if it is below he is assigned to the other. Hence the name "discriminant analysis": the function f is defined so that it discriminates between members of the two groups in the most efficient fashion.

Let us assume we have measurements on two variables for a sample of 18 drawn equally from two populations, A and B. Figure 1 presents the hypothetical scatter diagram for this sample. Now imagine that we draw a nineteenth observation, but do not know whether it belongs to A or B. The problem is to assign the new observation to either A or B in a way that minimizes the probability of misclassification.

In this case we would base our estimate of the coefficients (the c's) of the discriminate function on the information provided by the original 18 observations. Having values for the c's allows us to assign a value of f to any possible combination of X and Y, whether from our original sample or a new sample. Next, we use mathematical methods to estimate the probability that, given a particular value of f, the observation would fall in A. This probability distribution for A might look like the one given by the solid curve in Figure 2, which also presents a similar distribution for B, shown by a dotted curve.

Further, Figure 2 contains a vertical line which represents the discriminant or break-point value of f. The break-point is set half way between the means of f for A and B, so at this point an observation has about an equal probability of falling in A or B. The shaded areas on either side of the break-point give the total probability of misclassifying a particular observation.

The logic of two-way discriminant analysis is presented in greater detail in Frank, Kuehn, and Massy (1962), along with computing formulas. More

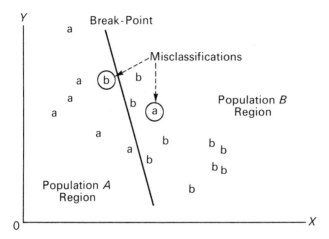

Figure 1.   Discrimination of Two Hypothetical Populations on Two
Variables

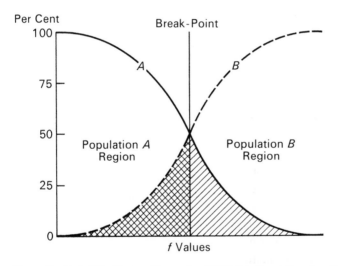

Figure 2.   Probability That an Observation Will Fall in Population A or B

detailed treatments can be found in the references cited in connection with
N-way analysis.

N-Way Analysis

Consider three populations of individuals (A, B, and C) describable in
terms of two variables (X and Y). The populations might refer to audiences
of three advertising media and the variables to audience attributes, such as

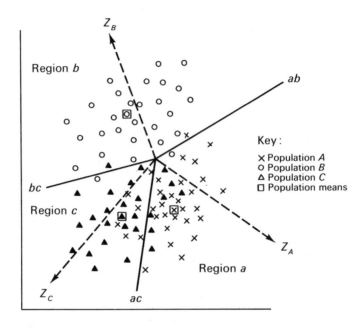

Figure 3. Acceptance Regions for Three Hypothetical Populations on Two Variables

family size and income. Figure 3 shows a hypothetical scatter diagram for the attribute values of individuals in each of the three populations.

The discriminant problem here is to define three mutually exclusive regions (a, b, and c) which exhaust the X-Y space. The region boundaries should be set up such that when the X and Y values put an individual into a given region, it is more probable that he actually is a member of that population than of any other population. The problem is soluble provided that the variables are approximately normally distributed in each population, their respective variance-covariance matrices are about equal, and that the a priori probability for membership in each (i.e., the relative incidence of the groups in the overall population) is known. (These conditions also are required for the two-way case.)

In Figure 3, the lines separating the three regions represent loci of equal probability for their respective pairs of regions. To report that a given observation lies to one side of the threshold line is to say that the probability that the observation belongs in this region is greater than for any other region. Obviously, this "maximum probability criterion" does not preclude mistakes in classification. Six population A individuals are erroneously put in group C and one in group B. On the other hand, if the classification process were repeated many times with similar samples of individuals, this procedure would result in the lowest possible proportion of errors.

How are the regions determined? As in the two-way case, the sample data are used to estimate the parameters of linear discriminant functions for the populations. These are denoted by the three broken half lines $(Z_A, Z_B,$ and $Z_C)$ in Figure 3. (Note: for the sake of simplicity, the discriminant function was not drawn in Figure 1; if it had been, it would be shown perpendicular to the break-point line.) Once the parameters of these functions have been estimated, the boundaries are set so that each discriminant line (Z) bisects the angle between its respective boundary lines: thus Z_A bisects the angle between *ab* and *ac*. (This is equivalent to taking half the distance between the discriminant means in the two-way case.) The analyst proceeds by first estimating the three sets of discriminant coefficients and then setting up boundaries for the acceptance regions on the basis of his initial results. While the means of the variables fall within the acceptance regions for their respective populations (this is a necessary condition), they do not have to lie on the discriminant lines.

Figure 3 also provides insight into using confusion matrices to evaluate the similarity of populations. Table 1 shows the correct and incorrect classifications for the example. The figures along the diagonal tell us that the

Table 1.   Predicted and Actual
Population Membership of
Hypothetical Example

Actual	Predicted			Total
	A	*B*	*C*	
A	20	1	6	27
B	1	25	1	27
C	7	1	19	27

number of correct predictions for *B* is greater than for either *A* or *C*. The off-diagonals indicate that a member of *A* is most likely to be misclassified as a *C*, and a member of *C* to be wrongly associated with *A*. Hence it makes sense to conclude that populations *A* and *C* are more nearly alike than are *A* and *B*, or *B* and *C*. Figure 3 corroborates this view, since the distance between the two swarms of points for the *A-C* pair is less than that between the points for either the *B-C* or *B-A* pair.

While the same conclusion could have been obtained by examining the six *t* ratios for the differences between the means of pairs of groups, this would greatly strain the analyst's ability to compare many numbers at once, even in this rather simple example. Another technique for measuring similarity, the Mahalanobis D^2 statistic (see Rao, 1952), is not as easy to understand and is not as closely related to the predictive efficacy of the discriminant analysis as the method of confusion matrices.

An Application

Similarity of FM Station Audiences

Confusion matrices were used to evaluate the similarities among the audiences of five FM ratio stations located in the Boston Metropolitan Area. The data for the study were collected by Herbert Taylor (1962) from a sample of families who owned at least one FM radio receiver. A mail questionnaire was used to obtain information on current station selections and some 47 socio-economic and consumption variables. Respondents were given a series of scales simulating the markings on a typical FM dial, and asked to note the position of the dial(s) on each FM receiver in the home, as of the time the questionnaire was filled out.

The sample consisted of returned questionnaires from about 380 families; 280 had sent in for Station A's program guide and the rest were selected at random. The results given here are based on the 239 families for whom the station tuned to at response time could be unambiguously determined. Since the sample probably contains substantial biases, which may lead to false impressions about audience characteristics, station call letters have been withheld.

The first step in the analysis was to reduce the number of potential explanatory variables from 47 to some more manageable number. Factor analysis was used to obtain 12 new variates that could serve as summaries of the original set. (The definitions of the factor score variables are presented below in Table 4.) The factor loadings matrix upon which they are based is the same as that reported by Massy (1963).

The 12 summary variates were subjected to a five-way multiple discriminant analysis to predict which types of respondents listen to what radio station.

Table 2 gives the confusion matrix for the 12-variate five-way discriminant run for the sample of 239 families, under the assumption that a priori probabilities are equal for membership in any of the five audiences. Entries on the main diagonal of the matrix denote correct classifications or hits,

Table 2.   Confusion Matrix for 12 Variates,
Assuming Equal Probabilities

Actual Audience	Predicted Audience Membership					Total
	A	B	C	D	E	
A	43	13	8	21	14	99
B	16	15	15	13	13	72
C	3	5	14	5	4	31
D	2	3	5	9	4	23
E	2	1	0	4	7	14

Total Hits = 88; Per Cent Hits = 36.8%; χ^2 (48) = 72.4

while the off-diagonal elements represent misses. The percentage of hits is 36.8 per cent. A χ^2 test based on the Mahalanobis D^2 statistic found the differences between the means among the five groups to be significant at the .025 critical level. Thus we may conclude that at least one pair of station audiences are different on at least one of our 12 variables.

We are better able to draw conclusions from the confusion matrix if we normalize the raw misclassification counts by dividing each by its row total. The new entries, presented in Table 3, represent the probabilities that an individual who is actually in a given station's audience will be so classified. Table 3 indicates that some combinations of stations are much more alike than others, as far as we can tell.

Table 3. Normalized Confusion Matrix for 12 Variates, Assuming Equal Probabilities

Actual Audience	Predicted Audience Membership					Total
	A	B	C	D	E	
A	.43	.13	.08	.21	.14	1.00
B	.22	.21	.21	.18	.18	1.00
C	.10	.16	.45	.16	.13	1.00
D	.08	.13	.22	.39	.17	1.00
E	.14	.07	.00	.29	.50	1.00

Station A has a fairly distinct audience profile, as indicated by the .43 on its diagonal; it is most strongly associated with Station D, and to a lesser extent with E and B. Station B's profile is little different from those of the other stations; it is somewhat more closely associated with A and C.

Station C has a strongly differentiated profile; its diagonal of .45 is almost three times as large as any of the misclassifications. C is weakly associated with B and D.

Station D has a fairly distinct profile, and is most nearly like Station C, followed by E. The Station E profile appears to be quite distinct, but the small sample size for E makes conclusions difficult.

It would be interesting to know whether the relationships given above are reciprocal. That is, if members of one group tend to be misclassified in a second group, are members of the second group in turn likely to be misassigned to the first group? In Figure 4 the arrows indicate the direction of misclassification for the two largest off-diagonal entries in each row of Table 3. The figure shows that, except for Station A, all relationships are reciprocal. Station A listeners tend to be disproportionately associated with Station D rather than B, even though B's listeners are more likely than D's to be associated (i.e., misclassified) with A.

Table 4 presents the coefficients of the 12 variables for the five discriminant functions. Each coefficient represents the effect of the variable on the probability of classification in the group corresponding to the particular

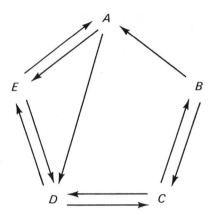

Figure 4. Association Diagram for 12 Variables
(Arrow Indicates Direction of Misses)

Table 4. Multiple Discriminant Coefficients for Five Stations and
12 Variates

Variables	Stations				
	A	*B*	*C*	*D*	*E*
1. Durables ownership (high scorers more likely to own dishwashers, freezers, washers, dryers, second cars)	−.18	−.53	+ .27	− .74	−1.01
2. Age—older (+)	−.89	−.79	+1.18	+ .38	−1.72
3. Social class I—higher occupational status	+.41	+.90	+ .21	+1.22	+1.11
4. Music preference I—classical and opera (+) vs. popular (−)	+.03	+.06	− .26	+ .11	− .01
5. Social class II—"lower middle class" (high scorers use credit, have low income and assets, tend to have older cars)	+.20	+.29	− .34	+ .57	+ .94
6. Automobile ownership (high scorers own newer cars, tend toward foreign, lower priced, and larger models)	+.96	−.01	−1.27	−1.04	+1.10
7. Music preference II—folk (+) vs. popular (−)	−.04	+.19	+ .60	+ .18	− .27
8. Source of entertainment (high scorers seldom "go out")	+.58	+.21	− .48	+ .24	+1.04
9. Wife's status—working wife (+)	+.36	−.09	− .06	− .69	+ .49
10. Music preference III—opera (+) vs. jazz (−)	+.28	+.35	− .55	− .13	+ .77
11. "Individualism" (high scorers tend to like folk music, dislike trading stamps, and not own TV set or shop in discount houses)	−.27	+.20	+ .71	+1.98	+ .20
12. Program guide—sent in for Station *A*'s guide (−)	+.31	+.43	+ .18	+ .25	+ .22
Constant	−.26	−.19	− .38	− .38	− .33

discriminant function. As such, the coefficients are more sensitive measures of audience characteristics than a similar table of the means of the variables. Moreover, the discriminant coefficients take into account correlations among variables. For example, since older people obviously have fewer children living at home, the means for these two variables would tend to be highly correlated from group to group. The discriminant coefficient, on the other hand, gives us the effect of number of children at home, holding age constant, and vice versa.

Certain audience characteristics can be observed by looking at the extreme values of the discriminant coefficients for each variable in Table 4. A variable contributes most to the probability of classification in that station audience for which it is most positive. Conversely, negative coefficients indicate the extent to which high scorers on a variable are *not* likely to be associated with the particular audience. Variables whose coefficients are near zero for any group do not much affect the probability for that group.

Key Audience Characteristics

An analysis of the extreme positive and negative coefficients in Table 4 produced the following audience profiles:

Station A   Ownership of a bigger or newer car, or more than one car, contributes most strongly to classification in A's audience. Families that seldom " go out " to movies, sports, or cultural events also are disproportionately likely to be "A's." The younger the family the higher its probability of being in the A audience.

Station B   The probability of classification in B increases as the family rises in occupational status. It is highest if the family did not send in for A's program guide. Younger families, and families that indicate a preference for opera over jazz, are more likely to be assigned to B.

Station C   Respondents assigned to C tend to be much older than average, and own fewer and/or older and smaller automobiles, and prefer jazz and popular music to opera. "Going out" contributes more to C's classification probability than to any other station. The same is true for sending in for A's program guide—Station C even is ahead of Station A.

Station D   "Individualism" contributes most strongly to the probability of classification in this audience. Next in importance is occupational status. Affluence in automobile ownership strongly inhibits the chances of being so classified.

Station E   High classification probabilities for E are strongly related to occupational status and automobile affluence, and inversely related to "going out" and durables ownership. Younger people are much more likely to be classified in this audience. The group is most likely to exhibit "lower middle class" values (Social class II). The extreme positive coefficient for opera versus jazz might best be regarded as a dislike for jazz.

Differences between pairs of coefficients indicate the extent to which the variable aids in discriminating the two audiences. The five stations permit ten different pair-wise comparisons of coefficients. Since this is an unwieldy number, we shall concentrate on the pairs that are not connected by any arrows in Figure 4. Our data indicate that the most widely separated stations in the discriminant space are *A-C*, *B-C*, *B-D*, and *C-E*.

A compared with *C*. *A* listeners are younger and much more likely to own newer, larger autos and/or more autos than *C* listeners. On the other hand, families that "go out" often are much more likely to be classified in *C*.

B compared with *C*. The probability of classification in *B* rather than *C* increases as automobile affluence increases, and decreases with age.

B compared with *D*. "Individualism" increases the probability of membership in *D* relative to *B*. On the other hand, the *B*'s tend to be younger and more affluent on automobile ownership.

C compared with *E*. Age, automobile affluence, and durables ownership increase the probability of being classified in *C* relative to *E*. The same is true for a stated preference for jazz over opera. The *E*'s tend to "go out" more than the *D*'s, and are more likely to exhibit "lower middle class" behavior.

While a more extensive analysis of audience differences would be necessary in an actual study, the foregoing shows how the confusion matrix can be used to narrow down the comparison of pairs of discriminant coefficients. The same approach could be used to determine what pairs of means are most likely to exhibit significant differences. It represents an important reduction of the dimensions of the problem of defining essential differences between audiences, especially when a large number of audiences are to be compared.

References

Anderson, T. W. *Introduction to Multivariate Statistical Analysis*, New York: Wiley, 1958.

Banks, S. Why People Buy Particular Brands. In Ferber, Robert, and Hugh Wales (Eds.). *Motivation and Market Behavior*. Homewood, Illinois: Richard D. Irwin, 1958.

Cooley, W. W., and P. R. Lohnes. *Multivariate Procedures for the Behavioral Sciences*. New York: Wiley, 1962.

Evans, F. B. Psychological and Objective Factors in the Prediction of Brand Choice: Ford versus Chevrolet. *Journal of Business*, Vol. 32, No. 4, October, 1959, pp. 340–369. Reprinted in Frank, R. E., A. A. Kuehn, and W. F. Massy (Eds.). *Quantitative Techniques in Marketing Analysis*. Homewood, Ill.: Richard D. Irwin, 1962.

Fisher, R. A. The Use of Multiple Measurements in Taxonomic Problems. *Annuals of Eugenics*, Vol. 7, 1936, p. 179.

Frank R. E., A. A. Kuehn, and W. F. Massy. *Quantitative Techniques in Marketing Analysis*. Homewood, Ill.: Richard D. Irwin, 1962.

Frank, R. E., and W. F. Massy. Innovation and Brand Choice: The Folgers' Invasion. *Proceedings* of the Winter Meeting of the American Marketing Association, Boston, December, 1963.

Kendall, M. G. *A Course in Multivariate Analysis.* London: Griffin, 1957.

Lipstein, B. The Dynamics of Brand Loyalty and Brand Switching. In *Proceedings: Fifth Annual Conference.* New York: Advertising Research Foundation, 1959, pp. 101–108. Reprinted in Britt, S. H., and H. W. Boyd, Jr. (Eds.). *Marketing Management and Administrative Action.* New York: McGraw-Hill, 1963.

Massy, W. F. Applying Factor Analysis to a Specific Marketing Problem. *Proceedings* of the Winter Meeting of the American Marketing Association, Boston, December, 1963.

Rao, C. R. *Advanced Statistical Methods in Biometric Research.* New York: Wiley, 1952.

11

Donald G. Morrison: On the
Interpretation of Discriminant
Analysis

Background

Many theoretical- and applications-oriented articles have been written on the multivariate statistical technique of linear discriminant analysis. However, on a practical level little has been written on how to evaluate results of a discriminant analysis—at least in managerial, as opposed to statistical, terminology. This article looks at the problem of evaluation from various viewpoints and thus highlights some features pertaining to other statistical techniques.

Overview of Discriminant Analysis

The objective of a discriminant analysis is to classify objects, by a set of independent variables, into one of two or more mutually exclusive and exhaustive categories. For example, on the basis of an applicant's age, income, length of time at present home, etc., a credit manager wishes to classify this person as either a good or poor credit risk. For expository purposes we will limit this discussion to two classifications; later we will comment on *n*-group discriminant analysis.

Reprinted from *Journal of Marketing Research*, published by the American Marketing Association. Donald G. Morrison, "On the Interpretation of Discriminant Analysis," *Journal of Marketing Research*, Vol. VI, May 1969, pp. 156–163.

For notation, let

X_{ji} be the ith individual's value of the jth independent variable
b_j be the discriminant coefficient for the jth variable
Z_i be the ith individual's discriminant score
$z_{\text{crit.}}$ be the critical value for the discriminant score

Linear Classification Procedure

Let each individual's discriminant score Z_i be a linear function of the independent variables. That is,

$$Z_i = b_0 + b_1 X_{1i} + b_2 X_{2i} + \cdots + b_n X_{ni} \tag{1}$$

The classification procedure follows:

if $Z_i > z_{\text{crit.}}$, classify Individual i as belonging to Group 1
if $Z_i < z_{\text{crit.}}$, classify Individual i as belonging to Group 2

The classification boundary will then be the locus of points, where

$$b_0 + b_1 X_{1i} + \cdots + b_n X_{ni} = z_{\text{crit.}}$$

When n (the number of independent variables) $= 2$, the classification boundary is a straight line. Every individual on one side of the line is classified as Group 1; on the other side, as Group 2. When $n = 3$, the classification boundary is a two-dimensional plane in 3-dimensional space; the classification boundary is generally an $n - 1$ dimensional hyperplane in n space.

Advantages of a Linear Classification Procedure

The particularly simple form of (1) allows a clear interpretation of the effect of each of the independent variables. Suppose the independent variable X_1 is income, and the classification procedure is if $Z_i > z_{\text{crit.}}$, classify the individual as being a good credit risk, i.e., the higher the value of Z_i, the more likely the individual is a good credit risk. If the sign of b_1 is positive, then higher income implies a better credit risk, and the larger the size of b_1, the more important variable X_1 is in discriminating between Group 1 and Group 2 individuals. Clearly, if $b_1 = 0$, then X_1 has no effect.

If we had a more complex discriminant function, we could not isolate the effect of each variable so easily. Suppose we had a nonlinear discriminant function, say

$$Z_i' = a + b X_i + c X_i^2 + d Y_i + e Y_i^2 + f X_i Y_i$$

The effect of Z_i' of increasing X_i by one unit depends on the value of X, b, c, f, and even Y.[1]

Hence, for interpretation, a linear discriminant function is highly desirable. This raises the following question.

When Is a Linear Classification Procedure Valid?

The technical details of this section are in the appendix. However, the essence of these details can be easily expressed. A linear classification procedure is optimal if the spreads (variance) of the independent variables (the X's) in Group 1 are the same as the spreads in Group 2 and if the interrelations (correlations) among the independent variables in Group 1 are the same as the interrelations in Group 2. Really we are saying that the covariance matrices of Group 1 and Group 2 are equal.

The appendix also gives a brief example of the kind of nonlinear classification region that can arise when the assumption of equal covariance matrices is not true.

Next is the discussion of evaluating the results after a discriminant analysis has been run.

Statistical Significance

Distance between Groups

One of the standard quantities that appears on the output of a discriminant analysis is a distance measure, the Mahalanobis D^2 statistic, between the two groups.[2] After a transformation this D^2 statistic becomes an F statistic, which is then used to see if the two groups are *statistically* different from each other. In fact this test is simply the multidimensional analog of the familiar t test for the statistical significance of the difference between one sample mean

---

[1] Some of the variables may have little influence on the discrimination, i.e., the b's associated with these variables are very close to zero. The main part of the discrimination will then occur in a space of lower dimensionality.

[2] The Mahalanobis D^2 statistic can be considered as a generalized distance between two groups, where each group is characterized by the same set of n variables and the variance-covariance structure is identical for both groups. Each group can be further characterized by its n-dimensional mean vector. In the special case where all n variables are mutually independent, D^2 is merely the square of the usual Euclidean distance between the two mean vectors, where the orthogonal coordinate system is normalized by the standard deviation of each variable. If the variables are collinear, the coordinate axes are also rotated so that the cosine of the angle between the two axes is equal to the correlation between the two variables associated with these axes.

Let μ_1 be the mean vector for Group I and μ_2 be the mean vector for Group II. If $(\mathbf{V})$ is the common covariance matrix, the Mahalanobis D^2 statistic is

$$(\mu_1 - \mu_2)\mathbf{V}^{-1}(\mu_1 - \mu_2)'$$

$\bar{x}_1$ and another sample mean $\bar{x}_2$. The D^2 (or transformed F) statistic tests the difference between the n-dimensional mean vector $\bar{x}_1$ for Group 1 and the corresponding n-dimensional mean vector $\bar{x}_2$ for Group 2. However, the statistical significance per se of the D^2 statistic means very little.

Suppose the two groups are significantly different at the .01 level. With large enough sample sizes, $\bar{x}_1$ could be virtually identical to $\bar{x}_2$, and we would still have statistical significance. In short, the D^2 statistic (or any of its transformed statistics) suffers the same drawbacks of all classical tests of hypotheses. The statistical significance of the D^2 statistic is a very poor indicator of the efficacy with which the independent variables can discriminate between Group 1 individuals and those in Group 2.

Percentage Correctly Classified

A Bias Exists in Many "Canned" Programs

One common source of misinterpretation of discriminant analysis results comes from the way in which most of the "canned" computer programs construct the classification table (sometimes called the confusion matrix). The computer will print out the table [shown below]. The entry n_{ij} is the number of individuals who are actually in Group i, but were classified under Group j. Then $(n_{11} + n_{22})/n$ is the proportion of individuals correctly classi-

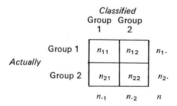

fied. However, the typical canned program uses all n observations to calculate the discriminant function and then classifies these *same* n individuals with this function. Frank, Massy, and Morrison [3] discuss in detail the upward biases that can occur in classification tables constructed in this way. One method of avoiding this bias is to fit a discriminant function to part of the data and then use this function to classify the remaining individuals. It is the classification table for these last individuals that we will discuss now.

Percent Correctly Classified by Chance

Suppose a researcher is interested in determining the socioeconomic variables that distinguish adopters of a new product from nonadopters. His "fresh" second half of the split sample contains 30 adopters and 70 nonadopters. He applies his discriminant function obtained in the first half of the split sample to this second half and gets 70 percent correct classifications. He then says, "By chance I could get 70 percent correct classifications; therefore, my discriminant function is not effective in separating adopters from nonadopters." Notice that the chance model has not been explicitly stated. The remainder of this section will develop a more appropriate chance model that will show that in a statistical sense this hypothetical researcher is being overly pessimistic.

Assume that there exists a population with only two types of individuals, Type I and Type II. Let p be the proportion of the population that is Type I, and $1 - p$ the proportion that is Type II. If the variables (age, income, etc.) actually have no effect on discriminating I's from II's, we can expect to get a proportion p correctly classified *if we classify everyone as Type I.* Hence, if $p > \frac{1}{2}$, we would classify everyone as Type I; if $p < \frac{1}{2}$, would classify everyone as Type II.

Our hypothetical researcher wishes to identify adopters. However, since his sample has only 30 percent adopters and 70 percent nonadopters, he defies the pure chance odds if he classifies an individual as an adopter. This is true because any individual has an a priori .7 probability of being a nonadopter and only a .3 probability of being an adopter. But what if the researcher says, "I want to try to identify the adopters. I believe my discriminant function has some merit; therefore, I am going to classify 30 percent of the individuals as adopters." Given this outlook, what is the appropriate chance model?

Let

> p be the true proportion of Type I individuals
> α be the proportion classified as Type I

Then the probability of an individual being classified correctly is

$$P(\text{Correct}) = P(\text{Correct}|\text{Classified Type I})P(\text{Classified Type I})$$
$$+ P(\text{Correct}|\text{Classified Type II})P(\text{Classified Type II})$$

$$P(\text{Correct}) = p\alpha + (1 - p)(1 - \alpha) \qquad (2)$$

For our researcher, $p = \alpha = 0.3$. Hence the chance proportion correctly classified is $(0.3)^2 + (0.7)^2 = .58$. *Note that when $p = .5$, i.e., two groups of equal size, $P(\text{Correct}) = .50$ regardless of the value of α.*[3]

More formally this *proportional chance criterion is*

$$C_{\text{pro.}} = \alpha^2 + (1 - \alpha)^2 \qquad (3)$$

---

[3] A generalization of (1) for N groups with n individuals in Group i, $i = 1, \ldots, N$ is found in [5]. This excellent article is worthwhile reading for anyone working with discriminant analysis or any other classification techniques. These more general results will be necessary for multiple discriminant analysis when the number of groups (or types) is greater than two.

where

$$\alpha \text{ is the proportion of individuals in Group 1}$$
$$1 - \alpha \text{ is the proportion of individuals in Group 2}$$

The researcher who said, "By chance I could get 70 percent correct," was using the *maximum* chance criterion,

$$C_{\text{max.}} = \max(\alpha, 1 - \alpha) \qquad (4)$$

where $\max(\alpha, 1 - \alpha)$ is read "the larger of α or $1 - \alpha$." For example, $\max(.3, .7) = .7$.

Situations Where $C_{\text{pro.}}$ and $C_{\text{max.}}$ Should Be Used

If the sole objective of the discriminant analysis is to maximize the percentage correctly classified, then clearly $C_{\text{max.}}$ is the appropriate chance criterion. If the discriminant function cannot do better than $C_{\text{max.}}$, you are wiser to disregard it and merely classify everyone as belonging to the larger of the two groups. Obviously, this is rarely true for a marketing research study. Usually a discriminant analysis is run because someone wishes to correctly identify members of *both* groups. As indicated, the discriminant function defies the odds by classifying an individual in the smaller group. The chance criterion should take this into account. Therefore, in most situations $C_{\text{pro.}}$ should be used. Recall that our discussion on chance models applies to individuals not used in calculating the discriminant function. If the individuals were used in calculating it, then some upward adjustment must be made on $C_{\text{pro.}}$ or $C_{\text{max.}}$. Frank, Massy, and Morrison [3] give methods for estimating these biases.

Analogy with Regression

Perhaps an analogy with regression will clarify these concepts. We have all read articles in which the author has found "significant" relations; however, he has "explained" only four percent of the variance, i.e., $R^2 = 0.04$. But since the sample size is large, this sample R^2 is statistically significantly different from zero. In discriminant analysis, the percentage correctly classified is somewhat analogous to R^2. One tells how well we classified the individual; the other tells how much variance we explained. Statistical significance of the R^2 is analogous to the statistical significance of the D^2 statistic. Clearly, with a large enough sample size in discriminant analysis we could classify 52 percent correctly (when chance was 50 percent) and yet have a statistically significant difference (distance) between the two groups.

Evaluation Criteria for Discriminant Analysis

When results of a discriminant analysis are obtained, there are three basic questions to ask: (1) Which independent variables are good discriminators? (2) How well do these independent variables discriminate among the two groups? (3) What decision rule should be used for classifying individuals? We have already discussed the first two questions; the third one obviously involves economic considerations. More complete answers to these questions require a synopsis of the theoretical derivation of the discriminant function.[4]

Deriving the Discriminant Function

Let us look at Individual i and observe his values of the n independent variables. That is, we see

$$x_i = (x_{1i}, x_{2i}, \ldots, x_{ni})$$

Let

$P(I)$ be the unconditional (prior) probability that an individual belongs to Group 1

$P(I|x_i)$ be the conditional (posterior) probability that an individual belongs to Group 1, given we have observed x_i

$l(x_i|I)$ be the likelihood that an individual has the vector of values x_i, given that he belongs to Group 1

Analogous definitions hold for Group 2. From Bayes' Theorem we have

$$\frac{P(I|x_i)}{P(II|x_i)} = \frac{l(x_i|I)}{l(x_i|II)} \cdot \frac{P(I)}{P(II)}$$

Or

Posterior Odds = Likelihood Ratio × Prior Odds   (5)

The classification procedure will then be as follows. If the odds are strongly enough in favor of Group 1, classify the individual as belonging to Group 1. (If the odds were 3 to 1 in favor of Group 1, this would mean a probability of .75 that the individual belongs to Group 1.) We may also use the logarithms of the odds as a criterion. For example, odds greater than one

---

[4] Mathematical details on this derivation are in [1, Chapter 6].

(a probability greater than .5) is equivalent to the logarithm of the odds being greater than zero. We may write (5) as

$$\log(\text{posterior odds}) = \log(\text{likelihood ratio}) + \log(\text{prior odds}) \qquad (6)$$

If the assumptions of normality and equal covariance matrices discussed earlier are true, the logarithm of the likelihood ratio is of the form

$$\log(\text{likelihood ratio}) = b_0 + b_1 X_1 + \cdots + b_n X_n \qquad (7)$$

This is the discriminant function. When the two groups are of equal size, each group's prior probabilities are equal. The prior odds are then one, and the posterior odds are merely the likelihood ratio. When the prior odds are different from one, then

$$\log(\text{posterior odds}) = b_0 + b_1 X_{1i} + \cdots + b_n X_{ni} + \log(\text{prior odds})$$

However, since the prior odds contain none of the independent variables, this quantity is a constant, and the discriminant function is

$$b_0' + b_1 X_{1i} + \cdots + b_n X_{ni}$$

where

$$b_0' = b_0 + \log(\text{prior odds}) \qquad (8)$$

An understanding of the foregoing nonmathematical material is sufficient to answer the three basic questions.

Determining the Effect of Independent Variables

The sign and size of the b_j's determine the effect of the independent variables X_j. The size of the coefficient b_j in the discriminant function

$$Z_i = b_0 + b_1 X_{1i} + \cdots + b_j X_{ji} + \cdots + b_n X_{ni}$$

will clearly be influenced by the scale that we use for X_j. Suppose X_j is family income. A change of X_j from \$6,000 to \$7,000 will have the same effect on Z_i whether or not X_j is scaled in dollars or thousands of dollars. Therefore if X_j is measured in thousands of dollars, b_j will be one thousand times larger than if the units of X_j are in dollars. However, if we normalized (divided) each variable by its standard deviation, the original units become irrelevant. As units are scaled by a factor k, the standard deviation is also scaled by the same factor k. That is, if the standard deviation of X_j is σ_j, then the standard deviation of kX_j is $k\sigma_j$. Then since $X_j/\sigma_j = kX_j/k\sigma_j$, we need not worry about the scale of X_j.

Let b_j^* be the discriminant coefficient that results when the standardized variables $X_j^* = X_j/\sigma_j$ are used.[5] Suppose $|b_j^*| > |b_k^*|$. Then variable X_j is a better discriminator between Group 1 and Group 2 than variable X_k. A unit change in X_j^* has more effect on Z_i than a unit change in X_k^*. The more a variable affects Z_i, the better it discriminates. We are justified in normalizing our variables by their standard deviations, since we are discriminating on the basis of *statistical* distance between the two groups and statistical distances are measured in units of standard deviations.[6]

If the discriminant analysis is run with nonstandardized variables, it is extremely easy to obtain b_j^* from b_j. We have seen that

$$b_j X_j = b_j^* X_j^* = b_j^* \frac{X_j}{\sigma_j}$$

Hence,

$$b_j^* = b_j \sigma_j \tag{9}$$

Recall that the sign of b_j^*, which is the same as that of b_j, determines the direction of the effect of X_j. If b_j^* is positive, as X_j increases, Z_i increases; the larger Z_i, the more likely that Individual i belongs to Group 1.

We want to obtain the best possible estimates b_j. As in all statistical estimation, the larger the sample size (assuming it is a representative sample), the better the estimates. Suppose we have 900 individuals in Group 1 and 100 individuals in Group 2. If we use only 100 of Group 1 individuals in calculating the discriminant function, the prior probability of an individual belong to Group 1 is 0.5. But if we use all 900 members of Group 1, this prior probability drops to 0.1. Does this affect any of the b_j's of interest? No. Recall from (8) that the prior probabilities affect only b_0 and have no effect on b_1, $b_2, \ldots, b_n$. Therefore, in determining which variables are the best discriminators, we should use all the data. (By this we mean all individuals and not necessarily all available independent variables. As in any multivariate technique, if X_j and X_k are highly correlated, they are measuring almost the same thing. The coefficients b_j and b_k will be unstable and hard to interpret.)

The advisability of using all data in calculating the b_j's is not surprising; in fact it is intuitively obvious. However, in assessing the discriminant function's performance, we may not want to use all the data.

---

[5] We assume that the variables form at least an interval scale. That is, any variable X can be transformed to a new variable $Y = a + bX$, where a and b are arbitrary constants, without affecting the analysis. The standardized coefficients b^* will remain unaffected by these linear transformations of the data. Some of the other multivariate methods, e.g., some cluster analysis techniques, do not require such strict assumptions about the scale of the independent variables.

[6] See [3] for a detailed discussion of distance concepts.

How Well Do the Variables Discriminate?

To answer this question we need to use the classification table and an appropriate chance criterion. Throughout this discussion we will assume that we either have fresh data or that we have adjusted for "fitting-the-discriminant-function-to-data" bias. The question of how to use the data arises when the two groups are of greatly unequal size.

We saw from (6) that when the two groups are of equal size, the likelihood ratio (which contains all sample information) completely determines the discriminant function. However, when the prior probabilities are unequal, this influences the classification procedure. If the groups are greatly unequal, the term log(prior odds) can completely dominate the term log(likelihood ratio). Here we cannot determine how well the independent variables discriminate. We would obtain the clearest picture if the prior odds were equal and, hence, did not affect the classification.

Assume that we were attempting to discriminate adopters of a new product from nonadopters. If we had a sample of 1,000 people, a result of 50 adopters and 950 nonadopters would not be unusual. If we attempted to

		Classified		
		1	2	
Actual	1	7	43	50
	2	13	937	950
		20	980	1,000

classify all 1,000 individuals, we might get a classification table like the one above. Here we classified 944 (or 94.4 percent) individuals correctly. The proportional chance criterion is (see (2))

$$C_{\text{pro.}} = (.05)^2 + (.95)^2 = .907$$

However, given that we classified 98 percent as Group 2, the outcome should have been

$$(.98)(.95) + (.02)(.05) = .932$$

or 93.2 percent correctly classified.

The maximum chance criterion is

$$C_{\text{max.}} = .95$$

Therefore our 94.4 percent correct classification is not too impressive. However, of the 20 individuals classified as Group 1, seven were correct. This is 35 percent compared with a chance percentage of 5. This last result is fairly impressive.

Now let us change the hypothetical classification slightly. Here, we still

		Classified		
		1	2	
Actual	1	1	49	50
	2	9	941	950
		10	990	1,000

classified slightly over 94 percent correctly; however, only one in ten was correct for Group 1 classifications.

In summary, when one group is much larger than the other, almost all individuals are classified as the larger group. This means several will automatically be correctly classified. When we allow the posterior odds to classify the individuals—see (5)—we usually get even fewer classified in the smaller group than actually belong in it. There is often more interest in the smaller group, and classification tables like the preceding two are not the best way to assess the discrimination power of the independent variables.

One possibility is to rank all 1,000 individuals by their Z values and put the 50 highest in Group 1. This assures that a sufficient number will be classified as Group 1. We can now see how well we classified these individuals.

Another method would be to randomly divide the 950 group 2 individuals into 19 groups, each with 50 members. We could construct 19 classification tables; the same 50 Group 1 members and the 19 different Group 2's. Then we could see on the average how well we did. This procedure has the advantage that the chance model is unambiguously 50 percent. Working with 50 percent chance models also makes interpretation easier. It is clear that correctly classifying 75 percent when chance is 50 percent is a good classification. (Of the 50 percent by which we could improve chance, we got half or 25 percent.) When the sample sizes were 50 and 950, the proportional chance criterion was 90 percent. Suppose we again obtain half of that remaining after chance and classify 95 percent correctly. This could occur by doing well with Group 1 individuals or by merely classifying everyone as Group 2. However, the interpretation is not as clear.

In summary we can say that (a) when the groups are of greatly unequal size, it may be difficult to interpret the classification table, and (b) regardless of the total sample size, the effective sample size (for determining ability to discriminate) is governed by the *smaller* of the two groups.

This last point is particularly relevant in the planning stages of a research project. A large total sample size is of little comfort without a sufficient number of individuals in each group.

Classification Decision

The last two sections dealt with which variables are good discriminators and their ability to discriminate. However, if the discriminant function is used to classify individuals, then clearly the misclassification costs must enter the decision.

As before, let

$P(I|x_i)$ be the posterior probability that an individual belongs to Group 1, given that we observed his vector of independent variables x_i

$P(II|x_i)$ be analogous definition for Group 2

C_{12} be the opportunity cost of classifying an individual in Group 2 when he actually belongs in Group 1

C_{21} be the opportunity cost of classifying an individual in Group 1 when he actually belongs in Group 2

Any rational cost structure would have $C_{11} = C_{22} = 0$.

If we classify Individual i as Group 1, the expected opportunity cost is

$$K_i(I) = P(II|x_i)C_{21}$$

Similarly, if we classify him as Group 2, the expected opportunity cost is

$$K_i(II) = P(I|x_i)C_{12}$$

The classification procedure becomes: if $K_i(I) < K_i(II)$, we classify Individual i as belonging in Group 1 and vice versa.

By the same reasoning used to examine the effect of prior probabilities on the discriminant function, it is clear that C_{12} and C_{21} affect only the b_0 term of the discriminant function (or equivalently it simply changes the $z_{crit.}$ value).

Let the logarithm of the likelihood ratio—see (6)—be log(likelihood ratio) $= b_0 + b_1 X_{1i} + b_2 X_{2i} + \cdots + b_n X_{ni}$

The classification rule is then:

classify Individual i as Group 1 if

$$b_0 + b_1 X_{1i} + b_2 X_{2i} + \cdots + b_n X_{ni} > \log k \qquad (10a)$$

classify Individual i as Group 2 if

$$b_0 + b_1 X_{1i} + b_2 X_{2i} + \cdots + b_n X_{ni} < \log k \qquad (10b)$$

where

$$k = \frac{P(II)C_{21}}{P(I)C_{12}} \qquad (11)$$

In a real application, the difficult problem will be obtaining good estimates for the opportunity costs C_{12} and C_{21}.

Implementation of the Results

One of the first successful business applications of discriminant analysis was in credit selection. Good credit risks were separated from poor credit risks on the basis of demographic and socioeconomic variables. Since on the credit application the individual fills in information on these same demographic and socioeconomic variables, the discriminant function can be applied directly to his application. The classification procedure (10a) and (10b) is then used to determine whether the application is to be given credit.

A main problem with this kind of project is obtaining representative past data. Chances are that the company only has data on individuals accepted as good credit risks. Of these previously screened individuals, some were actually good credit risks, others were not. However, this sample is not representative of the applicants applying for credit. In other words, the discriminant function for past data may not be the best for discriminating among current applicants. Of course, there is always the problem that the past discriminant function is outdated. Time or the competitive situation has changed the environment enough to make old results inapplicable. But at least for credit selection the variables used to discriminate were operational; the independent variables were used in decision making. This is not always true.

Suppose a researcher were able to discriminate adopters of a new product from nonadopters on the basis of demographic characteristics. If the product is sold through supermarkets and advertised in the mass media, it may be difficult to direct in-store displays and ads specifically at the likely adopters. However, if cents-off coupons are mailed, it may be relatively easy to direct this mailing to the more likely adopters. If a discriminant analysis is to be considered a decision-making aid (as opposed to a strictly research-oriented study), management needs a clear idea how the results will be implemented before the project is undertaken.

When the independent variables are obtained by personal interviews, there is a whole new set of problems.[7] It may be particularly hard to get comparability across interviewers.

High degrees of collinearity (high correlations) among the independent variables should be avoided. The resulting discriminant coefficients will be

---

[7] Ferber discusses these problems in detail in [2, pp. 251–9].

unstable, and it will be more difficult to interpret the contribution of each independent variable. Hence, if two independent variables are highly correlated, e.g., $r = .95$, only one of these variables should be included in the analysis. Otherwise the variances of the b's (the discriminant coefficients) will be unnecessarily large.

Discussion

In summary some considerations follow:

1. A linear discriminant function is appropriate only when the groups' covariance matrices are equal (or nearly equal).
2. The D^2 statistic (which may be transformed to an F statistic) only tests the statistical significance of the difference between groups. Recall the effect of the sample size on statistical significance.
3. Beware of the upward bias that results from classifying the same individuals used to calculate the discriminant function.
4. Beware of the different chance models that can result when groups have different sizes. Remember that greatly unequal-sized groups make interpretation of the classification table difficult.
5. The effective sample size is really governed by the smaller group.
6. Have the discriminant coefficients been normalized by the standard deviations of the independent variables?
7. In forming the classification decision, be sure that prior probabilities and opportunity costs of misclassification have been considered.
8. Will the independent variables used for discrimination be operational?

All of these apply to multiple discriminant analysis, i.e., when we are classifying individuals into more than two groups. The only main difference is that it is not as easy to assess the effect of the independent variables in discriminating among the groups. For example, variable j might be the best discriminator for Group 1 and Group 2, but variable k is best between Group 2 and Group 3. Strictly speaking, all eight points also apply to discriminant analysis for more than two groups.

Appendix

Conditions Required for Optimal Linear Classification

Let

μ_{j1} be the mean of the jth variable for individuals who belong to Group 1

σ_{jk}^1 be the covariance between variables j and k for individuals who belong to Group 1

The mean vector μ_1 is formed as follows:

$$\mu_1 = (\mu_{11}, \mu_{21}, \ldots, \mu_{n1})$$

The covariance matrix $\mathbf{V}_1$ is

$$\mathbf{V}_1 = \begin{bmatrix} \sigma_{11}^1 & \sigma_{12}^1 & \cdots & \sigma_{1n}^1 \\ \sigma_{12}^1 & \sigma_{22}^1 & \cdots & \sigma_{2n}^1 \\ \vdots & \vdots & & \vdots \\ \sigma_{1n}^1 & \sigma_{2n}^1 & \cdots & \sigma_{nn}^1 \end{bmatrix}$$

σ_{11}^1 is merely the variance of X_1. The covariance between X_j and X_k is equal to the covariance between X_k and X_j; hence the matrix is symmetrical. Finally, the covariance is related to the simple correlation between two variables. Letting r_{jk} be the correlation between variables X_j and X_k, we have

$$r_{jk} = \frac{\sigma_{jk}}{\sqrt{\sigma_{jj}\sigma_{kk}}}$$

Analogous definitions hold for the mean vector μ_2 and covariance matrix $\mathbf{V}_2$. With these preliminaries we can now state the conditions for optimality of a linear classification procedure.

A linear classification procedure is optimal if: (a) the independent variables in Groups 1 and 2 are multivariate normal with mean vectors μ_1 and μ_2 and covariance matrices $\mathbf{V}_1$ and $\mathbf{V}_2$, respectively, and (b) $\mathbf{V}_1 = \mathbf{V}_2$.

We will now illustrate how unequal covariance matrices can lead to nonlinear classification boundaries. Suppose we are classifying two groups on the basis of two variables X_1 and X_2. Assume that the mean vectors μ_1 and μ_2 are equal, but that the covariance matrices are of the form

$$\mathbf{V}_1 = \begin{bmatrix} \sigma_{11} & 0 \\ 0 & \sigma_{22} \end{bmatrix}$$

$$\mathbf{V}_2 = \begin{bmatrix} \alpha\sigma_{11} & 0 \\ 0 & \alpha\sigma_{22} \end{bmatrix}$$

where

$$\alpha > 1$$

Then intuitively, the farther an individual's x_i is from the common mean vector μ, the more likely it is that he belongs to Group 2. Mathematically we would calculate the distance from μ at which the likelihood functions for both groups were equal. Because the covariance matrices are symmetrical, the locus of such points will be a circle with μ as the center. The classification boundary will be this circle. If the prior probabilities favor Group 1, the radius of the circle will increase and vice versa.

Interpretation of the variables is very difficult (or at least not simple). An increase in X_1 may increase or decrease the likelihood of an individual belonging to Group 1; it depends on the previous values of X_1 and X_2.

References

1. T. W. Anderson, *Introduction to Multivariate Statistical Analysis*, John Wiley & Sons, Inc., 1958.
2. Robert Ferber, *The Reliability of Consumer Reports of Financial Assets*, Studies in Consumer Savings No. 6, Urbana, Ill.: Bureau of Economic and Business Research, University of Illinois, 1966.
3. Ronald E. Frank, William F. Massy, and Donald G. Morrison, "Bias in Multiple Discriminant Analysis," *Journal of Marketing Research*, 2 (August 1965), 250–8.
4. Donald G. Morrison, "Measurement Problems in Cluster Analysis," *Management Science*, 13 (August 1967), B775–80.
5. Frederick Mosteller and Robert R. Bush, "Selective Quantitative Techniques," *Handbook of Social Psychology*, Vol. 1, in Gardner Lindzey, ed., Reading, Mass.: Addison-Wesley, 1954.

12

Thomas S. Robertson and James N. Kennedy: Prediction of Consumer Innovators: Application of Multiple Discriminant Analysis

Introduction

The successful diffusion of new products depends on an understanding of the consumer innovator. This article reports on using multiple discriminant analysis to predict innovators and to assess the importance of several innovator characteristics.

Reprinted from *Journal of Marketing Research*, published by the American Marketing Association. Thomas S. Robertson and James N. Kennedy, "Prediction of Consumer Innovators: Application of Multiple Discriminant Analysis," *Journal of Marketing Research*, Vol. V, February, 1968, pp. 64–69. The research for this article was supported by the Illinois Bell and Michigan Bell Telephone Companies and the Bureau of Business and Economic Research, UCLA. Prof. Douglas J. Dalrymple and Daniel Greeno of UCLA, C. T. Smith and E. N. Asmann, business research administrators of A.T. & T. and Illinois Bell Telephone Company, respectively, gave helpful criticism.

Two multiple discriminant equations are generated. The first, a short-cut method permitting manual calculation, is based on the assumption that the variables studied are independent. The second requires a computer but considers whatever interdependence is present.

The findings here are based on an empirical inquiry into the adoption of a new small home appliance product. The characteristics studied came from literature on new product diffusion from various academic disciplines.

Innovator Characteristics

The characteristics of consumer innovators are ill-defined. Although some 800 studies on the diffusion of new ideas and practices have been reported in sociology, direct application of these findings to the marketing of consumer products is questionable.

As defined in sociology, innovators are the first 2.5 percent of the community's potential adopters to purchase. In marketing, a 10 percent figure has gained some recognition. An innovation is loosely defined as any product that consumers perceive to be new. Adoption or innovative behavior is the process of accepting and purchasing the innovation. Diffusion means the spread of the item from the manufacturer to ultimate users.

A model of innovator characteristics follows. This model is based on agricultural findings summarized by Everett M. Rogers [18], on a major research effort tracing a new drug's diffusion in the medical community [6], and on four innovative behavior studies in the marketing discipline [1, 4, 10, 16]. The characteristics selected are not exhaustive but are of most general importance in previous research.

Venturesomeness

Rogers uses venturesomeness as a summary concept to characterize agricultural innovators. "The major value of the innovator is venturesomeness. He must desire the hazardous, the rash, the daring, and the risking" [18, p.169]. Venturesomeness is operationally defined in this study as willingness to take risks in the purchase of new products. Risk-taking by consumers has been investigated in several recent marketing studies [3, 8].

Social Mobility

The Tastemaker studies by Opinion Research Corporation conclude that innovators are the mobiles in society [1]. Social mobility means movement on the societal status hierarchy. Here, upward social mobility is measured and defined by prior and anticipated movement on the social class ladder.

Privilegedness

Income level frequently has correlated with innovative behavior [4, 19]. Privilegedness is financial standing *relative* to other community members. Richard P. Coleman applied the privilegedness concept to the compact car and color television markets and found, for example, that color television innovators were overprivileged members of each social class [7].

Social Integration

Social integration is defined as the person's degree of participation with other community members. This variable has been important in the agricultural studies and the medical diffusion study [18, 6], but it has not been directly tested in the consumer goods area.

Interest Range

Katz and Lazarsfeld found degree of interest in a consumption area to be "strongly related" to opinion leadership [14]. A common assumption has been that innovators are more interested in the consumption area in which they innovate [22]. The Tastemaker studies further suggest that innovators may be committed to a wider range of interests or values than non-innovators [1]. The hypothesis of interest range will be studied here.

Status Concern

Status concern is the person's need to be noticed and admired. The variable is not explicitly derived from diffusion research but from Veblen's treatise on conspicuous consumption [20]. The conspicuousness of innovations and the resulting attention may prompt innovative behavior. Air-conditioners, for example, were a highly conspicuous item and this affected their pattern of diffusion in the Philadelphia neighborhood studied by Whyte [21]. Bourne, on reference group influence, cites the product's conspicuousness as perhaps the main attribute in whether purchase will be susceptible to reference group effect [5].

Cosmopolitanism

How oriented the person is beyond his community is referred to as cosmopolitanism. Findings from the agricultural and medical studies emphasize that innovators have cosmopolitan outlooks. The physician innovator, for example, subscribed to more medical journals, attended more out-of-town professional meetings, and visited more out-of-town medical institutions and teaching hospitals [13].

Hypotheses

Innovators will have distinguishing characteristics from non-innovators. The formulation and direction of each hypothesis is based on previous research findings. Innovators will be:

1. More venturesome in their consumption behavior than non-innovators.
2. More socially mobile.
3. Relatively more financially privileged.
4. More socially integrated.
5. Interested in a wider range of consumption areas.
6. More status concerned.
7. More cosmopolitan in outlook.

Research Design

Research was done in one reasonably well defined social system, the middle class suburban community of Deerfield, Illinois. Innovators were operationally defined as the first ten percent of the community's members to adopt the small home appliance innovation under investigation. Penetration of this product in the community was 11 percent at the time of the study, one year after the product's introduction. Non-innovators were those who did not purchase the product.

The sample had 60 innovators and 40 non-innovators. This breakdown was preferred to allow more opportunity to trace the flow of information that innovators used. Innovators were chosen systematically from the community's geographic areas where the product's penetration was greatest. The sampling procedure selected every other household owning the innovation for inclusion in the sample. By a random number procedure, non-innovators were selected from each block on which an innovator was chosen. Thus it was hoped that certain demographic variables would be controlled for the innovator and non-innovator subsamples.

A telephone street-address directory was used in sample selection and interviews were arranged by telephone. Under these controlled procedures, response rate was about 80 percent. The only known biases are the exclusion of unlisted telephone number households, no telephone households, and some working-wife households.

In-home personal interviews, lasting about 90 minutes each, were done by professional interviewers. The female head of household was the spokesman for each family consumption unit because she represented the family's opinions best and she was more open to depth interviewing.

Table 1 gives the questionnaire items measuring venturesomeness and social mobility characteristics. For example, the venturesomeness characteristic is assessed by four measurement components. The answers to these components can all be arranged on seven-point scales from highly venturesome to highly non-venturesome. The mean of the several components gives an overall venturesomeness score for the person. The same procedure was followed for the remaining variables.

Table 1.   Examples of Questionnaire Items

Characteristic	Measurement Components	Questionnaire Items
Venturesomeness	Attitude toward innovative behavior	How do you feel about buying new things that come out for the home?
	Actual adoptions of home appliances	Which of the following items do you have for your home?
	Willingness to buy hypothetical innovations	How willing would you be to buy the following items immediately after they come on the market?
	Self-perception on represented innovator characteristics	In regard to new products on the market, I am: (last-first . . . leader-follower, etc.)
Social mobility	Continuity or change in friendship patterns	What about *your* friends and the friends that *you and your husband* have together. Where do you know them from? How long have you known them?
	Neighborhood mobility patterns	What do you dislike about your neighborhood? If you move, what kind of neighborhood would you like to move to? Why?
	Occupational mobility	What is your husband's occupation? What position did your husband hold before this one?
	Locational mobility	How long have you lived at this address? How often have you moved within the last five years?
	Organizational mobility	How often do you give up one organization and join another?

Four coders handled the coding of the open-ended material. Over 90 percent consistency was obtained using guidelines set by the head researcher.

Linear Discriminant Function

The objective of the multiple discriminant analysis is to produce a linear function that will distinguish innovators from non-innovators. Weights are assigned to the variables such that the ratio of the difference between the means of the two groups to the standard deviation within groups is maximized. The discrete nature of the dependent variable suggests discriminant analysis rather than regression analysis, which has as an assumption that the dependent variable is a random variate.

The linear discriminant function can be expressed as [9]:

$$Z = w_1 x_1 + w_2 x_2 \cdots + w_n x_n \tag{1}$$

Here, $x_1 \cdots x_n$ represent the independent variables while $w_1 \cdots w_n$ represent the discriminant coefficients, or *weights*, to be applied to the independent variables. Z will be called the person's point score. Based on the point score, it should be possible to predict innovators and non-innovators.

Discriminant analysis also allows the researcher to determine the relative importance of the independent variables. The importance value, proposed by Mosteller and Wallace [17], measures the contribution of each variable to the difference in the average point scores between the two groups $(\bar{Z}_I - \bar{Z}_N)$.

Given that one mean value is exactly at the average of the innovator group and another at the average of the non-innovator group, then the difference in score is a measure of the importance $[Y_i]$ of the variables, indicating the contribution it makes to the total difference in innovator versus non-innovator point scores.

$$Y_i = w_i \bar{x}_{i_I} - w_i \bar{x}_{i_N} = w_i(\bar{x}_{i_I} - \bar{x}_{i_N}) \tag{2}$$

Here, w_i is the discriminant weight for the variable under consideration while $\bar{x}_{i_I}$ is the mean score of the innovator sample for this variable and $\bar{x}_{i_N}$ is the mean score of the non-innovator sample. The discriminant weight may be determined manually if the covariance of the variables involved is assumed to be zero. Otherwise, the computations should be made using a regression analysis or discriminant analysis program.

Thus, if independence of the variables is assumed, the weights may be computed directly from the relationship:

$$w_i = (\bar{x}_{i_I} - \bar{x}_{i_N})/(\sigma_{i_I}^2 + \sigma_{i_N}^2) \tag{3}$$

where $\bar{x}_{i_I}$ is the average for the ith characteristic in the innovator sample and $\bar{x}_{i_N}$ is the average in the non-innovator sample. The respective variances of the ith characteristic are represented by $\sigma_{i_N}^2$ and $\sigma_{i_N}^2$ [17].

Significance of the point-score distributions is tested using the difference between the average point scores for innovators and non-innovators.

$$D = \bar{Z}_I - \bar{Z}_N \tag{4}$$

Using this value and the appropriate degrees of freedom, the various significance tests can be approximated [12, p. 379].

Application

Manual Technique

The first step in the analysis was to compute discriminant weights using (3), assuming zero covariance among the variables. The objective was to quickly identify the important variables and to provide guidelines for the final computer analysis.

Mean scores and manually computed weights for innovators and non-innovators are summarized in Table 2. Means are based on a maximum

Table 2.   Mean Values of Characteristics, Discriminant Weights, and Importance Values*

Characteristic	Innovator Mean ($N = 60$)	Non-innovator Mean ($N = 40$)	Manual Computations	
			Weight	Importance
Venturesomeness†	4.88	4.12	3.59	2.73
Social mobility†	3.93	3.20	2.02	1.47
Privilegedness‡	3.68	3.25	1.77	0.76
Social integration‡	4.13	3.78	1.97	0.69
Status concern	2.00	1.73	1.72	0.46
Interest range	5.27	5.00	1.25	0.34
Cosmopolitanism	2.77	3.03	−1.41	0.37
Unweighted total	26.66	24.11	Difference	6.82

* Mean values based on a seven-point scale except status concern where a three-point scale was used.
† Difference between means significant at $p < .01$ (t test).
‡ Difference between means significant at $p < .05$ (t test).

possible score of 7, except for the status concern variable, where the maximum possible score is 3. Differences in mean scores from variable to variable may be comparable; yet, as will be seen, the importance values resulting can vary significantly as a function of the variances.

The discriminant function is designed to give high point scores (Z values) to the innovator group and to give low point scores to the non-innovator group. These Z values represent the combination of weighted characteristics for each person. It is possible to set a cutoff point so that the cost effects of misclassifying innovators and non-innovators are minimized. This cutoff point can then be used to predict innovators and non-innovators from other samples. The model's functioning, therefore, gives maximum significant difference between the means of the two groups by assigning optimum weights to the independent variables.

Based on the manually derived discriminant function and optimum cutoff points, 82 percent of the innovator group and 63 percent of the non-innovator group could be correctly classified. This discriminant function also gave importance values for the several variables, which indicated that venturesomeness and social mobility together accounted for about 62 percent of the point score difference between innovators and non-innovators.

The manually derived discriminant function, therefore, proved useful for gaining insight concerning the data. Its value is that of an approximating device. It is also helpful in evaluating the effects of various methods of coding and parameterizing the variables.

Computer Technique

The input data for the computer analysis were respondent scores on the seven characteristics (independent variables) and a dummy dependent variable. The dependent variable was assigned values of $(100)\,(n_2)/(n_1 + n_2)$ for innovators and $(100)\,(-n_1)/(n_1 + n_2)$ for non-innovators. A regression analysis program was then used to generate discriminant function weights (actually regression coefficients), the coefficient of multiple correlation, and a test of significance (F test). The covariance among the variables was, of course, considered. Discriminant function weights and importance values are in Table 3. Each importance value is also transformed into its relative importance compared with the other variables.

Table 3. Discriminant Weights and Importance Values by Computer

Characteristic	Weight	Importance	Relative Importance
Venturesomeness	3.59	2.73	35%
Social mobility	3.08	2.25	29
Privilegedness	2.04	0.88	11
Social integration	2.44	0.85	11
Status concern	0.95	0.26	3
Interest range	0.59	0.16	2
Cosmopolitanism	−2.86	0.74	9
Total		7.87	100%

Venturesomeness makes the greatest contribution in discriminating between the two groups. Its importance value, 2.73, may be interpreted as the contribution this variable makes toward overall innovative behavior, or, more strictly, the contribution toward the overall difference between the average point scores of innovators and non-innovators. Its relative value is 35 percent.

The social mobility characteristic with an importance score of 2.25 accounts for 29 percent of the point score difference between innovators and non-innovators, while privilegedness and social integration each have relative contribution values of 11 percent. Status concern and interest range account for only 3 percent and 2 percent, respectively, of the difference between innovator and non-innovator point scores, and are of minor importance here.

Cosmopolitanism, finally, has a negative weight with an importance value of .74. This value can be interpreted as a positive localism score and accounts for 9 percent of the difference between group point scores. A high cosmopolitanism score reduces the likelihood of innovative behavior.

The Z score distributions are in Table 4. The cutoff point that minimizes cost effects of misclassification is dependent on: (a) the proportion of innovators and non-innovators in the population and (b) the cost of misclassifying a member of either group. The two misclassification costs may be considered as: (1) the loss of profit from not selling an appliance to an innovator and (2) the cost involved in canvassing a nonbuyer. Members of a population are classified as innovators if the following relationship is satisfied [2]:

$$p_{I(Z)}/p_{N(Z)} \geq (C_c/C_{LP})(q_N/q_I) \qquad (6)$$

The values $p_{I(Z)}$ and $p_{N(Z)}$ are the percentages of innovators and non-innovators in the sample with point score Z. The frequency or *density ratios*, $p_{I(Z)}/p_{N(Z)}$, are in the last column, Table 4, for each of the groupings. The proportion of innovators and non-innovators are represented by q_I and q_N, respectively; the canvassing and loss-of-profit costs are C_c and C_{LP}.

Table 4.   Point Score Distributions

Point Score Range	Innovators		Non-innovators		Density Ratio P_I/P_N
	Percent P_I	Cumulative	Percent P_N	Cumulative	
57.6–60.0	1.7				∞
55.1–57.5	5.0	6.7			∞
52.6–55.0	8.4	15.1			∞
50.1–52.5	11.7	26.8	7.5		1.56
47.6–50.0	18.3	45.1	5.0	12.5	3.66
45.1–47.5	23.3	68.4	20.0	32.5	1.17
42.6–45.0	18.3	86.7	17.5	50.0	1.05
40.1–42.5	10.0	96.7	7.5	57.5	1.33
	*				
37.6–40.0	0.0	96.7	20.0	77.5	0.00
35.1–37.5	3.3	100.0	7.5	85.0	0.44
32.6–35.0			7.5	92.5	0.00
30.1–32.5			5.0	97.5	0.00
27.6–30.0			0.0	97.5	0.00
25.1–27.5			2.5	100.0	0.00

* Cutoff score that minimizes misclassification cost if the population contains 10 percent innovators and the ratio of costs, C_c/C_{LP}, is .10.

For example, if the ratio of canvassing cost to loss-of-profit is .10, and ten percent of the population are innovators, the value for the right-hand side of (6) is .90. The ratios, computed in Table 4, exceed this value in the class intervals for point scores above 40. The estimated cutoff that minimizes the cost of misclassification is, therefore, 40. That is, if the point score of a particular respondent is above 40, he would be called an innovator and canvassed; if his score is 40 or below, he would be called a non-innovator and not canvassed. This strategy minimizes the cost effects of misclassification for the sample estimates.

The cutoff point that minimizes the number of respondents misclassified in the sample can also be determined by (6). Here, the cost effects are considered to be equal, and the ratio C_c/C_{LP} is, therefore, 1. Since the sample has 60 innovators and 40 non-innovators, the ratio of q_N/q_I is assumed to be .67. The optimum cutoff point, minimizing misclassification in the sample is also 40 since the ratios for point scores above 40 in Table 4 exceed .67.

It can also be seen that the density ratios do not decrease steadily, as might be expected, because of the relatively small sample number of innovators and non-innovators.

The significance of the discriminant function was evaluated by an F test [15]. The F value obtained, 2.767, suggests that the discriminant function could discriminate between innovators and non-innovators ($P < .05$). The multiple correlation coefficient was .417.

The task of validation is not yet finished, however. As shown by Frank, Massy, and Morrison [11] and by Mosteller and Wallace [17], bias can occur in multiple discriminant analysis if the discriminant function is applied to the same sample data used to estimate the function. "The primary cause of this bias is due to errors of sampling when estimating the means of the population, upon which the discriminant coefficients are based" [11, p. 252].

A further possible source of bias is search bias which enters when a researcher seeks the best predictive variables. This bias is of no significance in this study because all hypothesized variables were used in the discriminant function.

The method for validation consists of splitting the sample data and using one-half the data to derive the discriminant function and then applying this function to the remaining data [11]. This procedure can help isolate the effect of sampling errors by the decrease in discriminant power from the analysis subsample to the applied subsample.

Here, two validation runs were made. Data were divided into two series—odd and even. A linear discriminant function was computed for each series and applied against the analysis series and the applied series. Thus four combinations emerge: odd-odd, odd-even, even-even, and even-odd.

Results (Table 5) show a drop in the percentage of correct classifications when the discriminant function is applied to new data. This is caused by sampling variation in the original computation of the weights. The F tests were not significant because of reduced sample sizes. Overall results based on the discriminant function should be regarded as tentative rather than conclusive. There is evidence that predictive ability was improved. Each percentage improvement can potentially translate into an increase in sales volume.

Table 5. Results of Validation Tests

	Total	Even Data		Odd Data	
		Even-Even	Even-Odd	Odd-Odd	Odd-Even
Percentage correctly classified					
Innovators (N = 60)	96.7%	83.3%	76.7%	100.0%	93.4%
Non-innovators (N = 40)	42.5	65.0	60.0	45.0	30.0
Total (N = 100)	75.0	76.0	70.0	78.0	68.0
F value	2.767	1.004		0.928	
Multiple correlation coefficient	.417	.379		.366	

Discussion

Review of the innovative behavior literature from several disciplines suggested probable characteristics of consumer innovators. These characteristics were measured for consumer innovators and non-innovators, and discriminant analysis was applied to test the value of the composite of characteristics for predictive purposes and the discriminating value of each characteristic.

Results of manual and computer techniques did not differ greatly, despite the assumption of zero-covariance in the manual method. The manual method is a good approximating device and at an early stage in a research project can be used to test the value of the hypotheses in discriminating ability.

For the present set of findings, it appears that two variables, venturesomeness (willingness to take new product risks) and social mobility (movement up the social class hierarchy) account for most of the innovative behavior difference between innovators and non-innovators of new home appliances. The astute marketer of such product innovations would seem to have his best chance for initial sales success with an appeal to venturesome, socially mobile people.

Characteristics also important are social integration (degree of participation with others), privilegedness (financial standing relative to other community members), and cosmopolitanism (orientation beyond the local community), the only negative related variable. The status concern and interest range variables are of minor importance here. The marketing program for an appliance innovation should perhaps further emphasize the socially integrated, privileged, and non-cosmopolitan characteristics of innovators.

The present set of findings about adoption of new home appliances suggests, therefore, promotional and market segmentation strategies. Achieving initial market penetration would seem to depend on appeals to the characteristics of importance. A revised marketing strategy would be needed after the innovator penetration level was secured in order to appeal directly to the characteristics of non-innovators. In fact, varying promotional appeals might be appropriate throughout the buildup of market share.

References

1. *America's Tastemakers*, Research Reports Nos. 1 and 2, Princeton, N.J.: Opinion Research Corporation, 1959.
2. T. W. Anderson, *An Introduction to Multivariate Statistical Analysis*, New York: John Wiley & Sons, Inc., 1958, 130–1.
3. Raymond A. Bauer, "Consumer Behavior as Risk Taking," in Robert S. Hancock, ed., *Proceedings of the American Marketing Association*, Chicago, June 1960, 389–98.

4. William E. Bell, "Consumer Innovators: A Unique Market for Newness," in Stephen A. Greyser, ed., *Proceedings of the Winter Conference of the American Marketing Association*, Chicago, 1963, 85–95.

5. Francis S. Bourne, "Group Influence in Marketing and Public Relations," in Rensis Likert and Samuel P. Hayes, Jr., eds., *Some Applications of Behavioral Science Research*, Paris: UNESCO, 1957, 217–24.

6. James S. Coleman, Elihu Katz, and Herbert Menzel, *Medical Innovation: A Diffusion Study*, Indianapolis: The Bobbs-Merrill Company, 1966.

7. Richard P. Coleman, "The Significance of Social Stratification in Selling," in Martin L. Bell, ed., *Proceedings of the 43rd National Conference of the American Marketing Association*, Chicago, December 1960, 171–84.

8. Scott M. Cunningham, "Perceived Risk as a Factor in the Diffusion of New Product Information," in Raymond M. Haas, ed., *1966 Fall Proceedings of the American Marketing Association*, Chicago, 1966, 698–721.

9. Ronald A. Fisher, *Statistical Methods for Research Workers*, London: Oliver and Boyd, 1958, 285–9.

10. Ronald E. Frank and William F. Massy, "Innovation and Brand Choice: The Folger's Invasion," in Stephen A. Greyser, ed., *Proceedings of the Winter Conference of the American Marketing Association*, Chicago, 1963, 96–107.

11. ——— and Donald G. Morrison, "Bias in Multiple Discriminant Analysis," *Journal of Marketing Research*, 2 (August 1965), 250–8.

12. Cyril H. Goulden, *Methods of Statistical Analysis*, New York: John Wiley & Sons., Inc., 1952, 378–93.

13. Elihu Katz, "The Social Itinery of Technical Change: Two Studies on the Diffusion of Innovation," *Human Organization*, 20 (Summer 1961), 70–82.

14. ——— and Paul F. Lazarsfeld, *Personal Influence*, Glencoe, Ill.: The Free Press, 1955.

15. Maurice G. Kendall, *A Course in Multivariate Analysis*, London: Charles Griffin and Co., Limited, 1957.

16. Charles W. King, "Fashion Adoption: A Rebuttal to the 'Trickle Down' Theory," in Stephen A. Greyser, ed., *Proceedings of the Winter Conference of the American Marketing Association*, Chicago, 1963, 108–25.

17. Frederick Mosteller and David L. Wallace, "Inference in an Authorship Problem," *Journal of the American Statistical Association*, 58 (June 1963), 275–309.

18. Everett M. Rogers, *Diffusion of Innovations*, New York: The Free Press, 1962.

19. ———, "Characteristics of Agricultural Innovators and Other Adopter Categories," *Studies of Innovation and of Communication to the Public*, in Wilbur Schramm, ed., Stanford: Stanford University Press, 1962, 63–97.

20. Thorstein Veblen, *The Theory of the Leisure Class*, New York: The Macmillan Company, 1912.

21. William H. Whyte, Jr., "The Web of Word of Mouth," *Fortune*, 50 (November 1954), 140–3, 204–12.

22. Gerald Zaltman, *Marketing: Contributions from the Behavioral Sciences*, New York: Harcourt, Brace & World, 1965, Ch. 3.

D. Canonical Analysis

In this type of analysis, the focus is upon the relationship between two sets of interval-scaled variables. Unlike the other single-equation techniques in the analysis of dependence, canonical analysis includes more than one dependent variable. Like regression analysis, a set of weights or canonical coefficients is found for the independent variables such that the weighted sum is maximally correlated with a number representing a construct to be explained or predicted. However, this construct is itself a weighted sum of dependent variables instead of a single variable. Consequently, two sets of weights or coefficients must be found.

Green, Halbert, and Robinson present an exposition of canonical analysis and its underlying assumptions in the context of an illustrative example. Perry and Hamm present an application in which the relationship between socioeconomic risk and personal influence in purchase decisions is studied. As both papers imply, the interpretation of canonical analysis is delicate. The problem is that the construct to be predicted or explained is not usually obvious and predefined like sales, but rather must be interpreted on the basis of the canonical coefficients obtained. This subjectivity has perhaps inhibited the application of the technique. However, since a simple univariate dependent variable is inappropriate in an increasing number of situations, we can safely forecast wider use of canonical analysis.

13

Paul E. Green, Michael H. Halbert,
and Patrick J. Robinson: Canonical
Analysis: An Exposition and Illustrative
Application

The purpose of this article is to describe a specific multivariate procedure —canonical analysis—and to illustrate its use in a correlation study which grew out of an attempt to relate information buying behavior to various personality characteristics of subjects who participated in an experimental game. Unlike some other multivariate statistical techniques, such as factor analysis and discriminatory analysis, canonical correlation has received little attention in past reports of marketing research studies. Its potential advantages and limitations, and its relationship to other multivariate techniques, constitute the emphasis of this article.

The reader is no doubt familiar with multiple linear regression analysis, which can be appropriate when one wishes to predict the value of a single criterion variable from a linear function of a set of predictor variables.[1] In some instances, however, interest may not center on a single criterion variable; that is, the analyst may be interested in relationships between *sets* of variables or relationships within a single set. Canonical correlation is a subclass of multivariate analysis which, as defined by Kendall is that " branch of statistical analysis which is concerned with relationships of sets of dependent variates [12]."

In *canonical analysis* [5], the analyst is not concerned with a single criterion, multiple predictor relationship (as in ordinary multiple linear correlation) but, rather, with relationships among sets of criterion variables and predictor variables. His objectives are to:

1. Determine the maximum correlation between a set (of more than one element) of criterion variables and predictor variables.
2. Derive "weights" for each set of criterion and predictor variables, such that the weighted sums are maximally correlated.

Abridged from *Journal of Marketing Research*, published by the American Marketing Association. Paul E. Green, Michael H. Halbert, and Patrick J. Robinson, "Canonical Analysis: An Exposition and Illustrative Application," *Journal of Marketing Research*, Vol. III, February, 1966, pp. 32–39. The authors are indebted to Professor Donald F. Morrison, University of Pennsylvania, for a critical review of this article, and to the Chemstrand Company for providing financial support for this project.

[1] Strictly speaking, multiple linear regression is to be distinguished from multivariate correlation in terms of assumptions underlying the model-fixed values for the predictor variables in the former, versus multinormal distributions in the latter.

3. Derive additional linear functions which maximize the remaining correlation, subject to being independent of the preceding set(s) of linear compounds.
4. Test statistical significance of the correlation measures.

As can be noted from the above description, canonical analysis is a technique for dealing mainly with *composite* association between sets of criterion and predictor variables. Geometrically, it may be viewed as a measure of the extent to which a group of individuals occupies the same relative position in the space spanned by the criterion variables as it does in the space spanned by the predictor variables. The technique, then, does not force the investigator, on an *a priori* basis, to develop a single index to represent the set of criterion variables (in order, say, to run a single, " global, " multiple linear correlation), or to compute a set of correlations for each criterion variable taken separately. Canonical analysis can also be used in prediction and, hence, can fill a function that traditional multiple regression serves.

An Illustrative Application of Canonical Analysis

In order to describe canonical analysis more adequately, a numerical illustration seems most appropriate. The data for this application were obtained from an experimental game [7]. Essentially, the subjects (36 business graduate students) were given prior information about the likelihood that a set of ten card decks belonged to one of two possible classes. They had the option, on the basis of prior information alone, to guess which class the deck they chose for betting purposes belonged to, or could, for a fixed cost per card, see some or all of the cards before placing their bet. The main purpose of the experiment was to see to what extent subjects' intuitive behavior was consistent with current statistical decision models.

In this article interest centers not on average play, but on *individual* subject behavior and the possible relationship of this behavior to various personality variables; that is, attempting to explain *intersubject* differences in mode of play. Surprisingly, relatively little work has been reported on the relationship of risk taking and uncertainty reduction to personality characteristics. Scodel, Ratoosh, and Minas [15] have reported the results of a set of betting exercises in which subject behavior was related to a set of personality test scores. They concluded that conservative (low payoff-high probability) players were more " other directed, socially assimilated " than less conservative (high payoff-low probability) players. Atkinson, *et al.* [2] and Becker and Siegel [4] have conducted various experiments related to risk taking and personality variables, but as Edwards [6] points out, little experimentation has been undertaken on the relationship of risk taking and personality.

In this study individual subject scores on several personality tests for each game participant were obtained. The relationship between a subject's "personality profile" and two behavioral characteristics which summarized each subject's game performance were of interest.

Characteristic 1: the subject's "sensitivity" attribute is a categorical indicant of whether or not a subject varied the amount of information purchased in the experiment as a function of his prior uncertainty. For example, some subjects, having once decided upon some number of cards to purchase, continued to purchase this fixed number (or close to it) *independently* of the prior information which they received regarding the likelihood that the deck belonged to one of two possible classes. Other subjects *varied* the amount of additional information which they requested as a function of their prior information, buying less when prior uncertainty was low than when it was high.

Characteristic 2: the subject's "bias," is a measured indicant of how much information, in total, a subject bought over the whole trial sequence. Some subjects, for example, elected to purchase large amounts of information, whether or not purchasing variability about their specific average was related to prior information. Other subjects, of course, purchased relatively little information before placing their bets.

Thus, two criterion variables, sensitivity and bias, appeared to be describing different things about subject behavior. Moreover, the sample correlation between these two response variables was virtually zero. No strong *a priori* grounds existed for combining these variables into a single criterion measure. That is, no logical basis was available for assigning so much weight to the sensitivity attribute and so much weight to the bias measure. Thus, if the association between these variables (*as a set*) with the set of predictor variables (personality test scores) is studied, a technique would have to be used which would permit description of an *overall* relationship between a set of two criterion variables and a set of several predictor variables. Canonical analysis is just such a technique. Moreover, its use would permit objective discovery of the weights to be assigned to each criterion variable, such that the resulting linear compound would be maximally correlated with the set of predictor variables.

The predictor variables (personality test scores) were represented by the following:

1. The Atwell and Wells Wide Range Vocabulary Test. Reputed to be a good indicator of general intelligence.

2. The Shipley Institute of Living Test. Purports to (conceptual portion) measure a subject's ability to "see patterns" or deal with abstraction and constitutes another type of intelligence measure.

3. The Gough-Sanford Rigidity Test. Attempts to measure the extent of a subject's open-mindedness versus close-mindedness; that is, degree of attitude rigidity.
4. The Rotter Social Reaction Inventory Test. Purports to measure the degree of one's "felt control over his environment;" that is, the extent to which he feels that he can influence events versus viewing uncertainty in a more fatalistic manner.
5. The Hierarchy of Needs Test. Attempts to rate subjects with regard to need level, ranging from "lower-level" physiological needs to "higher-level" needs, such as esteem from others and self-actualization.
6. The Allport, Vernon, and Lindzey Study of Values Test. Purports to classify subjects according to scores in the following classifications: theoretical, economic, aesthetic, social, political, and religious.
7. The Gordon Personal Profile Tests. Attempts to classify subjects according to tests scores in personality classifications: ascendancy, responsibility, emotional stability, and sociability.

All of the above tests are of the self-administered type. Subjects required, on the average, about two hours to complete the test battery. Some of the tests, *e.g.*, the Allport-Vernon-Lindzey, have separate scores for various subparts. In total, 20 predictor scores were available for each subject. In combination with the two criterion variables, sensitivity and bias, a 22×22 matrix was required to summarize the intercorrelations. As might be surmised, however, many correlation coefficients were not significant. Those test scores which did not correlate well (alpha risk equal to 0.15 for the null hypothesis $\rho = 0$) with at least one predictor were eliminated.

This step resulted in five-predictor variables: (a) the Atwell-Wells intelligence measure; (b) the Gordon measure for responsibility; (c) the Gough-Sanford measure of open-mindedness; (d) the Rotter measure of "felt control over one's environment;" and (e) the Gordon measure for sociability, which were used in the canonical analysis. (Subsequent work using all 20 predictor variables indicated, as expected, little improvement over the canonical correlation coefficients based on only these five variables.)

The starting point for the canonical analysis is the correlation matrix in Table 1.

Table 1. Correlation Matrix of Experimental Game Results

	1	2	3	4	5	6	7
Sensitivity measure	1.00	0.09	−0.27	−0.36	0.19	0.44	−0.23
Bias measure		1.00	−0.29	−0.23	−0.09	0.05	−0.29
Atwell-Wells I. Q.			1.00	0.22	−0.23	−0.23	0.07
Gordon responsibility				1.00	0.18	−0.17	0.07
Gough-Sanford rigidity					1.00	0.24	0.01
Rotter social reaction						1.00	−0.25
Gordon sociability							1.00

Looking at the sample intercorrelations in Table 1, the following can be seen:

1. The criterion variables, sensitivity and bias, are practically uncorrelated, the sample correlation coefficient being only 0.09.
2. Sensitivity (coded 0) versus nonsensitivity (coded 1) seems to be associated with the predictor variables in the following way: The higher the subject's I.Q., responsibility, and sociability, the greater his tendency to be sensitive to prior information; the higher his attitude rigidity and degree of fatalism with respect to uncontrollable events, the greater his tendency to be nonsensitive to prior information.
3. Bias (total amount of information purchased) seems to be associated with the predictor variables in the following way: The higher the subject's I.Q., responsibility, and sociability, the less the tendency to exhibit high positive biases in information purchasing. (The correlation coefficients relating the bias measure to the Gough-Sanford and Rotter scores are so small as to be insignificant at the 0.15 alpha risk level.)

On an *a priori* basis the observed relationships appear to make sense, but the problem is to determine the overall correlation between the *set* of criterion variables (sensitivity and bias) and the set of predictor variables. This is analogous to finding a coefficient of multiple correlation if each criterion variable was considered separately.

Essentially, two sets of weighting coefficients (a set for the criterion variables and a set for the predictor variables) were sought, such that if linear combinations of each set were formed (thus arriving at a *composite* variable representing each set) and correlated in a *two-variable* linear correlation, a higher correlation *for this particular set* of composite variables would be obtained than for any other set of combinations which could be formed. As would be surmised, specific numbers satisfying the above criterion are called canonical coefficients. The technique develops these coefficients and also computes the canonical correlation index which would be obtained if the two composite variables were formed and carried through a two-variable linear correlation.

Two other considerations should also be mentioned before presenting the results. First, we were not necessarily limited to finding only one set of canonical coefficients for the criterion and predictor variables. In this problem another set of coefficients could be "extracted" for which the linear compounds would also be maximally correlated, subject to being independent of all previously obtained compounds within the criterion or predictor set, as the case may be. In general, if there are r criterion variables and s predictor variables, as many sets of canonical coefficients can be obtained as are represented by the smaller of the two numbers, r or s. Each new canonical correlation index, however, will be smaller than the preceding value. That is, the highest canonical correlation index will be related to the *first* set of canonical coefficients which are obtained by the technique.

Second, formulas are available for testing the significance of the canonical correlation indexes under the usual assumptions involving multivariate statistical inference. (In this problem both canonical indexes turned out to be significant at the 0.05 alpha level; although, in view of the coded categorical variable, sensitivity, some question arises as to the appropriateness of the test.)

Proceeding now to the results, a canonical analysis was performed on the correlation matrix of Table 1. For illustrative purposes, a description of only the results for the first (maximally correlated) set of canonical coefficients and the associated canonical correlation index is given.[2] The canonical correlation index for this problem turned out to be 0.61. This index is interpreted as a measure of the *overall* correlation between the two sets of criterion and predictor variables. (As in the usual case of multiple linear correlation, it has an upper limit of unity.) Notice that this value is higher than the correlation indexes for the original variables taken singly (see Table 1).

The set of canonical coefficients, also found by the technique, is shown in Table 2.

Table 2. Set of Canonical Correlation Coefficients for Criterion and Predictor Variables

Variable	Canonical Coefficient
Sensitivity measure	0.842
Bias measure	0.465
Atwell-Wells I.Q.	−0.341
Gordon responsibility	−0.516
Gough-Sanford rigidity	0.117
Rotter social reaction	0.358
Gordon sociability	−0.381

To show how the canonical coefficients in Table 2 are used, the standardized scores (mean equal to zero and standard deviation equal to one) of the first subject in the experiment are shown in Table 3. The linear compounds for the criterion and predictor sets, using the coefficients of Table 2, are also computed, leading to the two composite scores for Subject One:

−0.89 (criterion set)
−0.80 (predictor set)

Similarly, for the remaining 35 subjects, two composite values, $\overset{*}{x}_i$ and $\overset{*}{y}_i$ ($i = 2, 3, \ldots, 36$), can be computed. Then, if desired, these pairs can

[2] The analyst may wish to extract additional canonical indexes if his interpretation of the resultant relationships is improved in so doing. In this respect the motivation is similar to extracting more than one factor in principal components analysis.

be plotted in conventional scatter diagram form. This two-variable plot is in Figure 1.

If the two composite variables were now correlated, the same canonical correlation index (0.61) would be obtained as derived from the original analysis. The figure shows the regression lines for the linear regression of the criterion set Y on the predictor set X, and vice versa.

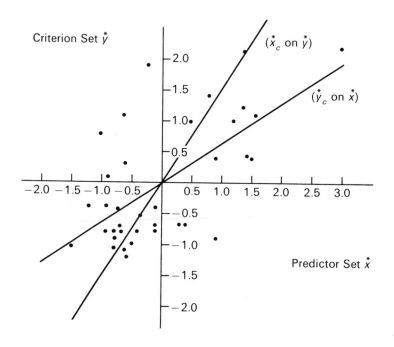

Figure 1.   Scatter Plot of Linear Compounds

The slope coefficients for the two regression lines plotted in the figure are again:

$$\overset{*}{y}_c = 0.61\ \overset{*}{x}$$

$$\overset{*}{x}_c = 0.61\ \overset{*}{y}$$

Since we are dealing with standardized variates, both regression lines will pass through the origin of the coordinate system and the slope coefficients will equal the canonical correlation index, 0.61, by the relationships

$$r_{y \cdot x} = b_{y \cdot x}\frac{\sigma_x}{\sigma_y}$$

$$r_{x \cdot y} = b_{x \cdot y}\frac{\sigma_y}{\sigma_x}$$

These equations could be used for traditional prediction purposes. That is, if there was a set of personality test scores, say for some *new* individual, the linear compound $\overset{*}{y}_c$ could be estimated in two steps. First, compute the linear compound $\overset{*}{x}$ by substituting the subject's (standardized) test scores in the equation in Table 3. Then substitute this numerical value in the first of the

Table 3.   Illustration of Linear Compound Computation for Subject One

	Standard Scores	Linear Compounds
Sensitivity measure	−0.722	$\hat{y}_1$: 0.842 (−0.722) = −0.608
Bias measure	−0.605	0.465 (−0.605) = −0.281
		$\hat{y}_1$ = −0.889
Atwell-Wells I.Q.	0.741	$\hat{x}_1$: −0.341 (0.741) = −0.253
Gordon responsibility	−0.183	−0.516 (−0.183) = 0.094
Gough-Sanford rigidity	−1.124	0.117 (−1.124) = −0.132
Rotter social reaction	−0.776	0.358 (−0.776) = −0.278
Gordon sociability	0.606	−0.381 (0.606) = −0.231
		$\hat{x}_1$ = −0.800

above regression equations and find the appropriate $\overset{*}{y}_c$ value. This predicted value could then be compared with the linear compound obtained by substituting the subject's sensitivity and bias measures (in standardized form) in the linear compound $\overset{*}{y}$.

A few comments should also be made on the canonical coefficients of the predictor and criterion variables in the linear compounds, illustrated in Table 3. With respect to the predictor set note that the highest coefficient (−0.516) is associated with the Gordon responsibility test score, and the next highest coefficient (−0.381) is associated with the Gordon sociability score. With regard to the criterion set of variables, it appears that the sensitivity measure carries the higher coefficient (0.842), which is probably not surprising judging from the correlation coefficients summarized in Table 1. Thus, the appropriate weights to assign to the sensitivity attribute and bias measure are found, which result in maximal correlation with the set of predictor variables.

More important, the canonical coefficients enable one to ascertain the overall relationship between sensitivity-bias and the set of personality variables. It appears as though sensitivity and " unbiasedness " tend to increase with higher scores on I.Q., responsibility and sociability, and decrease with higher scores on attitude rigidity and degree of fatalism with respect to uncontrollable events. This behavior is consistent with the interpretation given to the original correlation matrix in Table 1, but is now applicable to the overall relationship between the two sets of variables.

Additional Considerations in Canonical Correlation

The foregoing illustration hardly exhausts the various aspects of canonical analysis. For example, the technique can be extended to deal with correlations among *more* than two sets of data. That is, if in addition to the present variables, information is known about various socioeconomic variables for each subject, the technique could be extended to handle association among all three sets of data [11].

Furthermore, canonical analysis can be combined with other multivariate techniques for more efficient analysis, should the problem justify it. As an illustration, if one were dealing with a very large set of criterion and predictor variables, one could first conduct a factor analysis on each set and then run a canonical analysis on the principal components. One could also combine all variables into one factor analysis, separating the extracted factors into criterion-predictor versus independent factors for criterion and predictor variables, respectively. The analyst could then run a canonical analysis on the resultant sets.[3] Finally, one might wish to avoid canonical analysis altogether by finding the *first* principal component of the criterion set (by factor analysis) and then correlating scores on this component with the predictor variables, not unlike an ordinary multiple correlation problem.

Canonical analysis, like other multivariate techniques, is not without limitations. The two major assumptions underlying the model (when canonical correlation indexes are to be tested for statistical significance) are:

1. Both criterion and predictor sets are made up of interval-scaled variables.
2. The observed data represent a random sample of observation vectors drawn from the same multinormal universe.

In the illustrative application covered earlier the sensitivity attribute was a coded variable. As such, tests of significance of the canonical indexes are not strictly appropriate.

The assumption of multinormality (and, hence, linearity) can also be restrictive if statistical significance is to be ascertained. As in traditional multiple correlation, the analyst may be able to make suitable transformations in order to achieve linearity, but in dealing with small samples, the linearity assumption must usually be made by necessity; experimental error is typically large enough to mask the possibility that nonlinearity is present. As the number of variates increases, however, the multivariate extension of the central

---

[3] It should be mentioned that, in general, one would not obtain the same results by using this method. As a matter of fact, dissatisfaction with some aspects of factor analysis gave rise to the development of canonical analysis in the first place. These alternative techniques are merely listed to show some of the possible ways in which a given multivariate problem might be analyzed.

limit theorem indicates that moderate departures from multinormality probably do not lead to serious errors in the application of significance tests which are based on multinormal distributions.

The computational labor involved in conducting canonical analysis is usually such as to require a computer for handling problems of any realistic size. Fortunately, many "canned" programs are available. The particular program used in the above illustrative problem was part of the "Biomedical Package" of U.C.L.A.. Cooley and Lohnes [5] also provide flow charts and FORTRAN programs for canonical analysis.

The use of canonical analysis in marketing research has been virtually nonexistent to date, although other multivariate techniques (discriminatory analysis, factor analysis) are beginning to find increasing application. It would seem that the limitations of canonical analysis are no more or less than those of other multivariate procedures, and that lack of application in marketing research studies to date is principally due to lack of familiarity with the technique. If the analyst is primarily interested in the *overall* relationship between *sets* of dependent variables, canonical analysis is an appropriate method to describe this relationship. Its use can free the investigator from (a) having to pick a single criterion variable from two or more possible criterion variables or (b) arbitrarily weighting the set of criterion variables in order to fit the problem into the standard format of multiple correlation analysis.

References

1. T. W. Anderson, *Introduction to Multivariate Statistical Analysis*, New York: John Wiley & Sons Inc., 1958.
2. J. W. Atkinson, *et al.*, "The Achievement Motive, Goal Setting, and Probability Preferences," *Journal of Abnormal Social Psychology*, 60 (1960), 27–36.
3. M. S. Bartlett, "The Statistical Significance of Canonical Correlation," *Biometrica*, 32 (1941), 29–38.
4. S. W. Becker and Sidney Siegel, "Utility of Grades: Level of Aspiration in a Decision Theory Context," *Journal of Experimental Psychology*, 55 (1958), 81–5.
5. W. W. Cooley and P. R. Lohnes, *Multivariate Procedures for the Behavioral Sciences*, New York: John Wiley & Sons Inc., 1962.
6. Ward Edwards, "Behavioral Decision Theory," *Annual Review of Psychology*, 12 (1961), 473–98.
7. P. E. Green, M. H. Halbert, and J. S. Minas, "An Experiment in Information Buying," *Journal of Advertising Research*, 4 (September, 1964), 17–23.
8. H. H. Harmon, *Modern Factor Analysis*, Chicago, Ill.: University of Chicago Press, 1960.
9. D. L. Heck, "Charts of Some Upper Percentage Points of the Distribution of the Largest Characteristic Root," *Annals of Mathematical Statistics*, 31 (1960), 625–42.

10. R. N. Howard, "Classifying A Population into Homogeneous Groups," *Proceedings of the Cambridge Conference on Operations Research*, Cambridge, England, September 14–8, 1964.

11. Paul Horst, "Relations Among *m* Sets of Measures," *Psychometrika*, 26 (1961) 129–49.

12. M. G. Kendall, *A Course in Multivariate Analysis*, New York: Hafner, 1957.

13. D. N. Lawley and A. E. Maxwell, *Factor Analysis as a Statistical Method*, London: Butterworths, 1963.

14. W. F. Massy, "On Methods: Discriminant Analysis of Audience Characteristics," *Journal of Advertising Research*, 5 (March, 1965), 39–48.

15. A. P. Scodel, Philburn Ratoosh, and J. S. Minas, "Some Personality Correlates of Decision Making Under Conditions of Risk," in D. Willner, ed., *Decision, Values and Groups*, New York: Pergamon Press, 1960, 37–69.

16. Hilary Seal, *Multivariate Statistical Analysis for Biologists*, New York: John Wiley & Sons Inc., 1964.

17. L. L. Thurstone, *Multiple Factor Analysis*, Chicago, Ill.: University of Chicago Press, 1947.

14

Michael Perry and B. Curtis Hamm:
Canonical Analysis of Relations
between Socioeconomic Risk and
Personal Influence in Purchase
Decisions

The concept of perceived risk in consumer behavior was introduced by Bauer [2]. He argued that consumer behavior involves risk in the sense that any action of a consumer will produce mainly social and economic consequences that he cannot anticipate with certainty, some of which are likely to be unpleasant. Thus, socioeconomic risk can be defined as the possibility of significant social or economic injury associated with making an incorrect purchase decision in a particular situation of consumer uncertainty.

The notion of perceived risk has received empirical support by Bauer [3], Cox [5], Cox and Rich [6], Cunningham [7, 8], Arndt [1], and Popielarz [11]. It has also been found that to cope with the hazards of buying, consumers tend to develop risk-handling strategies. One such strategy of reducing risk is

Reprinted from *Journal of Marketing Research*, published by the American Marketing Association. Michael Perry and B. Curtis Hamm, "Canonical Analysis of Relations between Socioeconomic Risk and Personal Influence in Purchase Decisions," *Journal of Marketing Research*, Vol. VI, August 1969, pp. 351–354. The authors acknowledge the Oklahoma State University Research Foundation for its support in this study. The research assistance of James Tempero is also gratefully acknowledged.

repeated purchase of the same brand, i.e., brand loyalty [7]. A more active strategy is seeking additional information with respect to the decision problem [6].

On selection of the second strategy, several sources of information are available to the consumer, such as advertising in general media, advertising in narrow media, e.g., brochure, *Consumer's Report*, and word-of-mouth. An interesting question is whether there are any relations between the importance of each information source and the degree of perceived risk in a specific purchase situation. Arndt studied the relations between perceived risk and word-of-mouth and found that "the high-risk perceivers tended to make more effort to seek word-of-mouth information" [1, p. 294].

This study investigates the relations between the importance of personal influence and the degree of risk in 25 purchase decisions. Personal influence here includes both verbal (word-of-mouth) and observed opinion, and perceived risk combines both social and economic risk.

The hypothesis tested states that the higher the socio-economic risk involved in a particular purchase decision, the greater the importance of personal influence, as compared with other sources of influence.

Methodology

To test the hypothesis, a sample of 101 male Oklahoma State University undergraduates was selected. They were given a questionnaire that asked them to rate the socioeconomic risk and interpersonal influence in 25 purchasing decisions. The rating was done on a seven-point scale, with the score of 1 indicating very little or no significance and the score of 7 indicating high significance. This technique resembles the one used by the Wallach team [12] in the study of group influence on individual risk taking.

The questionnaire had two parts. In the first part the respondents were asked to rate, separately, the significance of social risk and that of economic risk for each decision. The two kinds of risk were explained as follows:

> *Social significance* refers to how the purchase decision will affect the opinion other people hold of the individual. Thus social significance varies with such factors as a product's social importance and its social conspicuousness.
> *Economic significance* refers to how the purchase will affect the individual's ability to make other purchases. Thus, economic significance varies with the financial considerations of price in relation to factors such as the individual's income, ability to pay, and alternate uses for the money.

In the second part of the questionnaire, respondents were given the following instructions:

A good friend and fellow student has been impressed by an advertisement for Product L. He is now in the process of deciding whether or not to purchase it. Listed below are seven possible sources of information from which the student might draw to assist him in making the decision. With the same seven-point rating scale used in Part I, estimate the significance of *each* source as an influence upon your friend's purchase decision. . . .

By placing a friend, rather than the respondent himself, in the hypothetical risk situation, a more objective evaluation of the decision process was anticipated. This was based on McKenna's [10] finding that there is a closer congruence between a person's concept of a close friend and his ideal self than there is between that of his ideal self and his own self concept.

The seven information sources for the purchase decision were:

1. Information contained in the ad.
2. Information contained in a different ad (either for the product or a competitor).
3. Unbiased information sources (such as *Consumer's Report*).
4. Observed attitude of others toward the product (such as the product's ownership and use by others).
5. Verbal opinion of others toward the product (such as a friend's personal recommendation).
6. Past personal experience.
7. Information from some source other than (1–6).

Sources (4) and (5) were selected to represent the interpersonal influence on the purchase decision, and only they were included in the final analysis.

The purchase decisions, on which the rating was done, were chosen on the following bases:

1. Each must be the kind of a purchase decision that the respondent might face as a college student.
2. Each must be the kind of purchase decision that would be suitable for advertising promotion.
3. The list must include purchase decisions on both goods and services.
4. The list of decisions must cover a significant range of potential socio-economic risks.

Using these requirements, the 25 purchases listed in Table 1 were selected and presented randomly to the respondents.

Table 1. Rank and Correlation of Purchase Decisions

Purchase Decision	Socioeconomic Risk Weighted Index	Rank	Interpersonal Influence Weighted Index	Rank	Canonical Correlation Coefficient
Color TV	6.82	1	6.15	2	.445*
Automobile	6.48	2	4.50	7	.314†
Sport coat	4.94	3	4.37	8	.111
Men's cologne	4.50	4	5.06	4	.738*
Apartment	4.22	5	6.39	1	.208
Suit	4.19	6	1.98	15	.125
Stereo hi-fi	4.12	7	0.45	22	.243
Beer	3.40	8	3.41	11	.199
Haircut	3.04	9	4.89	5	.293†
Class ring	2.87	10	0.79	21	.201
Man's hair spray	2.73	11	3.90	9	.233
Automobile battery	2.35	12	3.79	10	.155
Black socks	2.18	13	2.12	14	.375*
Contact lenses	2.14	14	2.66	13	.240
Cigarettes	1.51	15	1.92	17	.350*
Shoe brush	1.45	16	1.80	18	.301†
Watch	1.40	17	5.59	3	.109
Sun glasses	1.37	18	2.77	12	.184
Ballpoint pen	1.02	19	1.94	16	.169
Extra comb	0.98	20	0.90	20	.281†
Magazine	0.95	21	1.46	19	.282†
Sweat shirt	−0.84	22	−1.02	23	.197
Life insurance	−0.88	23	−1.50	25	.197
Italian meal	−1.56	24	4.86	6	.183
Golf clubs	−1.98	25	−1.41	24	.329†

* Significant at .01 level.
† Significant at .05 level.

Analysis of Data

The final data for the analysis consisted of four scores for each respondent and each purchase decision. These scores were designated as follows:

X_s is the rate of social risk
X_e is the rate of economic risk
Y_a is the significance of observed attitude
Y_v is the significance of verbal opinion

Some method to combine the first two scores into an index of total risk and the last two scores into one of total personal influence was needed. The simplest method of constructing such indexes is to sum each pair of scores for each individual, and then sum the combined scores of all individuals for each product. This procedure will yield two indexes for each product, which can be described as:

$$X_{..j} = \sum_i (X_{sij} \pm X_{eij}) \qquad Y_{..j} = \sum_i (Y_{aij} \pm Y_{vij})$$

where

i is the individual
j is the purchase
$X_{..j}$ is the index to total purchase risk
$Y_{..j}$ is the index of personal influence for the purchase

After the two indexes were computed, the products were ranked once according to the magnitude of the risk value and once according to the personal influence value. Spearman's rank-order correlation coefficient between the two indexes was found to be .959, which has a probability of less than .001 being due to chance.

Unfortunately, the deficiency of this procedure is its assumption that the scales have the same origin and scale factor, not just that they are equal interval scales, as is usually assumed in scale construction and manipulation. Therefore, an alternative method, such as canonical analysis, was required here to solve the scaling problem.

Canonical analysis is not widely used in marketing research [9] despite some advantages it has over other methods of multivariate analysis. Its objective is to find two sets of coefficients, represented by the vectors a and b, which maximize the correlation between linear functions of two sets of variables [4].

Here, these functions can be expressed by using the preceding notations as:

$$A_{s \cdot j} X_{sij} \pm A_{e \cdot j} X_{eij} = B_{a \cdot j} Y_{aij} \pm B_{v \cdot j} Y_{vij}$$

Canonical analysis would determine the a's and b's for each product and also the degree of correlation. Then the indexes of total risk and personal influence will be computed as:

$$X_{..j} = \sum_i \left(\frac{A_{s \cdot j} X_{sij} \pm A_{e \cdot j} X_{eij}}{N} \right)$$

$$Y_{..j} = \sum_i \left(\frac{B_{a \cdot j} Y_{aij} \pm B_{v \cdot j} Y_{vij}}{N} \right)$$

for each j(= purchase), where N(=101) is the sample size. The use of the a and b weights would be optimal in terms of maximum linear correlations between the two sets of variables.

Findings

In the present case, the score of the risk and influence indexes for each of the 25 purchase decisions was computed on each purchase separately, using the individuals' scores for that purchase alone. The purpose of this procedure was to find the a and b weights that would maximize the canonical correlation for each of the 25 purchases.

Subsequently, all 25 purchase decisions were ranked—first according to their score on the risk index $(X.._j)$ and then according to their score on the personal influence index $(Y.._j)$. These scores and ranks are given in Table 1. Spearman's rank-order correlation coefficient was found to be .573, which has a probability of less than .01 being due to chance. This is a significant rank correlation between risk and influence and supports the hypothesis that the higher the socioeconomic risk in a purchase decision, the greater the personal influence on that decision.

The canonical analysis provided an opportunity to examine, besides the rank order of all products, the relation between risk and influence for each product separately. Consequently, the canonical correlation was computed for each product, the coefficients of which are also reported in Table 1. Only ten of these coefficients were significant at or below the .05 level. The reason might be that the functional relations between the two sets of variables are nonlinear; and since the canonical analysis assumes linear relations, it will yield insignificant correlation whenever the actual correlation is nonlinar.

The coefficients of the canonical functions, i.e., the a and the b weights, indicate each variable's contribution to the canonical correlations. These weights can be interpreted as the importance of each variable in forming the general index.

Table 2 presents the canonical coefficients for the purchase decisions with significant correlation $(p < .05)$. It reveals that in all but one decision (color

Table 2.   Canonical Results on Selected Purchase Decisions

Purchase Decision	Correlation Coefficient	Canonical Weight			
		Risk		Influence	
		Social	Economic	Observed	Verbal
Men's cologne	.738	1.24	0.06	0.44	0.89
Color TV	.445	0.54	0.83	0.89	0.44
Black socks	.375	1.08	−0.23	0.99	−0.03
Cigarettes	.350	1.03	−0.38	0.97	−0.23
Golf clubs	.329	−0.72	0.24	−0.86	0.50
Automobile	.314	0.83	0.37	0.05	0.99
Shoe brush	.301	0.99	−0.01	−0.01	0.99
Haircut	.293	1.07	−0.44	0.26	0.96
Magazine	.283	0.75	0.56	0.93	0.35
Extra comb	.281	0.76	0.05	−0.27	0.96

TV), social risk played a more important role in forming the risk index than economic risk. With respect to the kind of personal influence, no significant pattern has been found.

Summary and Conclusions

The relations between socioeconomic risk and personal influence were studied, using canonical analysis. It was found that the higher the risk involved in a particular purchase decision, the greater the importance of personal influence. This supports previous findings by Arndt [1]. However, the canonical correlation between the two concepts was found in most cases to be not significant, which might be because of the nonlinear relations between them. In those cases in which the correlation was significant, the social risk contributed more than the economic risk.

These findings suggest that promotional strategies in a high-risk purchase situation should try to reach the consumers through personal channels (opinion leaders, word-of-mouth), rather than general media. They should also emphasize the social benefits of the purchase more than the economic ones.

References

1. Johan Arndt, "Role of Product-Related Conversations in the Diffusion of a New Product," *Journal of Marketing Research*, 4 (August 1967), 291–5.
2. Raymond A. Bauer, "Consumer Behavior as Risk Taking," in R. S. Hancock, ed., *Dynamic Marketing for a Changing World*, Proceedings, 43rd National Conference, American Marketing Association, 1960, 389–98.
3. ———, "Risk Handling in Drug Adoption: The Role of Company Preference," *Public Opinion Quarterly*, 25 (Winter 1961), 546–59.
4. William W. Cooley and Paul R. Lohnes, *Multivariate Procedures for the Behavioral Sciences*, New York: John Wiley & Sons, Inc., 1962.
5. Donald F. Cox, "The Measurement of Information Value: A Study in Consumer Decision-Making," Proceedings, Annual Conference, American Marketing Association, 1962.
6. ——— and S. U. Rich, "Perceived Risk and Consumer Decision-Making— The Case of Telephone Shopping," *Journal of Marketing Research*, 1 (November 1964), 32–9.
7. Scott M. Cunningham, "Perceived Risk as a Factor in Product-Oriented Word-of-Mouth Behavior: A First Step," in L. G. Smith, ed., *Reflections on Progress in Marketing*, Proceedings, 1964, Educators Conference, American Marketing Association, 1965.
8. ———, "Perceived Risk as a Factor in the Diffusion of New Product Information," in R. M. Hass, ed., *Science, Technology and Marketing*, Proceedings, Annual Conference, American Marketing Association, 1966.
9. Paul E. Green, M. H. Halbert, and Patrick J. Robinson, "Canonical Analysis: An Exposition and Illustrative Application," *Journal of Marketing Research*, 3 (February 1966), 32–9.
10. Helen V. McKenna, Peter R. Hofstaetter, and James P. O'Connor, "The Concept of Ideal Self and of a Friend," *Journal of Personality*, 24 (April 1956), 262–71.

11. Donald T. Popielarz, "An Exploration of Perceived Risk and Willingness to Try New Products," *Journal of Marketing Research*, 4 (November 1967), 368–72.

12. Michael A. Wallach, Nathan Kogan, and D. T. Bem, "Group Influence on Risk Taking," *Journal of Abnormal and Social Psychology*, 65 (July 1962), 75–86.

E. Experimental Design

In the experimental design model, the dependent variable is interval scaled, while the independent variables are nominal. In this respect it is the reverse of discriminant analysis.

In the analysis of dependence, the influence of certain independent variables—such as advertising—on a dependent variable—such as sales—is sought. In the design of experiments, of course, the advertising variable would have to be nominal—like heavy versus light advertising. The problem is that there are usually nuisance variables present that effect the dependent variable and distort the results. There are generally four methods for controlling such variables. One is the statistical control used in regression analysis. If the nuisance variable were price, it would be included as an independent variable in the regression model. The advertising variable would then be interpreted as the effect of advertising when price was held constant. The other three methods of control for a nuisance variable are called techniques of experimental control and form the basis for the design of experiments.

One of these three approaches is simply to hold price constant over all the test areas. Such an approach is rarely practical. A second is to assign test areas randomly to the experimental conditions—namely, heavy advertising and light advertising. It would be hoped that price and other sources of variation or bias would not have any net influence on the resulting sales measures. A third would be to consider price a second treatment or experimental variable. The experimental design would then be called upon to measure separately the impact of price (i.e., high, medium, and low) and advertising on sales.

Lipstein presents the basic experimental design model and discusses some practical considerations in applying experimental design to marketing problems. Barclay describes factorial design in the context of a pricing experiment. Cox uses a randomized block design to explore the effect of shelf space upon sales and comes to a very unexpected conclusion.

There are situations in the design of experiments when it is not possible to control experimentally for all nuisance variables, for some might be interval scaled and beyond the experimenter's control. In such cases, statistical control is also utilized by adding one or more interval-scaled variables to the set of independent variables. A model of this type is considered an analysis-of-covariance model. In effect, the added variable or covariate is placed as the sole independent variable in a regression model. The residual terms or differences between the dependent variable values and the corresponding predicted values then represent the dependent variable with the influence of the covariate removed. This residual can then become the dependent variable in a conventional experimental design model. Barrows presents a good introduction to the analysis of covariance in the context of an illustrative problem.

15

Benjamin Lipstein: The Design of Test Marketing Experiments

There are two levels at which test market experiments must be designed: one is the arrangement and selection of markets, the other is the measurement system to be used within the market. This paper is concerned with the structure and selection of markets for experimentation.

Although test marketing of a new product may be undertaken for a number of reasons, there are two purposes most of us would consider of paramount importance and which have clear design implications: one is to derive an estimate of the brand share which the product may achieve on a national level; the second is to evaluate alternative strategies for subsequent use on a national scale. The brand share projection problem is essentially a problem of estimation in contrast with the second which is a test of a specific set of alternatives or hypotheses. While the projection problem may also be regarded as a test of a hypothesis, the problem of estimation remains dominant in its implications for design.

The Evaluation of Alternative Strategies

It is in the area of alternative strategies that experimental design has much to contribute to the test market experiment. The issue is the relative performance of two different marketing activities. For example, which will be more effective, a coupon or a sample, in the introduction of a new product?

Reprinted from the *Journal of Advertising Research*. © Copyrighted 1965 by the Advertising Research Foundation.

Should the price be set at $.75 or $.98? Will one kind of copy approach produce a more rapid trial rate than an alternative copy approach? In these situations one is not so much concerned with the absolute share achievement, though this kind of information is often estimated, as with the relative performance of the two strategies in terms of brand share, consumer awareness, and consumer trials.

Within the context of this problem, it is meaningful to talk about the consequences and the cost of an erroneous decision. For example, if we choose couponing in preference to sampling, and if the decision is incorrect, the consequences may be a specific dollar cost of marketing or a lower achievement in brand share. It is these risks that must be related to what statisticians refer to as the Type I and Type II errors. A Type I error is the case in which no difference exists between two merchandising approaches, but we erroneously believe there to be a difference. A Type II error is committed when we fail to recognize a difference that exists. There are different cost consequences for each of these two kinds of errors, and the probabilities must accordingly be fixed against these costs. The fixing of these probabilities is a joint responsibility of the researcher and marketing management. They are often arrived at by negotiation. The ultimate value of a test may depend upon management's awareness of the likelihood of these two probabilities. This does not call for confounding management with technical jargon—management is often quite familiar with these issues—the problem is only one of communication.

Treatment Variations within the Market

Once these probability levels have been fixed we are prepared to tackle the specific questions of the design of a test market experiment. One of the first issues to be considered is, can the alternative strategies such as couponing and sampling be tested in the same market? One cannot mix two different copy strategies within the same media market and hope to measure any differences. If the issue *can* be tested within the market, such as the case of couponing and sampling, then we have much greater latitude in the choice of cities for experimental purposes. From a design point of view, such an experiment is concerned with comparisons within the experimental block or city.

Typically in such a situation the city might be divided into two, three, or four parts. Coupons would be used in one part, samples in another part, and perhaps no promotions in still another part of the city. Separate measurements would be taken in each part of the city and comparisons could then be made between each of the parts to provide an estimate of the effect of one vs. the other. Such results could then be combined over a number of test cities. The important thing is that the comparisons are always made within the city and hence the city effects or city differences do not confound or conceal the experimental effects.

Many arrangements of treatments can be used in a complete block design. The randomized complete block design might call for a division of the city into two or more segments for the application of separate treatments. For instance, in Syracuse, the railroad divides the city and the metropolitan area in the two halves (north and south) which are fairly comparable on a demographic basis. In the case of Columbus, such a division can be made on the north/south axis and again, very conveniently, the railroad divides the metropolitan area into two approximately equivalent parts.

The effect of testing couponing vs. sampling in the same city is best observed by examining the experimental design model. The model identifies the following variables:

U = Overall mean of the entire city
B = City or block effect
S = Sampling effect
C = Couponing effect

Let us assume that we are estimating brand share using retail store audits in both halves of the city. The observed share for the coupon half of the city is represented by X_c and for sample half by X_s.

The observed shares have the following model representation:

$$X_c = U + B + C + e \tag{1}$$

$$X_s = U + B + S + e \tag{2}$$

where e is the random error. To compute the effect of the couponing vs. sampling, we subtract one equation from the other to obtain:

$$X_c - X_s = C - S \tag{3}$$

We can thus measure the effect of couponing vs. sampling within the city or block, subject only to sampling variation. A variation of the split city design is to use a checkerboard design where segments of the city are randomly selected and assigned to sample or coupon exposure. In this kind of application a consumer panel would be needed to measure the effects since retail store audits could not be clearly attributed to the effects of couponing or sampling.

If it is desired to vary two factors simultaneously, a factorial arrangement might be used, say, two levels of sampling and two price levels if they can be controlled within the same market. Such an arrangement would provide estimates of the differential effects of sampling levels, prices, and the possible interaction of the two.

Assuming that we have divided a test city into four parts for purposes of this factorial design, we would have the following equations:

$$X_1 = U + SP_1 + e \tag{4}$$

$$X_2 = U + SP_2 + e \tag{5}$$

$$X_3 = U + CP_1 + e \tag{6}$$

$$X_4 = U + CP_2 + e \tag{7}$$

where X_1, X_2, X_3, and X_4 represent the brand shares for each segment of the city, U, S, and C are as defined above, and P_1 and P_2 represent the lower and higher prices in the test. One estimate of price effect is equation (4) minus equation (5):

$$X_1 - X_2 = SP_1 - SP_2 \tag{8}$$

Similarly, we have for equations (6) and (7):

$$X_3 - X_4 = CP_1 - CP_2 \tag{9}$$

Since both are equally acceptable estimates of price we can combine equations (8) and (9) to obtain the effect of the price difference, namely:

$$\text{Effect of price} = {}^1/_2[(SP_1 - SP_2) + (CP_1 - CP_2)] \tag{10}$$

Similarly, by subtracting equation (6) from (4) and (7) from (5) and averaging the results we have:

$$\text{Effect of sample vs. coupon} = {}^1/_2[(SP_1 - CP_1) + (SP_2 - CP_2)] \tag{11}$$

Lastly, adding equations (4) and (7) and subtracting equations (5) from (6) provides an estimate of the interaction of couponing/sampling with changes in price:

$$\text{Interaction effect} = {}^1/_2[(SP_1 + CP_2) - (SP_2 + CP_1)] \tag{12}$$

The statistical analysis of this experiment is very direct. The details are readily available in most books on design of experiments. The reader should be cautioned, however, that at least two markets are required with these experiments to provide a bona fide error term for testing of the effects.

If the market can only absorb two treatment variations, but three are under consideration, an incomplete block design using groups of three cities can be used. In such a case, let us assume that one test market contains a test of sampling vs. couponing, another contains sampling vs. control, and the third contains couponing vs. control. If sampling proves to be superior to couponing in the first market and couponing is superior to control in the second market, and couponing is superior to control in the third market, then we have a unique ranking:

$$\text{Sampling} > \text{Couponing} > \text{Control}$$

In effect, although all treatments are not included in the same block, comparisons can be made between the three experimental variations.

A great many test variations can be considered within the context of viewing the test city as an experimental block. The key to such designing is that the variation between cities, which is generally very large, is excluded from the comparisons. However, this type of experiment provides only relative performance of the treatment. It is of course understood that all other factors such as dollars of advertising and sales effort are held constant. Throughout this section I have assumed that at least two markets with the same treatment arrangements will be used so that variances and tests of significance can be computed. The size of the Type I and Type II errors one is willing to accept, and the order of difference sought will determine the number of test markets.

Treatment Variations between Markets

Where the issue to be tested affects the entire market, such as copy or levels of advertising expenditures, the entire test market becomes the experimental unit. The design must then contend with and attempt to control between city variation. In general, for a given level of reliability, the number of test cities for this type of problem is substantially greater than for test market variables which can be tested in the same market.

Since the comparisons are to be made between markets, every effort must be made to reduce the variability which is a function of the selected markets. In this case, many of the dictums which we frequently hear are relevant. Ideally, markets to be used in the test should be as similar as possible. Where possible, the following restraints should be placed upon the selection of markets. They should be similar in population size, family income, demographic characteristics, and ethnic background; similar in trade factors and media facilities; and, hopefully, all in the same geographic region. Our willingness to forego any of these controls will be related to our evaluation of the degree to which differences in these characteristics may affect the test results. It now becomes self-evident why certain cities are used repeatedly for test market operations.

Having selected the cities for the test, the next step is the selection of the experimental design. Latin squares are frequently useful because they provide a means for controlling variations between cities, which could not be controlled by selection. For example, the rows of the Latin square might control for geographic variation, while the columns could be used for controlling competitive activity or media facility variations. The treatments within the Latin square in this case might be three levels of advertising expenditures or three different kinds of copy. The Latin square design implies independence of controls and treatments or that an interaction effect is not present. By way of example, we may obtain from retail store audits an estimate of brand share for each segment of the Latin square as in Table 1.

Table 1.   Latin Square

Competitive	Geographic Region		
Activity	East	North Central	West
Level 1	A	B	C
Level 2	B	C	A
Level 3	C	A	B

where $A =$ High level of advertising expenditure
$B =$ Medium level of advertising expenditure
$C =$ Low level of advertising expenditure

These brand shares are functions of geographic region, competitive activity, and the experimental level of advertising. By summing the rows we would be averaging out the effect of regions and levels of advertising; by summing the columns, the average effect of competitive activity and levels of advertising would be eliminated; and lastly, by summing the advertising expenditure level for each of the treatments we would average out the effect of geographic region, and competitive activity for a direct comparison of levels of advertising. The Latin square design operates to reduce the variation in the experiment in the same way that stratification does for sample surveys. In this case, the experimental error which is derived from the experiment for testing the treatment effects is due to the variation between cities. We would expect that the variation between cities would be substantially greater than the within variation to be found in the complete block experiments described above.

If the test issues are levels of advertising vs. levels of promotion, a factorial arrangement might be considered. The advantage of the factorial design is that it would provide an estimate of the interaction of these two treatment variations with no additional increase in sample size.

The structure of factorial designs when the entire city is used as the experimental unit is similar to the factorial design described above. However, only one treatment is used for each city, in contrast with complete block designs in which all treatments are used within a single city. The main problem when the entire city is used as the experimental unit is again the variation which cities contribute to the experimental error.

The experimental variations for these situations are many and varied. Because the between city variation is likely to be large, it is always desirable that advance estimates of variation be made to indicate the reasonableness of the sample of cities for the decision issues. Again, consideration must be given to the expected magnitude of the Type I and Type II errors as well as the degree of difference expected.

Other Considerations in Design

There are a great variety of experimental designs and estimation procedures, such as covariance analysis and regression methods, which the statistician can draw upon for designing test market experiments. The variations in design and estimation are only limited by our imagination and the cost restraints of the project. In addition, there are a number of other important considerations in test market design which are beyond the scope of this paper, such as length of test, benchmark measurements, related measurements, policing of your own activities, and competition.

External Disturbances to Test Markets

Since the problems of test marketing are not only in design, but also in execution, there is some merit in enumerating some of the things that may obscure the effects to be measured in a test market.

1. The sales force may discover that they have a poor brand showing in one of the cities, and may decide to improve the picture.
2. The test product may go out of stock, and not be replenished in time.
3. A newspaper strike may affect the media program.
4. Your competitor may be in an overstocked position.
5. Price cutting to clear stocks may be the pattern of the day.
6. Your competitor may be out of stock for the test period. This, of course, would exaggerate the success of the audit.
7. Special promotions or deals may be run by your competitor. This may have the effect of obscuring the normal success of the new product or test feature.
8. Competitor changes in price, whether up or down, would have an impact.
9. Unusual climatic conditions or other natural phenomena would obviously interrupt the progress of the test.

The main point of this listing of some of the causes of disruption of a test city audit is that we cannot, and should not, attempt to analyze the data without consideration of all of these unpredictable events. Awareness of these occurrences in a test city program provides the opportunity for evaluating these uncontrollable and extraneous events in a test market experiment.

The simple facts of life are that we never have enough test cities from a statistical point of view. Hence, it is all the more important to recognize factors which could distort the test results.

Test marketing can be a dangerous and misleading tool, but if designed and used intelligently it can provide management with essential guidance which will assure success in the long run.[1]

---

[1] Editor's note: In a section deleted due to space constraints, Dr. Lipstein stressed the importance of using multiple test markets which are representative of significant segments if reliable national market share projections are to be obtained. He also suggested that multiple measurements be built into the test markets to ensure against erroneous interpretation.

16

William D. Barclay: Factorial Design in a Pricing Experiment

Introduction

This article describes an application of factorial design to a pricing experiment conducted at the retail store level. Although factorial design has long been applied in biological and industrial experimentation [2, 3, 4, 6], comparatively few marketing research applications have been reported [1, 5].

The need for the pricing experiment discussed here arose as follows:[1] For one of its product lines, the Quaker Oats Company manufactures three items: A, B, and C. These items comprise a " line " since they fulfill a similar, broad consumer need. They compete with one another and with other brands in the same general category.

Financial analysis of these items revealed a wide discrepancy in profit productivity. Item C was evaluated as adequately profitable, but neither A nor B was so judged. Translated to retail price levels, increases of four cents per package for A and four cents per package for B were desired.

Reprinted from *Journal of Marketing Research*, Published by the American Marketing Association. William P. Barclay, " Factorial Design in a Pricing Experiment," *Journal of Marketing Research*, Vol. VI, November, 1969, pp. 427–429. The author acknowledges the advice and participation of James L. Spangenberg, Carolyn Cleath, and H. Maurice Jones, all of Quaker Oats, in the development and conduct of the experiment.

[1] The situation has been modified for simplicity and security.

Given this marketing background, the research problem was formulated this way. Assuming that total line profits (of A, B, and C combined) are the suitable criterion:

1. What would be the effect on total line profits of increasing the price of A by four cents per unit at retail?
2. What would be the corresponding effect of increasing the price of B by four cents per unit?
3. Is there interaction between these two factors, i.e., would the effect of increasing one price depend on the level of the other price?

This article describes the experimental design used to answer these questions (a factorial design in randomized blocks) and the analysis. The focus will be on a description of methodology and its rationale. For full computational detail, the reader will be referred to appropriate sources.

The Experimental Design and its Execution

Because two factors were of interest here (the consequences of increasing the prices of A and B), the study might have been designed as two separate experiments, each dealing with one factor. This classical, single-factor-at-a-time approach was rejected in favor of a complete factorial design [1, 3, 4, 5, 6] that involved the use of four treatment combinations as shown below.

Treatment Combination	Symbol	Description of Package Prices	
		Price of A	Price of B
1	$a_0 b_0$	Present	Present
2	$a_0 b_1$	Present	Present $+ 4¢$
3	$a_1 b_0$	Present $+ 4¢$	Present
4	$a_1 b_1$	Present $+ 4¢$	Present $+ 4¢$

Factorial design was adopted principally because we anticipated the possibility of interaction between the two price increases. Detecting interaction would have been impossible with the single factor approach, since factors are not simultaneously varied in that method. If (as later developed) there were no interaction, then factorial design would be more efficient.

Experimental Layout and Its Development

A completely randomized experimental layout would have been inefficient. The Latin Square layout and similar designs, involving changing treatments over time, were eliminated because of administrative difficulty and possible consumer confusion about shifting prices. The randomized block design [1, 2, 3, 4, 5, 6] was chosen because it was more efficient than complete randomization and avoided the problems associated with Latin Square type designs.

For sample size, no directly relevant information about the magnitude of experimental error was available. However, related knowledge indicated that 30 test stores per treatment combination, or 120 in all, were needed for comparisons among pairs of treatment combinations. The 120 test stores were chosen from among medium to large grocery stores in an area with high distribution on test items.

With 120 stores and randomized blocks of four treatments, there were 30 blocks to be constructed. A three-week sales audit of the stores provided a stratification basis. For each store, Quaker sales and market share were calculated. Stores were listed in order of Quaker sales divided into consecutive groups of eight. Within each group, stores were then ranked by Quaker share. Finally, successive subgroups of four stores were defined as blocks. Within each block, randomization was used to decide which store would receive each treatment combination.

Physical Conduct of the Experiment

Three weeks after pretest audit, experimental price changes were made. Simultaneously, some distribution gaps in test stores were filled so that the experiment was conducted under 100 percent distribution conditions. Prices assigned to products introduced at this time equalled average high or low prices specified by the treatment assigned.

Three monthly sales audits were conducted. Standard procedures were used to maintain Quaker items in stock at correct prices.

Analysis of Data

The key response observation in this experiment was line profits. However, the analysis was conducted in terms of the logarithms of profits rather than the original observations on the following rationale:[2]

1. Since test stores varied widely in size, it was anticipated that treatment effects would more likely be additive on a log scale than on the original scale.
2. For each level of B pricing the sum of the two A price observations in each block was plotted against their difference. For each B price level the plot was approximately linear, suggesting that these observations should be transformed to a log scale for analysis.[3]

---

[2] See Cox [3, Chapter 2] and Snedecor and Cochran [6, Chapter 11] for further discussion.

[3] See Bliss [2, Chapter 11] for discussion of graphical evaluation of additivity.

Also, the main analysis was in log profits for the combined second and third test months. First month's data was omitted so that consumers could adapt to experimental changes.

Estimates of Factor Effects

The analysis was standard for a 2×2 factorial in randomized blocks [4, 6]. Denoting the treatment combination means (in coded log profit units) by the same symbols used earlier to identify the treatment combinations, the experimental means were: $a_0 b_0 = 3.0128$ units, $a_0 b_1 = 3.0255$, $a_1 b_0 = 2.9863$, and $a_1 b_1 = 2.9441$ units. Factor effects were estimated as follows:

1. Increasing the price of A by four cents was estimated to change profits by:
   $\frac{1}{2}(a_1 b_0 - a_0 b_0) + \frac{1}{2}(a_1 b_1 - a_0 b_1) = -0.0540$ units.
2. Increasing the price of B by four cents was estimated to yield:
   $\frac{1}{2}(a_0 b_1 - a_0 b_0) + \frac{1}{2}(a_1 b_1 - a_1 b_0) = -0.0148$ units.
3. The interaction between the two factors was evaluated to be:
   $\frac{1}{2}(a_1 b_1 - a_0 b_1) - \frac{1}{2}(a_1 b_0 - a_0 b_0) = -0.0274$ units.

Confidence Intervals for Factor Effects

The preceding estimates of factor effects are, of course, subject to sampling fluctuations. From the variance analysis below the experimental error variance was estimated to be $s^2 = .030334 = (0.174)^2$ with 87 degrees of freedom.

Source	Degrees of Freedom	Sum of Squares	Mean Square
Blocks	29	3.922590	
Treatments	3	0.116546	
Error	87	2.639099	.030334

Ninety percent confidence intervals were constructed using the formula:

$$\text{Estimated effect} \pm ts/(r)^{\frac{1}{2}}$$

where

$t = 1.66$ is Student's t value for 87 degrees of freedom and 90 percent confidence
$s = 0.174$ units
$r = 30$ blocks

Since the width of the half-interval was $(1.66)(0.174)/5.477 = 0.0528$ units, the 90 percent confidence intervals were as shown below.

Effect	90% Confidence Interval (Log Units)
Price of A	−0.0012 to −0.1068
Price of B	−0.0676 to +0.0380
Interaction	−0.0802 to +0.0254

From the standpoint of questions in this experiment, these confidence intervals may be interpreted as follows:

1. Increasing the price of Item A by four cents at retail would (with 90 percent confidence) reduce total line profits. In log units, the loss in profits would range from .0012 to 0.1068 units per store. In percentage terms (obtained by taking the antilogarithms of these losses), the profit reduction would be between less than 0.1 percent and about 22 percent. (The magnitude of the probable loss is poorly determined because of high experimental error, but its existence is well established.)
2. There was no evidence that increasing the price of B would significantly change total profits. Similarly, interaction between the two factors was not statistically established.

Commentary

It is believed that the factorial approach is worth consideration whenever a marketing experiment evaluates two or more factors, each at two or more levels. It would appear especially useful for pricing experiments involving several items in a line, in which the possibility of interaction of effects is usually present.

The experiment was somewhat disappointing because the results were subject to comparatively high experimental error, but this is generally true in marketing experimentation. In any case, the results of the experiment were sufficiently precise to be used for the pricing decisions that were made.[4] It was decided to hold the price of A at the lower level and to increase the price of B, but by less than the amount tested.

References

1. Seymour Banks, *Experimentation in Marketing*, New York: McGraw-Hill Book Co., 1965.
2. Charles I. Bliss, *Statistics In Biology*, Volume One, New York: McGraw-Hill Book Co., 1967.

---

[4] To conserve space, only part of the analysis has been reported. Covariance analysis was also used to improve results.

3. David R. Cox, *Planning of Experiments*, New York: John Wiley & Sons, Inc., 1958.
4. Owen L. Davies, ed., *The Design and Analysis of Industrial Experiments*, London: Oliver and Boyd, 1956.
5. Paul E. Green and Ronald E. Frank, *A Manager's Guide to Marketing Research: Survey of Recent Developments*, New York: John Wiley & Sons, Inc., 1967.
6. George W. Snedecor and William G. Cochran, *Statistical Methods*, Ames, The Iowa State University Press, 1967.

17   Keith K. Cox: The Effect of Shelf Space upon Sales of Branded Products

One of the scarcest resources in a self-service store is shelf space. In allocating shelf space, many food manufacturers and supermarket retailers employ decision rules which assume a positive relationship between the amount of shelf space given to a product and its sales [5, 13]. The ideal decision rule for shelf space allocations for retailers would consider contribution to profit and opportunity cost concepts. A brand should be given more shelf space if (1) its additional revenue is greater than its additional cost (contribution to profit concept), and (2) there are no other alternative uses of that additional shelf space that will add more profit (opportunity cost concept). The same concepts imply that manufacturers should strive for additional shelf space for their brands if (1) the additional revenue gained is greater than the additional cost to acquire the shelf space, and (2) there are no alternative ways of increasing revenue for their brands that will add more contribution to profit.

A retailer may be considered as a seller of shelf space to various buyers. Cairns shows how this idea can be combined with the appropriate cost concepts [4, p. 34]:

> To induce a retailer to sell him space, a supplier must offer a price for a unit of space which exceeds the "opportunity cost" of this space. This opportunity cost of a unit of retail space is the gross profit the retailer can obtain by allocating this space to the most profitable item not now in his assortment, or to the most profitable combination of items already stocked.

Reprinted from *Journal of Marketing Research*, published by the American Marketing Association. Keith K. Cox, "The Effect of Shelf Space upon Sales of Branded Products, *Journal of Marketing Research*, Vol. VII, February, 1970, pp. 55–58. The author expresses his appreciation to Mr. Bernard Weingarten and Mr. Virgil Reynolds, President and Vice President of Weingarten Supermarkets, for their permission to use six supermarkets in the field experiments. Mr. John Burton assisted in the daily audit of the experiments.

Therefore, it is the marginal revenue and not the average revenue that should be considered in the decision rules for retailers and manufacturers.[1] There is very little published information on measuring the additional revenue an individual brand gains when given additional shelf space.

In the absence of much empirical data, a "battle of the shelf space" occurs frequently between manufacturers and retailers. The manufacturer is interested in maximizing the revenue and profit of his brand, but the retailer is interested in maximizing the revenue and profit of the total product category. Previous research by the author has shown that the retailer's increasing the amount of shelf space for a product category beyond a certain minimal level may be an inefficient method of space allocation [6].

The objective of this article is to measure the relationship between sales of an individual product brand and its shelf space. Therefore, this research is primarily oriented toward a manufacturer with a national brand or a retailer with a private brand who is interested in maximizing sales of his own brand. Three hypotheses were tested in a field experiment.

1. There is no relationship between the amount of shelf space given to a staple product brand and total unit sales of that product brand.

This hypothesis is based on the assumption that consumers buy staple goods primarily by habit. Consequently, the amount of shelf space allocated to a staple brand is a very weak stimulus as long as the brand has some minimum amount of shelf space.[2]

2. There is a relationship between the amount of shelf space given to an impulse product brand that has high consumer acceptance and total unit sales of that product brand.[3]
3. There is no relationship between the amount of shelf space given to an impulse product brand that has low consumer acceptance and total unit sales of that product brand.

Merely by classifying a brand as an impulse brand, one which may influence the consumer in a spur-of-the-moment decision, it is a logical assumption that sales of that brand should be influenced by changing amounts of shelf space. However, a product brand with high consumer acceptance may have a lower threshold level in terms of the influence of shelf space than would a product brand with low consumer acceptance.

---

[1] Kotler [14] discusses the appropriate decision rules for allocation of marketing effort, pp. 274-6.

[2] Buzzell, *et al.* [3] shows how a minimum level of shelf space should be allocated to any brand. See Exhibit 7, pp. 51-52.

[3] One operational way to classify whether a product brand has high consumer acceptance is by using a share of market criteria.

Table 1. Shelf Treatments for Powdered Coffee Cream and Salt Experiments

Treatment	Powdered Coffee Cream		Salt	
	Coffee-mate	Creamora	Morton	Food Club
	Proportion of shelf space			
1	⅓	⅔	⅓	⅔
2	½	½	½	½
3	⅔	⅓	⅔	⅓

Because past research has shown that the effect of shelf space upon product sales may be relatively minor, a 25% level of significance was selected in testing the three hypotheses.[4] Although this higher level of significance increases the probability of a Type I error, it decreases the probability of a Type II error. A Type II error would occur if the hypothesis that there was no relationship between the amount of shelf space and product brand sales was accepted, when in reality, there was a relationship between the amount of shelf space and product brand sales.

Research Methodology

The present experiment measured the relationship between the sales of a product brand (i.e., Coffeemate) and shelf space, whereas a previous experiment measured the relationship between the sales of a product category (i.e., all powdered coffee cream) and shelf space [6]. The two product categories chosen for the test were powdered coffee cream and salt, with powdered coffee cream considered an impulse product and salt considered a staple product. Two leading brands were tested in each product category. Morton and Food Club salt brands were selected to test the first hypothesis; Coffee-mate powdered coffee cream was selected to test the second hypothesis; and Creamora powdered coffee cream was selected to test the third hypothesis.

Selection of Research Design

Many past field experiments in supermarkets have utilized some type of Latin square design [2, 9, 11, 12]. This is a logical design, since differences among stores and among time periods can be statistically controlled through a randomized process and replication of the test treatments. In the present experiment, the Latin square design was not selected because of its limitation that the number of treatments, stores, and time periods have to be equal. Based upon past experimental results, the decision was made not to control

---

[4] See Cox and Enis [7, pp. 9–11], Richmond [17, Chapter 10], and Banks [1, pp. 223–5].

for time differences.[5] A randomized blocks design was selected, with the stores treated as the blocks, so that one important type of extraneous variation (differences among stores) could be separated from the experimental error.

Six large supermarkets within the Weingarten food chain in Houston, Texas, were selected as test stores. Each store was assigned all test treatments on a random basis, with each treatment lasting for one week. A shelf inventory of the test products was made each day during the life of the experiment.

Selection of Shelf Treatments

The total shelf space for the two product categories was kept constant throughout the experiment. Different allocations of shelf space were made between the two brands of salt and powdered coffee cream (Table 1). Although most food manufacturers would not normally consider such a wide variation of shelf space alternatives for their brands, the test treatments ranged from a low of one-third to a high of two-thirds of the total shelf space available for the top two brands; these extremes were intended to make the experimental results as powerful as possible.

To obtain the necessary shelf treatments, all test stores had to have some multiple of six in total shelf space for the two brands tested within each product category. For example, if the total shelf space allocation was 24 shelf facings for the two brands, the test treatments for each brand would be 8, 12, and 16 shelf spaces. If a test store actually had 22 spaces before the experiment started, the amount of space for the two brands would be adjusted to 24 spaces for the life of the experiment.

The experiment lasted three weeks in October and November of 1968.

Experimental Model

A fixed effect model for a randomized blocks design was selected for the experiments, where a single observation is given by

$$Y_{ij} = M + T_j + B_i + E_{ij}$$

where

Y_{ij} = the jth observation in the ith block
M = overall mean
T_j = effect of jth treatment
B_i = 3 effect of ith block
E_{ij} = effect of experimental error in the ith block
subjected to jth treatment
$i = 1, 2, \ldots, n$
$j = 1, 2, \ldots, t$

---

[5] See Cox [6], especially Table 2, p. 65.

In the randomized blocks design, the following statistical relationships are used:

Total sum of squares = Treatment sum of squares
+ Block sum of squares
+ Residual error sum of squares

$$\sum_i^n \sum_j^t (Y_{ij} - M)^2 = n \sum_j^t (\overline{Y}_{.j} - M)^2$$
$$+ t \sum_i^n (\overline{Y}_{i.} - M)^2 + \sum_i^n \sum_j^t (Y_{ij} - \overline{Y}_{.j} - \overline{Y}_{i.} + M)^2$$

where

$\overline{Y}_{.j}$ = treatment mean
$\overline{Y}_{i.}$ = block mean
t = number of treatments
n = number of replications

Each sum of squares is divided by the appropriate degrees of freedom to obtain the mean square. The F-ratio formula is

$$F = \frac{\text{Treatment mean square}}{\text{Residual error mean square}}.$$

Using a 25% level of significance with 2 and 10 degrees of freedom, the null hypothesis should be rejected when the F-ratio is greater than 1.60.

Test Results

The test results of the supermarket experiments are shown in Tables 2 and 3. Table 2 summarizes the total unit sales of each product brand for each shelf space treatment in the experiment. Table 3 gives the degrees of freedom, mean squares, and F-ratio for all four product brands tested. The following are the results.

Table 2. Total Unit Sales of Product Brands in Six Supermarkets over Three Weeks

Brands	Shelf Space		
	1/3	1/2	2/3
Coffeemate	366	409	442
Creamora	155	158	146
Morton salt	672	639	675
Food Club salt	249	286	283

Hypothesis 1 was accepted. There was no relationship between the amount of shelf space given to Morton and Food Club salt and total unit sales of the two product brands.

Hypothesis 2 was accepted. There was a relationship between the amount of shelf space given to Coffeemate and its total unit sales. The F-ratio was 3.49 greater than required for the 25% level of significance.

Hypothesis 3 was accepted. There was no relationship between the amount of shelf space given to Creamora and total unit sales of Creamora.

The F-ratio for differences in product sales among stores was significant at the 1% level for all four brands. These results point out how difficult it is to execute a quasi-experimental design, where a group of equivalent control stores and test stores are used in the experiment.

Analysis and Implications of Results

Using the contribution to profit and opportunity cost concepts, what decisions might be implied to retailers and manufacturers from the research results? For staple products and impulse brands with low consumer acceptance, the additional marginal revenue gained from additional space was insignificant. Given this information retailers should limit their shelf allocations for these brands to some minimal level; such a level for any brand should be influenced by such constraints as out-of-stock conditions and the ability to stock a full case at one time.

Table 3. Mean Squares and F-Ratios for Four Brands Tested

Source	Degrees of Freedom	Coffeemate		Creamora		Morton		Food Club	
		Mean Square	F-Ratio	Mean Square	F-Ratio	Mean Square	F-Ratio	Mean Square	F-Ratio
Blocks (stores)	5	1,644.8	23.70*	400.0	7.94*	5,817.2	16.29*	912.8	9.78*
Treatments (shelf spaces)	2	242.0	3.49†	6.5	.13	66.5	.19	70.5	.76
Residual error	10	69.4		50.4		357.1		93.3	
Total	17								

* Significant at .01 level.
† Significant at .10 level.

Suppose that Morton salt sold twice as much as Food Club salt, and that the minimal level for any brand of salt was six shelf spaces. One decision rule would be to give the Morton brand twice as much shelf space as the Food Club brand, since it sold twice as much. If there were eighteen spaces allocated to salt, Morton salt would be allocated twelve spaces and Food Club salt would get six spaces. The Dillon study suggests the use of this decision rule for allocating shelf space to products based upon past sales history [8].

Using the contribution to profit and opportunity cost concepts, an alternative decision rule would be for the retailer to give both Morton and

Food Club brands the minimum six shelf spaces, and stock the Morton brand twice as often. The extra six spaces would then be available for new products or other alternatives (opportunity cost) which would contribute more profit to the retailer.

For many manufacturers, the additional revenue generated by extra shelf spaces for a brand may not compensate for the cost of obtaining the shelf space. In terms of opportunity cost, the brand salesman may need to spend more time keeping his brand in stock and seeing that the retailer carries his full product line rather than spending his time obtaining more shelf space beyond a minimal level.

Conclusions

There are a number of limitations to the present experiment. First, sale of many other brands may respond differently to changes in shelf space than the brands tested in this experiment. Also, this experiment was conducted in six stores of one supermarket chain in only one city. Still, the results imply that many of the existing decision rules in use by manufacturers and retailers in allocating shelf space may need to be reevaluated.

References

1. Seymour Banks, *Experimentation in Marketing*, New York: McGraw-Hill, 1965.
2. D. G. Burgoyne and C. B. Johnston, "Are Shelf Space and Shelf Location Really Important?" *The Business Quarterly*, (Summer 1968), 56–60.
3. Robert D. Buzzell, Walter J. Salmon, and Richard F. Vancil, *Product Profitability Measurement and Merchandising Decisions*, Boston: Harvard University, 1965.
4. James P. Cairns, "Suppliers, Retailers, and Shelf Space," *Journal of Marketing*, (July 1962), 34–6.
5. *COSMOS*, National Association of Food Chains, 1968.
6. Keith Cox, "The Responsiveness of Food Sales to Supermarket Shelf Space Changes," *Journal of Marketing Research*, (May 1964), 63–7.
7. ——— and Ben M. Enis, *Experimentation for Marketing Decisions*, Scranton, Pa.: International Textbook, 1969.
8. *The Dillon Study*, Progressive Grocer, New York: The Butterick Co., 1960.
9. Bennett Dominick, Jr., *An Illustration of the Use of the Latin Square in Measuring the Effectiveness of Retail Merchandising Practices*, Methods of Research in Marketing, Paper No. 2, Cornell University, June 1952.
10. James F. Engel, David T. Kollat, and Roger D. Blackwell, *Consumer Behavior*, New York: Holt, Rinehart and Winston, 1968, Chapters 21 and 22.
11. Peter Henderson, James Hind, and Sidney Brown, "Sales Effects of Two Campaign Themes," *Journal of Advertising Research*, (March 1961), 15–22.
12. William S. Hoofnagle, "Experimental Designs in Measuring the Effectiveness of Promotion," *Journal of Marketing Research*, (May 1965), 154–62.

13. "How to Allocate Shelf Space and Maintain Inventory Controls," *Food Topics*, May 1961.

14. Philip Kotler, *Marketing Management*, Englewood Cliffs, New Jersey: Prentice Hall, 1967.

15. Wayne Lee, "Space Management in Retail Stores and Implications to Agriculture," in Wenzil K. Colva, ed., *Marketing—Key to Profits in the 1960's*, American Marketing Association, 1960, 523–33.

16. *McKinsey—General Foods Study*, General Foods Corporation, October 1963.

17. Samuel B. Richmond, *Statistical Analysis*, (2nd ed.), New York: Ronald Press, 1964.

18. U.S. Department of Agriculture, *Better Utilization of Selling Space in Food Stores*, Marketing Research Report No. 30, November 1952.

18

Lionel C. Barrow, Jr.: New Uses of Covariance Analysis

Research is frequently conducted to determine which of several possible treatments (such as several themes, packages, products, commercials, advertising expenditure levels, and ad campaigns) produces the best score on some key criterion. These criteria may be brand awareness, beliefs about the product, interest in buying it, sales, etc.

Researchers know that the treatments to be manipulated are not the only phenomena that can affect these criteria. For example, a person's past experience with a brand or service will probably have as pronounced an effect upon awareness and beliefs, and upon intent to use or buy the product, as seeing one or more commercials. Therefore, a researcher typically tries to design the studies to control for the effects of these other factors or covariates. Having done so to the best of his ability, the researcher then proceeds to apply his different treatments and infers that the differences he observes in, for example, interest in buying the test product, are due to the differences in the treatments administered rather than to any inherent differences in the kinds of people who received a particular treatment.

The usual way of trying to make "other things equal" is to assign respondents randomly to each treatment. However, it is just as unreasonable to expect random assignment to yield a perfect match as it is to expect exactly 50 heads and 50 tails in every 100 tosses of an unbiased coin. Just as the actual values obtained from such an experiment will vary by chance from the theoretical 50-50 value, so the actual values of the key covariates will vary by chance in an advertising experiment. With small samples, this random fluctuation can be quite large. Thus, for example, there are five chances in 100 that they will vary from six to 11 percentage points if the samples contain 150 respondents, and from eight to 14 percentage points if the samples contain only 100 respondents.

Attempts are therefore made to improve on the basic assignment procedures by making sure that an equal number of respondents with key characteristics receive each treatment.

But often sampling does not do the job. Randomly dropping or replicating a few respondents to equalize the distribution for one key variable quite often creates disproportionality in other variables.

What, then, can be done when sampling fails, when our treatment groups—whatever they are—are not comparable, are not matched on one or more key variables?

At Foote, Cone & Belding, we have been using analysis of covariance to match treatment groups as part of the normal computerized tabulation and analysis procedures in studies requiring matched groups.

Green and Tull (1966) present an excellent discussion of the rationale for using covariance analysis and of the mathematics involved. This present article summarizes some of FC&B's experiences with the procedure (which we recommend highly) and, in addition, presents some of the situations not covered by Green and Tull in which the procedure should not be used. Cochran (1957) and Smith (1957) both credit the noted British statistician, R. A. Fisher, with being the first to introduce analysis of covariance in 1934. Cochran quotes Fisher as saying that the procedure "combines the advantages and reconciles the requirements of two very widely applicable procedures known as regression and analysis of variance."

The technique equates samples for the effects of as many key variables (such as previous usage of a brand) as we are able to identify and measure. It therefore enables us to say with confidence that a given treatment is or is not better than another treatment because we have, to the best of our ability, made "all other things equal" by controlling for the influence of those extraneous variables.

The extent to which statistical controls are exercised depends upon two factors:

1. The *size* of the relationship between the matching variable (or covariate) and the dependent variable (as determined by a regression coefficient).

2. The extent to which a given group average differs on the covariate from the average for the entire sample.

Thus, let:

$\overline{Y}_a$ and $\overline{Y}_b$ = the *unadjusted* scores obtained by each of two groups (Group A and Group B) on the dependent variable

$\overline{Y}_a{}'$ and $\overline{Y}_b{}'$ = the *adjusted* scores for the same groups on the same variable

$\overline{X}_a$ and $\overline{X}_b$ = the scores obtained by each group on the covariate

$\overline{X}$ = the scores obtained by the entire sample on the covariate

b_{xy} = the regression coefficient indicating the size of the relationship

Then, a simplified formula for the adjustment would be:

$$\overline{Y}_a{}' = \overline{Y}_a - b_{xy}(\overline{X}_a - \overline{X})$$
$$\overline{Y}_b{}' = \overline{Y}_b - b_{xy}(\overline{X}_b - \overline{X})$$

Covariance may also be used to reduce sampling or experimental error thereby enabling an experimenter to discover significant differences that might otherwise have been missed.

The reduction in the estimate of sampling or experimental error is affected only by the extent to which the covariate is correlated with the dependent variable.

As Winer (1962) points out, "if this correlation is equal to p, and the experimental error per unit, disregarding the covariate, is σ_y^2, then the experimental error after the adjustment is:

$$\sigma_y^2 (1 - p^2)\left[1 + \frac{1}{f_e - 2}\right]$$

where f_e represents the degrees of freedom for the estimation of σ_y^2."

Use of Covariance to Correct Mismatched Samples

Table 1 presents the results of analysis of covariance adjustments on the first eight FC&B copy research studies in which the procedure was used.

These scores represent the expression of interest in buying the test product, using the seven-point scale below.

Scale Position	Index Score	Code for Machine Analysis
Definitely will buy	100	6
Almost definitely will buy	83	5
Probably will buy	67	4
Not sure will buy or not	50	3
Probably will not buy	33	2
Almost definitely will not buy	17	1
Definitely will not buy	00	0

Table 1. Effect of Covariance Adjustment on Purchase Intent Scores

	Purchase Intent Index Scores		
Study Number	Unadjusted	Adjusted	Difference
I			
Test Group	43	39	−4
Control Group	18	22	+4
II			
Test Group A	30	30	—
Test Group B	36	35	−1
III			
Test Group A	70	70	—
Test Group B	65	65	—
IV			
Test Group A	80	81	+1
Test Group B	80	80	—
Test Group C	79	79	—
Test Group D	81	81	—
V			
Test Group A	76	76	—
Control Group	69	69	—
VI			
Test Group A	64	63	−1
Test Group B	57	57	—
Control Group	51	52	+1
VII			
Test Group A	73	72	−1
Test Group B	70	69	−1
Control Group	65	67	+2
VIII			
Test Group A	52	51	−1
Control Group	41	42	+1
Average change*			.9*

* Computed without regard to the plus or minus sign.

As Table 1 indicates, on the average the adjustments were minor (less than one index point). This is probably because the copy research sampling procedures (random selection of sampling points; interviewing at every nth household; rotating the order in which respondents are assigned to a test or control group; and obtaining an equal number of interviews in each sampling cluster for each test and control group) were designed to achieve as close a match as is possible "in the field."

Thus, in most instances, the adjustments did not lead to a change in our conclusions. However, this was not always the case. For example, the data for Study VII were taken from a copy research test of two commercials. In this study two groups of 150 housewives were interviewed to obtain their interest in buying the product and their beliefs about the product after seeing a commercial. The same data were obtained from a third (control) group of housewives who did not see a test commercial. The interviews were conducted in the home in four cities (New York, Chicago, St. Louis, and Los Angeles). Each test group respondent saw one and only one of the test commercials on an 8 mm. rear-screen projector along with a short entertainment film.

The key covariate was the response to the five-point brand usage scale below which bore a high relationship (beta weight = .926 for the coded scores) to purchase intent.

Scale Position	Index Score	Code for Machine Analysis
Always	100	4
Often	75	3
Sometimes	50	2
Seldom	25	1
Never	00	0

The unadjusted purchase intent data indicated that both commercials significantly increased interest in buying the test product. If no adjustments had been made we would have concluded that both commercials were good enough to run, on the strength of the following data:

Commercial	Unadjusted Purchase Intent Differences between Test and Control Groups
"A"	+8 *
"B"	+5 *

* Significant at .05 level

However, the control group contained fewer users of the test product than did either of the test groups and, as a result, had a lower brand usage score. When covariance adjustments were made for this and other differences, the control group score went up and the score for test group " B " went down. The adjusted difference was an insignificant two index points. The adjusted difference of +5 index points between Commercial "A" and the Control, while smaller than the unadjusted difference, was still large enough to be significant. Thus, the adjustments resulted in a change in our conclusions. "A" was deemed good enough to run but " B " was not.

The correctness of these adjustments was partially confirmed by an FC&B validation study. These respondents were reinterviewed six weeks later to ascertain what products and brands they had purchased since the original interview. Commercial "A" produced a significant increase in reported purchasing of the test brand while Commercial " B " did not. More Commercial "A" respondents than control group respondents reported buying the test brand. (The difference was 12 percentage points.) The Commercial " B " difference over the control group, on the other hand, was an insignificant two percentage points.

Failure to match samples can also lead to picking the wrong winner. McNemar (1955) gives such an example. He reports a study in which the unadjusted means were:

Test Treatment	Unadjusted Score
1	7.30
2	5.60
3	4.40

From the above data it would appear that Treatment 1 was the clear winner. However, the group that received Treatment 1 also had a higher score on a covariate which bore a close relationship to the criterion (beta weight = .687). When the criterion scores were adjusted for the difference on the covariate, the adjusted means became:

Treatment	Adjusted Score
1	5.95
2	4.86
3	6.48

In other words, Treatment 3 was the better treatment, *not* Treatment 1. Treatment 1's score was spuriously inflated by the covariate, and its apparent superiority disappeared as soon as an adjustment was made for the difference on the covariate.

Covariate analysis can thus prevent a researcher from making erroneous judgments about findings from supposedly matched samples. It can also give him more confidence in the judgments that he does make.

Improving the Chances of Finding Significant Differences

The term "precision" is used in research to refer to the preciseness or accuracy with which one measures some variable (such as interest in buying the product, beliefs about the product, etc.). Since in advertising research we are dealing with data gathered from samples (rather than with data gathered from everyone in the population) some of the variation observed is due to sampling error. That is, the proportions saying that they are "willing to buy Product X" may not be exactly the same in any two samples of housewives. Thus, there is a certain amount of sampling "error" in any of our estimates of the effects of any of the advertising treatments being assessed.

As Green and Tull (1966) point out, covariance procedures can be used to reduce experimental error, and thereby increase the preciseness of one's measurements. In fact, in the eight FC&B research studies previously mentioned, covariance procedures have resulted in an error reduction of from five per cent to 63 per cent for the key measure (purchase intent), with the average reduction being 33 per cent.

The covariates responsible for this have for the most part been those related to a respondent's previous experience with and/or awareness of the test brand. Demographic characteristics have not played an important role to date in reducing error in FC&B research studies.

Obviously there are other ways of attempting to obtain the same end. One could (for example) reduce sampling error by:

1. Stratifying the sample beforehand on the key covariates into meaningful subgroups and randomly assigning members of each subgroup to the test and control conditions.
2. Increasing sampling size.

Table 2. Effect of Covariance Adjustments on Experimental Error

Study Number	Error Mean Square		Per Cent Reduced*	Covariance Efficiency†
	Unadjusted	Adjusted		
I	3.3100	2.0143	61%	164%
II	3.2116	2.3079	22	139
III	2.3024	1.9141	17	120
IV	1.4886	1.4072	5	106
V	3.7347	1.8189	51	205
VI	3.3723	1.7592	48	192
VII	3.7527	1.3729	63	273
VIII	2.7760	2.5251	9	110
Average			33%	164%

* Adjusted/Unadjusted.
† Unadjusted/Adjusted.

The first procedure complicates matters for an already overburdened interviewer and may not be feasible, especially if one wishes to match on several variables at the same time.

The second procedure is feasible but quite costly. Snedecor (1956) offers a method of estimating the difference in cost afforded by a change in experimental procedure. He computes an efficiency index by reversing the procedures used in Table 2 and dividing the unadjusted error mean square by the adjusted. In an example he uses, the unadjusted mean square = 0.0270 while the adjusted mean squares = 0.0214. The ratio between the two equaled 126 per cent.

Snedecor concludes that without covariance, 26 per cent more sampling units (pigs in his example) "would have been required to achieve the same precision."

Following the same logic, the efficiency index for covariance ranged from 106 per cent to 273 per cent, and averaged 164 per cent.

To accomplish a similar reduction in error by increasing sampling size would have required an average increase of 64 per cent or 90 additional interviews per group. Depending on the incidence of eligible respondents, FC&B pays, on the average, from $9 to $12 an interview for the field work on a copy research job. Since usually one control and at least one test group is included in every job, the extra cost for the typical job could range from $1728 to $2304. Covariance analysis seldom costs more than $200. The cost advantage of the procedure is, therefore, considerable.

Limitations

Covariance analysis may be used:

1. When one wants to make sure the different samples are matched on key covariates.
2. When one wishes to reduce error variance and thereby increase one's chances of finding significant differences.

However, the blind use of the procedure will not guarantee that either of the above goals will be reached.

It should be obvious that covariance analysis is usable only if the covariates can be measured. When the covariates cannot be measured, the only way to increase the precision of your study is to increase sample size.

It should be equally obvious that covariance analysis may lead to improper results if, as Green and Tull point out, the basic assumption of the procedures are not met. Covariance procedures assume that the relationship between the covariate and the criterion is the same for all samples in the study.

Although Atiqullah (1964) indicates that violating this assumption " does not seem to have serious effect " when large samples are used, it is our recommendation that problems of this sort be handled wherever possible by including the covariate as a secondary factor.

Covariance analysis also assumes that the relationships between the covariates and the dependent variable are linear. Thus, an inspection of the cross-tabs prior to doing the covariance analysis might indicate that some transformation of the data will increase the extent of the relationship and thereby increase the usefulness of the covariance analysis.

However, there are two less obvious circumstances in which covariance analysis should definitely not be used which were not discussed by Green and Tull. H. Fairchild Smith (1957) points out these two problem areas:

1. When the potential covariates are themselves affected by the experimental manipulation.
2. When the variation in the covariate is imposed along with the experimental manipulation.

With reference to the first problem area, in FC&B's copy research studies, brand usage or brand awareness data gathered before exposure to a test commercial are prime candidates for use as covariates. Experience has shown that they are related to the basic copy research criteria (purchase intent and beliefs about the product), and they cannot be affected by the experimental manipulation (showing or not showing a given commercial) since they are gathered before the manipulation takes place.

However, it would not be appropriate to use these as covariates in a study of the effect of an advertising campaign (measured at several points in time). The campaign may not only be affecting purchase intent, it may also be affecting brand usage and awareness.

Smith (1957) says that under these conditions, covariance analysis is not only meaningless but might be misleading.

He says:

When treatments induce simultaneous variation in all characters to estimate their effects on one while " holding another constant " is artificially fictitious. To my mind such estimates are anything but illuminating.

The commonly occurring phrase "corrected means," with its implication that more correct comparisons are thereby made, is misleading; "fictitious means" might be less deceptive. In absence of experimental control to demonstrate what in fact would happen if a given character were "held constant," one can seldom demonstrate that actually false conclusions are reached, but treatment means "adjusted" by error regressions seem to yield no information which cannot be gleaned from simpler statistics unconfused by distortions whose interpretation is dubious.

Smith also discusses the other instance in which covariance analysis is neither proper nor useful. This occurs if the covariate is imposed with the treatment. For example, in a study of advertising weights one might establish:

1. A "normal" weight spot schedule (i.e., where the schedule is one that would normally be purchased for this client).
2. A spot schedule that varies from the normal such as a "double" weight schedule.

The usual method for establishing a "double" weight schedule would be to try to buy twice as many "impressions" as purchased for the "normal" schedule. However, it probably will not be possible to do this on the same programs with the same adjacencies. An attempt would then be made to buy comparable programs and/or time periods but ultimately one may wind up buying the additional impressions wherever one can—even if it means buying in fringe time or on fringe stations that ordinarily would not be considered for the client's schedule.

Thus, the advertising weight study may involve not only a test of different potential impressions, but it may also involve a test of different types of schedules.

At first glance it would seem that analysis of covariance could be used—if desired—to "control" for the last unintended variation. Not so, says Smith:

If one wants to use an observed regression to allow for an ancillary environmental effect which cannot conveniently be randomized with treatments and may vary systematically from one treatment to another, the only safe procedure is to arrange for it to be deliberately varied....
The ideal arrangement, if an ancillary factor may seriously affect results, is to factorize it with treatments even if its levels may not be precisely controlled.

In spite of the problems discussed above, there are a sufficiently large number of cases where covariance analysis is both proper and useful. It is, therefore, recommended highly to researchers faced with the twin problems of matching samples and reducing experimental error.

References

Atiqullah, M. The Robustness of the Covariance Analysis of a One-Way Classification. *Biometrika*, Vol. 51, Nos. 3 and 4, 1964, pp. 365–372.

Cochran, William F. Analysis of Covariance: Its Nature and Use. *Biometrics*, Vol. 13, September 1957, pp. 261–281.

Green, Paul E. and Donald S. Tull. Covariance Analysis in Marketing Experimentation. *Journal of Advertising Research*, Vol. 6, No. 2, June 1966, pp. 45–53.

McNemar, Quinn. *Psychological Statistics.* 2nd Edition, New York: John Wiley, 1955.

Smith, H. Fairfield. Interpretation of Adjusted Treatment Means and Regressions in Analysis of Covariance. *Biometrics*, Vol. 13, September 1957, pp. 281–308.

Snedecor, George W. *Statistical Methods.* 5th Edition, Ames, Iowa: The Iowa State College Press, 1956.

Winer, B. J. *Statistical Principles in Experimental Design.* New York: McGraw-Hill, 1962.

The Analysis of
Interdependence

2

In the analysis of interdependence, there is no one variable or variable subset that is the focus of study—that differs in importance from the others. A variable or set of variables is not to be predicted from the others or explained by them. The goal, rather, is to give meaning to a set of variables or objects.

If many variables describe a set of objects, some may be redundant—really measuring the same construct. To determine which are redundant and what they are measuring, the analyst may employ principal components, described in this introduction and in the Aaker paper. A more general technique is that of factor analysis, which usually starts with principal components analysis, but then often modifies the conclusion to improve the interpretability of the resulting constructs. Principal components and factor analysis are two techniques of multidimensional scaling, the objective of which is to position objects such as brands or consumers in an interpretable, multidimensional space. Other techniques are introduced in Section B. A more direct approach to the question of what variables are similar or what objects form natural groupings or clusters is cluster analysis, described in Section C.

As an introduction to the analysis of interdependence, let us consider principal components analysis in the context of one particularly important application area—market structure analysis. An approach to determining market structure involves the identification of the perceptual dimensions of the market and how the brands are perceived by various market segments with respect to these dimensions. From this information, insights can be obtained into the nature of competition. When coupled with segment preference information, it can lead to product strategy development.

Let us assume that a market structure analysis of the economy automobile market is desired. The first concern should probably be with the boundaries of the product class. That is not so obvious as one might think. Should all foreign models be included? What about economy versions of medium priced cars? Where do you draw the line between a sports car and an economy car? The issue is which models are viewed as alternatives by the economy car buyer. It is often useful to do some preliminary research to determine accurately the appropriate product class boundaries. As Barnett notes, Stefflre has done some innovative research looking into this question.[1]

With the product class established, the next task is to determine some meaningful variables upon which to measure the perception of the product class user or potential user. Is styling relevant? What about gas mileage and trunk space? A brand manager's or researcher's intuition is a good place to start, but it is seldom as good as insights obtained from some sort of unstructured interviews. It is not uncommon to determine 60 or 80 candidates for inclusion. A problem of the analysis of interdependence is to reduce these variables to a smaller, more meaningful set.

Principal Components

A basic approach to this problem is geometrical in nature. It is described in some detail in the Aaker paper. The approach basically is one of axis rotation. Suppose economy automobile models were rated by groups of people along two dimensions, price and gas mileage, and the resulting measures then plotted, as in Figure 1. At this point, someone might ask of the analyst two related questions. First, are there really two dimensions operating, or are both variables really measuring the same thing? If a model perceived to be low priced by a certain respondent will be very likely to be also perceived as generating good gas mileage, then the two dimensions could be measuring the same underlying characteristic. If so, can a new dimension be formed that will represent this characteristic, which might be described as overall economy? Second, the number of original variables may often simply be too large to be manageable. A smaller, more workable set must be found. In our example, suppose only one number is desired to describe the product class. If such a constraint existed, what number should be selected? One of the two variables or a combination of the two?

Principal components provide an approach to these questions. It will generate a new dimension shown as v_1 in Figure 1, which retains as nearly as possible the interpoint distance information or variance that was contained in the original two dimensions. The new axis or principal component can be viewed as one of the old or original dimensions rotated 30 degrees. The coordinate with respect to the new dimension for a brand is its projection onto this dimension. For example, the Model 17 coordinate on dimension v_1 is shown as d in Figure 1. If we start with many dimensions instead of just two, we might have to introduce another principal component (perpendicular or orthogonal to the first one) to provide adequate representation. In Figure 1, such a component would be v_2. Although it becomes difficult to represent

---

[1] See also Volney Stefflre, "Market Structure Studies: New Products for Old Markets and New Markets (Foreign) for Old Products," in Frank M. Bass, Charles W. King, and Edgar A. Pessemier (eds.), *Applications of the Sciences in Marketing Management* (New York: John Wiley & Sons, Inc.), 1968.

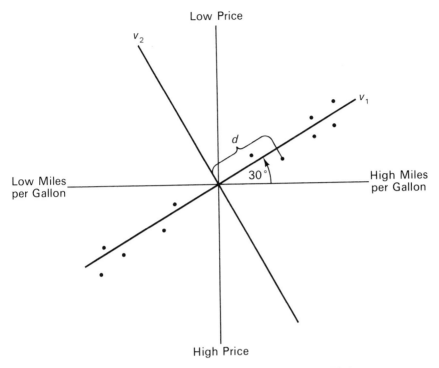

Figure 1.   Perceptual Map of the Economy Automobile Market

more than two dimensions graphically, there is no mathematical reason why more dimensions cannot be found. Each brand will have a set of coordinates for each of the resulting dimensions. Each new dimension becomes a combination of the original variables. The original variables having the greatest correlation with a new dimension are most closely related to it.

The original data have a certain amount of variance which is related to the sum of the squared interobject distances. The reduced space representation will sacrifice some of this variation, but as little as possible. For example, in Figure 1, the v_1 component might contain 90 percent of the variance in the original two-dimensional representation. This statistic, the percent of the variance explained by the components in the reduced space representation, is similar to the R^2 of regression analysis. It provides an indication of how " good " the lower space representation is. It also provides one mechanism for deciding how many dimensions should be included in the analysis. Basically, the analyst will attempt to retain a reasonable percent of the original variance. The marginal component or dimension which contributes a relatively small amount of variance will be examined critically to determine if it is worthwhile. Unless it represents an interpretable construct known to be important, it will be deleted from the analysis.

A. Factor Analysis

Factor analysis is primarily a tool to reduce a large number of variables to a few interpretable constructs. One approach to factor analysis is principal components. When principal components is used in this context, the components or dimensions are called factors. The coordinates of object or individual i with respect to factor k, F_{ik}, are called factor scores. For example, in Figure 1, dimension v_1 would be factor 1, and the score on factor 1 for object 17 is d. The original variables can be expressed in terms of the factors and an error term. If x_{ij} is the value of variable j for individual i, we can write:

$$x_{ij} = a_{j1}F_{i1} + a_{j2}F_{i2} + \cdots + a_{jm}F_{im} + e_{ij}$$

The a_{jk} terms are called factor loadings; each is a measure of the importance of factor k in measuring variable j. As long as the factors are orthogonal (perpendicular) and the original variables are reduced (the variable mean subtracted) and standardized (divided by the variable standard deviation), the factor loading, a_{jk}, represents the correlation between factor k and variable j. If such is not the case, a separate matrix of factor-variable correlations, termed the factor structure, is often calculated to help the analyst interpret the factors. To interpret a factor, the variables that are highly correlated (positively or negatively) with it are identified from the factor structure. These variables then hopefully offer clues as to what the factor represents. In Figure 1 the first factor would be highly correlated with the two original economy variables.

Factor analysis differs from principal components analysis in two respects. First, the variables are assumed to be analyzable into a small set of factors and an error term. This error term, e_{ij} in Equation (1), does not appear in principal components. Similar to the error term in regression analysis, it is expected to include all sources of residual variation not absorbed by the factors. A portion of e_{ij} associated with variable j is often identified as being a specific factor. The remaining factors are then termed common factors. Communalities provide a measure of how much variable variation is absorbed by the common factors. They represent that portion of the variable variation which contributes to the correlation with other variables or is "common" with other variables.

The second difference involves the process of rotating factors to new orthogonal, or even nonorthogonal, axes, if such a rotation will improve the interpretability of the resulting factors. The original principal components solution might have generated factors which were difficult to interpret in that they were only moderately correlated with many variables which did not logically fit together. Axis rotation will hopefully generate new dimensions and a new factor structure that will have more meaning. Suppose brands of beer were evaluated on the nine dimensions shown in Table 1. A factor analysis is performed, and three factors representing 0.65 (0.30 + 0.21 + 0.14) of the original variance are obtained. The first factor might be interpreted as "body." It has a high correlation with the strong-weak and heavy-light attributes and a very high correlation with the aftertaste attribute scale. However, the second and third factors are not easy to interpret. A solution is to rotate the factors or dimensions so that their relationship to the original attributes changes. There are several rotational schemes available, such as varimax and quartimax. Virtually all of them attempt to maximize the number of factor-variable correlations that are either high or low. Some also attempt to minimize the number of factors with which a variable is associated. As a result, a factor can be uniquely and strongly associated with a limited number of variables.

In Table 1 a hypothetical rotation has taken place. Notice that the total variance explained by the three factors (0.23 + 0.22 + 0.20 = 0.65) remains the same although the amount of variation associated with the individual factors does change. If these data were real, we might interpret Factors 2 and 3 as "price-quality" and "social" dimensions, respectively. These could be important factors which might easily have been ignored if a rotation had not been performed.

In principal components analysis, dimensions or components are found that recover the original interpoint distance as nearly as possible. In factor

Table 1.   A Hypothetical Example of Factor Rotation

| Attribute* | Factors | | | | | |
| | Before Rotation | | | After Rotation | | |
	1	2	3	1	2	3
Strong	0.9†	0.5	0.4	0.8	−0.2	−0.2
Heavy	0.8	0.6	0.3	0.8	0.0	−0.1
Aftertaste	0.9	0.7	−0.4	0.9	−0.2	0.3
Price	0.2	−0.5	0.2	−0.1	0.8	−0.2
Quality	−0.4	−0.4	0.4	−0.2	0.8	0.1
Popular	0.3	0.5	−0.5	−0.1	0.3	0.7
Fun	−0.5	0.3	−0.6	−0.3	−0.1	0.8
Friends	0.2	0.6	−0.3	0.2	−0.3	0.9
Sophisticated	−0.4	0.4	0.4	0.1	0.8	0.1
Variance explained	0.30	0.21	.14	0.23	0.22	0.20

* Assuming that each attribute is presented as a polar opposite: strong smelling–weak smelling, heavy–light, and so on.

† The correlation of Factor 1 with the first attribute.

analysis, the dimensions or factors are found that have maximum interpretability. Factor analysis involves a statistical model with an error term, whereas principal components is a well-defined geometric operation. Kendall explains the difference as follows:

> In component analysis, we begin with the observations and look for components in the hope that we may be able to reduce the dimensions of variation and also that our components may, in some cases, be given a physical meaning. We work from the data toward a hypothetical model. In factor analysis, we work the other way around; that is to say, we begin with a model and require to see whether it agrees with the data and, if so, to estimate its parameters.[1]

We have considered plotting objects. It is possible to reverse the process—to consider variables plotted with respect to objects. Thus, the variable price will have a coordinate value along the dimension of Brand A and another on the Brand B axis. When factor analysis is then applied, the effect is to obtain factors which are combinations of objects instead of variables. Factor analysis so applied is termed Q-analysis, in contrast to the more common R-analysis.

Wells and Sheth present a good overview of factor analysis emphasizing how to interpret the various terms introduced here and commenting on some of the difficulties. Factor analysis is somewhat unique in the field of multivariate analysis because it was developed in the early 1900s within psychology and still remains largely outside the realm of statisticians. Ekleblad and Stasch discuss factor analysis in the context of one of the classic psychological problems. They also provide in this context an introduction to rotation criteria. Massy suggests several factor analysis applications, including the use of factor scores as inputs to successive stages of analysis. If many variables were used as independent variables in a regression analysis, it would be difficult to separate the effects of any individual variable (the multicollinearity problem). If, however, the variables are first factor analyzed, and the variables are replaced by a smaller set of factor scores, the multicollinearity problem is reduced. The remaining two factor analysis papers present examples of factor analysis applied to semantic differential data. One provides the analysis on several groups of people, while the other shows the results of several different rotational schemes.

---

[1] M. G. Kendall, *A Course in Multivariate Analysis* (New York: Hafner Publishing Company), 1961.

19

William D. Wells and Jagdish N.
Sheth: Factor Analysis in Marketing
Research

When it works well, factor analysis helps the marketing analyst make sense of large bodies of intertwined data. When it works unusually well, it also points out some interesting relationships that might not be obvious from examination of the input data.

Factor analysis can be useful to the analyst in four ways. First, it can point out the latent factors or dimensions that determine the relationship among a set of observed or manifest values. For example, suppose we have no idea as to what people look for in choosing among types of liquors, and we simply ask a sample of respondents to rank order several types of liquors (Scotch, gin, rum, liqueurs, etc.) according to their relative preferences. By factor analyzing these preference data, the analyst may discover some salient characteristics of liquors that determine the relative preferences. These characteristics could be tangible attributes, such as degree of sweetness or sourness of types of liquors, or intangible attributes, such as their stereotype images.

The second way factor-analysis can be helpful is by pointing out relationships among observed values that were there all the time but not easy to see. For example, a factor analysis of cosmetic use suggested that hair spray is more closely associated with face cosmetics, such as eye shadow and lipstick, than with other products women use specifically for their hair. It also showed that hair spray, eye shadow, and lipstick belong in a group of purchases and activities that includes number of movies attended in the past month. This grouping suggested the presence in the population of a special type of consumer with a set of buying habits and activities that might be worth some follow-up research. It also suggested some immediate applications: a lipstick instead of a comb as a hair spray premium; movie themes, or movie related prizes, as sales promotions for face cosmetics. In the long run the unforseen general relationship is of more value than the specific immediate application, but on a good day one can have both.

Third, factor analysis is useful when things need to be grouped. Suppose, for example, that some television commercials have been rated on 50 or 60 rating scales, and the problem is to present these ratings to someone who does not have three weeks to study them. If the 50 or 60 scales are employed for consistency purposes, it is highly likely that several of them are heavily correlated with one another because they are all indicators of the same aspect of a commercial. To illustrate, there may be seven to eight scales dealing with the attractiveness of the commercial. Factor analysis summarizes information of these highly correlated scales in a very small number of basic ideas which may be easier to grasp.

Finally, and related to the third function, factor analysis can be used for empirical clustering of observations. In the previous example, our interest may be to cluster a large number of commercials based upon the ratings in the hope that some uncommon clustering may be discovered.

What Is Factor Analysis?

Factor analysis is a multivariate statistical technique that addresses itself to the study of interrelationships among a total set of observed variables. None of these variables is treated differently than others, unlike the case in multiple regression, in which one variable is explicitly considered the criterion (dependent) variable and all others the predictor (independent) variables. However, factor analysis, in a sense, does consider each of the observed variables as a dependent variable which is a function of some underlying, latent, and hypothetical factors. Conversely, one can look at each factor as the dependent variable which is a function of the observed variables.

The primary purpose of factor analysis is the resolution of a set of observed variables in terms of new categories called factors. Such factors then can prove to be useful for any of the four functions described earlier. Several methods are available for this resolution, and therefore derivation of factors, which do not necessarily give the same results. In this sense, factor analysis is indeed a *set of techniques* rather than a single unique method. These options will be described later in the paper.

Factor analysis has some basic concepts and terminology unique to itself. A *factor* is a linear combination of the observed variables.[1] In other words,

$$F = a_1 x_1 + a_2 x_2 + a_3 x_3 + \cdots + a_n x_n$$

In this respect, a factor resembles the predicted dependent variable ($\hat{y}$) in multiple regression. In fact, if the derivation of $a_j's$ ($j = 1 \cdots n$) is based on the same principle of least squares as in multiple regression, a factor is the predicted dependent variable and the $a_j's$ are regression coefficients. The only difference is that the total observed variables are grouped in such a manner

---

[1] Editor's note: As noted in the introduction and in the Ekeblad and Stasch article, the variables can also be viewed as being linear combinations of the factors. There is no contradiction here. The linear combinations (that is, the coefficients—the a's) will be different, of course. The type of relationship considered depends only on the interpretation problem being addressed.

that we obtain more than *one* factor. Thus we may have the following relationship:

$$F_1 = a_{11}x_1 + a_{21}x_2 + a_{31}x_3$$
$$F_2 = \qquad\qquad\qquad\quad a_{52}x_4 + a_{52}x_5$$
$$F_3 = \qquad\qquad\qquad\qquad\qquad\qquad a_{63}x_6 + a_{73}x_7$$

Here, a total of seven variables are grouped in three factors in which the first factor consists of the first three variables (x_1, x_2, x_3), the second factor, the next two variables (x_4, x_5), and the third factor, the last two variables (x_6, x_7). It should be remembered that each factor has, in fact, coefficients for all the variables in the analysis but that these may be zero or close to zero for all variables other than those grouped in that factor.

If this is the case, then just as every individual in a sample is assigned a predicted score ($\hat{y}_i$) in multiple regression, so in factor analysis each individual is assigned a *factor score*. Thus

$$F_i = a_1 x_{1i} + a_2 x_{2i} + a_3 x_{3i} + \cdots + a_n x_n$$

Once again, the difference is that each individual will be assigned as many factor scores as there are factors and not just one score. These scores are summarized in a "factor scores" matrix for the sample. When the factor score is correlated with the observed score on each variable, the resultant correlation is called a *factor loading*. If there are n variables and r factors, there will be a total of ($n \times r$) factor loadings. These are summarized in a matrix called the "factor loadings" matrix. It is a matrix of correlations among observed variables and factors.

In addition to these three basic concepts, there are some others that can be described by the example shown in Table 1. First, if we square the loadings of each factor and sum it, we get a "sum of squares" which is technically called the *eigenvalue* of that factor. Each eigenvalue summarizes a fraction of total variance in the six variables. When the variables are standardized

Table 1. A Factor Loadings Matrix

Variable	Factors		h^2 (Communality)
	A	*B*	
1	.71	.40	.66
2	.70	.46	.70
3	.70	.37	.63
4	.69	−.41	.64
5	.65	−.43	.61
6	.71	−.39	.66
Sum of squares (eigenvalue)	2.89	1.01	3.90
Variance summarized (eigenvalue/no. of variables)	.48	.17	.65

(which is most common in factor analysis because what is usually factored is a matrix of correlations among observed variables), each variable's variance is equal to 1 (unity). The total variance in our example then is equal to 6 or the number of variables. This means that the first factor summarizes 48 percent of total variance (2.89/6) and the second factor summarizes 17 percent of total variance (1.01/6). Together, the two factors summarize 65 percent of total variance. Mathematically, this is identical to R^2 in multiple regression.

Second, the variance of each variable summarized by the two factors is called its communality (h^2). It is that percentage of total variance (unity in the example) which is summarized in *common factors*. Common factors are those which are shared by at least two variables. All other factors are called *unique factors*.[2] The total variance of a variable then can be considered to be divided into two types of factors: common and unique.

Third, as mentioned before, each factor loading represents a correlation between a variable and a factor. We can therefore obtain the observed correlation between two variables by multiplying their factor loadings on each factor and summing them. For example, the correlation between variable 1 and 2 is computed to be .68 [(.71 × .70) + (.40 × .46)]. This computed value is not likely to be identical with the observed correlation in our example because the two factors do not summarize total variance but only a large percentage of it. Similar computations then can reproduce the original correlation matrix among a set of observed variables.

Decisions, Decisions

The name factor analysis is applied to a variety of procedures. While the mathematical analysis is pretty much the same, the procedures provide a large number of options to the analyst to suit the method with the assumptions of his data. Unfortunately, the results from these options vary considerably, so that it is easy to get confused. The trick is to pick the procedure that best does the job at hand. Among the options on which the analyst must decide are these.

What to Correlate with What?

Factor analysis is concerned with relations among observations, and hence it commonly starts with a matrix of correlations as its input. In marketing research, most data are collected along three dimensions: on people or entities, with respect to some characteristics of attributes, and repeated measures of these over time. In other words, marketing data typically consist of a *data cube*. Then, the analyst can make six types of correlations by holding

---

[2] Editor's note: Also called specific factors.

one side of the cube constant and using the other side as replications (Cattell, 1952). For example, on a sample of 1,000 housewives, we have measures for 12 monthly periods, the expenditures on about 20 items including foods, drugs, services, etc. Then holding time constant, we can obtain a matrix that summarizes correlations among items by treating the sample as replicate observations. Or we can correlate 1,000 housewives by treating the 20 items as replicate observations. The first type of input matrix (correlations among variables) results in R-type factor analysis, which is most common. The second type (correlations among entities) results in Q-type factor analysis, which is known, but not used extensively in marketing research because of large samples. The other four types are called O-type (correlations of time periods for one entity or person), P-type (correlations among variables for one entity), S-type (correlations among entities on a single variable), and T-type (correlations among occasions on a single variable) analyses.

The analyst must decide, based on his research objectives, which correlation matrix he wishes to factor analyze.

Correlation, Covariance, or Cross-Products Matrix?

Although it is most common to factor analyze a matrix of correlations, it is not mandatory. The reader may remember that a correlation coefficient is derived from standard scores in which the averages of all variables are set equal to zero and the variances equal to one. This means that we lose two of the three types of information contained in a data matrix, namely the levels and dispersions of variables.

In some cases, however, it may be desirable to retain one or both of these types of information in analyzing data. In such cases, a covariance matrix (only means set equal to zero, but variance not standardized) or a cross-products (unstandardized data matrix) may be appropriate as input to factor analysis. Generally, if the units of measurement are quite disparate among observed variables (as for example between income and education), it is advisable to standardize the data and hence use a matrix of correlations. By the same token if the units of measurement are identical or very similar across variables and if individual differences are expected, it is better to factor analyze a matrix of covariances or cross-products. Another, and more common reason for using correlations matrix as input to factor analysis, is the ease with which factor loadings can be interpreted or evaluated in terms of correlations between variables and factors ranging in value from −1 to +1 only.

What Goes in the Diagonal of Correlation Matrix?

If the researcher chooses the option of having a matrix of correlations as the input to factor analysis, one more option on which he must decide is: What value should he put in the diagonal of the matrix which represents the correlation of a variable with itself. This may come as a surprise to some readers because, by statistical definition, correlation value in the diagonal has to be one. However, there are two reasons why a value other than one may be desired. First, if the measure were repeated, it is unlikely to get a perfect correlation on the same variable due to errors of measurement. Hence for the sake of reliability, the diagonal value may be chosen that is less than one. Second, and more importantly, it may be based on the reasoning that all the variance of a variable may not be summarized by common factors; a fraction of it may be unique. Placing ones in the diagonal presumes that variance is partitioned only among the common factors obtained by doing principal components analysis. It is this concern which has led to the use of other values than one in the diagonal. The reader is asked to read Harman (1967) for a variety of such other values, technically referred to as the communality problem.

Current practice in marketing research seems to be the tendency toward inserting ones in the diagonal presumably because systematic theories are lacking and because most research is empirical.

Rotation

Another substantive option is the derivation of "new" factors from the initial results by the methods of rotation. As a very rough analogy, rotation is something like staining a microscope slide. Just as different stains reveal different structures in the tissue, different rotations reveal different structures in the data, even though in both cases all the structures were always actually there. Similar to the stains, there are a set of guidelines called the principles of simple structure in factor analysis. These principles are now quantified into a series of analytical rotational options. The most widely known and used in marketing research is the varimax rotation, in which the principle used is that of simplifying the factors rather than variables. Different rotations give entirely different results. From a statistical point of view, all results are equal, none superior or inferior to others; but from the point of view of making sense of results of factor analysis, rotation is extremely important.

The results of the first factor analysis on the six variables were rotated, and both unrotated and rotated factor loadings are presented in Table 2. It will be noted that while unrotated factor analysis was unclear and ambiguous in terms of interpretation, it now is quite meaningful in terms of rotated factors. Factor A is the underlying common dimension for variables 4, 5, and 6; factor B is the underlying dimension for variables 1, 2, and 3. Suppose that the six variables were rating scales evaluating a brand of freeze-dried coffee. The first three variables may be various aspects of convenience, for example, ease of preparation, ease of cleaning, and less time consumption. Similarly, the last three variables may be various aspects of taste, for example, flavor, aroma, and taste. Then, the rotated factor analysis seems plausible and

Table 2. Factors

	Variable	Unrotated			Rotated		
		A	*B*	h^2	*A*	*B*	h^2
	1	.71	.40	.66	.23	.78	.66
	2	.70	.46	.70	.18	.82	.70
	3	.70	.37	.63	.25	.75	.63
	4	.69	−.41	.64	.78	.18	.64
	5	.65	−.43	.61	.77	.14	.61
	6	.71	−.39	.66	.78	.21	.66
Sum of squares (eigenvalue)		2.89	1.01	3.90	1.98	1.92	3.90
Variance summarized		.48	.17	.65	.33	.32	.65

meaningful in terms of the structure and grouping of variables. It is now even tempting for us to label the factors as convenience and taste, which without prior theory or some external validating evidence may not be correct.

More importantly, notice that the total variance summarized by the two factors remains invariant in rotations; however, the amount summarized by each factor usually changes. Also, the communality of each variable remains invariant, but its distribution among the two factors changed substantially. In short, what happens in rotations is internal shifting of variables and their correlations among factors, but with the outer boundaries remaining the same.

When to Stop Factoring

When a large unorganized set of variables is factored, as is often the case in marketing research, the analysis will extract the largest and most interesting combinations of variables first and then proceed to smaller combinations. For example, in an analysis of grocery product use, the first factor extracted was a group of food and laundry products consumed in quantity by large, middle income families. The next factor consisted of products used for wrapping and preserving food. The next was a group of foods used heavily by relatively low income families, and the next was a group of products that are supposed to germproof and deodorize the home. All of these product groups were interesting and meaningful, but as the analysis proceeded the groups became smaller and smaller and less and less understandable, until finally the "groups" consisted of only one product each.

Carrying an analysis too far has two penalties. It is exceedingly wasteful of computer time, and it obscures the meaning of the findings because it affects the rotation adversely. When many factors are involved in varimax rotation, the tendency is to produce rotated factors that have loadings very high on a very few variables. This tends to produce fragments. On the other hand, if very few factors are involved, the tendency is to have loadings on quite a few variables, so that no meaningful interpretation is possible. To return to the microscope analogy, adjusting to stop factoring is something like focusing. Too high or too low an adjustment will obscure a structure that is obvious when the adjustment is just right.

Four stopping criteria may be employed. When the analyst already knows enough about his data so that he knows how many factors are actually there, he can have the analysis stopped after that number of factors has been extracted. In marketing research this situation is rare. Secondly, if he has a clear idea in advance about the amount of variance the factors can explain (also a rare privilege in marketing research), he can stop when that criterion is reached. Most commonly, however, if he does not know very much about his data to begin with, he will want to keep factoring until factors get small and meaningless.

The other two criteria are statistical rules of thumb. The third one is an incremental approach. After a first set of factors has explained a large percentage of variance, say 75 percent, if the next factor adds only a small percentage of total variance, say less than five percent, it may be discarded and we could stop factoring. The final criterion is most objective. It states that all factors whose eigenvalues are greater than one when a correlation matrix is factored can be considered as significant and meaningful factors.

The reader who has come this far will know why critics of factor analysis have insisted that it is an art rather than a properly objective scientific method. What to correlate, the type of data input, the entries in the diagonal, the type of rotation used, and the stopping criterion are all decisions the analyst must make. The decisions create numerous combinations, and are not easy or automatic. Along with the data they determine the results.

An Example

Factor analysis is useful when there is a large number of variables and the correlations among these are distributed from very high to very low levels. Take, for example, the matrix of correlation shown in Table 3. It consists of correlations in reported reading of 30 magazines by a large sample of adult males. The fact that variable 1, *Business Week*, correlates .19 with *Life* and .31 with *New Yorker* says that *Business Week* and *New Yorker* have more in common than do *Business Week* and *Life*, at least in this sample. Note that the correlations are not much distinct from one another and, therefore, eyeballing the matrix does not show any obvious simple groups. When the relationships are as complex and as many as these (and this is a comparatively simple and small matrix), factor analysis will help sort them out.

This matrix of correlations was factor analyzed by the principal components method in which ones were placed in the diagonal.

Table 3. Correlation Matrix*

Variable Description	Var. No.	1	2	3	4	5	6	7	8	9	10	11	12	13	14	15
Bus. Week	1															
Life	2	19														
New Yorker	3	31	14													
Time	4	30	31	23												
Newsweek	5	33	27	26	25											
U.S. News and World Report	6	23	10	16	15	29										
Sat. Review	7	12	10	36	12	18	15									
Look	8	09	38	08	18	23	18	15								
Sat. Ev. Post	9	07	35	09	16	15	11	13	39							
Forbes	10	24	06	20	25	09	16	14	04	05						
Argosy	11	04	21	00	08	18	05	10	16	16	-00					
Atl. Mthly.	12	09	08	17	13	15	13	-00	13	12	14	02				
Car and Driver	13	04	07	00	02	02	04	22	06	-01	-01	27	04			
Fld. and Stream	14	08	11	01	09	12	10	-01	16	15	03	16	12	05		
Farm Jrnl.	15	-05	-04	-08	-05	-01	15	-01	01	-01	-02	-00	14	-04	02	
Fortune	16	29	12	33	34	14	07	02	06	08	25	-01	02	02	09	-05
Harper's	17	08	08	27	07	13	02	12	10	08	09	-01	-02	06	01	-04
Mech. Illus.	18	07	16	01	06	10	04	19	14	11	08	18	04	27	-01	-08
Pop. Mech.	19	09	09	02	07	12	03	-00	14	09	05	17	-03	20	22	-05
Pop. Science	20	11	13	04	05	11	02	09	13	11	03	12	15	19	26	-01
Outdoor Life	21	-06	06	01	02	06	03	08	11	10	02	22	01	04	59	10
Prog. Farmer	22	11	-03	-07	-06	-07	09	01	-06	01	-03	00	-02	-05	06	02
Reader's Dgst.	23	03	16	03	08	20	-04	06	16	20	11	13	02	-11	03	00
Road and Track	24	19	10	03	01	02	05	04	04	04	-01	13	-02	55	13	-01
Sci. Amer.	25	-06	06	19	10	11	05	25	05	03	08	04	03	03	04	-02
Succ. Farming	26	02	-06	-07	-08	01	03	01	01	-01	-03	05	01	-06	08	58
Sports Afield	27	04	11	02	05	10	02	-00	13	12	-01	18	12	06	56	09
True	28	-01	16	02	12	11	-03	-00	19	18	-03	41	-02	06	08	00
Hot Rod	29	04	01	-01	-04	01	-03	-01	07	02	-03	16	00	35	09	-04
Motor Trend	30	04	05	02	03	05	-02	03	10	03	-04	20	05	45	11	-01

* The decimal points in the correlation coefficients have been suppressed.

Table 3 (cont.).

Variable Description	Var. No.	16	17	18	19	20	21	22	23	24	25	26	27	28	29	30
Bus. Week	1	29	08	07	09	11	03	-06	11	03	19	-06	02	04	-01	04
Life	2	12	08	16	09	13	06	-03	16	10	06	-06	11	16	-01	05
New Yorker	3	33	27	01	02	04	01	-07	03	03	19	-07	02	02	-01	02
Time	4	34	07	07	07	06	02	-06	18	01	10	-08	05	12	-04	03
Newsweek	5	14	13	10	12	11	06	-06	20	02	11	01	10	11	-01	05
U.S. News and World Report	6	15	07	02	04	03	02	03	19	-04	05	05	03	02	-03	-02
Sat. Review	7	12	19	-00	09	08	01	06	03	04	25	01	-00	-00	-01	03
Look	8	06	10	14	14	13	11	-06	16	04	05	-01	13	19	07	10
Sat. Ev. Post	9	08	08	11	09	11	10	01	20	04	03	-03	12	18	02	03
Forbes	10	25	09	08	05	03	02	-03	11	-01	08	05	-01	01	-03	-04
Argosy	11	04	-01	18	17	12	22	00	13	13	04	-02	18	41	16	20
Atl. Mthly.	12	15	38	01	02	-02	04	-02	03	01	12	-06	02	01	00	05
Car and Driver	13	02	06	27	20	19	04	-05	-11	55	-03	-06	06	06	35	47
Fld. and Stream	14	01	-01	22	26	12	59	06	03	13	04	08	56	28	09	11
Farm Jrnl.	15	-05	-04	-01	01	-03	06	34	07	-05	13	58	09	00	-04	-01
Fortune	16		24	06	04	03	01	-00	05	04	11	-06	00	07	00	01
Harper's	17	24		-02	-05	-04	-03	01	04	07	11	-04	00	02	00	03
Mech. Illus.	18	06	-02		56	46	20	00	07	24	09	-02	20	18	25	31
Pop. Mech.	19	04	-05	56		58	23	01	06	19	07	-01	21	17	22	28
Pop. Science	20	03	-04	46	58		13	-02	10	16	09	-04	13	15	17	24
Outdoor Life	21	01	-03	20	23	13		08	03	11	04	07	47	26	05	13
Prog. Farmer	22	-00	01	00	01	-02	08		02	-03	-02	13	06	-04	-01	-01
Reader's Dgst.	23	05	04	07	06	10	03	02		-10	03	08	04	14	-08	-04
Road and Track	24	04	07	24	19	16	11	-03	-10		13	-05	12	12	36	49
Sci. Amer.	25	11	11	09	07	09	04	-02	03	13		-02	05	06	05	09
Succ. Farming	26	-06	-04	-02	-01	-04	07	13	08	-05	-02		15	02	-03	01
Sports Afield	27	00	00	20	21	13	47	06	04	12	05	15		23	08	14
True	28	07	02	18	17	15	26	-04	14	12	06	02	23		10	13
Hot Rod	29	00	00	25	22	17	05	-01	-08	36	05	-03	08	10		54
Motor Trend	30	01	03	31	28	24	13	-01	-04	49	09	01	14	13	54	

Table 4. Principal Components Factor Loadings*

Variable Description	Var. No.	1	2	3	4	5	6	7	8	9	10	Communality
Bus. Week	1	35	43	−12	04	06	−28	−33	17	15	00	56
Life	2	45	26	07	−27	16	33	−03	−05	21	−28	61
New Yorker	3	30	51	−21	19	−19	−13	04	17	00	−11	52
Time	4	37	45	−04	−12	05	−08	−32	−20	05	−21	55
Newsweek	5	43	38	05	−03	12	05	−10	33	11	32	58
U.S. News and World Report	6	24	37	11	15	23	00	−12	14	18	47	57
Sat. Review	7	25	36	−10	32	−03	04	41	32	−01	−20	61
Look	8	45	18	15	−20	16	41	18	−05	22	−02	58
Sat. Ev. Post	9	39	20	20	−23	12	38	23	−16	14	−21	58
Forbes	10	20	36	−07	08	01	−31	−22	−37	−05	04	47
Argosy	11	45	−13	19	−18	−07	23	−19	10	−49	05	64
Atl. Mthly.	12	21	35	−10	23	−24	18	35	−25	−14	36	65
Car and Driver	13	37	−38	−46	17	04	19	−21	−05	17	01	63
Fld. and Stream	14	50	−21	46	−02	−43	−14	−04	00	18	04	75
Farm Jrnl.	15	−02	−09	49	63	32	09	−11	−06	−01	−08	77
Fortune	16	29	44	−17	14	−12	−19	−25	−32	−15	−16	58
Harper's	17	17	35	−21	29	−32	22	28	−27	−13	19	63
Mech. Illus.	18	57	−31	−09	−06	24	−29	18	−16	−04	02	63
Pop. Mech.	19	57	−30	−03	−04	26	−40	31	−08	−04	06	75
Pop. Science	20	50	−23	−10	−10	36	−36	33	−01	−05	−01	69
Outdoor Life	21	43	−24	43	−00	−44	−19	01	01	13	01	67
Prog. Farmer	22	−03	−08	30	44	13	00	07	−24	04	−30	46
Reader's Dgst.	23	21	25	29	−16	40	02	−09	02	−23	13	45
Road and Track	24	42	−37	−41	19	−09	21	−18	02	11	−10	63
Sci. Amer.	25	26	18	−16	22	−10	−12	11	45	−22	−35	58
Succ. Farming	26	−01	−11	48	54	25	12	−13	06	−10	04	63
Sports Afield	27	44	−23	43	05	−39	−10	−01	05	22	03	64
True	28	45	−11	24	−22	−13	15	−12	03	−52	−05	65
Hot Rod	29	36	−41	36	15	04	18	−12	00	−05	09	51
Motor Trend	30	48	−42	−37	21	04	16	−13	03	−01	06	65
Eigenvalues		413	292	225	169	150	144	125	106	101	100	1823

* Decimal points suppressed.

The first output of factor analysis appears in Table 4.

The columns represent the factors. The items being analyzed are listed down the side. The entries in the columns are factor loadings which represent the correlation between each item and the factor. The first ten factors have eigenvalues (sum of squares) greater than one, and together they explain about 61 percent of total variance in the 30 variables. Also, for a given variable the ten factors summarize between 45 and 77 percent variance. This is an unrotated matrix and, as usual, its meaning is not especially clear.

The matrix [shown in Table 5] is the product of a varimax rotation. The rotation has clarified the factors, and they can now be interpreted as follows.

Factor 1 has high loadings on *Car and Driver*, *Road and Track*, *Motor Trend*, and *Hot Rod*. This means that respondents who say they read *Car and Driver* also tend to say they read the other magazines that load high on Factor 1. In other words, these four magazines form a group based on some degree of common audience.

Factor 2 has relatively high loadings on *Fortune*, *Forbes*, *Time*, and *Business Week*. Again, the interpretation is that magazines in this group have more audience overlap with each other than with magazines that load high on other factors. The inference is that they, like the first group, represent some common core of interests.

Table 5. Factor Analysis of Magazine Readership

Variable Description	Var. No.	1	2	3	4	5	6	7	8	9	10
Bus. Week	1	05	51	06	−10	02	03	−15	26	−06	43
Life	2	07	20	04	−06	73	01	−09	08	09	10
New Yorker	3	00	37	04	−11	05	−05	21	53	−07	19
Time	4	−00	65	02	−06	31	−01	−07	07	08	12
Newsweek	5	03	10	09	−09	20	04	05	20	11	68
U.S. News and World Report	6	−03	12	00	12	07	03	14	−02	−06	72
Sat. Review	7	−04	−03	−03	09	17	09	26	69	−11	10
Look	8	06	−05	09	−01	71	09	13	00	08	20
Sat. Ev. Post	9	−05	03	07	03	74	08	11	03	10	−01
Forbes	10	−07	64	−00	02	−06	12	15	−07	−03	09
Argosy	11	17	00	17	−01	12	04	01	01	75	07
Atl. Mthly.	12	−02	08	02	−02	07	02	78	07	03	13
Car and Driver	13	78	04	01	−04	04	10	−02	−04	−06	01
Fld. and Stream	14	05	04	84	04	09	10	−00	−02	14	04
Farm Jrnl.	15	−01	−03	05	87	−02	−02	−04	−02	−00	09
Fortune	16	03	72	−02	−00	01	−01	19	14	07	−03
Harper's	17	08	15	−01	−03	07	−09	75	15	−02	−01
Mech. Illus.	18	26	10	15	−01	09	72	−01	−03	09	−01
Pop. Mech.	19	16	03	19	00	03	82	00	04	05	05
Pop. Science	20	12	00	03	−04	09	81	−07	10	04	05
Outdoor Life	21	02	01	80	04	01	13	01	01	13	−02
Prog. Farmer	22	−04	07	07	61	07	05	02	03	−13	−25
Reader's Dgst.	23	−24	12	−14	15	21	18	−07	−08	36	34
Road and Track	24	77	03	10	−03	06	04	−01	10	01	−07
Sci. Amer.	25	07	08	01	−00	−05	06	−04	74	14	−01
Succ. Farming	26	−01	−11	07	75	−08	−06	−03	−01	12	17
Sports Afield	27	08	−03	78	10	08	08	−00	01	07	06
True	28	06	05	23	−03	13	10	02	04	75	−06
Hot Rod	29	68	−07	−01	−01	−04	16	05	−03	13	01
Motor Trend	30	77	−03	05	03	01	20	04	03	12	04

Factor 3 has high loadings on *Field and Stream, Outdoor Life*, and *Sports Afield*. Factor 4 has high loadings on *Farm Journal, Successful Farming*, and *Progressive Farmer*. Thus, one can proceed through the whole matrix, factor by factor, looking for high loadings to determine what the various factors "mean."

The Meaning of "Loading"

Note that all the magazines have a loading of some size on every factor, and that for any one factor the loadings of a few magazines are large while the loadings of the other magazines are small. This result is exactly what a varimax rotation is intended to achieve. Other rotation systems, designed to achieve other outcomes, would have produced a different configuration from the same unrotated matrix. The loadings portray the degree to which the individual items (magazines in this case) represent the factor as a whole. Thus, *Fortune* and *Forbes* serve better than *Business Week* as representatives of whatever Factor 2 is. If the high loaded items on a factor are thought of as a group, the highest loaded items are the best instances of whatever it is that holds the group together. In the present example, the cement that glues the groups is presumably editorial content that makes magazines within groups appealing to somewhat the same group of readers.

Note that *Reader's Digest* does not have a high loading on any of the factors. Instead its positive loadings are divided among the news group (Factor 10) best typified by *U.S. News* and *Newsweek*, a "general reading" group (Factor 5, *Life, Look, Saturday Evening Post*), a men's fiction group (Factor 9, *Argosy* and *True*), and Factor 4, a group of farm magazines. This result implies that *Reader's Digest* has an appeal that spreads broadly through readers of at least four magazine types. *Reader's Digest* also has small negative loadings on the sports car factor (Factor 1) and the hunting and fishing factor (Factor 3). This finding shows that *Reader's Digest*'s broad appeal is not unlimited—that in fact men who are heavy readers of the two magazine types represented by *Motor Trend* and *Field and Stream* tend *not* to read *Reader's Digest*.

Communality

The column to the far right of the matrix (Table 4), after Factor 10, shows the degree to which the factors account for or "explain" each of the variables. Thus the factors extracted in this analysis account for the reported readership of *Life* somewhat better than they account for the reported readership of *Business Week*, and they account for *Outdoor Life* better than they account for *Progressive Farmer* or *Reader's Digest*. The size of the communality is a useful index to how much of the variable is in a sense "left over" after what it has in common with other variables has been taken out. The comparatively low communality of *Reader's Digest*, for example, shows that it has relatively little in common with the other magazines included in this analysis, while the relatively high loadings of *Field and Stream* and *Farm Journal* show that they have much in common with the magazine groups, *taken as groups*, that the factors represent.

Factor Scores

Most factor analysis computer programs compute factor scores for each respondent on each factor. The factor score represents the degree to which each *respondent* gets high scores on the *group* of items that load high on each factor. In the present illustration, each respondent's factor score on Factor 1 would reflect the degree to which he reports himself to be a heavy reader of *Car and Driver, Road and Track, Motor Trend*, and *Hot Rod* taken together. His score on this factor would also be influenced by his reported readership of all the other magazines, but since the highest loaded items have by far the most influence on the factor score, the remaining low-loaded items would not count much toward his score on Factor 1. His score on Factor 2 would portray mainly his readership of *Fortune, Forbes*, and *Time*, and so on. As described earlier, there would be one score on each factor for each person.

Factor scores have a variety of uses. Because they can be cross-tabulated with other variables, they can help explain what the factors mean. In one study, for example, the underlying difference between two groups of cosmetics became obvious when it was found that one group was used primarily by younger women, while the other group was used by women past their prime. In another study the distinction between two groups of grocery items was clarified when it was found that one group was heavily used by middle income families, while the other group was heavily used by low income families. These relationships were obvious once the factor scores had pointed them out, but without the factor scores as a guide through the tangle of correlations between products and demographic variables, it was hard to know where to look.

Since factor scores are shorthand summaries of items, they can facilitate comparisons among groups as groups. For example, the availability of factor scores makes it possible to say what types of TV programs are viewed by readers of what types of magazines, or what types of recreational interests go with what types of taste in clothes.

Finally, factor scores can be treated as if they were raw scores to perform any of a number of multivariate analyses. These include multiple regression, multiple discriminant analysis, and clustering. One advantage is that factor scores tend to be more stable measures than the raw scores.

Comments on Q Analysis

The analysis just described, the reader will note, is R-type factor analysis, by far the most common. In R analysis high correlations occur when respondents who score high on variable 1 also score high on variable 2, and respondents who score low on variable 1 also score low on variable 2. Factors emerge when there are (relatively) high correlations within groups of variables.

In Q analysis, the correlations are computed between pairs of respondents instead of pairs of variables. High correlations occur when respondent 1's pattern of responses *on all the variables* is much like respondent 2's pattern of responses. Factors emerge when there are relatively high correlations within groups of *people*.

Q analysis is useful when the object is to sort people into groups based on their *simultaneous* responses on a number of variables. It is therefore being increasingly employed in studies aimed at market segmentation.

Two difficulties with Q analysis have limited its use to date. Currently available Q-analysis computer programs do not handle even moderately large samples of respondents easily, and reliability tests have suggested that Q factors are disappointingly unstable from sample to sample. It seems reasonable to expect that these problems will be overcome or at least better understood, and that Q analysis or one of its mathematical relatives will become a standard and important market research technique. For more on Q analysis see (Stephenson).

Difficulties, Problems, and Cautions

Cost

A factor analysis of even moderate size requires a great amount of number crunching. Before the advent of computers, factor analytic studies employing 50 or more variables were almost never attempted, and even much smaller studies required so many hours of labor on a hand calculator that they were seldom replicated, checked for reliability, or even examined for arithmetic errors. Perhaps it was the heroic amount of effort required that led some of the early analysts to believe that their work had revealed the Truth.

Although computerized factor analysis is now much faster and much easier, it is still not costless. The cost increases roughly linearly with the number of respondents, and it increases much faster than linearly with the number of variables. Large analyses therefore are likely to be expensive, and adding variables to an already large analysis is apt to increase the cost far faster than it increases value.

Reliability

Like any other statistical procedure, a factor analysis starts with a set of imperfect data. When the data change because of changes in the sample, changes in data gathering procedures, or any of the numerous kinds of measurement errors, the results of the analysis will change too. The results of any single analysis are therefore *always* less than perfectly dependable.

This problem is especially pernicious because the results of a single factor analysis usually look plausible. In fact they sometimes look so plausible that the analyst is too readily tempted to say to himself, " What's interesting about this? I knew it all the time."

But plausibility is no guarantee of validity or even stability. A factor analysis of data generated *entirely by chance* will seem to make some sense when stared at long enough and hopefully enough. A factor solution computed from one randomly selected half of the respondents may seem to be an obvious representation of reality until it is placed beside a somewhat different but equally plausible solution computed from the remaining respondents. The moral is: do the analysis at least twice. As a minimum, divide the respondents into two groups at random and check one group against the other. When different samples produce similar results, confidence increases.

The sampling problem extends to the set of variables used in the analysis. It should be obvious that a dimension cannot emerge from a factor analysis unless at least two variables are in the analysis to represent it. It is perhaps less obvious that putting variables in and taking them out will influence the patterns formed by other variables. If some variables are added that have a strong relationship with some variables that would otherwise have formed a group, the group may break into two parts, one containing the new and some of the " old " variables, the other containing only the old.

Judgment

It has been said that sending data out to be factor analyzed is much like sending suits to the cleaners—you don't have to know anything about what was done to the suits or the data as long as they come back clean and free from wrinkles. It should be clear by now that the problem is not that simple. The user of factor analysis makes decisions that determine how the analysis will come out, or else the decisions are made for him. Even with a given set of decisions, different findings will come from different groups of respondents, different ways of obtaining data, and different mixes of variables.

All this is highly disconcerting to anyone who needs to believe that the results of any one factor analysis will be Revealed Universal Truth Forever Enduring, and it has sometimes led to disappointment and even indignant rejection of the method.

If on the other hand factor analysis is regarded as one of several fairly complicated tools that may help untangle badly tangled data, the user is much less liable to feel cheated when he tries to line up the results of a factor analysis against the real world.

References

Cattell, R. B. "The Three Basic Factor Analytic Research Designs—Their Inter-relationships and Derivatives," *Psychological Bulletin*, 49 (1952), 449–520.

Harman, Harry H. *Modern Factor Analysis*, 2nd ed., rev. Chicago: University of Chicago Press, 1967.

Stephenson, William. *The Study of Behavior*. Chicago: University of Chicago Press, 1953.

20

Frederick A. Ekeblad and Stanley F.
Stasch: Criteria in Factor Analysis

Increasing attention has recently been given to application of factor analysis to marketing problems. A review of the literature reveals the existence of two needs.

1. If marketing and advertising researchers are to read, understand, and evaluate research which utilizes factor analysis, they should be able to turn to a clear description of the basic factor analysis model, including its inputs, what is to be determined or calculated, how this determination is made, and what remains undetermined.

Ramond (1963) and Collins (1961) have both made a contribution in this direction. This paper expands their contribution by incorporating and reviewing why psychologists developed factor analysis. This approach is quite different from that of Ramond and Collins and, we believe, facilitates a clearer presentation.

2. If reports of research utilizing factor analysis are to be properly evaluated, a reader of such reports should understand the function of criteria in optimization problem solving in general, the paramount importance of optimizing criteria in factor analysis, and the appropriateness of various factor analysis criteria for various problem types.

Only Collins (1961) makes mention of the existence of more than one type of factor analysis criterion, and his discussion is brief. On the other hand, most reports of research utilizing factor analysis do not specify the criterion used in the analysis. It is frequently not clear what criterion is appropriate for the problem at hand.

The Basic Factor Analysis Model

It is most convenient to study the technique of factor analysis by first referring to the way it has been used in psychological research.

Assume that k individuals are exposed to n tests to determine if the tests have any common factors or elements. For example, 30 students might be given a statistics test, a marketing test, a finance test, a production test, and an accounting test. Presumably each test will have some element of "verbal

Abridged from the *Journal of Advertising Research*. © Copyrighted 1967 by the Advertising Research Foundation.

ability" because all the tests have questions that required knowledge of language. Each test will also have some element of "mathematical ability" because all the tests require the student to comprehend figures and to do some figuring in producing answers. Other common elements may be found in the tests. Each test will also have some unique elements. For example, the statistics test presumably has some questions on "statistics" that are quite unrelated to the "marketing" questions on the marketing test. Finally, each test may have a random error element in addition to the common and unique elements. We can therefore distinguish three classes of factors or elements that contribute to the composition of each test.

Common Factors

It is assumed that two or more of the tests possess some factors in common, e.g. verbal ability may affect an individual's scores on two or more of the tests. For example, Test 1 may have a *loading* (called a_{11}) of 0.15 of verbal ability, plus a loading (called a_{12}) of 0.57 of mathematics ability. Similarly, Test 2 may have a verbal ability loading of 0.93 (a_{21}) and a mathematics ability loading of 0.04 (a_{22}). The symbol a_{ij} is used to refer to the magnitude of the loadings. The first subscript refers to the test number, the second subscript to the factor number. Thus an $a_{21} = 0.93$ says that Factor 1 (verbal ability) has a loading of 0.93 on Test 2. These loadings can be visualized as the proportion of test content which reflects the abilities associated with these common factors.

Specific Factors

It is assumed that each test has some factor specific to itself. For example, Test 1 may have a specific loading of $s_1 = 0.46$. That is, statistics would constitute about 46 per cent of Test 1. Presumably all other tests would have a loading of zero on this factor.

Random Error Factor

This is a residual. It is assumed to consist of undefined or undefinable factors. For example, Test 1 may have a random error of $e_1 = 0.07$.

Composition of an Individual's Test Score

Each person taking the battery of tests possesses a given amount of ability on each factor with which the tests are loaded. The factor analysis model assumes that this ability is constant from test to test. The score of an individual on a given test is the product of his ability on a given factor and the loading of that test with that factor, plus the product of his ability on the second factor combined with the loading of that test with the second factor, etc. It is customary to assume that these combinations of loading and ability can properly be *added* together to determine the total score of the individual on the given test. If we define F_{11} as the measure of the ability of individual 1 on Factor 1 and a_{11} as representing the loading of Factor 1 on Test 1, then the product of $a_{11}F_{11}$ is the theoretical " subscore " of individual 1 on that part of Test 1 that is loaded with Factor 1. Similarly, $a_{34}F_{84}$ is the theoretical subscore which individual 8 receives on Test 3 because of his ability on Factor 4. If k individuals take Test 1, the factor analysis model assumes that their individual net scores (identified below by the symbol z_{hi}) can be explained by the following pattern of underlying subscores, each subscore being the product of that individual's ability on a given factor and the loading of that test with that factor:

$$z_{11} = a_{11}F_{11} + a_{12}F_{12} + \cdots + a_{1m}F_{1m} + s_1 S_{11} + e_1 E_{11}$$
$$z_{21} = a_{11}F_{21} + a_{12}F_{22} + \cdots + a_{1m}F_{2m} + s_1 S_{21} + e_1 E_{21} \qquad (1)$$
$$\cdots$$
$$z_{k1} = a_{11}F_{k1} + a_{12}F_{k2} + \cdots + a_{1m}F_{km} + s_1 S_{k1} + e_1 E_{k1}$$

The z's refer to so-called " z-scores," or " standard scores." If we let X_{11} equal the raw score of individual 1 on Test 1, and let sd_1 represent standard deviation of all such raw scores on Test 1, then z_{11} is defined as:

$$z_{11} = \frac{X_{11} - \bar{X}_1}{sd_1},$$

where the first subscript on the symbol z identifies the individual. It is useful to note that the z's for a given test have a mean of zero and a standard deviation (and variance) of 1. The F scores on the theoretical factors are defined in a manner similar to that used to define " z-scores." With respect to a given theoretical factor, each individual is measured in terms of his deviation from the average of all k individuals on that factor. For example, an individual might be $+ 0.80$ standard deviations on his verbal ability and $- 1.63$ standard deviations on his mathematical ability.

If the k individuals now took Test 2, it would be assumed that their individual net scores on that test would be explained by an underlying pattern similar to that in expression (1). The only changes would be:

1. The second subscript on the z's would be changed to 2.
2. The first subscript on the a's would be changed to 2.
3. The subscript on the specific and error factor symbols would be changed to 2.

Properties of Individuals and Properties of Tests

Examination of the z scores of a given set of k individuals on two tests reveals that:

1. The a's are properties of the tests and hence are constant from individual to individual on a given test.
2. The F's are properties of the individuals and hence are constant from test to test for a given individual.

In the normal application of factor analysis interest centers on the factors —both common and specific—assumed to be inherent in the various tests. To be more specific, the analyst is primarily interested in the various properties of each test, and the composition of each test in terms of these properties. Hence, the analyst is interested in determining the various loadings associated with each test. He is normally not interested in determining the values of the F's, which are properties of the individuals.

Factor Analysis Pattern

As seen earlier, there is one pattern of underlying subscores for each test, and it is seen there that the loadings associated with each factor are constant from individual to individual on a given test. Since the primary interest is to determine the values of the loadings for each test in the battery of tests, the analyst must work with as many patterns of underlying scores as there are tests in the battery unless a more abbreviated method of illustration can be used. Such an illustration is possible because the emphasis is on the tests rather than on the individuals. Hence by sacrificing—in a notational sense only—the identification of individuals, the factor analysis pattern shown below can be used to identify all the information the factor analyst seeks (see equation 2).

Each row in the above pattern is associated with one test and is representative of a set of underlying subscores such as that shown in expression (1) for Test 1. In the factor pattern of expression (2), individuals are no longer explicitly identifiable in the sense that their z scores and F scores were explicitly identifiable in expression (1). On the other hand, the factor pattern of expression (2) illustrates the loadings of the entire battery of n tests and the manner in which each test is broken down into its component parts. Expression (2) is normally referred to as the basic factor analysis model. The fact that a set such as expression (1) underlies each row of the factor analysis pattern found in expression (2) is important to the reader if he is to understand the basic fundamentals of factor analysis.

Unknown Variables, Input Data, and Indeterminate Variables

The factor analysis pattern in expression (2) embodies the three types of parameters listed in the sub-heading title. Factor analysis literature does not always state clearly which variables are unknown, what data are used as input, and whether or not it is possible to determine all the unknowns in the basic factor analysis model.

$$z_1 = a_{11} F_1 + a_{12} F_2 + \cdots + a_{1m} F_m + s_1 S_1 \qquad\qquad + e_1 F_1$$
$$z_2 = a_{21} F_1 + a_{22} F_2 + \cdots + a_{2m} F_m \qquad + s_2 S_2 \qquad\qquad + e_2 F_2 \qquad (2)$$
$$\cdots$$
$$z_n = a_{n1} F_1 + a_{n2} F_2 + \cdots + a_{nm} F_m \qquad\qquad + s_n S_n \qquad\qquad + e_n F_n$$

The unknown variables to be determined as a result of the factor analysis are the factor-loadings—the a_{ij} values, the s_i values, and the e_i values. (For convenience, the s_i values and the e_i values are frequently combined.) The factor analysis pattern in expression (2) illustrates all these unknown variables. For each of the n tests, these unknown variables include the influence or loading of each common element, and the influence or loading of the specific element, *and* the influence or loading of the random or error element.

The input data in a factor analysis are essentially the z_{hi} scores received by the k individuals taking the n tests. However, these data are treated before they actually become input to the factor analysis model. The k scores are used to calculate a correlation coefficient for each possible pair of tests taken. Thus, the z scores received by the k individuals taking the n tests are transformed to an $n \times n$ matrix of correlation coefficients, and the latter becomes the input data to the factor analysis. Referring to the example given at the beginning of this paper, this step would result in a five by five correlation matrix because there were five tests. Each correlation coefficient will be the result of the scores made by the thirty students on each possible pair of tests.

In the factor analysis technique being discussed in this paper, it is assumed that there is zero correlation between an individual's possession of one factor and his possession of another factor. In the example given at the beginning of the paper, we assume that verbal ability is uncorrelated with mathematical ability in the general population and that ability in statistics is uncorrelated with ability in marketing. Because of this assumption of independence between factors, it can be shown that the correlation coefficients of two tests is equal to the inner product of the factor loadings associated with these two tests. For example:

$$r_{23} = a_{21}a_{31} + a_{22} a_{32} + a_{23} a_{33} + \cdots + a_{2m} a_{3m}.$$

Because of this relationship a matrix of correlation coefficients is used as input data to a factor analysis.

Finally, it should be noted that a matrix of correlation coefficients has a value of unity in all the elements on the main diagonal. These unity elements are not used as part of the input data. Instead, they are replaced with certain estimated values called communalities. Because of the complexity of the problem, the issue of estimating communalities will not be discussed in this paper. Interested readers should refer to chapter 5 of Harman (1960).

There is a third class of variable which cannot be measured by normal factor analysis. The variables in a factor analysis falling into this category are the F's. These common factors are not determined quantitatively, because no provision is made for their determination. Qualitatively they remain unidentifiable as there is no way of identifying the first factor as "verbal ability," and the second factor as "math ability," or vice versa. These factors can be defined only in the mind of the researcher. This point will be further discussed in the following section.

To summarize, the factor analysis technique uses a matrix of correlation coefficients to determine the factor loadings found in the factor analysis pattern illustrated by expression (2). The normal use of the factor analysis technique does not concern itself with the quantitative determination of the F's. The identification of the F's is left entirely to the analyst.

Uses of Factor Analysis

Reasons for the Development of Factor Analysis

One of the primary reasons for the development of factor analysis was the interest psychologists had in evaluating tests. Given a number of tests (m) which purport to measure a number of different traits (n, where $m \geq n$) or characteristics, which tests do in fact measure what they purport to measure, and how well do they measure these traits?

In the simple example stated earlier in this paper the situation was one of five tests which measured, it was hoped, the ability of students in the areas of statistics, marketing, finance, production, and accounting. Each test possibly included certain elements common to all tests—that is, certain elements pertaining to verbal ability, math ability, etc., were assumed to be found in each test. To the extent that a test consists predominantly of common elements rather than the specific element appropriate to it, that test does not measure what it purports to measure. Assuming that such tests are undesirable, one can easily see the utility of a technique which can help test designers or users to evaluate the traits or characteristics various tests do in fact measure.

As an example, given the five tests mentioned above, factor analysis could be used to determine to what extent each of these five tests is loaded with statistics, marketing, finance, production, and accounting content respectively. If these five tests measure what they purport to measure, the factor loadings in the factor analysis solution would display a certain pattern (see expression (2), page 50). For example, in the row of the factor pattern associated with the statistics test, the final solution would display a high loading (near unity) on one specific factor and a near zero loading on verbal ability, math ability, and all other elements. In the row of the factor pattern associated with the marketing test, the final solution would display a high loading on one specific factor—but not the same specific factor as that associated with the statistics test—and a near zero loading on all the other factors. Similar statements apply to the other three tests. The factor pattern of the final solution could then be visualized as one with near zero values everywhere except for one, and only one, near unity value in each of the specific factor columns. This would tell us that we have five tests which measure something specific to each individual test. We cannot say with certainty just what these specific elements are, but if we choose we can identify them with statistics content, marketing content, etc.

The display of near zero values and near unity values mentioned in the preceding paragraph might be termed the "simple structure" of a factor pattern. (The formal definition of simple structure is usually credited to Thurston (1935). See also Harman (1960), pp. 112–4. It is more complex than that stated here. The term is not used here in any rigorous sense. Rather, it is used for illustrative purposes.) When such a structure results, the analyst knows that he has a number of tests which measure different things. This is what psychologists wish to know when they have a whole battery of tests which measure intelligence, personality, and other traits. In other words, they wish to know which tests are useful because they measure one specific thing, and which of the tests are of less value because they measure more than one thing. This need led to the development of factor analysis.

Application and Test Evaluation

The foregoing discussion dealt with a situation which was assumed to come in a nice package, neatly wrapped. Consider now the case where several tests are factor analyzed, and no amount of analysis yields a simple structure. How might the findings of the factor analysis technique be used? Basically, factor analysis would be used in a continuing process which selects, evaluates, and eliminates tests until one arrives at a battery of tests which display simple structure in their factor patterns. The key role played by factor analysis in this continuing process is to help the analyst decide which test to eliminate.

Any given test would be eliminated for either of two reasons:

1. If a test has moderate values for the loadings on a number of factors, it could be said that this test measures a number of things equally well. For example, if a test has a 0.25 loading on verbal ability, a 0.25 loading on math ability, and a 0.25 loading on spatial ability, it would

probably not be considered very useful for measuring any one of those traits individually.

2. If two rows in the factor structure exhibit essentially the same values term by term, it could be said that the two "different" tests associated with these two rows are tests which measure essentially the same thing. Both of these tests might be eliminated for reason 1 above. However, if both of those tests were not eliminated for this reason, at least one of the tests could be discarded as redundant.

Thus, factor analysis makes possible the evaluation of a series of tests. Those which do not measure specifically what they purport to measure can be discarded, replaced, or re-designed. This process can be continued until a "simple structure" is obtained.

Factor Analysis Criteria

A persistent problem in applying factor analysis has been to define a statistical standard that could be equated with simple structure and which could also be calculated in a routine way, particularly by use of an electronic computer. Several standards have been developed, some to simulate simple structure and some apparently just to make some objective solution possible. The following discussion considers the three most prominent standards, plus the technique of "rotation."

Principal Component Criterion (Centroid Method)

The principal component method is probably the most frequently used method today. Yet it does not and will not lead the analyst to the best possible simple structure. Instead, the principal component method uses a criterion which maximizes the sum of the squares of the loadings on an individual factor. In terms of the factor pattern, this method will maximize the squares of the a_{ij} values in a column. That column or factor is then considered to be the principal factor or principal component. The reader will recall that simple structure calls for, at most, a single near-unity value in any one column, with all other values being near-zero. These two criteria are expressed mathematically in Exhibit 1. A comparison of these two criteria indicates that they are not identical or even nearly identical.

The principal component method is not conducive to the determination of the best possible simple structure. There is no proof that it would be impossible for a principal component solution to show the loadings on a single factor to be all near-zero with the exception of one, which would be a near-unity value. Nevertheless, such an occurrence would be highly unlikely because of the criterion used in this method. A comparison of the two criteria as shown in Exhibit 1 will indicate this.

When expressed in terms of the principal component criterion, simple structure would result when the sum of the squares of the a_{ij} values in a column approaches unity and when all values in that column approach zero, with the exception of one near-unity value. However, there is nothing in the principal component criterion which says the sum of the squares of the a_{ij} values in a column must approach one, nor is there anything in this criterion which says all values in a column must approach zero with the exception of one near-unity value. Hence it can be said that if the analyst is searching for simple structure, the principal component method will not lead him to it.

Although the principal component method falls short in the search for simple structure, the method is useful if the analyst wishes to inquire into the dominant element or factor common to each of a number of tests. Where the analyst has a number of tests which he feels include a common element, a factor analysis using the principal component method can be used to identify and measure the intensity of the common element. Note that the analyst must change his emphasis from a search for a battery of tests, each of which measures something specific, to a search for the intensity of a common element in a battery of tests. However, if the analyst wants to eliminate tests which measure essentially the same thing, this means he is basically interested in simple structure. But by using the principal component criterion, he can only eliminate tests and must look elsewhere for a criterion which will help him determine how far any of the tests measure specific factors.

Because the centroid method is an approximation of the principal component method, the former has not been treated separately. Since the centroid method is the less rigorous of the two, the discussion of the principal component method also applies to it, but with less reliability.

Varimax Criterion

The varimax criterion comes closer than the principal component criterion to determining simple structure. Like the principal component criterion, it also concerns itself with a column of loadings in the factor pattern. However, this criterion strives to maximize the variance of the square of the loadings in each column in the factor pattern. (The square of the loadings is used in order to overcome the calculational difficulties associated with absolute values. This approach of squaring the loadings is common to all three criteria discussed in this paper.) The mathematical expression for this criterion is shown in Exhibit 1. Outwardly it does not appear to resemble the criterion requirements of simple structure. Yet the effect of maximizing the variance of the square of the loadings in a column can be seen if it is recalled that this variance (1) will approach zero when all the loadings of a column are approximately equal, and (2) will approach a maximum when all but one loading approach zero and the remaining loading approaches unity. Thus, maximizing this variance has the same effect as minimizing the number of high loadings in a column. When the varimax criterion is viewed in this light, it is seen to resemble simple structure in some respects.

Yet the varimax criterion is not ideal for use in the search for simple structure. It will help the analyst to find a test which best measures a certain factor. While this is an improvement over the principal component method, this criterion does not seem to take into consideration two aspects of simple structure. First, the common factors in simple structure should all have loadings of near-zero values. Consequently, the variance of the square of these loadings should approach a near-zero value. This is contradictory to the varimax criterion. Second, the varimax criterion will not prevent a solution in which a test has high loadings on two or more factors. For example, for any row in the factor pattern, the varimax criterion will not prevent a solution where $a_{i,j}$ and $a_{i,j+1}$ both approach unity. Tests which display either of these weaknesses do not conform to the requirements of simple structure. It should be noted that the varimax criterion does not make any specific attempt to establish the kind of relationships between factors (between columns) found in simple structure.

In spite of these apparent weaknesses the varimax criterion does seem to be an improvement over the principal component criterion when simple structure is being sought.

Quartimax Criterion

To obtain simple structure, the quartimax criterion is an improvement over the varimax criterion. The quartimax criterion strives to maximize the variance of the square of the loadings in each row of the factor pattern. Hence both of these last two methods are concerned with maximizing a variance. This similarity is seen in Exhibit 1 by comparing their mathematical expressions. However, in this criterion, the emphasis is on maximizing the variance in a row of the factor pattern instead of maximizing the variance in a column of the factor pattern. Maximizing the variance in a row has the same effect as maximizing the variance in a column—in the sense that the maximum is achieved when all but one loading approach zero and the remaining loading approaches unity. The significant difference is that with the quartimax criterion the number of high loadings in a row will be minimized. Since each row represents a test, the use of this criterion is more likely to lead to a factor pattern in which each row has all near-zero values with the exception of one near-unity value. Consequently, compared with the varimax criterion, the quartimax criterion is more likely to lead to the discovery of tests each of which measures a single specific factor. This is a further improvement over the varimax method because, as previously mentioned, that method will not prevent a solution in which a test will have high loadings on two or more factors. Furthermore, the quartimax method will permit all near-zero values in the columns associated with common factors. That also was not possible using the varimax method. Hence of the three available criteria, the quartimax method is the one most likely to arrive at the best possible simple structure.

It should be noted that the quartimax criterion is not synonymous with simple structure. Its principal weakness is that it does not explicitly include any reference to the relationships which exist between the rows of a factor pattern associated with simple structure. Thus it is possible to arrive at a solution in which two tests have high loadings on the same factor. This of course is contrary to simple structure. Nevertheless, the possibility of two tests being nearly identical is real. If a perfect criterion existed for the determination of simple structure, it too would show two tests with high loadings on the same factor if those two tests were quite similar. Consequently, this does not seem to be a serious limitation, especially when viewed in terms of what the quartimax criterion will achieve. By minimizing the number of high values in a row, the criterion is likely to lead to a solution where the loadings in a row all approach zero, with the exception of one near-unity value. Furthermore, this criterion is not likely to allow high loadings on two factors in the same row. Finally, it is also possible to arrive at a solution with all near-zero loadings in the columns associated with the common factors. This very closely resembles simple structure.

On the other hand, since the relationships between rows are not made explicit, it is possible for two tests to have similar loadings. When this occurs, the analyst need only discard, replace, or re-design one of the tests and then repeat the analysis in his search for simple structure.

The evidence seems to indicate that this last criterion would be the most useful of all three when the analyst's goal is simple structure.[1]

A number of writers have suggested different approaches which have been termed quartimax criteria. See Harman (1960), pp. 289–301. Some of these approaches maximize the variance of the square of *all* the loadings in a factor pattern. This is something quite different from maximizing the variance of the square of all the loadings in a row of a factor pattern. The view taken in this paper is that the former approaches do not even come close to simple structure except by chance. For that reason, they are not treated in this paper.

---

[1] Editor's note: In this exposition Ekeblad and Stasch are pointing out that the ideal situation is to have one test measure one unique factor and have defined simple structure in this context. In a more common situation there are many "tests" (or variables), and the objective is to reduce them to a few common factors. In this situation an alternative and perhaps more common definition of simple structure contains several criteria, including the following: (1) Each factor will have a high loading (a_{ij}) on several tests (or variables) and close to zero loadings on the rest. (2) Each test (or variable) will have loadings on only a few factors. When simple structure is so defined, the interpretability of the factors is usually maximized, and the objective of reducing many redundant tests (or variables) to a few underlying factors is accomplished. With this definition of simple structure, the conclusions reached by Ekelblad and Stasch regarding quartimax must be qualified. In fact, Harman (1960) observed, "This procedure [varimax] . . . does a better job of approximating the classical simple structure principles."

For those analysts who use the quartimax criterion, caution is suggested in selecting an appropriate approach.

Rotation without a Criterion

Frequently in the literature the reader will find reference to the term "rotation." This usually refers to an attempt by the analyst to move from one solution to another, presumably because the former solution was not satisfactory. When this rotation is achieved with the use of a criterion, the solution is just as objective and scientific as the solution derived directly from the raw data using the same criterion. On the other hand, when rotation is used without a criterion the resulting solution is subjective. With such a procedure, different analysts using the same input data are not likely to give the same solution. Such solutions may be helpful to the analyst, but they do not reflect objective research. If marketing or advertising researchers are to use factor analysis in an objective manner, rotation of solutions without the use of criteria must be avoided.

Exhibit 1.   Simplified Comparison of Factor Analysis Criteria

To facilitate the comparison of the various factor analysis criteria, all of the loadings shown in expression (2) of the text will be identified by the symbol a_{ij}. Furthermore, the specific and random elements will be combined into one term. This in no way changes the loadings on the m common factors found in expression (2). The reader need only bear in mind the fact that in the columns associated with the combined specific and random elements, all but one of the loadings are assumed to be zero.

I. *Simple Structure*
    a. Columns associated with common factors

$$a_{ij} \to 0, \qquad \text{for all } i$$
$$\sum_i a_{ij} \to 0$$

    b. Columns associated with combined specific-random factors

$$\begin{cases} a_{i \cdot j} \to 1, & \text{for any one } i = i* \\ a_{ij} \to 0, & \text{for all } i \neq i* \end{cases}$$
$$\sum_i a_{ij} \to 1$$

    c. For each row

$$\sum_j a_{ij} \to 1, \qquad \text{for all } i$$

II. *Principal Component Criterion* (for each column)

    Maximize $(a_{1j}^2 + a_{2j}^2 + a_{3j}^2 + \cdots)$, or Maximize $\sum_i a_{ij}^2$

III. *Varimax Criterion* (for each column)

$$\text{Maximize } \sigma_{aj}{}^2 = \frac{1}{n}\sum_{i=1}^{n}(a_{ij}{}^2 - \bar{a}_j{}^2)^2, \qquad \text{for all } j$$

IV. *Quartimax Criterion* (for each row)

$$\text{Maximize } \sigma_{ai}{}^2 = \frac{1}{m}\sum_{j=1}^{m}(a_{ij}{}^2 - \bar{a}_i{}^2)^2, \qquad \text{for all } i$$

References

Baggoley, Andrew R. *Intermediate Correlational Methods.* New York: John Wiley & Sons Inc., 1964.

Collins, Gwyn. On Methods: Factor Analysis. *Journal of Advertising Research,* Vol. 1, No. 5, September 1961.

Dudek, Frank J. Relations Among Television Rating Indices. *Journal of Advertising Research,* Vol. 4, No. 3, September 1964.

Farley, John. Why Does Brand Loyalty Vary Over Products? *Journal of Marketing Research,* Vol. 1, No. 4, November 1964.

Massy, William. Statistical Analysis of Relations between Variables. In R. E. Frank, A. A. Kuehn, and W. Massy, *Quantitative Techniques in Marketing Analysis,* Homewood: Richard D. Irwin, 1962.

Harman, Harry H. *Modern Factor Analysis,* Chicago: The University of Chicago Press, 1960.

Kirsch, Arthur D. and Seymour Banks. Program Types Defined by Factor Analysis. *Journal of Advertising Research,* Vol. 2, No. 3, September 1962.

Ramond, Charles K. Factor Analysis: When to Use It. In Shuchman, Abe, *Scientific Decision Making in Business,* New York: Holt, Rinehart and Winston, Inc., 1963.

Rothman, James. Formulation of an Index of Propensity to Buy. *Journal of Marketing Research,* Vol. 1, No. 2, May 1964.

Stephenson, William. Public Images of Public Utilities. *Journal of Advertising Research,* Vol. 3, No. 4, December 1963.

Stoetzel, Jean. A Factor Analysis of the Liquor Preferences of French Consumers. *Journal of Advertising Research,* Vol. 1, No. 2, December 1960.

Thurstone, L. L. *The Vectors of the Mind.* Chicago: The University of Chicago Press, 1935.

Twedt, Dik W. A Multiple Factor Analysis of Advertising Readership. *Journal of Applied Psychology,* June 1952.

Vincent, Norman L. A Note on Stoetzel's Factor Analysis of Liquor Preferences. *Journal of Advertising Research,* Vol. 2, No. 1, March 1962.

21

William F. Massy: What is Factor
Analysis?

Factor analysis is basically a method for reducing a set of data into a
more compact form, while throwing certain properties of the data into bold
relief. The user of factor analysis focuses on the set of variables for which
information has been collected and poses the question: Can the information
contained in the original variables be summarized in a smaller number of new
variables? The technique was originally developed for use in psychology,
where attempts were being made to summarize or "explain" subjects' scores
on a wide variety of test variables in terms of a relatively few underlying
dimensions or behavior traits. Scores for 50 or more questions on an intelligence test might be used to define a few basic intelligence factors like verbal or
mathematical ability, for example. In this case, the statistical problem is to
reduce the dimension of the problem from 50 variables (say) to 2 variables
with minimal loss of information. Factor analysis was designed to accomplish
this goal.[1]

Many of the simultaneous relationships between variables that are
brought into view by the techniques of factor analysis could not have been
uncovered through examination of the simple correlations among their raw
scores. This is why factor analysis is recognized as a powerful multivariate
statistical technique.

Ways to Apply Factor Analysis

Factor analysis methods provide estimates of factor loadings, which may
be extended to yield values for the underlying factors themselves. But how
can this statistical machinery be applied to problems of marketing research?
Will factor analysis become really useful as a method for interpreting marketing data, or is it just a passing fad?

Abridged from *Proceedings of the AMA Conference*, 1964, published by the American
Marketing Association. William F. Massy, "Applying Factor Analysis to a Specific
Marketing Problem," *Proceedings of the AMA Conference*, 1964, pp. 291–307.

[1] A most useful reference for almost all the topics connected with factor analysis,
including computational methods, is Harry H. Harman, *Modern Factor Analysis* (Chicago:
The University of Chicago Press, 1960). For a simplified treatment see Ronald E. Frank,
Alfred A. Kuehn, and William F. Massy, *Quantitative Techniques in Marketing Analysis*
(Homewood Ill.: Richard D. Irwin, Inc., 1962), pp. 100–104.

Of course no definitive answer to the latter question is possible now; the acceptability of any technique must be proved in practice, and as yet we have had little experience in the application of factor analysis to problems in marketing. On the other hand, it is possible to identify at least four distinct ways in which the technique promises to be useful. They are:

1. Separation and analysis of distinct dimensions that are latent in a larger set of *variables*.
2. Separation and analysis of distinctly different groups of *people* which exist in a larger population.
3. Identification of certain likely variables for subsequent regression or discriminant analysis, from among a much larger set of potential independent variables.
4. Summarization of the common parts of a set of explanatory variables into a smaller number of new variables which can be used in regression or discriminant analysis.

Approaches (1) and (2) take the identification of the underlying dimensions or factors as ends in themselves; the estimates of the factor loadings are all that is required for the analysis. Method (3) also relies on the factor loadings, but uses them as the basis for identifying variables for subsequent analysis with other techniques. Method (4) requires that estimates of the factors themselves be obtained; then the F's are used as independent variables in a regression or discriminant analysis. Examples of the application of each approach to marketing problems will be discussed in the following paragraphs.

Method 1

Factorization of a set of variables into a smaller number of dimensions is the classical approach to factor analysis, as handed down to us from the field of psychology. The intelligence testing example given in the previous section is an example of this approach. The method has come to be called "R-factor analysis" or simply "R-technique," to distinguish it from approach (2) below.

The work of Stroetzel provides an example of the application of R-technique to a marketing problem. He suggests that, "If complex behavior is caused by a few simple motives, they can be found in the patterns of that behavior." He "illustrates this premise with a factor analysis which tentatively explains consumer preference for nine liquors in terms of their sweetness, price, and regional popularity."[2] In this case, the relative rankings of a sample of consumers for the set of nine liquors served as original variables and the dimensions of sweetness, price and region were the three summary factors.

---

[2] Jean Stroetzel, "A Factor Analysis of the Liquor Preferences of French Consumers," *Journal of Advertising Research*, Vol. 1, No. 2 (December, 1960). p. 7.

Harper's[3] article on tests of quality for Cheshire Cheeses uses factor analysis in a similar manner; the results from 13 complicated tests on the cheeses were factored to find three critical dimensions of product quality that could be used in a practical quality control program.

Method 2

Factorization of a group of people, rather than a set of variables, is another application of factor analysis. Here the object is to separate a population of individuals into a set of independent groups on the basis of their attributes or responses to test questions. The procedure is called " Q-Factor Analysis." The difference between the R and Q technique lies in the manner of calculating the correlation coefficients upon which the factor analysis is based. In the former, they are calculated in the usual manner:

$$(R\text{-technique}) \ r_{ij} = \sum_{k=1}^{n} z_{ik} z_{jk}, \qquad i, j = 1, \ldots, 4$$

The coefficient r_{ij} represents the correlation of the ith and jth variables; it is calculated by summing over the sample of individuals. This procedure is reversed in " Q-Factor analysis," where correlations between the pth and qth individuals are desired:

$$(Q\text{-technique}) \ r_{pq} = \sum_{i=1}^{4} z_{ip} z_{iq}, \qquad p, q = 1, \ldots, n$$

Note that the summation is now over the variables and that the coefficients refer to the association between individuals, as averaged over the variables on the test.

The problem of identifying meaningful market segments seems to provide an opportunity for the fruitful application of Q-technique. Imagine that a company has data on the response of a sample of consumers to its marketing efforts (changes in relative price, promotions, etc.). It might like to know how many distinct sub-groupings of people can be made on the basis of these response patterns; each such group represents a market segment, which could presumably be singled out for separate consideration when the firm plans its future promotional strategy. If the sample size is small enough (say 120 or less), Q-factor analysis can provide direct answers to the questions: (a) How many distinct groups of people exist in the population? and (b) Which people in the sample are in what group? Q-factor analysis on larger samples poses insuperable computational burdens, but progress through indirect means appears to be possible. Professor Thomas Lodahl from Cornell and I

---

[3] Roland Harper, "Factor Analysis as a Technique for Examining Complex Data on Foodstuffs," *Applied Statistics*, Vol. V, No. 1, (March, 1956), pp. 32–48. Reprinted in the Frank, Kuehn, and Massy reference, pp. 409–426.

are working on a paper discussing the methodological aspects of the *Q*-technique as it may be applied in marketing. William Duhamel, one of our marketing Ph.D. candidates at Stanford, is writing a dissertation on their application to a practical problem of market segmentation.

Method 3

Factor analysis can be used as a device for determining which of a large group of potential explanatory variables should be included in a regression or discriminant analysis. Dik Warren Twedt's[4] analysis of advertising readership provides us with an illustrative example of this approach. He studied the relationship between the per cent of a sample of respondents who said they had read a particular magazine advertisement and some 34 variables representing the characteristics of the ad. The potential explanatory variables included mechanical attributes like the number of colors in the ad, square inches of illustration, and the size of the largest type used, together with content measures such as the number of facts and benefits represented in the ad and the readership interest of the surrounding copy.

First, 19 of these 34 variables were selected for further study on the basis of their simple correlations with the criterion variable, readership. These 19, plus the readership criterion, were subjected to an *R*-factor analysis. Six factors representing *picture and color, size of ad, typographic size, information content*, the *field around the ad* (readership of surrounding copy), and the influence of the previous schedule of the ad in that magazine, were obtained. They accounted for about two-thirds of the variance of the readership criterion, as measured by the loadings of the criterion on the factors. The explanatory power of the set of 19 independent variables was concentrated on the first three factors, which together explained almost 61% of the variance of readership in the sample (as opposed to 67% for all six factors).

On the basis of the factor analysis, the author selected a subset of three of the 19 explanatory variables for use in a multiple regression aimed at predicting readership. The variables chosen were *numbers of colors in the ad, size of the ad*, and the *number of square inches of illustration*: one variable for each of the first three factors, which were found to be strongly related to readership. The resulting regression yielded a multiple correlation coefficient of .76. When six more variables were added to the regression, the value of *R* jumped to only .79; this increment of 0.03 in the multiple correlation was too small to warrant the work involved in adding the extra variables.

Twedt used factor analysis to explore the interactions among a large set of explanatory variables and advertising readership, prior to multiple regression. Factor analysis was worthwhile because the manifold relationships

---

[4] Dik Warren Twedt, "A Multiple Factor Analysis of Advertising Readership," *Journal of Applied Psychology*, Vol. XXXVI, No. 3 (June, 1952), pp. 207–215. Reprinted in the Frank, Kuehn, and Massy reference, pp. 427–439.

between all the variables could be studied at one time without running into the problems of multicollinearity that are so often encountered in regression analysis. Once a relatively "clean" subset of independent variables was identified, the greater predictive power and hypothesis testing ability of multiple regression could be brought into play.

Method 4

Factor analysis can be used for the summarization of a complex set of potential explanatory variables in yet another way. Instead of using the estimated factor loadings for the identification of relevant variables, it is possible to find values for the factors themselves—and then use them as inputs to the multiple regression or discriminant analysis. The multiple regression might be:[5]

$$y_k = b_0 + b_1 F_{1k} + b_2 F_{2k} + v_k$$

The dependent variable in the study (y) is not included in the factor analysis that serves to determine the F's: this procedure is just the opposite of the one discussed under (3) above.

My earlier paper on the analysis of television ownership utilized regressions on factor scores.[6]

---

[5] Where y is the original standardized variable; F_1 and F_2 are the summary factors; b_i ($i = 0, 2$) are parameters to be determined by the analysis; v is the residual part of the y not accounted for by the factor.

[6] William F. Massy, "Television Ownership in 1950; Results of a Factor Analytic Study." In the Frank, Kuehn, and Massy reference, pp. 440–460.

22

Bishwa Nath Mukherjee: A Factor Analysis of Some Qualitative Attributes of Coffee

---

Factor analysis has been used recently to study consumers' preference for different varieties of liquor (Stoetzel, 1960) and food (Pilgrim and Kamen, 1959). The results of such analyses not only throw light on consumers' preferences, which may be very useful in estimating market trends, but more

---

Reprinted from the *Journal of Advertising Research*. © Copyrighted 1965 by the Advertising Research Foundation. The study was carried out at the Psychometric Laboratory of the University of North Carolina. Sincere appreciation is due to Professor Lyle V. Jones, who made available the data and critically read the first draft of the report. The assistance of Miss Elizabeth Niehl in carrying out part of the analysis is also gratefully acknowledged.

important, provide knowledge regarding the crucial attributes of the product, i.e., attributes which determine the consumers' preferences. Such knowledge not only may improve the product, but also may help in planning more effective advertising. Further, to safeguard the consumer franchise, the quality-control section at the factory should give special attention to the key attributes.

Though the data obtained for the present study were not especially suited for demonstrating the scope of factor analysis in picking out key product attributes, an initial attempt was made to isolate and identify, from subjects' ratings, those attributes of a particular brand of coffee which are primarily involved in determining preference for the product. Apart from this, the study aimed at determining which of the attributes have factorial patterns which are similar to the one yielded by the overall preference rating.

Method

We first developed a list of coffee attributes by questioning, in an open response manner, a group of consumers. The attributes mentioned most frequently, and thus chosen for this study, are listed in Table 1. An overall preference attribute was also included for rating. The attributes were rated on ten-point semantic differential scales.

Table 1. 14 Coffee Attributes Investigated

Pleasant flavor — Unpleasant flavor
Stagnant, muggy taste — Sparkling, refreshing taste
Mellow taste — Bitter taste
Cheap taste — Expensive taste
Comforting, harmonious, — Irritating, discordant,
smooth, friendly taste   rough, hostile taste
Dead, lifeless, dull taste — Alive, lively, peppy taste
Tastes artificial — Tastes like real coffee
Deep, distinct flavor — Shallow, indistinct flavor
Tastes warmed over — Tastes just brewed
Hearty, full-bodied, full flavor — Watery, thin, empty flavor
Pure, clear taste — Muddy, swampy taste
Raw taste — Roasted taste
Fresh taste — Stale taste
Overall preference:
Excellent quality — Very poor quality

Note: ten blank boxes separated each set of opposing statements. Subjects checked the position which came closest to describing how they felt toward the product.

We randomly selected 94 consumers, who rated each of the 14 attributes after drinking a cup of coffee. They were not told which brand they were drinking. Only one brand was tested.

The scale categories were assigned successive integers and the ratings thus were treated quantitatively. The mean and standard deviation of the ratings on each of the attributes were calculated and appear in Table 2. The ratings

Table 2. Intercorrelations among Attribute Ratings

	1	2	3	4	5	6	7	8	9	10	11	12	13	14
1. Pleasant flavor	1.00	.76	.81	.79	.83	.81	.74	.66	.65	.71	.76	.65	.71	.75
2. Sparkling taste		1.00	.78	.85	.77	.87	.83	.65	.70	.78	.85	.69	.74	.83
3. Mellow taste			1.00	.77	.85	.81	.77	.60	.65	.64	.75	.69	.69	.74
4. Expensive taste				1.00	.78	.87	.83	.76	.69	.81	.81	.64	.71	.87
5. Comforting taste					1.00	.82	.77	.66	.60	.69	.82	.69	.69	.74
6. Alive taste						1.00	.88	.70	.74	.80	.81	.65	.77	.87
7. Tastes like real coffee							1.00	.67	.76	.75	.79	.62	.76	.87
8. Deep distinct flavor								1.00	.51	.84	.70	.54	.59	.70
9. Tastes just brewed									1.00	.67	.65	.67	.80	.75
10. Hearty flavor										1.00	.83	.65	.72	.76
11. Pure clear taste											1.00	.66	.73	.76
12. Roasted taste												1.00	.78	.61
13. Fresh taste													1.00	.73
14. Overall preference														1.00
Mean rating*	4.5	4.3	4.4	4.6	4.4	4.2	4.2	4.3	4.3	4.2	4.3	4.4	4.6	6.9
Standard deviation	1.6	1.3	1.4	1.4	1.3	1.4	1.6	1.5	1.5	1.5	1.4	1.2	1.4	2.7

* The ten scale categories were assigned successive integers beginning with one at the favorable side of the scale. Thus ratings could vary from one (very "good") to nine (very "bad") on an attribute.

on the different attributes were then intercorrelated, producing a 14×14 matrix of product-moment intercorrelations.

The matrix of intercorrelation among the 14 attributes as shown in Table 2 was analyzed by means of the principal axes method (Harman, 1960) using the squared multiple correlations (SMC) as the communality estimates. These SMC values, which indicate squared multiple correlation between a particular variable and the remaining $(n - 1)$ variables, were obtained using a matrix inversion program. Refactorization was not performed because the obtained communalities did not differ appreciably from the SMC values. The average of the absolute differences between the SMC and obtained communalities for the corresponding pairs was only .022 and the largest discrepancy was only .05.

The principal axes solution was derived by an electronic computer, the Royal McBee LGP-30, using a program prepared by Johnson (1960). For the following three reasons only the first four principal factors were considered: (1) the contribution of the fifth principal factor to the total variance was not even one per cent; (2) the magnitude of the largest loading in the fifth principal factor was .06, which was considered insignificant; and (3) successive rotation of increasing numbers of the principal axes, satisfying in each case the varimax criterion, indicated that the inclusion of the fifth factor in the rotation did not yield a new factor having at least two factor saturations appreciably different from zero.

Table 3. Factor Loadings

	Principal Factor Matrix						Rotated (Varimax) Matrix				Oblique Factor Matrix			
	I	II	III	IV	h^2	SMC	A	B	C	D	A	B	C	D
1.	.86	−.01	−.20	.04	.78	.78	.63	.38	.36	.34	.34	.01	.07	−.03
2.	.91	−.01	−.01	−.09	.83	.85	.48	.43	.53	.38	.14	.04	.23	−.04
3.	.86	−.11	−.28	.002	.83	.80	.70	.26	.38	.36	.36	.13	−.003	−.01
4.	.91	.15	−.001	−.10	.87	.86	.46	.53	.54	.29	.16	−.05	.34	−.07
5.	.87	.002	.31	.10	.87	.84	.74	.38	.30	.32	.47	.01	−.004	−.08
6.	.93	.03	−.02	−.16	.90	.89	.49	.43	.59	.35	.12	.07	.30	−.01
7.	.90	−.02	.04	−.21	.86	.85	.42	.38	.64	.37	.03	.11	.33	−.04
8.	.77	.36	.11	.16	.77	.76	.31	.74	.27	.22	.24	−.40	.32	−.10
9.	.79	−.28	.24	−.09	.76	.73	.23	.24	.52	.62	−.15	.11	.14	.37
10.	.87	.25	.22	.17	.89	.86	.28	.75	.33	.39	.14	.38	.31	.07
11.	.89	.11	−.05	.10	.82	.85	.51	.55	.36	.36	.28	−.15	.17	−.01
12.	.76	−.29	.04	.27	.74	.71	.43	.28	.16	.67	.18	−.08	−.18	.38
13.	.84	−.27	.19	.12	.83	.79	.33	.32	.36	.70	.01	−.03	−.001	.41
14.	.90	.04	.08	−.23	.86	.84	.38	.43	.65	.34	.002	.08	.39	.01
% common variance	90.0	4.1	3.3	2.6			27.5	25.6	24.5	22.4				
% total variance	74.6	3.4	2.7	2.6			22.9	21.3	20.4	18.7				

Two methods were used to obtain the simple structure (Thurstone, 1947) from the principal factor matrix: (1) a machine orthogonal solution which satisfies Kaiser's (1958) varimax criterion, and (2) an algebraic oblique solution following the single plane method of graphical transformation (Thurstone, 1947).

Results

The left-hand portion of Table 3 shows the projections of all the coffee attributes on the first four principal factors. The h^2 column indicates the communalities obtained for each attribute after the first factorization. Table 3 also gives the machine varimax solution and the oblique solution, each showing the projections of all the attributes on the rotated axes A, B, C, and D. Table 4 shows the correlations between factors in the oblique solution.

Table 4. Oblique Solution—Correlations between Factors

	A	B	C	D
A	1.00	−.26	− .44	−.46
B		1.00	−.03	−.02
C			1.00	−.44
D				1.00

Factors are interpreted mainly on the basis of the factor contents. In defining a factor, we considered variables having projections of .50 or over on the rotated varimax axis, or of .30 or over on an oblique axis. Subjective evaluations of possible underlying processes influencing subjects' judgments were made, and each factor is discussed below with reference to the attributes having high loadings as obtained for the two methods of rotation. The interpretations must be considered highly tentative.

Factor A (Comforting Quality)

Variable	Attribute	Varimax	Oblique
1.	Pleasant flavor	.625	.340
3.	Mellow taste	.698	.359
5.	Comforting taste	.736	.465
11.	Pure clear taste	.512	.283

Factor A shows very high positive loadings on attributes like "comforting taste," "mellow taste," and "pleasant flavor," as is evident from both the solutions. This factor seems to be related to the "comforting" or "soothing" aspect of coffee flavor.

Factor B (Heartiness)

Variable	Attribute	Varimax	Oblique
8.	Deep distinct flavor	.742	.396
10.	Hearty flavor	.745	.380

Both the varimax and oblique solutions very clearly define this factor in terms of variables 8 and 10. The factor, it seems, can be interpreted as "heartiness" of coffee flavor.

Factor C (Genuineness)

Variable	Attribute	Varimax	Oblique
2.	Sparkling taste	.524	.232
4.	Expensive taste	.541	.334
6.	Alive taste	.594	.301
7.	Tastes like real coffee	.636	.328
8.	Deep distinct flavor	.268	.323
10.	Hearty flavor	.332	.310
14.	Overall preference	.653	.387

This factor is tentatively interpreted as a "genuineness" factor in view of its high loading on variable 7: "tastes like real coffee" versus "tastes artificial."

Factor D (Freshness)

Variable	Attribute	Varimax	Oblique
9.	Tastes just brewed	.621	.359
12.	Roasted taste	.670	.465
13.	Fresh taste	.698	.238

Both the solutions clearly define this factor in terms of the three attributes. Factor D may be regarded as a "freshness" quality of the coffee.

The factors are mentioned in order of importance in accounting for the total as well as the common variance. Collectively, these four factors account for 83.3 per cent of the total variance observed in subjects' ratings of the 14 attributes. Factor A alone accounts for 22.9 per cent of the total variance (varimax solution), compared with the 18.7 per cent for Factor D.

Conclusions

This study indicates that individual differences on coffee ratings can be best described in terms of the variation on comforting taste, heartiness of flavor, genuineness of product, and freshness. These four factors may be the important motivating principles governing consumers' coffee preferences.

Further, attributes like "alive taste" and "tastes like real coffee," both involved in defining the "genuiness" factor, exhibit factorial patterns very similar to the overall preference variable. This implies that a major factor behind coffee preference may be the distinction between pure coffee and artificial coffee. If this is true, then the manufacturer of the coffee tested in this study should give prime consideration to accentuating "genuineness," both in the product and in the advertising. Operations which make the coffee taste more like "real" coffee, and perhaps at the same time increase the "heartiness" of its flavor, will bring a positive change in the overall preference rating for the brand tested in the study.

References

Harman, H. *Modern Factor Analysis*. Chicago: University of Chicago Press, 1960.

Johnson, E. S. Characteristic Roots and Vectors of a Symmetric Matrix: A Computer Program for the LGP-30. University of North Carolina, Psychometric Laboratory Research Memorandum No. 1, 1960.

Kaiser, H. F. The Varimax Criterion for Analytic Rotation in Factor Analysis. *Psychometrika*, 1958, Vol. 23, pp. 187–200.

Pilgrim, F. J. and J. M. Kamen. Patterns of Food and Preferences through Factor Analysis. *Journal of Marketing*, Vol. 24, No. 2, October 1959, pp. 68–72.

Stoetzel, J. A Factor Analysis of the Liquor Preferences of French Consumers. *Journal of Advertising Research*, Vol. 1, No. 2, December 1960, pp. 7–11.

Thurstone, L. L. *Multiple Factor Analysis*. Chicago: University of Chicago, 1947.

23

Theodore Clevenger, Jr., Gilbert A. Lazier, and Margaret Leitner Clark: Measurement of Corporate Images by the Semantic Differential

The semantic differential was conceived as a device for measuring connotative meanings. Specifically, the process of semantic differentiation locates the connotative meaning of a concept in a multidimensional semantic space.

Reprinted from *Journal of Marketing Research*, published by the American Marketing Association. Theodore Clevenger, Jr., Gilbert A. Lazier and Margaret Leitner Clark, "Measurement of Corporate Images by the Semantic Differential," *Journal of Marketing Research*, Vol. II, February 1965, pp. 80–82. The research was supported in part by the National Science Foundation. The writers are grateful to the Computation and Data Processing Center, University of Pittsburgh, for technical assistance in computer analysis of these data.

While an extensive body of theory underlies the use and interpretation of such instruments [4], the development of any particular semantic differential proceeds along empirical lines. The raw materials for this development are: (1) a subject or group of subjects, (2) a concept or set of concepts to be rated

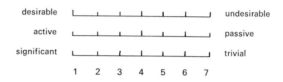

and, (3) a series of bipolar adjective scales such as the one above. Any number of bipolar scales may be included and their composition is limited only by the purposes and imagination of the investigator.

Each subject rates each concept on every scale. In the usual application, a factor analysis of the resulting data is performed across subjects and concepts. The correlations are run between each pairwise combination of scales (where N for the correlation coefficient is equal to the number of subjects times the number of concepts). The resulting matrix of intercorrelations is then subjected to factor analysis, a procedure which identifies clusters of scales which intercorrelate highly among themselves but relatively poorly with the scales of other factors. For every cluster of scales, or factors, a reference vector is established and each scale is then correlated with the reference vector of each factor. A scale is designated as belonging to a particular factor if the loading of the scale on that factor is relatively high and pure: that is, if the correlation of the scale with the reference vector of the factor in question is relatively high and its correlations with the reference vectors of the other factors are relatively low. Scales with ambiguous factor loadings are discarded. In general only those factors are retained which reduce the residual correlations to a substantial degree.

The result of this analysis is a set of factors (usually from two to four), each of which is measured by several of the scales (usually from two to six). The factors are said to represent dimensions in a semantic space. A score on each factor is obtained for a particular concept usually by averaging the scores of that concept on all of the scales of each factor respectively. The connotative meaning of the concept is then located as a particular point in a multidimensional space defined by the factors of this measuring instrument.

"The connotative meaning of General Motors" is so nearly identical with "the image of General Motors" that the semantic differential has been used to study corporate images. Such a study is usually concerned either with change in the image of a product or corporation over time (perhaps as a result of an advertising campaign); or comparison of the simultaneous images of two persons, products or corporations; or comparison of two or more groups of subjects (or consumers), such as a comparison of the late

John F. Kennedy's image among a group of university professors with his image among members of a labor union.

All such comparisons involve the assumption that the factor structure of the semantic differential in use is relatively stable from one group of subjects to another, and from one concept to another. "Osgood and his colleagues suggest that the semantic differential makes possible the measurement and comparison of various objects by diverse subjects. They imply that the measuring instrument is not grossly affected by the nature of the object being measured, or by the type of person using the scale [5]." If, however, the structure of the semantic space for the image of the Ford Motor Company is quite different from the structure of the semantic space for the Keystone Box Corporation, any effort to compare these two corporations on a semantic differential will lead to serious error. By the same token, if undergraduates at New York University attach a connotative structure to corporations different from that of Tucson housewives, any effort to compare the image of a particular corporation for these two groups of consumers will likewise lead to error. For this reason, there is some interest in the development of semantic differential measuring instruments which are "robust" in the sense that their factor structure remains relatively constant from one subject to another, and from one concept to another.

Recently it has been demonstrated that a semantic differential developed for applications in theatrical research fails to display these characteristics [3]. The purpose of the present research was to determine whether the factor structure of a semantic differential for institutional concepts was subject to a similar limitation.

Methodology

Forty undergraduate students and forty New York housewives were subjects for the experiment at the University of Pittsburgh. Each subject evaluated two corporate images: a nationally known tobacco company and a prominent electrical appliance manufacturer. Each corporation was rated on the bipolar scales: (1) *pleasant-unpleasant*, (2) *strong-weak*, (3) *sharp-dull*, (4) *good-bad*, (5) *heavy-light*, (6) *active-passive*, (7) *clean-dirty*, (8) *large-small*, (9) *fast-slow* and (10) *beautiful-ugly*. Scales 1, 4, 7, and 10 represent an "Evaluative" factor which appears quite commonly in semantic differential research; Scales 2, 5, and 8 are drawn from a "Potency" factor and Scales 3, 6, and 9 from an "Activity" factor which have frequently appeared in previous studies. Occasionally, the "Activity" and "Potency" factors have been collapsed into a single factor which is usually called "Dynamism."

In the first phase of the analysis the two groups of subjects were combined and separate factor analyses were performed for the two concepts. In the second phase of the analysis the two concepts were combined and separate factor analyses were performed for the two subject groups. The resulting factor structures were compared and conclusions were drawn concerning the similarity of factor structures for the two concepts and the similarity of semantic space for the two groups of subjects.

Results

Similarity of Factor Structures for the Two Concepts

Both the factor analysis for the electrical appliance manufacturer and that for the tobacco corporation produced two factors with roots greater than 1.0. As shown in Table 1, the factor structures of the two concepts are very

Table 1.   Rotated Factor Structure of
Combined Groups for Two Concepts

Scale	Tobacco Company		Appliance Manufacturer	
No.	I	II	I	II
1	.174	− .648	.863	−.041
2	.771	−.182	.131	.853
3	.697	−.208	.344	.732
4	.220	−.524	.822	.253
5	.430	−.059	−.101	.747
6	.568	−.480	.210	.796
7	−.009	.540	.809	.253
8	.749	.045	.415	.315
9	.436	−.522	.345	.445
10	.011	−.737	.859	.086

similar: that is, the pattern of factor loadings in each image is similar to that in the other.

The first column of each table lists the ten scales in the order mentioned above (Scale #1 is *pleasant-unpleasant*, #2 is *strong-weak, etc.*). In Table 1, the four columns of data list the factor loadings of every scale on each of the two factors for each concept. The first two columns of factor loadings come from the analysis of the tobacco company concept, and the last two columns are from the analysis of the appliance manufacturer concept.

The loading of a scale on a factor represents the correlation of the scale with the reference vector of that factor, and is customarily taken as a measure of the strength of association between the scale and the factor. For example, from the last 2 columns in Table 1, one concludes that Scale #1 (*pleasant-unpleasant*) is associated very strongly with Factor I of the appliance manufacturer's image (the loading is .863), and quite weakly with Factor II of the same image (the loading is − .041).

Factor I for the electrical appliance manufacturer and Factor II for the tobacco company both carry high loadings for the evaluative scales *pleasant-unpleasant, good-bad, clean-dirty*, and *beautiful-ugly*. Factor II for the electrical appliance manufacturer and Factor I for the tobacco corporation carry high loadings on the dynamism scales *strong-weak*, *sharp-dull*, and *heavy-light*. Thus, each analysis produced a factor similar to the Evaluative factor and each produced a factor similar to the Dynamism factor noted in previous studies.

Using a technique described by Ahmavaara, it is possible to test for the similarities of these factor structures in a more analytic fashion[1] [1]. Ahmavaara's technique calculates from transformation matrices the loadings of each factor from the first analysis upon each factor of the second analysis, and vice versa. The loadings of the Evaluative factor from each analysis upon the Evaluative factor of the other, and of the Dynamism factor of each analysis upon the Dynamism factor of the other all exceeded .99 in absolute magnitude. On the other hand, the loadings of the Evaluative factor from each analysis upon the Dynamism factor of the other, and of the Dynamism factor from each analysis upon the Evaluative factor of the other, were all smaller than .13 in absolute magnitude. This indicates substantial stability in factor structure from one concept to the other.

Stability of Factor Structure between Subject Groups   Both the factor analysis for the New York housewives and that for the Pitt undergraduates produced two factors with roots greater than 1.0. As can be seen from an examination of Table 2, Factor I for the undergraduates and Factor II for the housewives carry heavy loadings on the evaluative scales *pleasant-unpleasant*, *good-bad*, *clean-dirty*, and *beautiful-ugly*; the second factor for the undergraduates, along with the first factor for the housewives, contains heavy loadings on the dynamism scales *strong-weak*, *sharp-dull*, *active-passive*, *light-heavy*, and *fast-slow*.

Application of the Ahmavaara technique in this instance shows factor-to-factor loadings in excess of .97 for similarly-defined factors, and loadings smaller than .20 for oppositely designed factors. The results indicate substantial similarity in the structure of the semantic space from one group of subjects to another.

Discussion

The high degree of factorial similarity displayed by this semantic differential, both from concept to concept and from subject-group to subject-group, indicates that the instrument is quite robust within the range of differences sampled in this experiment. This finding lends support to the contention that the measuring ability of the instrument is not necessarily subverted by the characteristics of the respondents to whom it is administered, or the specific concepts measured.

---

[1] The computations were effected by means of the computer program described in A. W. Bendig's "IBM Orthogonal Factor Similarity Program [2]."

Table 2. Rotated Factor Structures of Combined Concepts for Two Subject-Groups

Scale No.	Housewives		Students	
	I	II	I	II
1	.020	.882	.857	.063
2	.723	.344	.170	.859
3	.561	.512	.172	.757
4	.285	.817	.803	.210
5	.748	.018	−.396	.587
6	.759	.140	.259	.801
7	.439	.754	.758	.114
8	.658	.400	.401	.219
9	.721	.313	.261	.340
10	.237	.713	.842	.075

Certainly the likelihood of obtaining stability in the images and in the semantic space of the subjects was enhanced by selecting scales to represent the factors most commonly obtained from analysis of semantic differential results. It has been argued that these dimensions of connotation are ubiquitous, and represent a substratum of meaning underlying our connotations for most if not all concepts. Nevertheless, there can be no guarantee that these general factors will appear in every instance. While the results of this study do not foreclose the need for pretesting in any marketing research project in which the semantic differential will be used, they do offer encouragement to those who plan to use it for the measurement of certain broad aspects of corporate images.

Advertisers and others interested in corporate images may frequently be concerned with subtler aspects of the image than these, in which case a different set of scales would have to be selected to measure more particular, and presumably less basic, dimensions of the image. Whether these subtle dimensions of meaning are sufficiently stable to allow comparisons between images for different concepts and different subject groups remains to be investigated.

References

1. Y. Ahmavaara, "Transformation Analysis of Factorial Data," *Annales Academia Scientiarum Fennica*, SER, B., No. 88 (1954).
2. A. W. Bendig, "IBM 7070 Orthogonal Factor Similarity Program." Unpublished paper, University of Pittsburgh, 1963.
3. G. A. Lazier, Theodore Clevenger, Jr., and M. L. Clark, "Stability of the Factor Structure of Smith's Semantic Differential for Theatre Concepts." Unpublished paper, Department of Speech and Theatre Arts, University of Pittsburgh, 1964.
4. Charles E. Osgood, George Suci, and Percy Tannenbaum, *The Measurement of Meaning*. Irbana: University of Illinois Press, 1957.
5. Claire Selltiz et al., *Research Methods in Social Relations*. (Rev. ed.; New York: Holt, Rinehart and Winston, 1959), 381–3.

B. Multidimensional Scaling

Torgerson noted that "The typical problem to be handled by the multi-dimensional-scaling procedures might be roughly stated as follows: Given a set of stimuli which vary with respect to an unknown number of dimensions, determine (1) the minimum dimensionality of the set and (2) projections of the stimuli (scale values) on each of the dimensions involved."[1] Thus, principal components and factor analysis are really techniques of multidimensional scaling. They address the problem of dimensionality and they provide coordinate values on the resulting dimensions. Each has desirable properties. In the case of principal components, the dimensions recover the original total variance as nearly as possible. In factor analysis, the interpretability of the dimensions is maximized. In this section other techniques of multidimensional scaling will be introduced which also have appealing properties.

Johnson develops a set of scales or a multidimensional perceptual map by using discriminant analysis. Like our examples of factor analysis, the raw data represent evaluations along a set of attributes. The objective of discriminant analysis in this context is to obtain a set of dimensions that will discriminate or separate the objects as much as possible. It has the advantage over principal components that a statistical test can be employed to determine if the observed perceptual differences among the objects could have occurred by chance. The actual output and its interpretation is very similar to that obtained with principal components or with factor analysis (with orthogonal factors).

Discriminant analysis is the one technique which is included in both the analysis of dependence and the analysis of interdependence. When Kendall originally made the distinction in 1950, he placed discriminant analysis in both categories.[2] In the analysis of dependence the focus was on predicting or explaining in which group an object belonged. In this context, the object is to identify dimensions or weighted sums of original variables that will discriminate as much as possible among the objects.

Johnson introduces the concept of an ideal point superimposed upon the perceptual map. A respondent is asked to indicate not only how he perceives

---

[1] Warren S. Torgerson, *Theory and Methods of Scaling* (New York: John Wiley & Sons, Inc. 1958), pp. 247–248.

[2] M. G. Kendall, "Factor Analysis as a Statistical Technique," *Journal of the Royal Statistical Society*, 12 (1950), 61.

brands or objects with respect to certain attributes but how an "ideal brand" would be perceived. This information provides useful guidance to marketing decision makers, especially when it is obtained for different market segments. It can suggest the creation of new brands to match the ideal brand of a worthwhile segment. It can also suggest communication strategies to change the brand perceptions of certain groups.

We have in the foregoing considered only attribute data. Johnson also observes that similarity (how similar are two objects) data can be used. When similarity data are used, the resulting perceptual map should have interobject distances that are monotonically related to the corresponding similarity index. The Aaker article discusses this relationship.

A problem with working with similarity data is that the interpretation of the resulting dimensions is considerably more difficult, since these dimensions are not related to any original set of attributes. Thus, the dimensions have to be identified either implicitly by the coordinates of the objects or by finding additional variables which might correlate with the coordinates along a certain dimension. When such variables are found, they can help the analyst interpret the dimensions.

Data can vary along an additional dimension. As observed in the introduction to Part One, there are four types of scales: nominal, ordinal, interval, and ratio. In the foregoing discussion we have assumed that all scales were interval. However, ordinal scales can also be used and have intuitive appeal. Respondents can have more difficulty rating an object in an absolute sense (along an interval scale) with respect to some variable than they would have in ranking it relative to other objects. If subjects are asked to rank a certain number of objects along a particular dimension, the resulting information is ordinal in nature. When such ordinal information provides the basis for a multidimensional scaling analysis, the results are described as nonmetric multidimensional scaling, as opposed to metric multidimensional scaling, which would involve the use of interval data.

It is possible to obtain a lower space representation of the subjects involved by using such nonmetric information. The set of tools used to obtain such a representation is discussed by Neidell. The output of nonmetric scaling is the same as that obtained from metric scaling. A set of dimensions and a corresponding set of coordinates for each object are obtained. If pairs of objects are rank ordered on the basis of similarity, the objective is to place the objects in space such that the rank order distance is the same as the rank order input as far as possible. If object A is regarded as more similar to object B than to any other object, then these two objects should be close together in the space generated by the nonmetric scaling program. As Doehlert shows, rank order preference data can be used to generate ideal points superimposed on such a perceptual map.

In Article 26 Barnett shows how multidimensional scaling can be used as the heart of a system designed to tailor scientifically a product for a target segment.

24

Richard M. Johnson: Market
Segmentation: A Strategic
Management Tool

Like motivation research in the late 1950's, market segmentation is
receiving much attention in research circles. Although this term evokes the
idea of cutting up a market into little pieces, the real role of such research is
more basic and potentially more valuable. In this discussion *market segmentation analysis* refers to examination of the structure of a market as perceived
by consumers, preferably using a geometric spatial model, and to forecasting
the intensity of demand for a potential product positioned anywhere in the
space.

The purpose of such a study, as seen by a marketing manager, might be:

1. To learn how the brands or products in a class are perceived with respect to strengths, weaknesses, similarities, etc.
2. To learn about consumers' desires, and how these are satisfied or
   unsatisfied by the current market.
3. To integrate these findings strategically, determining the greatest opportunities for new brands or products and how a product or its
   image should be modified to produce the greatest sales gain.

From the position of a marketing research technician, each of these three
goals translates into a separate technical problem:

1. To construct a product space, a geometric representation of consumers'
   perceptions of products or brands in a category.
2. To obtain a density distribution by positioning consumers' ideal
   points in the same space.
3. To construct a model which predicts preferences of groups of consumers toward new or modified products.

Reprinted from *Journal of Marketing Research*, published by the American Marketing
Association. Richard M. Johnson, "Market Segmentation—A Strategic Management
Tool," *Journal of Marketing Research*, Vol. IX, February, 1971, pp. 13–18.

This discussion will focus on each of these three problems in turn, suggesting solutions now available. Solutions to the first two problems can be illustrated with acutal data, although currently solutions for the third problem are more tentative. This will not be an exhaustive catalog of techniques, nor is this the only way of structuring the general problem of forecasting consumer demand for new or modified products.

Constructing the Product Space

A spatial representation or map of a product category provides the foundation on which other aspects of the solution are built. Many equally useful techniques are available for constructing product spaces which require different assumptions and possess different properties. The following is a list of useful properties of product spaces which may be used to evaluate alternative techniques:

1. *Metric:* distances between products in space should relate to perceived similarity between them.
2. *Identification:* directions in the space should correspond to identified product attributes.
3. *Uniqueness/reliability:* similar procedures applied to similar data should yield similar answers.
4. *Robustness/foolproofness:* procedures should work every time. It should not be necessary to switch techniques or make basic changes in order to cope with each new set of data.
5. *Freedom from improper assumptions:* other things being equal, a procedure that requires fewer assumptions is preferred.

One basic distinction has to do with the kinds of data to be analyzed. Three kinds of data are frequently used.

Similarity/Dissimilarity Data

Here a respondent is not concerned in any obvious way with dimensions or attributes which describe the products judged. He makes global judgments of relative similarity among products, with the theoretical advantage that there is no burden on the researcher to determine in advance the important attributes or dimensions within a product category. Examples of such data might be: (1) to present triples of products and ask which two are most or least similar, (2) to present pairs of products and ask which pair is most similar, or (3) to rank order k-1 products in terms of similarity with the kth.

Preference Data

Preference data can be used to construct a product space, given assumptions relating preference to distances. For instance, a frequent assumption is that an individual has ideal points in the same space and that product preference is related in some systematic way to distances from his ideal points to his perception of products' locations. As with similarity/dissimilarity data, preference data place no burden on the researcher to determine salient product attributes in advance. Examples of preference data which might lead to a product space are: (1) paired comparison data, (2) rank orders of preference, or (3) generalized overall ratings (as on a 1 to 9 scale).

Attribute Data

If the researcher knows in advance important product attributes by which consumers discriminate among products, or with which they form preferences, then he may ask respondents to describe products on scales relating to each attribute. For instance, they may use rating scales describing brands of beer with respect to price vs. quality, heaviness vs. lightness, or smoothness vs. bitterness.

In addition to these three kinds of data, *procedures* can be *metric* or *nonmetric*. Metric procedures make assumptions about the properties of data, as when in computing a mean one assumes that the difference between ratings of values one and two is the same as that between two and three, etc. Nonmetric procedures make fewer assumptions about the nature of the data; these are usually techniques in which the only operations on data are comparisons such as "greater than" or "less than." Nonmetric procedures are typically used with data from rank order or paired comparison methods.

Another issue is whether or not a *single product space* will adequately represent all respondents' perceptions. At the extreme, each respondent might require a unique product space to account for aspects of his perceptions. However, one of the main reasons for product spaces' utility is that they summarize a large amount of information in unusually tangible and compact form. Allowing a totally different product space for each respondent would certainly destroy much of the illustrative value of the result. A compromise would be to recognize that respondents might fall naturally into a relatively small number of subgroups with different product perceptions. In this case, a separate product space could be constructed for each subgroup.

Frequently a single product space is assumed to be adequate to account for important aspects of all respondents' *perceptions*. Differences in *preference* are then taken into account by considering each respondent's ideal product to have a unique location in the common product space, and by recognizing that different respondents may weight dimensions uniquely. This was the approach taken in the examples to follow.

Techniques which have received a great deal of use in constructing product spaces include nonmetric multidimensional scaling [3, 7, 8, 12], factor analysis [11], and multiple discriminant analysis [4]. Factor analysis has been available for this purpose for many years, and multidimensional scaling was discussed as early as 1938 [13]. *Nonmetric* multidimensional scaling, a comparatively recent development, has achieved great popularity because of the invention of ingenious computing methods requiring only the most minimal assumptions regarding the nature of the data. Discriminant analysis requires assumptions about the metric properties of data, but it appears to be particularly robust and foolproof in application.

These techniques produce similar results in most practical applications. The technique of multiple discriminant analysis will be illustrated here.

Examples of Product Spaces

Imagine settling on a number of attributes which together account for all of the important ways in which products in a set are seen to differ from each other. Suppose that each product has been rated on each attribute by several people, although each person has not necessarily described more than one product.

Given such data, multiple discriminant analysis is a powerful technique for constructing a spatial model of the product category. First, it finds the weighted combination of attributes which discriminates most among products maximizing an *F*-ratio of between-product to within-product variance. Then second and subsequent weighted combinations are found which discriminate maximally among products, within the constraint that they all be uncorrelated with one another. Having determined as many discriminating dimensions as possible, average scores can be used to plot products on each dimension. Distances between pairs of products in this space reflect the amount of discrimination between them.[1]

Figure 1 shows such a space for the Chicago beer market as perceived by members of Market Facts' Consumer Mail Panels in a pilot study, September 1968. Approximately 500 male beer drinkers described 8 brands of beer on each of 35 attributes. The data indicated that a third sizable dimension also existed, but the two dimensions pictured here account for approximately 90% of discrimination among images of these 8 products.

The location of each brand is indicated on these two major dimensions. The horizontal dimension contrasts premium quality on the right with popular price on the left. The vertical dimension reflects relative lightness. In addition, the mean rating of each product on each of the attributes is shown by relative

---

[1] McKeon [10] has shown that multiple discriminant analysis produces the same results as classic (metric) multidimensional scaling of Mahalanobis' distances based on the same data.

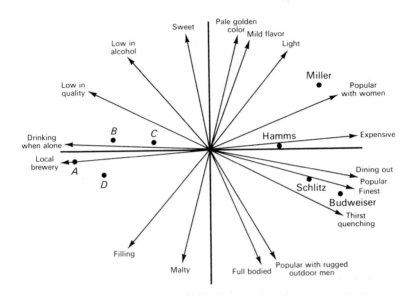

Figure 1. The Chicago Beer Market

position on each attribute vector. For instance, Miller is perceived as being most popular with women, followed by Budweiser, Schlitz, Hamms, and four unnamed, popularly priced beers.

As a second example, the same technique was applied to political data. During the weeks immediately preceding the 1968 presidential election, a questionnaire was sent to 1,000 Consumer Mail Panels households. Respondents were asked to agree or disagree with each of 35 political statements on a four-point scale. Topics were Vietnam, law and order, welfare, and other issues felt to be germane to current politics. Respondents also described two preselected political figures, according to their perceptions of each figure's stand on each issue. Discriminant analysis indicated two major dimensions accounting for 86% of the discrimination among 14 political figures.

The liberal vs. conservative dimension is apparent in the data, as shown in Figure 2. The remaining dimension apparently reflects perceived favorability of attitude toward government involvement in domestic and international matters. As in the beer space, it is only necessary to erect perpendiculars to each vector to observe each political figure's relative position on each of the 35 issues. Additional details are in [5].

Multiple discriminant analysis is a major competitor of nonmetric multi-dimensional scaling in constructing product spaces. The principal assumptions which the former requires are that: (1) perceptions be homogeneous across respondents, (2) attribute data be scaled at the interval level (equal intervals on rating scales), (3) attributes be linearly related to one another, and (4)

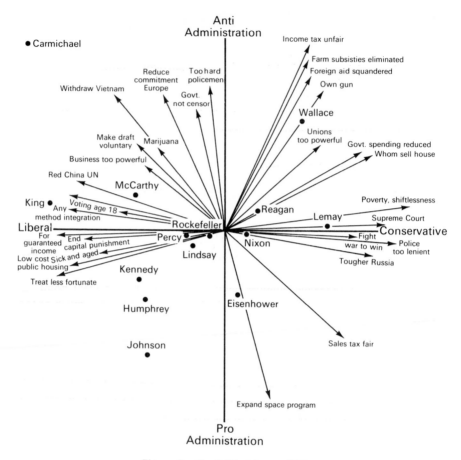

Figure 2.   The Political Space, 1968

amount of disagreement (error covariance matrix) be the same for each product.

Only the first of these assumptions is required by most nonmetric methods and some even relax that assumption. However, the space provided by multiple discriminant analysis has the following useful properties:

1. Given customary assumptions of multivariate normality, there is a test of significance for distance (dissimilarity) between any two products.
2. Unlike nonmetric procedures, distances estimated among a collection of products do not depend upon whether or not additional products are included in the analysis. Any of the brands of beer or political figures could have been deleted from the examples and the remaining object locations would have had the same relationships to one another and to the attribute vectors.
3. The technique is reliable and well known, and solutions are unique, since the technique cannot be misled any by local optimum.

Obtaining the Distribution of Consumers' Ideal Points

After constructing a product space, the next concern is estimating consumer demand for a product located at any particular point. The demand function over such a space is desired and can be approximated by one of several general approaches.

The first is to locate each person's ideal point in the region of the space implied by his rank ordered preferences. His ideal point would be closest to the product he likes best, second closest to the product he likes second best, etc. There are several procedures which show promise using this approach [2, 3, 7, 8, 12], although difficulties remain in practical execution. This approach has trouble dealing with individuals who behave in a manner contrary to the basic assumptions of the model, as when one chooses products first on the far left side of the space, second on the far right side, and third in the center. Most individuals giving rank orders of preference do display such non-monotonicity to some extent, understandably producing problems for the application of these techniques.

The second approach involves deducing the number of ideal points at each region in space by using data on whether a product has too much or too little of each attribute. This procedure has not yet been fully explored, but at present seems to be appropriate to the multidimensional case only when strong assumptions about the shape of the ideal point distribution are given.

The third approach is to have each person describe his ideal product, with the same attributes and rating scales as for existing products. If multiple discriminant analysis has been used to obtain a product space, each person's ideal product can then be inserted in the same space.

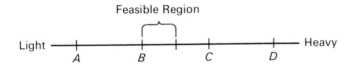

Figure 3. A One-Dimensional Product Space

There are considerable differences between an ideal point location inferred from a rank order of preference and one obtained directly from an attribute rating. To clarify matters, consider a single dimension, heaviness vs. lightness in beer. If a previous mapping has shown that Brands A, B, C, and D are equally spaced on this one dimension, and if a respondent ranks his preferences as B, C, A, and D, then his ideal must lie closer to B than to A or C and closer to C than to A. This narrows the feasible region for his ideal point down to the area indicated in Figure 3. Had he stated a preference for A, with D second, there would be no logically corresponding position for his ideal point in the space.

However, suppose these products have already been given the following scale positions on a heavy/light dimension: $A = 1.0$, $B = 2.0$, $C = 3.0$, and $D = 4.0$. If a respondent unambiguously specifies his ideal on this scale at 2.25, his ideal can be put directly on the scale, with no complexities. Of course, it does not follow *necessarily* that his stated rank order of preference will be predictable from the location of his ideal point.

There is no logical reason why individuals must be clustered into market segments. Mathematically, one can cope with the case where hundreds or thousands of individual ideal points are each located in the space. However, it is much easier to approximate such distributions by clustering respondents into groups. Cluster analysis [6] has been used with the present data to put individuals into a few groups with relatively similar product desires (beer) or points of view (politics).

Figure 4 shows an approximation to the density distribution of consumers' ideal points in the Chicago beer market, a "poor man's contour

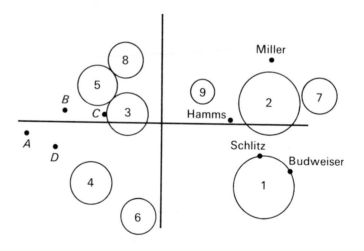

Figure 4. Distribution of Ideal Points in Product Space

map." Ideal points tended somewhat to group themselves (circles) into clusters. It is not implied that all ideal points lie within the circles, since they are really distributed to some extent throughout the entire space. Circle sizes indicate the relative sizes of clusters, and the center of each is located at the center of its circle.

A representation such as this contains much potentially useful marketing information. For instance, if people can be assumed to prefer products closer to their ideal points, there may be a ready market for a new brand on the lower or "heavy" side of the space, approximately neutral in price/quality.

Likewise, there may be opportunities for new brands in the upper middle region, decidedly light and neutral in price/quality. Perhaps popularly priced Brand *A* will have marketing problems, since this brand is closest to no cluster.

Figure 5 shows a similar representation for the political space, where circles represent concentrations of voters' points. These are not ideal points,

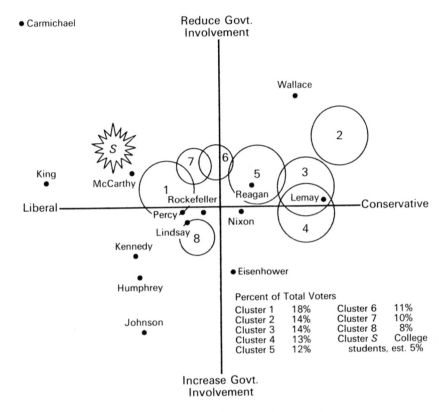

Figure 5. Voter Segment Positions Relative to Political Figures

but rather personally held positions on political issues. Clusters on the left side of the space intended to vote mostly for Humphrey and those on the right for Nixon in the 1968 election. Throughout the space, the percentage voting Republican increases generally from left to right.

It may be surprising that the center of the ideal points lies considerably to the right of that of the political figures. One possible explanation is that this study dealt solely with positions on *issues*, so matters of style or personality did not enter the definition of the space. It is entirely possible that members of clusters one and eight, the most liberal, found Nixon's position on issues approximately as attractive as Humphrey's, but they voted for Humphrey on the basis of preference for style, personality, or political party. Likewise, members of cluster two might have voted strongly for Wallace, given his position, but he received only 14% of this cluster's vote. He may have been rejected on the basis of other qualities. The clusters are described in more detail in [5].

A small experiment was undertaken to test the validity of this model. Responses from a class of sociology students in a western state university showed them to be more liberal and more for decreasing government involvement internationally than any of the eight voter clusters. Their position is close to McCarthy's, indicated by an " S."

Strategic Integration of Findings

Having determined the position of products in a space and seen where consumer ideal points are located, how can such findings be integrated to determine appropriate product strategy? A product's market share should be increased by repositioning: (1) closer to ideal points of sizable segments of the market, (2) farther from other products with which it must compete, and (3) on dimensions weighted heavily in consumers' preferences. Even these broad guidelines provide some basis for marketing strategy. For instance, in Figure 4, Brand A is clearly farthest from all clusters and should be repositioned.

In Figure 5, Humphrey, Kennedy, and Johnson could have increased their acceptance with this respondent sample by moving upwards and to the right, modifying their perceived position. Presumably, endorsement of any issue in the upper right quadrant or a negative position on any issue in the lower left quadrant of Figure 2 would have helped move Humphrey closer to the concentration of voters' ideal points.

Although the broad outlines of marketing strategy are suggested by spaces such as these, it would be desirable to make more precise quantitative forecasts of the effect of modifying a product's position. Unfortunately, the problem of constructing a model to explain product choice behavior based on locations of ideal points and products in a multidimensional space has not yet been completely solved, although some useful approaches are currently available.

As the first step, it is useful to concentrate on the behavior of clusters of respondents rather than that of individuals, especially if clusters are truly homogeneous. Data predicting behavior of groups are much smoother and results for a few groups are far more communicable to marketing management than findings stated in terms of large numbers of individual respondents.

If preference data are available for a collection of products, one can analyze the extent to which respondents' preferences are related to distances in the space. Using regression analysis, one can estimate a set of importance weights for each cluster or, if desired, for each respondent, to be applied to the dimensions of the product space. Weights would be chosen providing the best explanation of cluster or individual respondent preferences in terms of weighted distances between ideal points and each product's perceived location. If clusters, rather than individuals, are used, it may be desirable to first calculate preference scale values or utilities for each cluster [1, 9]. Importance weights can then be obtained using multiple regression to predict these values from distances. If explanations of product preference can be made for *existing products*, which depend only on locations in space, then the same approach should permit *predictions* of preference levels for new or modified products to be positioned at specific locations in the space.

Models of choice behavior clearly deserve more attention. Although the problem of constructing the product space has received much attention, we are denied the full potential of these powerful solutions unless we are able to quantify relationships between distances in such a space and consumer choice behavior.

Summary

Market segmentation studies can produce results which indicate desirable marketing action. Techniques which are presently available can: (1) construct a product space, (2) discover the shape of the distribution of consumers' ideal points throughout such a space, and (3) identify likely opportunities for new or modified products.

In the past, marketing research has often been restricted to *tactical* questions such as package design or pricing levels. However, with the advent of new techniques, marketing research can contribute directly to the development of *strategic* alternatives to current product marketing plans. There remains a need for improved technology, particularly in the development of models for explaining and predicting preferential choice behavior. The general problem has great practical significance, and provides a wealth of opportunity for development of new techniques and models.

References

1. Bradley, M. E. and R. A. Terry. "Rank Analysis of Incomplete Block Designs: The Method of Paired Comparisons," *Biometrika*, 39 (1952), 324–45.

2. Carroll, J. D. "Individual Differences and Multidimensional Scaling," Murray Hill, N.J.: Bell Telephone Laboratories, 1969.

3. Guttman, Louis. "A General Nonmetric Technique for Finding the Smallest Space for a Configuration of Points," *Psychometrika*, 33 (December 1968), 469–506.

4. Johnson, Richard M. "Multiple Discriminant Analysis," unpublished paper, Workshop on Multivariate Methods in Marketing, University of Chicago, 1970.

5. ———. "Political Segmentation," paper presented at Spring Conference on Research Methodology, American Marketing Association, New York, 1969.

6. Johnson, Stephen C. "Hierarchical Clustering Schemes," *Psychometrika*, 32 (September 1967), 241–54.

7. Kruskal, Joseph B. "Multidimensional Scaling by Optimizing Goodness of Fit to a Nonmetric Hypothesis," *Psychometrika*, 29 (March, 1964), 1–27.

8. ———. "Nonmetric Multidimensional Scaling: A Numerical Method," *Psychometrika*, 29 (June 1964), 115–29.

9. Luce, R. D. "A Choice Theory Analysis of Similarity Judgments," *Psychometrika*, 26 (September 1961), 325–32.

10. McKeon, James J. "Canonical Analysis," *Psychometric Monographs*, 13.

11. Tucker, Ledyard. "Dimensions of Preference," Research Memorandum RM-60-7, Princeton, N.J.: Educational Testing Service, 1960.

12. Young, F. W. "TORSCA, An IBM Program for Nonmetric Multidimensional Scaling," *Journal of Marketing Research*, 5 (August 1968), 319–21.

13. Young, G. and A. S. Householder. "Discussion of a Set of Points in Terms of Their Mutual Distances," *Psychometrika*, 3 (March 1938), 19–22.

25

Lester A. Neidell: The Use of
Nonmetric Multidimensional Scaling
in Marketing Analysis

Within the past two years marketing analysts have made increasing reference to new methodology, loosely referred to as "scaling."[1] These references are often confusing to the marketing executive for they do not pertain to the scaling procedures such as rating scales, paired comparisons, semantic differentiation, and scalogram analysis, which have been utilized previously in marketing studies. Instead, many analysts are now referring to the set of techniques called nonmetric multidimensional scaling which seems to be admirably suited to the analysis of several problem areas in marketing.

The purposes of this paper are: (1) to explain, in a nontechnical fashion, the theory and procedures underlying nonmetric multidimensional scaling; (2) to present an example of its use; and (3) to speculate on further marketing applications.

Reprinted from *Journal of Marketing*, published by the American Marketing Association. Lester A. Neidell, "The Use of Nonmetric Multidimensional Scaling in Marketing Analysis," *Journal of Marketing*, Vol. 33, October 1969, pp. 37–43.

[1] Yoram Wind, "Mathematical Analysis of Perception and Preference for Industrial Marketing," in Keith Cox and Ben M. Enis, eds., *A New Measure of Responsibility for Marketing* (Chicago, Ill.: American Marketing Association, June, 1968), pp. 284–294; James R. Taylor, "The Meaning and Structure of Data as Related to Scaling Models," in Robert L. King, ed., *Marketing and the New Science of Planning* (Chicago, Ill.: American Marketing Association, August, 1968), pp. 309–315.

The Problem of Measurement

Measurement involves the assignment of numbers to objects or properties of objects according to a set of rules. The rules by which numbers are assigned during measurement define the properties of the scales which are a result of measurement.[2] For example, road mileages represent a *ratio* scale, so-called because the ratios of distances among cities have meaning. A natural origin—zero point—exists from which all distances can be measured. In many instances of measurement, however, a natural zero does not exist, yet the size of the distance between *pairs* of objects has meaning. These are called *interval* scales. A very obvious example is the measurement of temperature in which different arbitrary zero points are established according to the rules of the measurement process one is using. Thus, regardless of the temperature scale being used, it is correct to say that the temperature difference from 20° to 40° is twice that of 20° to 30°, but it is not correct to say that 40° is twice as warm as 20°.

Ratio and interval scales are both *metric* scales because they contain information about equality relationships (that is, *how much* larger or smaller) among the objects being measured. Explicit distance functions are defined by the rules of measurement. It is possible, however, to generate scales by rules of measurement in which inter-object relationships are described simply by inequality or *nonmetric* relationships (that is, *which one* is larger or smaller), as will be shown. The rules of the measurement process which produce nonmetric scales are (1) objects can be ordered, and (2) (sometimes) intervals among objects can be ordered.

Relevance to the Marketing Situation

People cannot ordinarily provide accurate and reliable data about equality relationships among objects such as competing brands, or about brand characteristics. Psychological evidence of this is overwhelming.[3] Yet because of the ease of manipulating metric data, and because of the lack of nonmetric analytical procedures, marketing analysts have invariably assumed the existence of a metric scale. For example, analysts using a *t* test of significance applied to different rating scale scores frequently assume an interval (metric) scale where it is not appropriate.

At this point, it is entirely proper to ask, " So what? What harm is being done? And, do you have a better method?"

---

[2] Warren S. Torgerson, *Theory and Methods of Scaling* (New York: John Wiley and Sons, Inc., 1958), Chapter 1.

[3] Same reference as footnote 2, Chapters 4–10. Also Roger N. Shepard, "Metric Structures in Ordinal Data," *Journal of Mathematical Psychology*, Vol. 3 (July, 1966), pp. 287–315, at pp. 310–312; and Frank Restle, *Psychology of Judgment and Choice* (New York: John Wiley and Sons, Inc., 1961).

The lack of recognition that different assumptions can be made about data may account for some of the disappointing results which have been reported in attempts to predict market behavior. By assuming interval data when neither data nor theory supports it, the marketing analyst, in interpreting (for example) the results of consumer product evaluations, is quite liable to postulate that unnecessarily strong relationships exist between the evaluations and subsequent consumer behavior. When a relationship is not verified by empirical evidence, the validity of the relationship is questioned, when the error may lie instead in the *strength* of the postulated relationship.

Metric Results from Nonmetric Inputs

The techniques of nonmetric multidimensional scaling require only nonmetric (ordinal) input measures, yet metric (ratio scale) results are ordinarily obtained. This result, metrically invariant output from only ordinal input, stems from the reduction in the number of constraints needed to represent a k dimensional nonmetric solution in a metric space of less than k dimensions. This can be demonstrated intuitively.

All order relationships among n objects can be depicted in a space of n-1 dimensions.[4] As an example, the distance between any two objects can be represented by a straight line which is a unidimensional space. Similarly the distance relationships among any three objects can be completely described by a triangle which requires only a two-dimensional space to represent the three order relationships. As the number of objects (n) becomes large, the number of order relationships (that is, nonmetric constraints) required grows approximately with the *square* of n (actually $[n(n-1)/2]$). *However, the number of metric constraints required for complete specification of n points grows only linearly with n.* Thus, 45 *ordinal* relationships $[10(10-1)/2 = 45]$ are required to show completely the structure among ten objects. If one were to plot these same ten objects in a two-dimensional space, only 20 coordinates ($n \cdot k$ or $10 \cdot 2$) would be needed. The net result is that with large n a metric solution involving a space of considerably fewer dimensions may be obtained within the set of $[n(n-1)/2]$ relationships. In Shepard's words, "... the metric information was contained in the original numbers all along —only in such a dilute form that we did not recognize it. But when this same information is squeezed into a smaller set of numbers, it finally becomes concentrated enough to be recognized for what it is."[5]

---

[4] J. F. Bennett and W. L. Hays, "Multidimensional Unfolding: Determining the Dimensionality of Ranked Preference Data, *Psychometrika*, Vol. 25 (December, 1960), pp. 27–43.

[5] Roger N. Shepard, "Analysis of Proximities as a Technique for the Study of Information Processing in Man," *Human Factors* (February, 1963), pp. 33–48, at p. 35.

The Roadmap Problem—An Illustrative Example

A useful way of evaluating any new analytical procedure is to relate it to a problem with a known solution. In this case the problem to be considered was the placement of key cities on a map of the United States.[6]

In terms of nonmetric multidimensional scaling, the minimum data necessary to "solve" this problem are the rank orders of the inter-city distances. An atlas of the United States was used in calculating inter-city road mileages among all pairs of 15 cities. There are, therefore, 105 inter-city distances $[n(n-1)/2]$. Conversion of actual inter-city distances into rank order data was achieved by assigning the number "1" to the shortest road distance, that is, Boston-New York; the number "2" to the next shortest distance, that is, Kansas City-St. Louis; and so on, until all 105 inter-city distances were assigned a number. Ties were given equal numbers. This data base of rank orders was then utilized as input to a nonmetric multidimensional scaling program.

Clearly, the solution to the problem of city placement is known. What is required is a two-dimensional figure, with the axes labeled north-south and east-west. The nonmetric multidimensional scaling result should indicate clearly a two-dimensional solution and should place the cities in their correct geographic location on a United States map.

In Figure 1 the two-dimensional result obtained from a nonmetric multi-dimensional scaling program[7] is compared to the actual geographic locations of the cities. The correct geographic locations are identified by a dot (·) and the scaling solution by an "x." The fit between the scaling positions and actual geographic locations is quite good, although errors of approximately 200 miles are evident in the South and West. However, a substantial part of the error can be explained.

The differences are due primarily to imperfect data. Road distances often are *not* the shortest straight line distances between any pair of cities, but reflect natural detours such as mountain ranges and lakes, and the intricacy of the road network in any section of the country. The imperfections in the mileage data base affected some of the rank order placements. Thus, cities which are more inaccessible due to terrain and/or to being in more sparsely settled sections of the country are more likely to be "out of place" on the nonmetric scaling solution. This is indeed the case as shown by the locations of Miami, New Orleans, Phoenix, and Los Angeles.

In other words, the data base used for nonmetric multidimensional scaling in this example was both systematically and randomly biased, not unlike the data often available to marketing practitioners.

[6] Marshall G. Greenberg, "A Variety of Approaches to Nonmetric Multidimensional Scaling," Paper presented at the 16th International Meeting of the Institute of Management Sciences, New York (March, 1969).

[7] The actual program used was TORSCA. See F. W. Young and W. S. Torgerson, "TORSCA, A Fortran IV Program for Shepard-Kruskal Multidimensional Scaling Analysis," *Behavioral Science*, Vol. 12 (July, 1967), pp. 498–9.

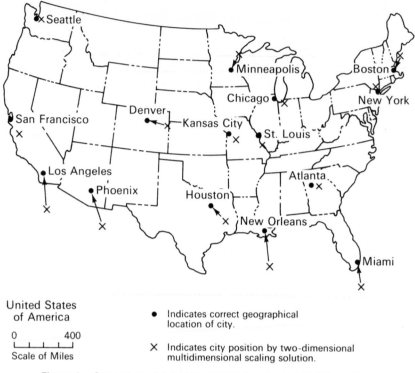

Figure 1. Comparison of Actual Geographic Locations of 15 Cities with the Locations Defined by the Two-Dimensional Multidimensional Scaling Solution

This roadmap has illustrated four aspects of nonmetric multidimensional scaling methods which must be understood in order to comprehend fully the novelty and the power of this set of techniques. These aspects are the nonmetric input, the metric output, the number of dimensions, and the interpretation of the dimensions.

The Number and Interpretation of Dimensions

In the roadmap example the true dimensionality of the solution was known. This is usually not the case in marketing analyses, as one of the variables under study *is* the number (and interpretation) of dimensions necessary to represent the data. Currently there are programmed statistical techniques[8]

---

[8] Same reference as footnote 7. Also Joseph B. Kruskal, "Multidimensional Scaling by Optimizing Goodness of Fit to a Nonmetric Hypothesis," *Psychometrika*, Vol. 29 (March, 1964), pp.–27, and "Nonmetric Multidimensional Scaling: A Numerical Method," *Psychometrika*, Vol. 29 (June, 1964), pp. 115–29.

which will assist the analyst in determining the appropriate number of dimensions required.

Interpretation of the dimensions is a matter of the investigator's judgment, as is true in factor analysis. Multidimensional scaling does not inherently provide any clues, but inspection of the objects in the extremes of the solution space or inclusion in the analysis of an object with "known" attributes can provide clues. Referring again to the roadmap example, one might look for the cities Miami and Seattle, knowing that they represent the extremes of Southeast and Northwest.

In summary, the techniques described in this paper utilize only order relationships among data, but can often provide metric information about distance relationships. Moreover, a *multi*dimensional solution may result even though the input measures were merely unidimensional (that is, the rank orders of the inter-object relationships).

Applications of Nonmetric Multidimensional Scaling to Marketing Problems

Marketing analyses often involve two distinct types of data bases. In one case the data such as sales, profits, or the presence or absence of a particular product feature are objectively determined. In the second case the data are defined by the perceptual processes of individuals. Examples of this type of data are perceptions, attitudes, and preferences. In many cases analysis of the same problem utilizing the two types of data can yield disparate results. A hypothetical problem will make this clear.

Suppose it were desirable to determine if the Chevrolet Camaro is more similar to the Pontiac Firebird than to the Ford Mustang. Clearly, there are several characteristics or attributes associated with all of these specialty cars. Each attribute, however, may be "more" or "less" associated with any one car. In order to evaluate the similarity among the three cars, a *set of* attributes (assuming that a common reference frame or set of attributes is suitable) must be considered. This set of attributes can possibly be represented (or modeled) geometrically, so that the "distance" between any of the three automobiles represents the degree to which they possess similar "scores" on the common attributes. This attribute space for specialty automobiles might be developed either by (1) asking consumers for their estimates (perceptions) of similarity, or by (2) objectively deriving it from measurement of horsepower, weight, and braking of the three automobiles.

The two attribute spaces may not be the same. People may not perceive differences in some of the objective measures, or their perceptions of these measures may not be "correct." In order to distinguish between objectively measured and people-derived attribute spaces, it is convenient to call the former "performance spaces" and the latter "perceptual spaces."

Development of a Perceptual Space

For many products purchasing behavior is believed to be related more to perceived product features (including something called "product image") than to actual performance characteristics. This might be true perhaps in explaining consumer purchasing patterns with respect to frequently purchased grocery items such as detergent, coffee, and beer. Similarly, it has been suggested that perceptions, rather than objective analysis of laboratory reports, can "explain" physician selection of competing brands of ethical pharmaceuticals.

In a recently completed pilot study, physician perceptions of, and preferences for, brands of drugs within two classes of ethical pharmaceuticals were analyzed.[9] Figure 2 illustrates a typical perceptual space derived in this

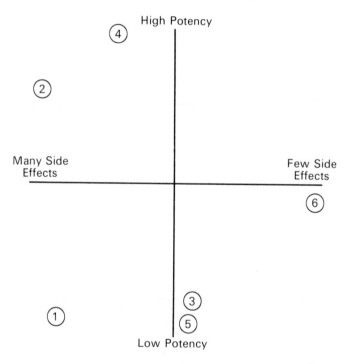

Figure 2. Perceptual Space of Brands of Ethical Pharmaceuticals

study. A composite space of only two dimensions based on a statistical goodness of fit measure and on interpretability appeared to be necessary to portray accurately inter-brand relationships.

---

[9] Lester A. Neidell, *Physician Perception and Evaluation of Selected Ethical Drugs: An Application of Nonmetric Multidimensional Scaling to Pharmaceutical Marketing*, unpublished doctoral dissertation, University of Pennsylvania, 1969.

To develop this perceptual space data were collected from a sample of general medical practitioners who were simply asked to render overall similarity judgments for all product pairs. Two methods of data collection were utilized successfully—triadic combinations and rating scales. These procedures are illustrated in Table 1. The critical aspect is that in neither method

Table 1. Illustration of the Methods of Data Collection Used in the Physician Study

Method of Triadic Combinations
  Instructions: Select the two *most* similar and the two *least* similar brands in each triple.

	Most Similar	Least Similar
Brand *A*	( )	( )
Brand *B*	( )	( )
Brand *C*	( )	( )

  All possible combinations of triples [(6!/3!3!) = 20] were included.

Rating Scale Method
  Instructions: Compare the five remaining brands to the brand acting as an anchor point by assigning a number which reflects your assessment of their overall similarity to the anchor point brand.

Reference Scale

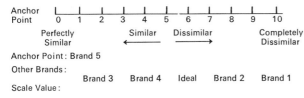

Anchor
Point   0   1   2   3   4   5   6   7   8   9   10

Perfectly   Similar   Dissimilar   Completely
Similar   ←———   ———→   Dissimilar

Anchor Point: Brand 5

Other Brands:
          Brand 3   Brand 4   Ideal   Brand 2   Brand 1
Scale Value:
          _____   _____   _____   _____   _____

Each brand in turn acted as an anchor point. While interval measures might be derived from this procedure only the ordinal results were utilized.

were the criteria for determining similarity stated. Individual response data were aggregated, and the aggregate or average perceptions were analyzed using a nonmetric multidimensional scaling program. Conceptually, the data used to develop this attribute space are vastly different from those used in performance space studies. However, after the similarity measures used for input are derived, the computational procedure is identical.

Figure 2 contains five "real" brands (Brands 1-5) which were identified during data collection, and one hypothetical brand (Brand 6) which was labeled the hypothetical "Ideal brand" during data collection. The concept of the "Ideal brand" is a simple one; it merely states that the closer a real brand is to the "Ideal brand," the more preferred is the real brand.[10] By definition, the "Ideal brand" is the most preferred brand.

This use of the "Ideal brand" concept introduces another aspect of nonmetric multidimensional scaling. *Preferences and/or preference distribution can*

---

[10] Clyde H. Coombs, *A Theory of Data* (New York: John Wiley and Sons, Inc., 1964), p. 141.

be super-imposed on, or jointly derived with, most attribute spaces, for both performance and perceptual data.[11]

The usefulness of this feature can be demonstrated by analyzing Figure 2. Suppose that this sample of physicians was actually a representative national sample, and further, that the two dimensions were equally important to the sample. Since by definition the "Ideal brand" would be most preferred, this suggests that Brands 3 and 5 would have the largest market shares of the five brands. If a drug manufacturer were to introduce a new brand in this product class, he would attempt to place it close to the "Ideal brand."

Labeling of the axes of this perceptual space was achieved by analyzing other data collected during the study and by relying on the advice of knowledgeable people in the pharmaceutical industry. The two dimensions were identified as "potency" and "side effects." Thus, Brands 2 and 4 were perceived to be highly potent, but also to induce (undesirable) side effects. Brands 1, 3, and 5 were perceived to be considerably weaker than the other two brands, but despite this, Brand 1 still had associated with it undesirable side effects.

Market Segmentation Analysis

In terms of marketing strategy, the position of the "Ideal brand" (Brand 6) suggests that a more "ideal" brand might be introduced. This implies, however, that a single "Ideal brand" exists which will be the "most preferred" brand for all respondents. Alternatively, *different* "Ideal brands" might exist. For example, suppose that the similarities data were collected from two distinct sets of physicians, one group of which placed the "Ideal brand" near Brands 2 and 4, while the other perceived their "Ideal brand" to be similar to Brands 3 and 5. If this were true, then the single "average Ideal" would be one that satisfies neither of these groups very well.

To further complicate marketing strategy decisions, the perceptual spaces of the *real brands* may not be similar. For example, on the average Brands 2 and 4 were perceived as similar; however, there may be a subset of respondents who did not believe this to be true. For this particular product class the possibility that different perceptual maps existed was supported by clinical evidence. According to this evidence, the interbrand relationships of Brands 1, 3, 4, and 5 were accurately portrayed, but the positioning of Brand 2 was inaccurate. Brand 2 should have been midway between Brand 4 and Brands 3 and 5 in both potency and side effects. Was it possible that some of the respondent physicians did in fact perceive the relationships of Brand 2 to the other four brands "correctly"?

---

[11] See Paul E. Green, Frank J. Carmone, and Patrick J. Robinson, *Analysis of Marketing Behavior Using Nonmetric Scaling and Related Techniques* (Cambridge, Massachusetts: Marketing Science Institute, March, 1968).

In summary, average perceptual maps may be a statistical artifact. In order to decide among alternative strategies it is necessary to assess the scatter or variability of perceptions.

A procedure called cluster analysis was utilized to determine if the aggregate perceptual maps did in fact disguise the existence of different perceptual maps. The objective of cluster analysis is to delineate any natural groupings that exist in a set of data.[12] No clearly defined rules exist, how-

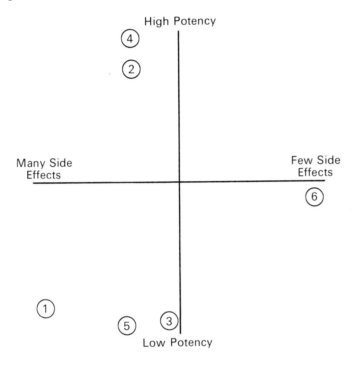

Figure 3.   Perceptual Map of First Market Segment

ever, to determine an "optimum" number of clusters to extract from any given data bank. In this particular product class, analysis of the volume of potential segments suggested that a maximum of two market segments could be profitably developed. Accordingly, only two clusters of respondents were developed. Similarities judgments were aggregated within each cluster, and again nonmetric multidimensional scaling was applied. The results are shown in Figures 3 and 4.

---

[12] See R. R. Sokal and P. H. A. Sneath, *Principles of Numerical Taxonomy* (San Francisco: Freeman and Company, 1963); Stephen C. Johnson, "Hierarchical Clustering Schemes," *Psychometrika*, Vol. 32 (March, 1965), pp. 241–254; and Paul E. Green, Ronald Frank, and Patrick Robinson, "Cluster Analysis in Test Market Selection," *Management Science*, Vol. 13 (April, 1967), pp. B387–B400.

Figures 2 (aggregate analysis) and 3 (first market segment) are quite similar with respect to interbrand relationships. However, in Figure 4 (which represents a second market segment) Brand 2 was perceived as being medium in potency and side effects, as suggested by the clinical evidence. The "Ideal brand" for this subset of respondents also "moved"; it was very similar to Brands 3 and 5.

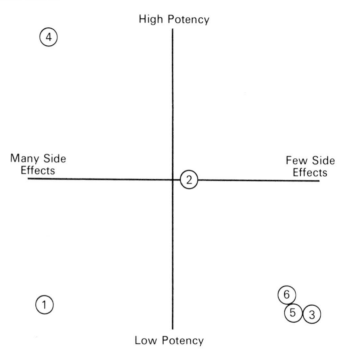

Figure 4. Perceptual Map of Second Market Segment

In both market segments, Brands 3 and 5 were closest to the "Ideal," suggesting that a single "optimum" brand choice might resemble either of these two brands. Such a choice, however, would leave a company very vulnerable to competition in segment one, since there is room for a brand to be "more ideal" in terms of the needs of these physicians. This choice would also face extremely stiff competition in segment two where it would be difficult to move a new brand into a position closer to the "Ideal" than either Brands 3 or 5. Thus, if this were a completely virgin market and if the brand placements were hypothetical entities, a brand resembling 3 and 5 might be considered optimum. Given the existing market structure, the preferred strategy would probably be to concentrate on segment one where the possibility of satisfying unfilled customer needs is much greater than in segment two.

In summary, different preferences (that is, "Ideal brand" locations) rather than different "real brand" perceptions would be the major consideration in implementing a segmentation strategy for this particular product class. In both segments, the "Ideal brand" is one with few side effects. Some physicians feel the "Ideal" should be medium in potency, perhaps in order to more easily control the dosage. Other physicians prefer a drug which is relatively ineffective, possibly because they feel this product is useful only as a placebo. Whatever the reasons for the different perceptual maps, it is clear that a strategy of market segmentation is feasible.

Additional Uses and Limitations

This example has only hinted at the range of possible applications of nonmetric multidimensional scaling in marketing. In addition to market segmentation analysis and new product studies, the techniques of nonmetric multidimensional scaling might be applied to the study of product life cycle. vendor and advertising evaluation, test marketing, salesmen and store image studies, and brand switching research.[13]

This is not to say that there are no limitations or problems to this methodology. There are. First of all there is a practical problem—data availability. This is particularly true in developing *perceptual spaces*, because the data must often be specially collected. Therefore, these analyses can be expensive, as anyone involved in empirical research can testify.

Second, there are computational problems. How unique are the attribute spaces given noisy and/or missing data? How reliable, statistically, are the solutions? It is clear that additional empirical and analytical work is needed in this area.

Third, there are theoretical questions. One of these concerns distance measurement. In the results discussed above, the ordinary Euclidean distance measure was utilized. There are other distance measures, which if utilized, might change drastically some of the interpretations earlier suggested.[14] One distance measure suggested in psychological literature is the "city-block" measure, in which distance between any two objects is *not* the shortest straight line distance, but is instead a function of the absolute distance traveled in terms of corners or right angles.

This limited discussion of the possible pitfalls of these new techniques is intended to indicate that, as with *any* set of analytical procedures, there are unresolved issues. Nonmetric multidimensional scaling offers the possibility of new insights into analysis of market behavior. It cannot, however, be used indiscriminately.

---

[13] Paul E. Green and Frank J. Carmone, "The Performance Structure of the Computer Market: A Multivariate Approach," *Economic and Business Bulletin*, Vol. 21 (Fall, 1969), pp. 1–11, and same reference as footnote 11, Chapter 1.

[14] Roger N. Shepard, "Attention and the Metric Structure of the Stimulus," *Journal of Mathematical Psychology*, Vol. 1 (February, 1964), pp. 54–87.

Summary

This paper has tried to introduce the reader to a set of new analytical procedures—nonmetric multidimensional scaling. An acquaintance with the specialized language of this technique is necessary to fully comprehend its possibilities. The central idea is that a multidimensional *attribute space* can be developed from a unidimensional data bank in which distances represent the degree of similarity among objects. Potential applications cover many facets of marketing. An example developed a *perceptual space* for competing ethical pharmaceuticals. Also in this example, the concept of a joint space, incorporating both perceptual and preference data, was introduced. In the example, the interpretation of the analyses, and their potential effects on marketing strategies, were stressed. The article concluded with a short discussion of some of the difficulties which might be encountered when utilizing these techniques.

26

Norman L. Barnett: Developing Effective Advertising for New Products

Advertising for a new product frequently sets out to maximize trial for the new brand. In this case, a major criterion in evaluating the effectiveness of the advertising is number of "triers per dollar." This particular approach overlooks one vital factor when other brands manufactured by the company have preceded the new entry; namely that a company has (or should have) more interest in maximizing its overall corporate share in a particular market than in maximizing the market share of the *new* brand, per se.

In addition to inducing trial for a new brand, the company should want to know from where the trial will come, i.e., which consumers will prefer the new brand over current brands. If the overall corporate share is to be maximized, the preference for the new brand must come from brands other than those the company currently has in the market. Of equal importance is "efficiency of trial," i.e., ensuring that those people persuaded to try the product are primarily those who will like it and, consequently, will repurchase it. In sum, it is essential that a new product draw minimally from consumers

Reprinted from the *Journal of Advertising Research.* © Copyrighted 1968 by the Advertising Research Foundaton. Based on a paper given at the American Marketing Association Conference, Bloomington. Indiana, September 1, 1966. Professor Volney J. Stefflre of the University of California, Irvine, was a frequent source of inspiration and guidance for much of the content of this article. But the author assumes total responsibility for the ideas contained herein.

of a company's current brands and, at the same time, satisfy those consumers who are attracted to it.

These strategic goals are easy to accept but have been difficult to operationalize. Recently, however, a research technology has been developed which promises to answer two basic questions:

1. How does a company design a new product with characteristics that attract users of competitive brands but *minimally* draw from consumers of its current brands?
2. How can a company design advertising to attract primarily people who will like and repurchase the new product?

The new technology, called Market Structure Analysis, has grown out of the academic research in psycholinguistics by Professor Volney J. Stefflre of the University of California at Irvine. It makes one basic assumption: in aggregate, consumer preference for a description of a new product versus current products will be approximately the same as consumer preference for the new product itself, as long as consumers see the new product as essentially matching the description. This implies that:

1. Researchers can determine the underlying characteristics which people use in differentiating among products.
2. Such characteristics and/or appropriate substitutes can be used in new combinations to form descriptions of feasible new products.
3. The new product descriptions so obtained can be screened for consumer preference with relative accuracy *before* a new product is built.
4. A product which *consumers* see as having the required characteristics can be developed.
5. Once a specific new product description is selected for development, it becomes the goal for advertising, i.e., advertising is developed so as to communicate the specific and unique characteristics of the new product, so that those who would prefer it to current brands can clearly identify it.

Figure 1 illustrates the research steps needed to develop an understanding of the differentiating characteristics which constitute basic market structure. Steps 1, 2, and 3 determine which items (products and brands) consumers see as constituting a market and the "position" of each item in the market vis-à-vis the other items. These steps provide the information necessary for building descriptions of feasible, strategically positioned new brands. In Step 4, descriptions of possible new products are built, and *their* "positions" within the market structure are determined by correlating rank order preference for current brands and products with rank order preference for the descriptions. Step 5 is a preference study which yields data both on the proportion of people preferring each of the current brands, and on the shifts in preference that occur when any of the new descriptions of potential brands are added to the array of current brands. The remainder of the research is devoted to developing a new brand which essentially matches the desired product description derived from the preference study.

Steps 1 through 4 are designed to develop an understanding of the market structure, i.e., the position of each brand in the market vis-à-vis the other

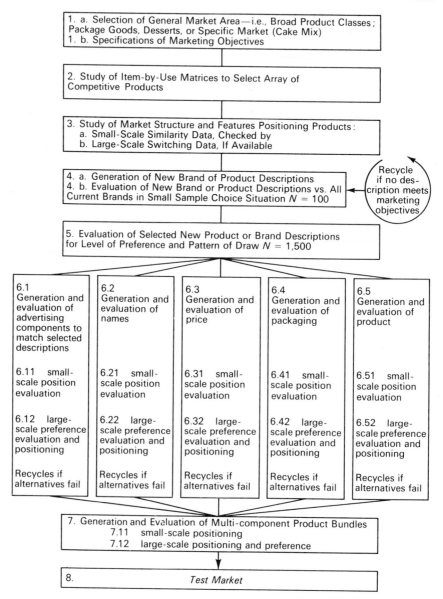

Figure 1. Market Structure Analysis Technology: General Chart of New Product Development

brands. Data as to the way in which consumers see brands can be developed from a study of judged similarity among items. Empirical evidence so far indicates that judgments of similarities collected from a relatively small sample will correlate highly with similarity data gathered from a large sample. Since good results have been obtained in studies of many consumer packaged goods markets, it seems probable that the stability of similarity judgments is a general rather than a specific phenomenon.

In the similarity study (Step 3), a small sample of perhaps 25, 50, or 100 consumers are asked to determine, for each brand, which other brands they

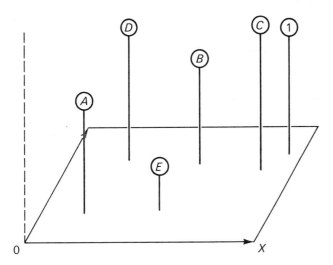

Figure 2. A Three-Dimensional Model Showing the Relative Positioning of Brands in a Market, as Derived from Consumer Judgments of Similarity

see as most similar. Once such judgments are made, the respondents are asked why pairs of brands which they saw as similar were so judged. Their verbatim responses suggest the causes of perceived similarity between brands.

One method, helpful in attaining a visual as well as an intellectual understanding of the way brands in a market relate to each other, is nonmetric multidimensional scaling. This method analyzes the similarity data on from 1 to 10 dimensions, locating each item on each dimension and indicating the residual "stress" when the items are positioned using any number of dimensions.

Suppose we actually build a physical model by locating each brand in a three-dimensional space, and by using any unit of measurement, e.g., inches, millimeters, etc., represent the values of each dimension. In this way a model may be constructed using consumers' original perceptions to show where each item "fits" relative to all other items. Figure 2 is a hypothetical representation of such a model and depicts consumers' "positioning" of hypothetical brands A, B, C, D, and E. The greater the agreement among perceivers that two items are similar, the smaller the distance between the points representing those items.

Note that, thus far, the analysis has been content free; we, as researchers, have made no assumptions as to how consumers might differentiate among brands, nor have we given consumers pre-chosen dimensions on which to evaluate brands. The positioning in the model is based purely upon *consumer's* perceptions.

In Figure 2, assume that a company is interested in introducing a new product into a market in which it already has a brand—Brand *A*. A major market shareholder is Brand *C*, and Brands *A* and *C* are located relatively far apart in this three-dimensional scheme. When the verbatim material, collected with the similarity data, are analyzed, hypotheses can be built as to the specific characteristics that cause items to locate as they do in this three-dimensional space. Once an understanding of these characteristics is obtained, new combinations of them can be created, perhaps with appropriate substitutions, to build descriptions of new products. (In addition to the current characteristics that consumers appear to use in differentiating among products, one can also use other qualities which would be seen by consumers as appropriate to the market being studied.) To illustrate, Brand *C* is a cake mix which is seen as rich, quick to bake, but requires careful preparation. If there is interest in locating in the market structure a new brand in a position competitive with Brand *C*, the new brand must have characteristics preferred by some *consumers* who currently choose Brand *C*.

Imagine that the current market share for each of these brands is as follows:

Brand *A* has 35%
Brand *B* has 10
Brand *C* has 30
Brand *D* has 15
Brand *E* has 10

The goal is to increase the corporate market share. To accomplish it a new brand will be placed on the market which should be seen as preferable to Brand *C* in a significant proportion of purchase situations. Moreover, the new brand will be developed so as to draw most of its share from brands other than Brand *A*.

When descriptions have been developed and screened, the few prime prospects (i.e., those which appear to have the potential to satisfy our goals), can be placed in a large-scale national probability preference study. This study will determine the share of choices consumers give to each brand, and subsequently the preference given to each description vis-à-vis each brand. Previous research suggests such preference data correlate well with audit estimates of current market share and that for descriptions of new brands, the preference received by the description approximates the market potential.

We are seeking a new brand that is seen by some consumers as preferable to Brand *C*, and we therefore select a description which tends to draw choices from Brand *C*. If a new product is built to match the successful description, results such as those shown below might be obtained.

Preference for Current Brands		vs	Preference for Current Brands plus Our New Product Description	
Brand	Share of Preference		Brand	Share of Preference
A	35%		A	35%
B	10		B	10
C	30		C	15
D	15		D	15
E	10		E	10
	100%		D_1 *	15
				100%

* Description 1 (our new description) would have 15 per cent of the market, essentially splitting the previous choices given to Brand *C*. This example is purposely oversimplified to illustrate strategic new product introduction. In the market situation, virtually all brands would be affected, although one might be more severely affected than others.

This process is used to determine which description should be used to develop a new product which will share choices with a specific current brand. It is also possible to develop either a new brand with unique characteristics that would draw its preference from several competitive brands, or a new product which competes with products in several *categories* for some uses, essentially forming a category of its own, such as a new kind of children's lunch-time food.

Having obtained a description that meets some stated marketing objective, the next problem is to develop all the components of the new product such that consumers perceive them, both individually and in combination, as essentially matching the chosen description. Knowing the key description provides a very strong and unique advantage. It has already been determined that a certain percentage of consumers prefer the description. If the new brand is built so that it is perceived as a better example of the target description than is any current brand, the new brand will be in position to obtain the preference enjoyed by the description. In the same fashion, the advertising, developed using research results, can be more effective in communicating the critical characteristics of the new brand than advertising designed without knowledge of such critical characteristics.

Appropriate Advertising

Rather than attempting simply to achieve trial of the new brand, the objective for advertising is to attract people who want what the new brand has to offer. This goal can be achieved when people understand correctly what is offered because the brand's advertising has *accurately* communicated the characteristic of the product. In other words, the aim is to communicate accurately, and by so doing to attract people who will like the new product and become frequent purchasers.

Development of appropriate advertising may be done through a number of simple research steps. First, one gathers psychological stimuli, e.g., colors, color combinations, shapes, forms, textures, illustrations, etc., of many different kinds. By projective research, one can determine which stimuli *consumers* see as being consistent with the desired product description. This can be accomplished by asking consumers which color is " X-est," or by asking consumers to rate each stimulus according to how " X " it is, where X represents the various characteristics in the desired product description. This research crudely identifies the stimuli that most accurately communicate the desired characteristics for every component of advertising—scenes, shapes, colors, words, etc. If, for example, the advertising goal is to develop illustrations for a friendly cake mix, consumers would be asked to identify which one of a large number of varied illustrations is the "friendliest." They are then asked to choose from an array of color combinations the one that is friendliest, and so forth for shapes, words, etc. The reader may find it difficult to believe that people can, in fact, report which color combination is friendliest, which package illustration or which photograph of a scene is friendliest. In fact, many consumers are reluctant at first to provide this strange type of information. However, Stefflre has found over a period of years remarkable unanimity among people in their identification of various stimuli which elicit for them a feeling of happiness, sadness, sweetness, sourness, or whatever other characteristics he is seeking to build into a brand.

Dictionary of Characteristics

Once the total range of research for these components is completed, a crude "dictionary" of forms, scenes, colors, and words will have been amassed which can then be given to creative people for guidance in building advertising, packaging, etc. Non-directive research of the kind described above, can again be used to ascertain whether a given component communicates the desired message and/or how it should be modified to be a better example of the target description. Ultimately, we can in the same manner determine when a mix of components that delivers that particular message we are trying to communicate has been developed.

When prototypes of this advertising are built, they are evaluated objectively by consumers in any of several ways. One effective yet simple method of evaluation is asking people to scale the degree to which each ad of a series of ads is "friendly," "warm," "light tasting," or whatever. By asking people to scale the newly developed ads against existing ads for current brands, it can be determined whether, in fact, one or more of our prototype ads is seen as being a better example of the target description than any other brand's advertising. That "better example" consumer judgment is a key criterion in evaluation. The successful ad does not have to be seen as "perfect" in the desired characteristics; it simply must be seen as a better example of the critical characteristics than is any other ad. It is also possible to measure the degree to which people who prefer a particular description like a particular package, product prototype, or coordinated ad, and so forth. This can be done by having consumers rank, in order of their preference, product, descriptions, and each of these other components. Early attempts will show what other kinds of things people prefer who like particular descriptions. Through a series of attempts, it should be possible to come up with coordinated components that:

1. Represent the desired set of characteristics,
2. Are liked by people who prefer the target description to current brands.

A fit among the components is achieved when each component helps communicate the desired message. The new brand is then in a position to be chosen or preferred by people who indicated their preference for the new product description in the large-scale preference study (Figure 1) and should get approximately the same proportion of choices as its description received when evaluated versus current brands.

Summary

This paper first discussed a new methodology for determining from consumers the characteristics a new brand should have in order to perform in a specific strategic fashion. Second, an approach was described for creating empirically the components of the brand, including the advertising. We described how the product's components can be evaluated by consumers to determine whether, in fact, they elicit the desired perceptions and how this process recycles until components that communicate the specific, desired message are achieved.

27

David H. Doehlert: Similarity and
Preference Mapping: A Color
Example

The Similarity Map

Du Pont is bringing out consumer products at an increasing rate. We have a large research and development effort to provide the consumer with the product he wants. We not only develop consumer products which we manufacture; we also provide end-use research for manufacturers who buy raw materials from us.

To guide our research and development on new and improved products, we must know what the consumer thinks. We must know what matters to the consumer and what he likes best. What we present to you today is the discovery that we can show by map what matters, and that we can show on the same map what each consumer likes best.

We claim that when a product is undergoing development, this kind of map can be used to assess where we stand relative to competition. And it can be used to measure our progress as we vary the product or its package or advertising. Finally, it can estimate market shares after development. So we say that at all stages it can provide guidance for research and development.

We have prepared 45 of these maps since 1963. Rather than use one of those cases for an example, we posed this problem: what colors of automobiles should be offered to the consumer? We could not test all kinds of colors, so we concentrated on some blues and greens and a gray and two browns.

We showed the colors, three at a time, and asked these questions:

Which pair is most alike?
Which pair is least alike?

We also asked about preference. The second part of this paper discusses preference data.

Each pair of colors appeared on four different cards in the course of the test. Suppose colors 3, 11, and 18 appeared together. Then if the subject

Reprinted from *Proceedings of the AMA Fall Conference, 1968*, published by the American Marketing Association. David H. Doehlert, " Similarity and Preference Mapping: A Color Example," *Proceedings of the AMA Fall Conference, 1968*.

declared 18 and 11 most alike all four times that he saw 18 with 11, we can conclude that, relative to other color differences, this difference is a small one. On our map, then, these two colors would be put close together.

Another pair of colors might always be declared least alike; on the map those two would be placed far apart. We have no coordinates in advance on which to map the colors. We only have information from the subjects about which pairs are most alike and which are least alike. That is, we have a similar score for each pair of items.

The map is prepared from this data by starting with an arbitrary scattering across the map of points to represent the nineteen colors. The computer program shifts the points until the pairs that were declared most alike are close together on the map and those less alike are farther apart. The program terminates iteration when further shifting of points cannot improve the map. This is the Kruskal-Shepard method of multidimensional scaling.

Later we will show which regions of this map are preferred. This will answer the question—which automobile colors should be offered. However, before discussing preference data, we will look closer at the process of developing this map.

The Data Collecting Method

We have standardized the data collection to make it fast, to reduce errors, and to make for quick analysis. Each set of three items is displayed on a single table. Three trays and six prepunched cards are provided for each person in the test to use in evaluating the three items. Suppose the subject has decided that 1 and 13 are most alike. She selects the card with 1 and 13 printed on the top edge, and drops that card in the tray labeled "most alike." The card for the least alike pair goes in the "least alike" tray, and the card for the third pair in the middle tray. Since the cards are prepunched with the subject's code number, the cards can go directly into analysis without any further handling. The cards are not marked by the subject, and can be used again for some other set of items.

There are nineteen such tables around the room in our experiment. The subjects went around the room twelve times in three hours. Less testing per person is needed when fewer than nineteen items are being tested. And in some applications, the testing can be divided among several groups of subjects so that it is less tiring for each subject.

Degree of Consensus about Similarity of the Colors

We checked our eighteen subjects for agreement about the similarities of these colors. That is, we computed correlation coefficients for all pairs of subjects. Then, using these correlations as measures of the similarity of subjects, we made a supplementary map.

It showed that subjects 2 and 12 were seeing the colors very differently from the others. We have checked their color vision, and we find that they are color blind. I expected to find that the others have normal color vision. Surprisingly, number 8 is also color blind. It is curious, indeed, that he gives data much like normal subjects, while 2 and 12 do not. Two and 12 are so different that we have made a separate map of the colors for them. Their map is different in that tans go over with greens. In other applications it might be possible to make just one map for all persons. We have always been able to do so. We invited trouble by using color for our example, because about 8% of all males have defective color vision.

The Number of Dimensions

We do not go into analysis with a preconceived idea of the number of dimensions needed to make a good map. Color is unusual in this respect. If you know anything about color, you know that colors have been represented as three-dimensional for a long time. However, in this example, we acted as if there were no ideas available as to the number of dimensions needed to map colors.

This approach makes the example more realistic, because in all our 45 applications we have never had prior information as to how many dimensions to expect. The analysis is the means of discovering the number of dimensions needed. In this color analysis we tried all maps of 2 to 8 dimensions. Figure 1 shows a statistic like the residual error, plotted against the number of dimensions.

It says that when you go below five dimensions the residual error goes up despite an increase of nineteen degrees of freedom at every step. This is the equivalent of saying that real effects are being lumped with the noise, when the fifth and fourth dimensions are dropped. So we conclude that these people see color in a five-dimensional way.

The Preference Map

We have shown a method for detecting differences that consumers see between items. We also wish to know which items they prefer. That is, we want our goals for developing new products to be the preferences of the consumers. The experimenter's personal reaction doesn't matter. What does matter is the opinions of those who buy. Therefore, preference data are needed.

We would like to present the preference data in a way that is easily seen and interpreted. We will show that this can be done by relating the preference results to the similarity map.

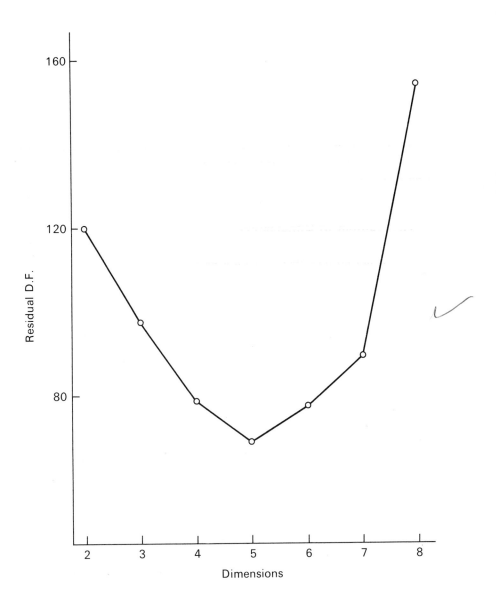

Figure 1. Lack of Fit versus Dimensions

Data Collection

The preference data were obtained at the same time that we collected the similarity data. A subject was asked to indicate which color he would like most for his next automobile, and which color he would like least for each group of three colors. He was asked to assume that the three colors were the only ones available. The preference data was recorded by voting with cards.

Subject Consistency

The eighteen subjects in this test were highly consistent. Each made a few contradictory remarks, but not many compared to the total number of comparisons made.

We can also examine their consistency in repeating preferences. Was each subject able to repeat his data? Or did he change his mind about what items he preferred as he saw them more and more times?

Table 1 shows that the correlation coefficients between tests for Person 18, for example, are quite high.

Table 1. Correlation of Preference Scores, Test to Test for Person 18

Test No.	Test No.			
	1	2	3	4
2		.81	.77	.76
3			.95	.92
				.95

Each subject saw every pair of colors four times. The coefficient between the first two tests (.81) is large, and only slightly smaller than the coefficients between tests 2 and 3 and between tests 3 and 4 (.95). This indicates that in the early tests Person 18 was changing somewhat, but in later tests his preferences for colors were firmly fixed.

All of the subjects had correlation coefficients as large or larger than those seen here. Many were in the high 90's. Thus, we can say that the subjects can repeat their performances from test to test. Since our data are consistent, we can use all eighteen of the subjects in the preference analysis.

Not all people like the same colors. Therefore, we should allow each subject to display his individual preferences and we do this.

We display these individual preferences graphically as were the colors themselves. Preference scores assigned to the nineteen colors by a subject were used to find a point for him on the similarity map. The location of this point represents his ideal automobile color. It will be close to the colors he likes and further away from those he dislikes. To see how ideal points are located, let us look at Person 18 again.

First, consider Person 18's location on the similarity map shown in Figure 2. As you can see, Person 18 is very close to item 9. That is, the distance between the ideal point for Person 18 and item 9 is quite small. This is one of

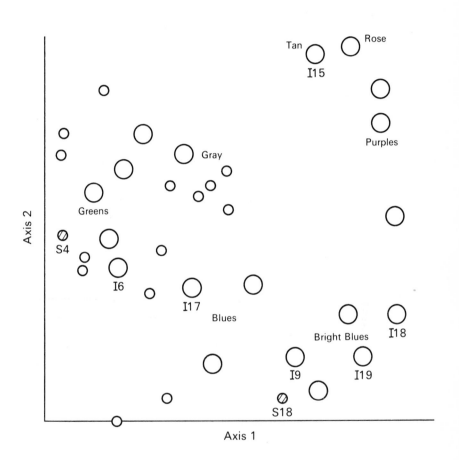

Figure 2. Preference Map Showing 19 Colors (Large Circles) and 16
Person Ideal Points (Small Circles)

the colors that he preferred, one which he gave a large preference score. We see that there exists a medium distance between his ideal point and item 18, and we have a large distance to item 15. Item 15 is one of his less preferred items and one that he gave a small preference score.

Now consider Table 2, which shows the preference score, and the corresponding map distances for Person 18.

Table 2. Preference Scores and Corresponding Map Distances, Ideal Point to Item Point, for Person 18

Items	Preference Score	Map Distance
1	66	.5
2	5	2.1
3	17	2.0
4	28	1.8
5	25	1.7
6	35	1.3
7	27	1.5
8	64	1.0
9	67	.4
10	45	1.2
11	35	1.5
12	21	1.8
13	20	1.8
14	12	2.2
15	11	2.0
16	56	.8
17	51	.9
18	40	1.1
19	59	.6

If our method of placing Person 18 on the similarity map is effective, then large preference scores will correspond to small distances. Notice that item 9 does have a large preference score and a small map distance. Item 18 has a smaller score and a larger distance, and the item 15 has a very small score and a still larger distance.

This tells us that the ideal point for Person 18 on the map represents his preference data quite well. That is, he is close to the colors he likes and far from those he dislikes. To show just how well his ideal point represents his data, we have plotted preference scores against distances in Figure 3.

As you can see the distances and scores are very well correlated. In fact, the coefficient of correlation is .97.

We have also included Person 9's scatter plot of distances and scores. His correlation coefficient is smaller (.78) than Person 18's. However, the correlation is very good except for item 7. Item 7 is the only gray that was included in the test. This indicates that we may need the fourth dimension to locate gray relative to the other colors.

The degree of correlation between the distances and scores is a measure of the effectiveness of presenting the preference data on the similarity map. The correlation coefficients for all subjects were above .75, and most of them were in the high 80's and 90's. Thus, we can say that our method is effective.

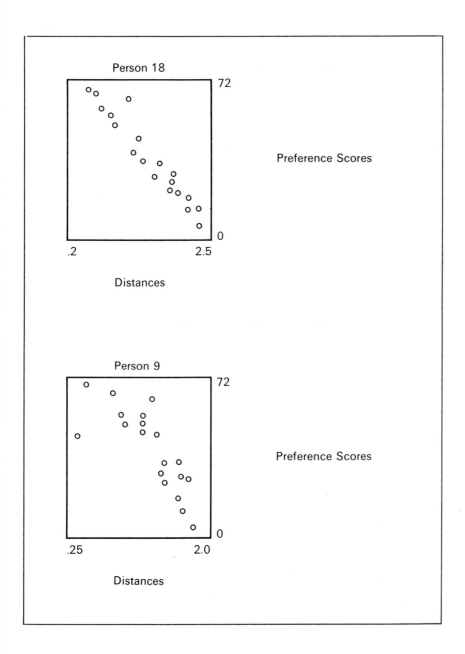

Figure 3. Preference Scores versus Distances for Two Subjects

Now we are ready to consider the total preference map. Each person has been placed on the similarity map at his optimum location within the range of the map. Perhaps the ideal color for a person was not included in the test. However, we may be able to conceive of it as some compromise between existing colors. If we could make this color, it would be preferred by him over all other colors, at least within the color space presented in the test.

If the person-points appear together in some region of the space, then the colors in or near that region are the best candidates to market. Looking at Figure 2, we can see that we have a very popular region with a large concentration of ideal points.

These are the colors (green, blues) that are most preferred by the majority of the subjects in our test. We also have a region preferred by a few people and we have a very unpopular region.

If we wished to choose colors to make or market for automobiles, we would want them to fall into the most preferred region of the map. In this case, we might try to make three or four that would satisfy the large region of ideal points and, perhaps, one that would fall into the zone preferred by a few people.

An interesting question might be posed here: "Does a subject consider items close to him distinguishably more preferred to those further away?"

For illustration, let us look at Person 4 and colors 6, 17, 9, and 19 on the map. You will notice that these colors range from more preferred to less preferred, respectively, for Person 4. Each pair of these items was seen four times by Person 4. For every pair, Person 4 consistently preferred the items in the order given above, all four times he saw the pair. This is significant at the .07 level. The differences shown on the map are, therefore, significant.

Summary

A study of the preference map gives us guidance in research as to what items to market. If a preferred item does not exist, the similarity map indicates the directions in which we should move to make items that will fall into the preferred regions of the map.

We would, of course, be cautious about the conclusions drawn from this experiment as we had only 18 subjects. We would not expect to be able to predict the preferred color regions for the total population of automobile buyers from such a small sample. This was used just for the purpose of demonstrating our method. Larger samples of subjects can be readily tested and analyzed.

C. Cluster Analysis

The purpose of cluster analysis is to identify objects (or variables) which are similar with respect to some criteria. The resulting object clusters should have high internal (within cluster) homogeneity and high external (between cluster) heterogeneity. Geometrically, the objects within a cluster should be close together and the objects in different clusters should be far apart. The choice of an appropriate distance measure is a crucial aspect of cluster analysis. Another is the choice of the criteria guiding the cluster program. What qualities should an optimal set of clusters for a particular problem have? As Frank and Green make clear, there are many distance measures and literally hundreds of cluster programs, each with its own criterion or objective function.

Still another decision parameter with which the analyst is faced is the level of clustering desired. At one extreme, all objects will be in the same cluster. At the other, each object will define its own cluster. The appropriate level will depend upon the problem and upon the overall structure of the object space. Usually, cluster analysis is performed on several levels, so that insights can be obtained into the object structure. If clusters combine as the level is decreased, then the structure forms a well-defined hierarchy. However, if objects of small clusters are dispersed as larger clusters are formed, then the underlying structure is less well defined and does not form a natural hierarchy. The Frost article illustrates the usefulness of obtaining sets of clusters at different levels.

Numerical taxonomy is often used as an alternative expression for cluster analysis. Taxonomy is defined by Webster to be the "classification especially of animals and plants according to their natural relationships." This definition contains the essence of the approach. In discriminant analysis, the objects are assigned to certain groups and other variables are found that will discriminate among them. In taxonomy or cluster analysis, groups or clusters are allowed to emerge on the basis of their natural relationships. As the definition implies, taxonomy is associated with biology and anthropology. In fact, most of the development of the techniques involved have come from these disciplines.

We might note in passing that it would be perfectly appropriate to follow cluster analysis with discriminant analysis to identify other variables which could then be used to exploit the cluster set found. For example, if consumers were clustered into segments, it might be useful to find media defining variables which discriminate among the segments to help implement the segmentation strategy.

As Wells and Sheth and Massy point out, factor analysis is often used to cluster variables or, in the case of Q-analysis, to cluster objects. If a group of variables has in common high loadings on one factor, then they are viewed as forming a cluster. Such an approach looks at only one factor or dimension at a time and, thus, must be used with care. However, if the factors are rotated so that variables will have high loadings on only one factor, then the interpretation problem is reduced. In any case, cluster analysis is a more direct way to obtain a set of clusters. It more directly deals with interobject distance. Further, most cluster programs provide quantitative measures of the quality of a cluster set and the stability of individual objects.

Frank and Green provide a good overview of numerical taxonomy or cluster analysis and present several applications. The Aaker article discusses two crude but useful clustering techniques which provide alternatives to formal cluster programs. An understanding of these techniques provides additional insights into the programs involved in applying cluster analysis. Frost presents an example of how cluster analysis can be applied to the problem of grouping TV programs. The Frost article, like the Massy article, illustrates how factor analysis can be productively used as a preliminary stage of analysis. Frost uses factor scores as inputs to his cluster program.

28

Ronald E. Frank and Paul E. Green:
Numerical Taxonomy in Marketing
Analysis: A Review Article

Marketing managers and researchers often comment on their difficulty in developing useful ways of classifying customers for formulating marketing policy. The source of the difficulty frequently stems from the abundance of alternative classification methods rather than from a lack of possibilities. Changes in our concepts of customer behavior have more often been associated with the generation of new measures of behavior than with the integra-

---

Abridged from *Journal of Marketing Research*, published by the American Marketing Association. Ronald E. Frank and Paul E. Green, "Numerical Taxonomy in Marketing Analysis: A Review Article," *Journal of Marketing Research*, Vol. V, February 1968, pp. 83–98.

tion of existing measures. In 50 years, researchers have stopped focusing almost exclusively on customer socioeconomic characteristics as a basis for policy formulation and have begun considering a wide range of measures of sociological and psychological phenomena (such as personality, preferences, buying intentions, perceived risk, interpersonal influence) and an increasing number of measures of actual buying behavior (such as total consumption and brand loyalty).

Much of customer behavior has many factors—it is multidimensional. Researchers often sidestep its complexity by picking some unidimensional attribute assumed to be an indicator of the more complex phenomena to be understood. For example, in studies of household brand loyalty (with respect to frequently purchased, branded food products), the researcher often finds variables used to measure brand loyalty such as the proportion of purchases spent on the most frequently purchased brand or the proportion spent on the brand that is of central interest to the researcher. For many purposes, however, these might be too limited a measure of loyalty since they fail to approximate a full description of a rather complex phenomenon. Customers do not typically buy a single brand or even two brands. Many households purchase three, four, or five brands of a product. In addition, the subset of brands chosen for consumption will vary from household to household.

What procedure could be used to study the clusters of brands that different households consume? All possible combinations of brands could be computed and households sorted into respective classes, but this approach presents a few problems. How many combinations are there in a market with twelve brands? There are over four million if the number of partitions resulting from grouping twelve brands into two or more clusters is added.[1] Even worse, one may want to measure the similarity of brand purchasing behavior not only for the combination of brands but also for the relative proportion of money spent on each brand.

This kind of classification problem is not unique to brand loyalty. How are television programs classified for similarity of audience profiles? Here, too, practitioners often use a single category as the basis for classification, such as the modal audience group (for example, teenagers loyal to "Rat Patrol"). How should market areas for choosing test markets be grouped? How can a potential purchaser compare the performance specifications of a wide range of computers? How should the readership characteristics of a number of alternative magazines be compared?

---

[1] The general formula [29] for finding all possible partitions of a given set of entities is

$$P(n, m) = [ml^n - \sum_{i-1}^{m-1} m_{(m-i)} P(i)]/m!$$

where

> m is number of partitions; $m \geq 2$
> n is number of entities in set to be clustered; $n \geq m$
> $P(m)$ is number of distinct partitions containing exactly m clusters
> $m_{(m-i)}$ is $m(m-1)(m-2) \cdots (m-i+1)$

Almost every major analytical problem requires the classification of objects by several characteristics—whether customers, products, cities, television programs or magazines. Seldom are explicit classification systems with some combination of attributes, such as those used for measuring a customer's social class or stage in life cycle, found. Such classification systems typically represent self-imposed taxonomies; that is, taxonomies the researcher believes to be relevant because of a theory or prior experience.[2] Although this approach can be useful it has limitations. Regardless of the complexity of reality, it is difficult to classify objects by more than two or three characteristics at a time. If reality requires greater complexity, researchers are severely constrained by their conceptual limitations.

The difficulty of seeing through this often bewildering maze is not unique to marketing (not to mention business problems), as indicated by Sokal, an entymologist:

> Classification is one of the fundamental concerns of science. Facts and objects must be arranged in an orderly fashion before their unifying principles can be discovered and used as a basis for prediction. Many phenomena occur in such variety and profusion that unless some system is created among them, they would be unlikely to provide any useful information [82].

A new technology, numerical taxonomy, has been developed, primarily in biology. It consists of a set of numerical procedures for classifying objects [83]. These taxonomic procedures may be called preclassification techniques since their purpose is to describe the natural groupings that occur in large masses of data. From these natural groupings (or clusters) the researcher can sometimes develop the requisite conceptual framework for classification.

Numerical taxonomy is still new, and to the authors' knowledge, only three articles in marketing have appeared [34, 50, 66]. This article introduces potential marketing applications of this set of techniques, giving some attention to their mathematical bases, current limitations, and assumptions. The following topics are discussed:

1. The nature of taxonomic procedures.
2. Illustrative applications of taxonomic methods to marketing problems.
3. The assumptions and limitations of the procedures.

The authors feel that taxonomic methods will be used increasingly to describe complex marketing data. Hopefully, this article will alert more researchers to the potential of these methods and to some of the cautions associated with use.

---

[2] Taxonomies can be distinguished from classifications since they denote interconnections (usually a hierarchy) among characteristics of the objects—a less generic term than classifications. In practice, however, the terms are often used interchangeably.

The Nature of Taxonomic Procedures

Assume that there is a set of objects, such as people, products, advertisements, and marketing channels, each of which can be characterized by a measurement (or more generally, by an attribute score) on each of a set of characteristics. The researcher has no external criterion for grouping the objects into subsets of similar objects; instead, he wants to identify natural groupings in the data, after which more formal models might be developed.

More formally stated, the problem is: How should objects be assigned to groups so there will be as much likeness within groups and as much difference among groups as possible? From this question four others arise: (1) what proximity measure is to be used to summarize the likeness of profiles, (2) after these likeness measures have been computed, how should the objects be grouped, (3) after the objects have been grouped, what descriptive measures are appropriate for summarizing the characteristics of each group, (4) are the groups formed really different from each other (the inferential problem)?

There are numerous taxonomic procedures for achieving the major objective. The following discussion illustrates the logic of one of them, followed by a brief overview of other kinds of procedures that have been developed. The purpose is to show the relevance of these techniques for establishing multidimensional classification systems, not to provide a definitive methodological statement.

An Example

Suppose that the objects of interest are television programs and the characteristics are (assumed independent) measures of the socioeconomic profile of each program. Let us start with measures of two characteristics, number of teenagers (X_1) and number of adult men (X_2), for each of ten programs. Our problem is to find a way of grouping the programs by the similarity of their audience profiles. Figure 1 plots the programs in two dimensions.

Assume that two clusters of five programs each are desired. A start is to compute Euclidean distances of every point from every other point with the usual formula:

$$\Delta_{jk} = [(X_{1j} - X_{1k})^2 + (X_{2j} - X_{2k})^2]^{1/2}$$

Points 1 and 2 in Figure 1 appear to be closest together. The first cluster would then be formed by finding the midpoint between Points 1 and 2, the centroid of the point coordinates. Then the distance of each point from this average would be computed and the point closest to this average would be added (here, Point 3). Similarly, Point 4 and then Point 5 would be added, giving a cluster of five programs as desired.

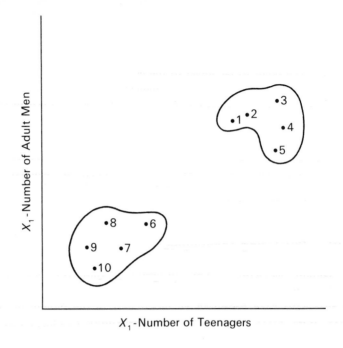

Figure 1. Illustration of Taxonomic Techniques (Hypothetical)

Generalizing to More than Two Dimensions

In the previous illustration, only two measurements were considered for each point (television program). It is relatively easy to follow the procedure visually.[3] In practice there may be many measurements for each program; hence, the graphical procedure must be supplemented by a computational technique that can deal with several characteristics.

Several computer routines are available for this type of taxonomic analysis often called cluster analysis. For example, one computer routine used involves these steps:

1. Each characteristic is first converted to a standardized variate with zero mean and unit standard deviation.
2. Euclidean distances are then computed for each of all possible pairs of points.
3. The pair with the smallest distance is chosen as the node of the first cluster, and the average of this pair is computed.

---

[3] The typical Euclidean distance measure can be easily generalized to more than two dimensions as:

$$\Delta_{jk} = [\Sigma_{i=1}^{n} (X_{ij} - X_{ik})^2]^{1/2}$$

4. Additional points are added to this cluster (based on closeness to the last-computed average) until:
    a. Some prespecified number of points has been clustered.
    b. The point to be added to the cluster exceeds some prespecified distance-cutoff or threshold number.
5. The program then proceeds to the next pair of points which are closest together of all unclustered points, and the above process is repeated.
6. If desired, the program can be modified to allow points to be in more than one cluster.
7. The program can be further modified to shift points from cluster to cluster to obtain final clusters which are best in the sense of having the lowest average within-cluster distance summed over all clusters at a given stage in the clustering.

Other Clustering Techniques

Proximity Measure   This program is only one way to cluster points in multidimensional space. Other proximity measures and clustering techniques have been proposed by researchers in the biological and social sciences. With some simplification, the proximity measures can be categorized as:

1. Distance measures.
2. Correlation measures.
3. Similarity measures for attribute data.

The input data—nominal, ordinal, interval, ratio or mixed scales—often determines the proximity measure used to express pairwise relationships among the elements.

Distance Measures   One kind of clustering technique based on Euclidean distance has already been described. Two problems exist with regard to this kind of measure: (1) correlated characteristics and (2) non-comparability of the original units in which the characteristics are measured [69]. The second problem is usually "solved" by standardizing all characteristics to mean zero and unit standard deviation. Thus it is assumed that mean and variance among characteristics is not important in the grouping process.

The first problem can be handled two ways. A principal component analysis may be run on the characteristics and factor scores computed for the objects. Each component score may then be weighted by the square root of the eigenvalue associated with that component before computing the distance measure. A second approach uses the Mahalanobis [60] generalized distance in which the squared distances between objects is measured as a linear combination of the correlated measurements expressed in units of the estimated population dispersion of the composite measure. If the characteristics are uncorrelated and measurements are first standardized (mean zero and unit standard deviation), the square root of the Mahalanobis measure is equivalent to the Euclidean measure discussed.

In practice, distance measures of the kind just described are usually used when data are at least intervally scaled. Kendall [54], however, proposed a distance measure requiring only ordinally scaled measurements. Also, Restle [75] and others have shown that even nominally scaled data may be characterized in distance terms, in the sense of obeying the distance axioms. The resulting metric, however, may not be Euclidean.

Correlation Measures Probably the most widely used proximity measure in clustering procedures involves the correlation coefficient.[4] Inverse factor analysis, the Q-technique, is a fairly widely used procedure in which objects replace tests in the computation of factor loadings. Clusters may then be formed by grouping subjects with similar factor loadings. Three problems are associated with this class of techniques. First, correlation removes the elevation and scatter of each object, thereby losing information. Second, in grouping objects by factor loadings, the analyst risks obtaining some objects that are split among clusters. Finally, the analyst must usually resort to an R-technique to interpret the clusters' characteristics according to their correlations with underlying factors.

Similarity Measures Similarity measures are often used in clustering when the characteristics of each object are only nominally scaled, for example, dichotomous or multichotomous. The usual notion of distance seems less applicable here (although it is still possible to use multidimentional scaling techniques to "metricize" such data before clustering). Typically, however, the analyst tries to develop similarity coefficients based on attribute matching.

For example, if two objects are compared on each of eight attributes, the following might result:

Entity	Attribute							
	1	2	3	4	5	6	7	8
1	1	0	0	1	1	0	1	0
2	0	1	0	1	0	1	1	1

The fractional match coefficient would be:

$$S_{12} = \frac{M}{N} = \frac{3}{8}$$

---

[4] If the characteristics are expressed in standard scores, the Euclidean distance between two objects is a monotone transformation of their correlation (18).

where M denotes the number of attributes held in common (matching 1's or 0's) and N denotes the total number of attributes. If weak matches (non-possession of the attribute) are to be deemphasized, the Tanimoto [76] coefficient is appropriate:

$$\text{Tanimoto } S_{ij} = \frac{\text{No. of attributes which are 1 for both objects } i \text{ and } j}{\text{No. of attributes which are 1 for either } i \text{ or } j, \text{ or both}}$$

In this problem the coefficient would be $\frac{2}{7}$. Many other similarity measures have been developed that represent variations of the fractional match coefficient. (See [83].)

One interesting distance-type measure which can also be used for attribute matching is the pattern similarity coefficient, r_p, proposed by Cattell, Coulter, and Tsujioka [16]. In interval-scaled data, the coefficient compares the computed distance with that expected by chance alone:

$$r_{p(jk)} = \frac{E_i - \sum_{i=1}^{n} d_{(jk)}^2}{E_i + \sum_{i=1}^{n} d_{(jk)}^2}$$

where i is the number of dimensions, $d_{(jk)}^2$ is the squared Euclidean distance in standard units between entities j and k, and E_i is twice the median chi-square value for i degrees of freedom. Cattell's coefficient has the convenient property of varying from $+1$ for complete agreement, 0 for no agreement, to -1 for inverse agreement.

The coefficient may also be adapted for dichotomous items as:

$$r_p' = \frac{E_i - d}{E_i + d}$$

where d represents the number of disagreements on d items.

Finally, some mention should be made of the mixed scale problem in which the characteristics are measured in different modes. One possibility is to degrade interval-scaled data into categories and use similarity coefficients. Another possibility is to upgrade nominally or ordinally scaled data. There seems to be no satisfactory solution to this problem although it is conceivable that some highly general measure of proximity, perhaps one derived from information theory, may be appropriate.

Clustering Routines

After the analyst has decided on some measure of pairwise proximity, he must still contend with the grouping process itself. A variety of approaches are possible. One major class of approaches to the clustering problem consists of hierarchical routines. For example, Edwards and Cavalli-Sforza [24] describe a clustering procedure (based on a least-squares technique) which first clusters the data into two groups. The procedure is repeated sequentially so that progressively smaller clusters are formed sequentially by splitting the original clusters. A hierarchical array is obtained. A variant of this procedure starts with clusters of one object each and builds new clusters hierarchically until one overall cluster results. This approach was described by Ward [93].

Other grouping routines use threshold or cutoff measures similar to the algorithm described earlier. Some procedures, for example, suggest selecting an object closest to the centroid of all the data to serve as a prime node around which other points are clustered until some threshold distance level is reached. An unclustered object farthest from the centroid of the first cluster may then be chosen as a new prime node. The process is continued, the third and subsequent prime nodes being selected on the basis of largest average distance from the centroids of clusters already formed.

Some grouping routines [24, 93] are highly metric since effectiveness measures involve the computation of within-cluster variance around the centroid of the cluster members. Others [83] use only the proximity between an unclustered object and some single member of the clustered set as a criterion for set inclusion.

In Q-technique, objects are often clustered by highest factor loadings, a simple approach; but it does not use all available information.

Finally, there is the possibility of clustering by systematic space-density search routines in which the n-dimensional space is cut into hypercubes and the computer program counts the number of cases falling into each region. Relatively little work, however, has been done on this taxonomic routine.

Descriptive Characteristics of the Groups

Even after objects are grouped, each cluster must be characterized by its representative profile. In some instances the cluster's centroid is used as a description of its members. In others the actual profile of the object closest to the group's centroid may be used. As in choice of proximity measure and choice of grouping routine, however, the criteria for describing each group are usually ad hoc, a main problem being that *cluster* is still not a precisely defined term. Some of these problems and the inferential problem will be reconsidered later in this article.

Illustrative Marketing Applications

Some appreciation for the versatility and unresolved problems of taxonomic methods can be gained from the following short review of studies conducted by the authors in the past two years.

Clustering Analysis in Test Marketing

One of the earliest pilot applications involved the use of cluster analysis in the grouping of cities (standard metropolitan areas) for test marketing purposes [34]. Data for each of 88 cities were available on 14 measured characteristics, such as population, number of retail stores, percent non-white. A clustering program using the Euclidean distance measure grouped the cities into homogeneous five-point clusters. Centroids of each cluster in 14-space and average distances of each point from the grand centroid and from the centroid of its own cluster were obtained. As an alternative for comparison purposes, the original data matrix was factored, and cluster analysis was performed on the resultant (standardized) factor scores.

The cluster analysis yielded some interesting findings. First, the cluster of five cities closest to the grand mean of all 88—Dayton, Columbus, Indianapolis, Syracuse, and New Haven—agreed well with various lists of typical cities prepared by such magazines as *Sales Management* and *Printer's Ink* indicating results consistent with industry judgment. This method also provides homogeneous groups of cities with centroids quite distant from the grand origin. Second, the combined procedure of factor analysis (and subsequent clustering of factor scores) indicated that two major dimensions, a city size construct and a demographic construct, explained most of the variance in the data.

This study was only a pilot effort. In practice, the marketing manager would use those city characteristics most relevant to his product line. The clusters could then serve as homogeneous blocks from which individual cities could be chosen to serve as treatment and control units, that is, matched units for various experimental purposes.

Television Program Audience Profile Analysis

Grouping of television programs into clusters having similar audience profile, which was used to illustrate the nature of taxonomic procedures, comprises still another exploratory investigation currently in progress. American Research Bureau data for both day and evening programs in October, 1965, are the bases for this analysis. For each, program measures of the number of adult men and women in different age categories and the number of children and teenagers viewing the program are available. The primary objective is to group programs by viewer characteristics so that their grouping is a function of viewer reaction to content and casting—not to the effects of time of day, day of week, and lead-in programs.

The analysis is divided into two stages. The first is the adjustment of raw data for the effects of time of day, day of week, and lead-in programs. The adjustment is roughly analogous to making a cyclical adjustment in a time series analysis to ensure a cleaner set of data for studying trend movements.

When variations in audience profile from program to program are caused primarily by the effect of program content and casting, the adjusted data are subjected to a taxonomic analysis. The first stage of the study is complete, and the taxonomic work is about to begin. (It will soon appear as a working paper [30].)

Patterns of Customer Brand Loyalty

At the beginning of this article the study of brand loyalty was used to illustrate the tendency for letting unidimensional measures represent customer behavior that may be multidimensional. In this study cluster analysis and Kruskal's algorithm [56] is used to characterize customer brand purchasing behavior. The objective is to develop more comprehensive classification systems for analyzing brand choice.

Chicago Tribune panel data for three product categories (carbonated beverages, regular coffee, and ready-to-eat cereals) for 1961 were used in the analysis. For each product category for each of 480 households, the percentage of units (based on weight) purchased by brand was computed.

Two different approaches were then taken. A Euclidean distance measure was used to group households that had relatively similar percentage distributions of brand purchasing behavior within a product. This is equivalent to studying brand loyalty for the bundle of brands households purchase. The results showed that with only one exception in the regular coffee market each cluster of households bought only one brand at a rate greater than the brand's overall market share. Although other brands were purchased, none was given this degree of favor. The only exceptions are the clusters containing several private brands. Households that purchase one private brand at a greater rate than its overall share are likely to purchase another with a similar degree of concentration. Customers who buy them may be less sensitive to differences in product characteristics, or the products themselves may be more similar.

A second approach organized the data by brand instead of by customer. This part of the analysis started with the transpose of the data matrix used, that is, the data were organized by brand and within brand, by household. For each brand the percentage of purchases devoted to that brand by each of about 100 households was available. Euclidean distance measures characterized brand similarity by pattern of purchase requirements over households.

Results so far have provided few surprises and have raised more questions than can be answered here. For example in the cereal market, evidence appears that old standard brands (Kellogg's Corn Flakes, Cheerios, Wheaties) tend to serve segments which overlap, yet many health-oriented cereals (Special K, All Bran, Grape Nuts) tend to serve a somewhat different group of customers.

Operational Characterization of Inter-brand Competition

In another pilot study, cluster analysis helped to characterize inter-brand competition in the computer field [38]. Performance data were obtained for over 100 different computer models with installation date used to categorize them as first- or second-generation models. For each computer model, data were available on 12 measured characteristics, such as word length, execution time, digital storage, transfer rate, and 10 categorical characteristics, such as whether the computer possessed Boolean operations, table look-up, and indirect addressing.

The data's mixed character (continuous variables and dichotomous features data) required a different approach from that typically used in cluster analysis. First, the attribute data were metricized by a multidimensional scaling technique [56]. A two-dimensional representation revealed that each computer model could be characterized by the dimensions of capacity (number of different features) and orientation (scientific versus business), as based on the particular pattern of zeroes and ones.

The resultant clusters, developed by a hierarchical grouping technique, displayed interesting characteristics from the standpoint of intermodel competition. For example, a machine's cluster of features appears to be idiosyncratic to the particular manufacturer, that is, each manufacturer tends to build all his machines with a particular set of features. Each manufacturer's complex, however, may vary from that of his competitors. It is interesting that only IBM had a model in each of the major clusters. However, the time period comparison—first- versus second-generation computers—indicated a trend toward all models having a greater number of features.

The measured variables were then analyzed separately, yielding two main dimensions—speed and size of computers. Finally, the measured data were dichotomized about the median of each characteristic (taken separately) and submitted to a combination multidimensional scaling and cluster analysis.

Figure 2 shows a two-space configuration derived from applying a nonmetric program to proximity measures developed from the above steps. After adjusting for intercorrelation of the characteristics [39], similarity measures were developed by tabulating the number of (weighted) matches for all computer pairs. The higher this number, the more similar each pair was assumed to be with respect to all 22 performance characteristics. For $n = 55$, there are 1,485 interpoint proximities as input to the program; only their rank order is required.

The two-space configuration of Figure 2 shows the boundaries of clusters formed (by another means) on a more precise configuration obtained in four-space. Such compression of results (into two-space) seriously distorts the make-up of Cluster 8; otherwise the clusters are fairly compact. It is interesting to note that Cluster 5 is composed of small, fairly slow, business-oriented machines, but Cluster 7 is characterized by large, relatively fast, scientific machines.

The complete study on which Figure 2 is based revealed that four dimensions—speed, size, number of different features (qualitative characteristics), and orientation (scientific versus business)—appeared to adequately describe the computer market.

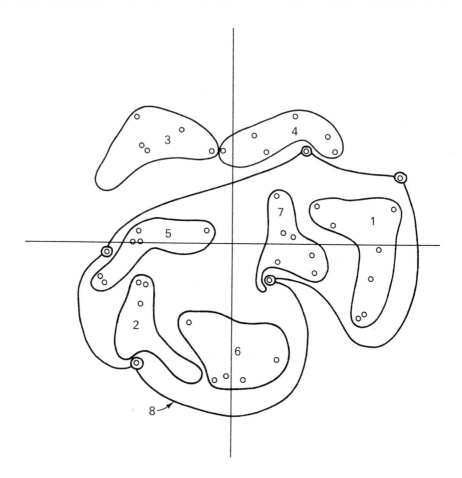

Figure 2. Two-Space Configuration of Computer Models in
"Performance Space"

The possibilities of such performance-space analyses over time have potential for the study of product innovation and modification—particularly industrial products like electric motors and machine tools. In this approach a whole series of performance spaces could be viewed through time—their dimensions, number of points (models), and interrelationships among points could all be changing, reflecting changes in technology and inter-model competition. Such an approach would seem to indicate the data's fine structure better than the more traditional reliance on S-curves to describe product life cycles.

Physicians' Media Reading Habits

In another study [41], numerical taxonomy was used to cluster reading profiles of both physicians and medical journals. The basic data consisted of zero-one matrixes in which each physician was classified as a light (zero) or heavy (one) reader of each of 19 medical journals. Each physician was also classified as one who lightly or heavily prescribed each of 29 therapeutic drug classes. Data were also available on the physician's specialty, age, and total weekly patient and prescription loads. The zero-one matrixes were again metricized by a multidimensional scaling program. Clusters of journals with similar, physician reading habits and clusters of physicians with similar journal profiles were developed.

Findings indicated that, within a given specialty, media reading profiles are not associated with such variables as physician age, total prescribing frequency, and product mix selection. However, the journal clusters provided an interesting output of the analysis by summarizing a diverse set of zero-one data. The marketing manager could use these clusters as a guide to media scheduling. For example, if he wishes to choose journals with high overlap of coverage, he can choose all journals within a given cluster. If, however, he wishes to emphasize diversity, he can choose one journal from each cluster.

From a methodological viewpoint, the interesting concept is the dual use of multidimensional scaling and cluster analysis. The first technique allows the researcher to make a concise description of the data—frequently interpretable in its own right—and the last allows him to organize the data into similar journal profiles that can then be subjected to further analysis.

Taxonomy in Psychometric Studies

Some mention should also be made of the usefulness of clustering procedures in psychometric studies involving perceptual and preference mapping. A recently completed study [36] involved the analysis of proximities data developed during a study of student perception of six graduate schools of business. Three modes of data collection—similarity triads, direct ratings, and the semantic differential—were used to collect proximity judgments.

In this study a hierarchical grouping method was used to develop clusters of respondents with similar perceptions of the six business schools. That is, although the main objective of this study was the development of perceptual maps, cluster analysis was useful in partitioning the respondents into homogeneous groups with similar perceptions.

The results indicated that a two-space solution adequately portrayed the respondents' perceptions. From other data collected in the study, the dimensions of the space could be characterized as prestige of school and quantitativeness of its curriculum. Not inconsequentially all three data collection methods yielded fairly similar perceptual maps, on an aggregate basis. Moreover, differences in perceptual mappings were not generally explainable by respondent personal data, such as undergraduate major, previous work experience, graduate major. Only one variable, home state of respondent, appeared to influence his perception of the business schools in any significant way.

A similar study [37] involved a multidimensional scaling of professional journals typically read by marketing academics and researchers. Perception and preference data were obtained for eight journals, and respondents were clustered on the basis of similarity of perception and preference.

Figure 3 shows the results of applying a nonmetric clustering routine to

```
                                    Subject Number

Proximity  0    0    1    0    0    0    1    0    0    0    0    1
Measure    9    0    1    8    6    2    1    3    4    7    5    2
1.8253     ·    ·    ·    ·    ·    ·    ·    ·    ·    ×  × ×   ·    ·    ·    ·
1.7745     ·    ·    ·    ·    ·    ·    ·    ·    ·    ×  × ×   ·    ·    ·    ×  ×   ·
1.7111     ·    ·    ·    ·    ·    ·    ·    ·    ·    ×  × ×   ·    ×  × × × ×   ·
1.6871     ·    ·    ·    ·    ·    ·    ·    ·    ·    ×  × ×   ·    ×  × × × ×   ·   × × ×
1.5961     ·    ·    ·    ·    ·    ·    ·    ×  × × × ×   ·    ×  × × × ×   ·   × × ×
1.4724     ·    ·    ·    ×  × ×   ·    ×  × × × ×   ·    ×  × × × ×   ·   × × ×
1.3715     ·    ·    ·    ×  × ×   ·    ×  × × × ×   ·    ×  × × × ×   ·   × × ×
1.2091     ·    ·    ·    ×  × ×   ·    ×  × × × × × ×   × × × × ×   × × × ×
1.1388     ·    ·    ·    ×  × ×   ×    × × × × × ×   × × × × ×   × × × ×
1.0558     ×  × ×   ·    ×  × × × × × ×   × × × × × ×   × × × ×
0.8077     ×  × × × ×   × × × × × ×   × × × × × ×   × × × ×
```

Figure 3. Illustration of Hierarchical Clustering Routine

the perception data [37]. Note that this program is hierarchical. Respondents 4 and 7 are first clustered because they had the highest proximity measure of the group. Respondents 2 and 11 are next clustered at level two, and so on, until all points are eventually in one large cluster. On the left-hand side of Figure 3 one can see how the proximity measure declines as more disparate points are clustered.

The results of this study indicated that preferences and perception were independent over stimuli, that is, respondents clustered by commonality of perception were unrelated to clusters formed by commonality of preference.

Assumptions and Limitations of Clustering Methods

Cluster analysis is not a single, cohesive set of techniques but rather a variety of procedures, each having a kind of ad hoc flavor and certain advantages and disadvantages. Some of the limitations are shared by all these techniques to some degree, but specific procedures have both advantages and disadvantages.

General Problems in Cluster Analysis

All clustering techniques have certain general analytical inadequacies because the data are used to generate the groupings. Illustrative questions are:

1. How many clusters should be formed?
2. If, as is usually the case, the characteristics of the objects are measured in different units, how can equivalence among metrics be achieved?

3. If the objects' scores along several dimensions are intercorrelated, how should these interdependencies be handled?

4. Even if the number of clusters can be determined in some satisfactory way, how does the analyst decide on the appropriate boundaries for clusters, summary measures of the characteristics of each cluster, and their statistical significance?

In some of the illustrative applications described here, the number of clusters was decided in advance. Increasing the number of clusters will tend to reduce the average within-cluster distance but, obviously, one must stop short of ending with each point being a cluster.

In addition, all data including variables originally interval-scaled were standardized to zero mean and unit standard deviation. Although this step enables the analyst to work with common metrics, it is assumed that central tendency and variability among dimensions are not important.

The problem of dealing with intercorrelated characteristics was pointed out in the test marketing illustration. In this study an alternative procedure was used in which the set of characteristics was first reduced to independent constructs by a principal component analysis before the cluster analysis. This procedure can lead to different clusters from those obtained by the first procedure that ignored the intercorrelations among characteristics. Finally, the researcher might wish to use the Mahalanobis generalized distance measure discussed by Morrison [66].

Appropriate boundaries and descriptive statistics of clusters are usually determined by the specific technique used—in many instances by a generalized distance function, the computation of centroids, and the use of a preset number of points or cutoff distances. Even so, it is fair to say that good measures of cluster compactness are not available. In the test marketing illustration each dimension included in the analysis was given (manifest) equal weight in determining similarity. In a given situation one might choose to give a single dimension or some subset of dimensions more weight than others in defining proximity measures. Cluster analysis can be easily modified to take into account unequal weights, but this approach still largely varies with circumstances.

Still less is known about the inferential characteristics of clustering techniques. Unlike other multivariate techniques, such as discriminant analysis and principal component analysis, clustering techniques are much less structured, and little investigation has been made to date of their statistical properties.

Limitations of Specific Proximity Measures

In earlier sections of this article, the characteristics of specific proximity measures—distance measures, correlation techniques, similarity coefficients—were briefly described. Each measure suffers from certain specific limitations.

Distance measures are usually restricted to instances in which the objects' characteristics to be measured can be expressed as interval-scaled variables. This represents a limitation on the kind of variable meaningfully handled although Kendall's nonparametric measure (mentioned earlier) could be used to handle data that are scaled only ordinally and the researcher could develop non-Euclidean metrics.

In addition, the Euclidean measure suffers from the disadvantage that two objects may be viewed as different solely because their values on one variable differ markedly. Finally, it should be reiterated that the researcher would, in general, obtain different results by using original versus standardized data for the characteristics of the objects being clustered by this method.

Correlative techniques, such as Q-factor analysis, have an even more serious limitation because one must standardize over objects, thus losing mean and scatter information. That is, in this technique, each object is given the same mean and variance.

A second disadvantage is that rotation of factor axes (to get purer loadings) lends a certain arbitrariness to the procedure. Finally, also mentioned earlier, in this procedure objects may be split on factors, leading to uncertainty of the placement of an object into a specific group.

Similarity measures are flexible since they can be adapted to handle nominal, ordinal, and interval-scaled data. Furthermore, it can be shown that similarity measures can be metricized by multidimensional-scaling procedures. Morever, similarity measures are generally less sensitive to the impact of a single characteristic on the resultant dissimilarity of two objects than are the Euclidean distance measures.

However, similarity measures have their set of limitations. First, if a group is to be formed on the basis of overall matches, two objects may not be grouped even if they match well on some subset of characteristics. Conversely, an object may be in a group because it is similar to different members of the group on different subsets of characteristics.

Second, if a large number of characteristics are involved, objects which match may do so for accidental reasons, reflecting the noise in the data; and third, if some variables are dichotomous and others are multichotomous, the two-state attributes will tend to be more heavily weighted in the similarity measures. For example, if one attribute were broken down into 100 states, we would rarely find matches. Hence this attribute would receive little importance in the overall similarity measure.

Finally, if continuous data are discretized in order to use similarity measures, valuable information can be lost. The analyst is thus plagued with the problem of deciding both the kinds of attributes to include in the analysis and the number of states to be associated with each.

Choosing Appropriate Techniques

Numerical taxonomy invites some ambivalence by the analyst wanting to use the techniques. On one hand, the procedures are designed to cope with a relevant aspect of marketing description—the orderly classification of multi-variate phenomena. On the other hand, the varying character of various proximity measures and clustering techniques—and the basic lack of structure at either the descriptive statistic or inferential statistic level—suggests that the analyst be cautious in applying them.

Until more structure is introduced, it seems prudent to conduct analyses in parallel where alternative proximity measures and grouping procedures are used [40]. Moreover, sensitivity analyses on synthetic data might be helpful in exploring the various idiosyncracies of alternative techniques. If the data are well clustered to begin with, similar results over alternative techniques will usually be obtained—but how often will these pleasant states of affairs exist? Though the authors believe numerical taxonomy can be useful in marketing analysis, they would urge prudence in its application and the systematic study of similarities and differences among alternative procedures. (The references may help to facilitate this study.)

References

1. G. H. Ball, "Data Analysis in the Social Sciences: What About the Details?" *Proceedings Fall Joint Computer Conference*, 1965, 533–59.

2. B. M. Bass, "Iterative Inverse Factor Analysis: A Rapid Method for Clustering Persons," *Psychometrika*, 22 (March 1957), 105.

3. J. F. Bennett and W. L. Hays, "Multidimensional Unfolding: Determining the Dimensionality of Ranked Preference Data," *Psychometrika*, 25 (March 1960), 27–43.

4. A. Birnbaum and A. E. Maxwell, "Classification Procedures Based on Bayes' Formula," *Applied Statistics*, 9 (November 1961), 152–68.

5. Jack Block, "The Difference Between Q and R," *Psychological Review*, 62 (1955), 356–8.

6. ———, Louis Levine and Quinn McNemar, "Testing for the Existence of Psychometric Patterns," *Journal of Abnormal Social Psychology*, 46 (July 1951), 356–9.

7. R. E. Bonner, "Some Clustering Techniques," *IBM Journal of Research and Development*, 8 (January 1964), 22–33.

8. A. D. Booth, "An Application of the Method of Steepest Descent to the Solution of Simultaneous Non-linear Equations," *Quarterly Journal of Mech. Applied Mathematics*, 2 (December 1949), 460–8.

9. G. E. P. Box, "The Exploration and Exploitation of Response Surfaces: Some General Considerations and Examples," *Biometrics*, 10 (March 1954), 16–60.

10. S. H. Brooks, "A Discussion of Random Methods of Seeking Maxima," *Journal of Operations Research Society*, 6 (1958), 244–51.

11. ———, "A Comparison of Maximum Seeking Methods," *Journal of Operations Research Society*, 7 (1959), 430–57.

12. Cyril L. Burt, "Correlations between Persons," *British Journal of Psychology*, 28 (July 1937), 59–96.

13. H. Cartwright, *Structural Models: An Introduction to the Theory of Directed Graphs*, New York: John Wiley & Sons, Inc., 1963.

14. Raymond B. Cattell, "r_P and Other Coefficients of Pattern Similarity," *Psychometrika*, 14 (December 1949), 279–98.

15. ———, "On the Disuse and Misuse of R, P, Q and O Techniques in Clinical Psychology," *Journal of Clinical Psychology*, 7 (1951), 203–14.

16. ———, M. A. Coulter and B. Tsujioka, "The Taxonometric Recognition of Types and Functional Emergents," in R. B. Cattell, ed., *Handbook of Multivariate Experimental Psychology*, Chicago: Rand McNally and Co., 1966, 288–329.

17. W. W. Cooley and Paul R. Lohnes, *Multivariate Procedures for the Behavioral Sciences*, New York: John Wiley & Sons, Inc., 1963.

18. C. H. Coombs, *A Theory of Data*, New York: John Wiley & Sons, Inc., 1964.

19. ———, "A Method for the Study of Interstimulus Similarity," *Psychometrika*, 19 (September 1954), 183–94.

20. Douglas R. Cox, "Note on Grouping," *Journal of American Statistical Association*, 52 (December 1957), 543–47.

21. Lee J. Cronbach and Goldine C. Gleser, "Assessing Similarity between Profiles," *Psychological Bulletin*, 50 (November 1953), 456–73.

22. Frank M. duMas, "A Quick Method of Analyzing the Similarity of Profiles," *Journal of Clinical Psychology*, 2 (January 1946), 80–3.

23. ———, "On the Interpretation of Personality Profiles," *Journal of Clinical Psychology*, 3 (1947), 57–65.

24. A. W. F. Edwards and L. L. Cavalli-Sforza, "A Method for Cluster Analysis," *Biometrics*, 52 (June 1965), 362–75.

25. G. A. Ferguson, "The Factorial Interpretation of Test Difficulty," *Psychometrika*, 6 (October 1941), 323–29.

26. R. A. Fisher, "The Use of Multiple Measurements in Taxonomic Problems," *American Eugenics*, 7 (1963), 179–88.

27. W. D. Fisher, "On Grouping for Maximum Homogeneity," *Journal of American Statistical Association*, 53 (December 1958), 789–98.

28. Claude Flament, *Applications of Graph Theory to Group Structure*, New Jersey: Prentice-Hall, Inc., 1963.

29. J. J. Fortier and H. Solomon, "Clustering Procedures," Unpublished paper, International Symposium on Multivariate Analysis, University of Dayton, June 1965.

30. Ronald E. Frank, "Television Program Audience Similarities: A Taxonomic Analysis," University of Pennsylvania, December 1967, mimeographed.

31. Eugene L. Gaier and Marilyn C. Lee, "Pattern Analysis: The Configural Approach to Predictive Measurement," *Psychological Bulletin*, 50 (March 1953), 140–8.

32. J. A. Gengerelli, "A Method for Detecting Subgroups in a Population and Specifying their Membership," *Journal of Psychology*, 55 (1953), 140–48.

33. L. A. Goodman and W. H. Kruskal, "Measures of Association for Cross Classifications," *Journal of American Statistical Association*, 59 (September 1964), 732–64.

34. Paul E. Green, Ronald E. Frank, and Patrick J. Robinson, "Cluster Analysis in Test Market Selection," *Management Science*, 13 (April 1967), 387–400.

35. ———, "A Behavioral Experiment in Risk Taking and Information Seeking," Working paper, University of Pennsylvania, January 1967.

36. Paul E. Green and P. J. Robinson, "Perceptual Structure of Graduate Business

Schools—An Application of Multidimensional Scaling," Working paper, June 1967.

37. ———, "Perceptual and Preference Mapping of Professional Journals," Working paper, May 1967.

38. ——— and F. J. Carmone, "Structural Characteristics of the Computer Market—An Application of Cluster and Reduced Space Analysis," Working paper, May 1967.

39. ———, "WAGS: An IBM 7040 Computer Program for Obtaining Weighted Agreement Scores for Multidimensional Scaling," Working paper, May 1967.

40. ———, "Cross Techniques Study—Computer Model Clustering," Working paper, August 1967.

41. ———, "A Reduced Space and Cluster Analysis of Physicians' Media Reading Habits," Working paper, September 1967.

42. H. H. Harman, *Modern Factor Analysis*, Chicago: University of Chicago Press, 1960.

43. C. W. Harris, "Characteristics of Two Measures of Profile Similarity," *Psychometrika*, 20 (1955), 289–97.

44. G. C. Helmstadter, "An Empirical Comparison of Methods for Estimating Profile Similarity," *Educational and Psychological Measurement*, 17 (1957), 71–82.

45. J. L. Hodges, Jr., "Discriminatory Analysis I: Survey of Discriminatory Analysis," USAF School of Aviation Medicine, Randolph, Texas, 1950.

46. Karl J. Holzinger, "Factoring Test Scores and Implications for the Method of Averages," *Psychometrika*, 9 (December 1944), 257–62.

47. Paul Horst, *Matrix Algebra for Social Scientists*, New York: Holt, Rinehart and Winston, 1963.

48. ———, "Pattern Analysis and Configural Scoring," *Journal of Clinical Psychology*, 10 (January 1954), 1–11.

49. K. J. Jones, *The Multivariate Statistical Analyzer*, Cambridge, Mass.: Harvard Cooperative Society, 1964.

50. J. Joyce and C. Channon, "Classifying Market Survey Respondents," *Applied Statistics*, 15 (November 1966), 191–215.

51. H. F. Kaiser, "Formulas for Component Scores," *Psychometrika*, 27 (March 1962), 83–7.

52. M. G. Kendall, *The Advanced Theory of Statistics*, Vol. 1, New York: Hafner Publishing Company, 1958.

53. ———, *Rank Correlation Methods*, London: Griffin Publishing Company, 1948.

54. ———, "Discrimination and Classification," London: CEIR Ltd., 1965.

55. J. B. Kruskal, "Nonmetric Multidimensional Scaling: A Numerical Scaling Method," *Psychometrika*, 29 (June 1964), 115–30.

56. ———, "Multidimensional Scaling by Optimizing Goodness of Fit to a Nonmetric Hypothesis," *Psychometrika*, 29 (March 1964), 1–28.

57. E. O. Laumann and L. Guttman, "The Relative Association Contiguity of Occupations in an Urban Setting," *American Sociological Review*, 31 (April 1966), 169–78.

58. J. C. Lingoes, "A Taxonometric Optimization Procedure: An IBM 7090 Classification Program," *Behavioral Science*, 8 (October 1963), 370.

59. ———, "An IBM 7090 program for Guttman-Lingoes Smallest Space Analysis," Computer Center, University of Michigan, 1965.

60. P. C. Mahalanobis, "On the Generalized Distance in Statistics," *Proceedings National Institute of Science*, Vol. 12, India, 1936, 49–58.

61. F. Massarik and P. Ratoosh, *Mathematical Explorations in Behavioral Science*, Homewood, Ill.: Richard D. Irwin, Inc., 1965.

62. P. McNaughton-Smith, *et al.*, "Dissimilarity Analysis: A New Technique of Hierarchical Subdivision," *Nature*, 202 (June 1964), 1033–4.

63. Louis L. McQuitty, "Hierarchical Syndrome Analysis," *Educational and Psychological Measurement*, 20 (1960), 293–304.

64. ———, "Typal Analysis," *Educational and Psychological Measurement*, 20 (1960), 293–304.

65. ———, "Best Classifying Every Individual at Every Level," *Educational and Psychological Measurement*, 23 (July 1963), 337–46.

66. Donald G. Morrison, "Measurement Problems in Cluster Analysis," *Management Science*, 13 (August 1967), B-775–80.

67. Jum Nunnally, "The Analysis of Profile Data," *Psychological Bulletin*, 59 (July 1962), 311–19.

68. Charles E. Osgood and George J. Suci, "A Measure of Relation Determined by Both Mean Difference and Profile Information," *Psychological Bulletin*, 49 (May 1952), 251–62.

69. J. E. Overall, "Note on Multivariate Methods of Profile Analysis," *Psychological Bulletin*, 61 (March 1964), 195–8.

70. K. Pearson, "On the Dissection of Assymetrical Frequency Curves," *Contributions to the Mathematical Theory of Evolution, Phil. Trans. of Royal Society* 1894.

71. ———, "On the Coefficient of Racial Likeness," *Biometrika*, 18 (July 1926), 105–17.

72. R. G. Pettit, "Clustering Program: Continuous Variables," Advanced Systems Development Division, IBM, Yorktown Heights, New York, 1964.

73. C. R. Rao, "Tests of Significance in Multivariate Analysis," *Biometrika*, 35 (May 1948), 58–79.

74. ———, "The Utilization of Multiple Measurements in Problems of Biological Classification," *Journal of Royal Statistical Society*, Section B, 10 (1948), 159–203.

75. F. Restle, *Psychology of Judgment and Choice*, New York: John Wiley & Sons, Inc., 1961.

76. D. J. Rogers and T. T. Tanimoto, "A Computer Program for Classifying Plants," *Science*, 132 (October 1960), 1115–22.

77. P. J. Rulon, "Distinctions Between Discriminant and Regression Analysis and a Geometric Interpretation of the Discriminant Function," *Harvard Educational Review*, 21 (June 1951), 80–90.

78. R. N. Shepard, "The Analysis of Proximities: Multidimensional Scaling With an Unknown Distance Functions: I and II," *Psychometrika*, 27 (June 1962, September 1962), 125–40, 219–46.

79. ———, "Analysis of Proximities as a Technique for the Study of Information Processing in Man," *Human Factors*, 5 (February 1963), 33–48.

80. G. G. Simpson, "Numerical Taxonomy and Biological Classification," *Science*, 144 (May 1964), 712–13.

81. P. H. A. Sneath, "The Application of Computers to Taxonomy," *Journal of General Micro-Biology*, 17 (August 1957), 201–27.

82. R. R. Sokal, "Numerical Taxonomy," *Scientific American*, 215 (December 1966), 106–16.

83. ———, and P. H. A. Sneath, *Principles of Numerical Taxonomy*, San Francisco: Freeman & Company, 1963.

84. William Stephenson, "Some Observations on Q Technique," *Psychological Bulletin*, 49 (September 1952), 483–98.

85. S. A. Stouffer, *et al.*, *Measurement and Prediction*, Princeton, N.J.: Princeton University Press, 1950.

86. Robert L. Thorndike, "Who Belongs in the Family?", *Psychometrika*, 18 (December 1953), 267–76.

87. Warren S. Torgerson, "Multidimensional Scaling: Theory and Method," *Psychometrika*, 17 (December 1952), 401–19.

88. ———, "Multidimensional Scaling of Similarity," *Psychometrika*, 30 (December 1965), 379–93.

89. Fred T. Tyler, "Some Examples of Multivariate Analysis in Educational and Psychological Research," *Psychometrika*, 17 (September 1952), 289–96.

90. Robert C. Tyron, *Cluster Analysis*, Edwards Bros. 1939.

91. ———, "Cumulative Communality Cluster Analysis," *Educational and Psychological Measurement*, 18 (March 1958), 3–35.

92. J. W. Tukey, "The Future of Data Analysis," *Annals of Mathematical Statistics*, 33 (March 1962), 1–67.

93. J. H. Ward, "Hierarchical Grouping to Optimize an Objective Function," *Journal of American Statistical Association*, 58 (March 1963), 236–44.

94. Joe E. Ward, Jr., and Marion E. Hook, "Application of an Hierarchical Grouping Procedure to a Problem of Grouping Profiles," *Educational and Psychological Measurement*, 23 (1963), 69–82.

95. Harold Webster, "A Note on Profile Similarity," *Psychological Bulletin*, 49 (September 1952), 538–9.

96. Joseph Zubin, "A Technique for Measuring Like-Mindedness," *Journal of Abnormal Social Psychology*, 33 (October 1938), 508–16.

29

David A. Aaker: Visual Clustering
Using Principal Components Analysis

Cluster analysis or numerical taxonomy, which has been introduced into the marketing literature only recently [5, 7], has shown promise of being a useful tool. The marketing applications of cluster analysis are pervasive and numerous. Brands can be clustered to obtain a feel for market structure.

Customers can be cluster analyzed to determine market segments. TV programs can be clustered to answer questions of audience composition more analytically. We could easily extend this list.

Literally hundreds of computer programs are available for performing cluster analysis. Several have been described in some detail in the marketing literature [1, 2, 5, 6, 7, 10]. Each systematically searches through different combinations of objects to try to get "similar" (with respect to a criterion or objective function) objects in the same clusters and "different" objects in different clusters. The number of clusters and the level of clustering will depend upon the data and the objective of the analysis. One can always specify a criterion that would imply only one cluster and another which would place each object in its own cluster. Thus, the researcher is required to specify in some manner the level of clustering desired. With the level specified, the cluster program can be applied to data, and a set of clusters will emerge that is optimal as far as that program is concerned. The user will obtain numerical values associated with the resulting clusters and their objects that provide additional insights into the cluster structure. Although powerful tools, nearly all cluster programs share some rather undesirable attributes. They are relatively difficult to use and interpret, and they are often expensive to set up and to run.

Recognizing these problems with large-scale cluster programs, Kamen [8] recently suggested a "simple but usable technique" for obtaining clusters from a data set. As Kamen observed, his technique, "quick clustering," is crude and its power is limited. However, he correctly notes that, for some researchers in some situations, it can have considerable value.

The purpose of this paper is twofold. First, Kamen's approach is described and a compromise between it and a formal cluster program is suggested. The compromise, termed visual clustering, involves obtaining a lower space representation of the objects and visually determining the clusters. Although requiring more effort, such an approach avoids several of the limitations of "quick clustering." It also has several advantages over cluster programs even though it lacks their power and is not presented as a substitute. In the following, visual clustering will be described and then compared with quick clustering in the context of an example. The second purpose of this paper is to present a practical exposition of principal components analysis, a basic multivariate tool. It provides a lower space representation of a set of objects which has several appealing properties.

Visual Clustering

Suppose that consumers' perceptions of brands of coffee were measured along two dimensions, taste (bitter-sweet) and color (dark-light). The brands could then be displayed in a "perceptual map" as in Figure 1. Clearly, three "clusters" of brands can be identified.

Visual clustering shares several problems with other clustering approaches. First, it is usually not so easy to determine which objects should be assigned to which clusters. A cluster program will have a very specific quantitative objective function and a search routine. In visual clustering there is no such aid. In crude terms, one simply stares at the result until clusters emerge. More scientifically, it means that the analyst develops his own heuristic or

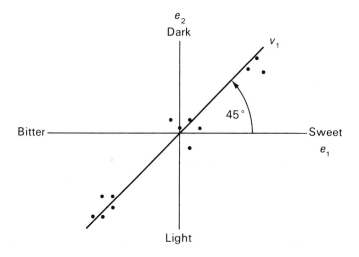

Figure 1. Perceptual Map of Coffee Brands

search procedure compatible with his project objective, to discern clusters from the graphical representation. Such a technique is certainly crude and subjective, but at least the heuristic is exposed. Too often, the objective function is not deliberately selected by the researcher but is simply the one used in a convenient cluster program and may not really be suitable. More important, a lack of structure is often easier to detect, since the user is not presented with an output listing each cluster member. Such an output can create an illusion of exactness even though one intimate with the program could readily discern the true state of affairs from other measures.

A second problem is how to select the appropriate number of clusters. Here, again, the determination of the number of clusters in visual clustering is entirely subjective, but the visual presentation does admit a good feel for the structure. Such a feel is much more difficult to achieve when working with a cluster program without a great deal of experience with it.

The selection of the original dimensions is a third problem. In the example, it must be determined that taste and color are somehow relevant for purposes of the investigation. In addition, it may be useful to make the resulting display independent of the choice of units. If the dimensions are standardized by dividing all the variables by their respective standard deviations, such independence will be achieved. After standardization, the measures will be the same whether the original units were in feet, yards, or miles. Further, the relative importance of the dimensions must be considered. It is quite appropriate to adjust one dimension (by multiplying its components by a positive constant) to reflect a subjective judgment about its importance (see Morrison [9]).

Principal Components

A problem unique to visual clustering is how to obtain a graphical representation. In most situations there will be many dimensions—the objects will be described by a set of many variables—and a two-dimensional representation will not be possible. In other situations, only interobject indexes of similarity or distance measures are available. In both cases, the appropriate tool is often principal components. It can be used to provide a lower space representation, it is easy to use and interpret, and computer programs are economical and readily available.

Principal components, unlike factor analysis, is not a statistical or conceptual model, but is only a set of geometric operations. The objective is to reduce the number of dimensions involved to a small number while retaining, as much as possible, the interpoint distance information contained in the original data set. A simple example will illustrate the axis rotation that is principal components.

Suppose, in Figure 1, it became desirable to work with one dimension instead of two. What single axes could be drawn that would retain as much of the two-dimensional interpoint distance as possible? Clearly, v_1, which can be viewed as e_1, rotated 45°, is the logical candidate. The v_1 component of the interobject distance is shorter than the true distance, but for most object pairs it is not a bad approximation.

More precisely, the object is to project the points from a two-dimensional space to a one-dimensional space so as to retain as much of the squared interpoint distance as possible. The v_1 is that one-dimensional space. When projecting to a two-dimensional space from a higher dimension, the axis v_1 is first found in the same manner. We then ask what axis perpendicular to v_1 should be included. The answer is the axis that will permit us to obtain the maximum amount of squared interpoint distance not contained in v_1. The process is continued until the desired number of dimensions is reached.

Interpoint Distance

The distance measure is central to any cluster analysis technique. To discuss distance concepts more precisely, it is necessary to introduce some notation. Assume that n objects are described by p variates. The value of the kth variate for object i will be denoted as y_{ik}. Let Y define the corresponding $n \times p$ matrix. The n objects may be plotted in a p-dimensional space. If p is more than 2 or 3, the plot must be at least somewhat conceptual. Nevertheless, it is well defined. The squared distance between objects i and j, $d_{ij}{}^2$, is given by:

$$d_{ij}{}^2 = \sum_{k=1}^{p} (y_{ik} - y_{jk})^2 = \sum_{k=1}^{p} (y_{ik} y_{ik}) +$$
$$\sum_{k=1}^{p} (y_{jk} y_{jk}) - 2 \sum_{k=1}^{p} (y_{ik} y_{jk}). \qquad (1)$$

The object of principal components is to find q dimensions ($q < p$) such that the squared interpoint distance is conserved as nearly as possible when the points are projected into the q-dimensional space.

Another general expression for distance is the following:

$$d_{ij}{}^2 = a_{ii} + a_{jj} - 2a_{ij} \qquad (2)$$

where a_{ij} is some predetermined coefficient of association between object i and object j. If a_{ij} is defined to be

$$a_{ij} = \sum_{k=1}^{p} y_{ik} y_{jk}$$

then the two expressions for distance are identical.

Several other possible definitions for a_{ij} yield useful distance measures. One of the most interesting is to let a_{ij} be an index of similarity, s_{ij}. An index of similarity is a number which indicates how "similar" two objects are to each other. It can be 1 if the objects are identical, 0 if the objects are perfectly dissimilar, and between 0 and 1 otherwise. For example, if we were dealing with qualitative variables, we might observe the number of matches between objects i and j. A match would occur on a variable if both objects had the same value. The total number of matches divided by the total number of variables would be one possible index of similarity. Frank and Green [1], Joyce and Channon [7], and Sokal and Sneath [12] provide descriptions of several useful similarity indexes.

What distance measure is implied by defining a_{ij} to be a similarity index? Observe that because of the nature of a similarity index:

$$a_{ii} = s_{ii} = 1$$

Thus, the distance squared becomes:

$$d_{ij}{}^2 = s_{ii} + s_{jj} - 2s_{ij} = 2(1 - s_{ij}) \qquad (3)$$

Such a distance measure has intuitive appeal. When $s_{ij} = 0$, the objects are at a maximum distance apart. When $s_{ij} = 1$, the objects are zero distance apart. When $0 \le s_{ij} \le 1$, distance squared is a linear function of s_{ij}.

It would also be possible to let a_{ij} equal the correlation coefficient, ρ_{ij}. Because $\rho_{ii} = 1$ by definition, the distance measure would be:

$$d_{ij}^2 = 2(1 - \rho_{ij}) \tag{4}$$

Because of the definition of the correlation coefficient, the distance of equation 4 is closely related to that of equation 1. In fact, if the matrix Y were reduced (variate means subtracted) and standardized by row or variate standard deviation, the distance of equations 1 and 4 would then be identical. Equation 4 is of the same form as equation 3 and, thus, has the same intuitive appeal. It should be noted that the correlation coefficient eliminates some information contained in the original data set. By reducing and standardizing the data, the characteristics of elevation and scatter are removed from the data. In some situations this information is important and should not be eliminated. In these cases, the analyst should work with the original data and not with correlation coefficients.

The distance expression of equation 2 will be of value only if a graphical representation can be found based upon that distance. Fortunately, such is the case. If the n by n matrix $A = [a_{ij}]$ is known, it is possible to find n points in an n-dimensional[1] Euclidean space with coordinates such that the squared distance between the ith and jth point is $a_{ii} + a_{jj} - 2a_{ij}$.[2] However, n dimensions will normally be too many to handle. Fortunately, principal components can be used to represent graphically these n points in a small number of dimensions, $q < n$, such that the sum of their squared interpoint distances is conserved as nearly as possible.

The Mechanics of Principal Components

As the above discussion suggests, two types of input data can be used. The first is the $n \times p$ matrix, Y, with components y_{ik}. The second is an $n \times n$ matrix A with components a_{ij}. The output format will depend upon which type of input is used and upon the specific computer program used. The ultimate objective is to obtain the coordinate values for the n objects with respect to the new dimensions. Let us first consider the use of the Y matrix as the input.

---

[1] Actually the points may be found in an r-dimension space where $r = $ rank $A \leq n - 1$. Remember that one can always plot n points in an $n - 1$ space just as two points define a line.

[2] For the Euclidean space to be real—that is, to contain no imaginary axes—the matrix A must be positive semi-definite. Fortunately, A will be positive semi-definite for most reasonable definitions of a_{ij}. If A is not positive semi-definite and if the negative eigenvalues associated with the imaginary axes are small, the analysis may still proceed.

It is desirable to use reduced data—data with variable means subtracted—so that:

$$\sum_{k=1}^{p} y_{ik} = 0 \qquad i = 1, 2, \ldots, n$$

If the data are not reduced, the objects will all have high coordinate values on the first principal component or dimension. The first dimension may then be regarded as allowing for the mean value of the variables and will actually not provide much interobject distance information.

The output will include p ordered p-component vectors which will be labeled principal components, eigenvectors, latent vectors, or characteristic vectors. Let us denote them by:

$$v_m = (v_{m1}, v_{m2}, \ldots, v_{mp}) \; m = 1, \ldots, p$$

These vectors should be normalized such that:

$$\sum_{k=1}^{p} v_{mk}^{2} = 1$$

The coordinates for the n objects with respect to the new dimensions are often also included in the output. The coordinate for the mth dimension for object i is simply:

$$\sum_{k=1}^{p} y_{ik} v_{mk}$$

The program will also print out a number associated with each dimension, λ_m, which will be labeled principal root, eigenvalue, latent root, or characteristic root. It has the property that the sum of the first q eigenvalues divided by the sum of all the eigenvalues represents the proportion of the squared interpoint distance that has been retained in the q dimension representation.

Let us now assume that a matrix of similarities, A, is used as the input. Again, the first component will reflect the mean value of all the elemets of A and will be of little interest. Gower [3] has shown that a simple transformation will eliminate this component. The transformation involves creating a new matrix B by subtracting from each component of matrix A its column mean and its row mean and adding back the grand mean:

$$b_{ij} = a_{ij} - \bar{a}_i - \bar{a}_j + \bar{a} \tag{5}$$

where $\bar{a}_k$ is the mean value of the kth row (or column) of A and $\bar{a}$ is the overall mean. It can be easily verified that the interpoint distance measure defined by equation 5 is not affected by the transformation. This transformation essentially "reduces" the similarity matrix.

When the input is an $n \times n$ similarity matrix, the principal components (or eigenvectors or latent vectors or characteristic vectors) will now be n

component vectors and there will be n of them. Let us denote them by

$$w_m = (w_{m1}, w_{m2}, \ldots, w_{mn}) \ m = 1, \ldots, n$$

The coordinates of the n objects for the mth dimension are simply the elements of the w_m vector multiplied by $\sqrt{\lambda_m}$, where λ_m is defined as before. If w_m is normalized such that

$$\sum_{i=1}^{p} w_{m1}^2 = \lambda_m$$

then the multiplication step is also eliminated.

Nonmetric Multidimensional Scaling

An alternate approach to providing a graphical representation is nonmetric multidimensional scaling. Its objective is to find a lower dimensional space such that the rank order of the interpoint distance is preserved as much as possible. The input need not be "distances" but can merely be their rank order. This approach is described by Green and Carmone [4] and by Neidell [11].

An Example

To illustrate visual clustering and principal components analysis, the 11 by 11 matrix of correlations shown in Table 1 which was used by Kamen to present quick clustering will be used. The eleven objects are gasoline brands which respondents were asked to rate along a scale from 7 (very favorable) to 1 (unfavorable). The matrix is actually the brand correlations which appeared in one market during a 1965 test.

In quick clustering, the highest entry in each column is underlined. Then the highest such number is noted (0.640), and the brands involved form a cluster (Martin-Owens). If another brand in either the Martin row or the Owens row has an underlined coefficient, it is added to the cluster with a link to the appropriate brand—a link that is weaker than that joining Martin and Owens. Clark is thus included in the Martin-Owens cluster with a link to Martin. The procedure then repeats itself on the matrix with brands already clustered deleted. By this method four clusters were found in the data set of Table 1: Owens-Martin-Clark, D-X–Phillips–Shell, Skelly-Mobil-Texaco, and Standard-Gulf. Quick clustering, of course, requires only a pencil and paper. The problem is that it doesn't take into consideration intercorrelations. Further, it provides little feel for the tightness of the clusters, the distance between clusters, and the relative positioning of clusters in the total market structure. Visual clustering overcomes many of these limitations.

Table 1. Correlations Among Gasoline Brands in Rockford, Illinois, in Terms of General Attitude

		Standard 1	Martin* 2	Shell 3	Texaco 4	Phillips 5	Mobil 6	D-X 7	Owens* 8	Skelly 9	Clark* 10	Gulf 11
Standard	1	—	.006	.358	.382	.325	.289	.262	.108	.368	.178	.404
Martin	2	.006	—	.157	.088	.134	.161	.130	.640	.184	.360	.200
Shell	3	.358	.157	—	.337	.375	.343	.340	.057	.322	.256	.336
Texaco	4	.382	.088	.337	—	.430	.452	.326	.053	.357	.266	.337
Phillips	5	.325	.134	.375	.430	—	.445	.484	.170	.432	.325	.281
Mobil	6	.289	.161	.343	.452	.445	—	.358	.119	.454	.177	.322
D-X	7	.262	.130	.340	.326	.484	.358	—	.110	.393	.300	.230
Owens	8	.108	.640	.057	.053	.170	.119	.110	—	.349	.301	.180
Skelly	9	.368	.184	.322	.357	.432	.454	.393	.349	—	.238	.307
Clark	10	.178	.360	.256	.266	.325	.177	.300	.301	.238	—	.208
Gulf	11	.404	.200	.336	.337	.281	.322	.230	.180	.307	.208	—

* Independent brands. All others are majors.

Reprinted from *Journal of Marketing Research*, published by the American Marketing Association. Joseph M. Kamen, "Quick Clustering," *Journal of Marketing Research*, VII, July 1970, pp. 199–204. Reprinted by permission of the publisher and author.

Principal components analysis was applied to the correlation matrix after the transformation defined by equation 5 was performed. The first five components (weighted by $\sqrt{\lambda_i}$) are presented in Table 2. They provide the coordinates for the first five dimensions in the spatial representation of the eleven objects. Also presented is the percent of total (squared) interpoint distance that is contained in each dimension. The first two dimensions, which are plotted in Figure 2, contain 37 percent of the interpoint distance infor-

Table 2.   Output of Principal Components Analysis

Brand	Components				
	1	2	3	4	5
Standard	−.33	.44	.04	.43	−.21
Martin	.76	.05	.02	−.18	.18
Shell	−.24	.06	.32	.10	.62
Texaco	−.35	.09	.05	−.41	−.29
Phillips	−.24	−.35	−.04	.01	−.09
Mobil	−.26	−.10	−.36	−.40	.15
D-X	−.20	−.48	.05	.20	.03
Owens	:74	.10	−.25	.13	−.05
Skelly	−.07	−.07	−.47	.25	−.05
Clark	.29	−.24	.55	−.03	−.31
Gulf	−.12	.55	.10	−.17	−.01
Eigenvalue	1.68	.95	.83	.71	.67
Percent of variation	23	14	11	10	10
Cumulative percent of variation	23	37	48	59	68

mation. All five dimensions together contain 68 percent. In many problems, there will be much more variation absorbed by the first few dimensions. However, even with such a diffused example, it will be worthwhile to proceed. The author has obtained sets of clusters from a 43 by 43 matrix, in which only 23 percent of the variation was contained in the first four components, which were consistent with those obtained from a formal cluster program.

From Figure 2, it seems clear that Owens and Martin belong in the same cluster. The balance of the figure is less obvious, but the following clusters seem plausible:

1. Owens-Martin
2. Phillips–D-X
3. Clark
4. Texaco–Mobil–Skelly–Shell
5. Standard–Gulf

If a high percent of the variation (ideally, 80 to 90 percent) were contained in the first two components or dimensions, the analysis would be complete.

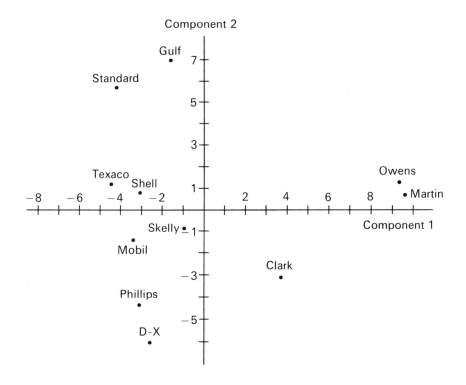

Figure 2. Components 1 and 2

However, in this example, such is not the case.

To pursue the analysis further, components 3 and 4 are plotted in Figure 3. Of course, Figures 2 and 3 are not comparable with a four-dimensional graph, and thus the actual "quantity of information" presented is something less than 58 percent. However, this approach does permit one to obtain considerable information on the effect of higher dimensions.

Figure 3 indicates that the structure is not really very well defined and that an unambiguous set of clusters does not exist. This observation, it should be noted, is not insignificant. Often an output which lists several clusters fails to convey this type of conclusion to those not intimate with the program. With the above qualification several judgments emerge. The Owens-Martin pair are still close together (as they are in dimension 5 recorded in Table 2). The same can be said for the Phillips–D-X pair. Clark again appears by itself and should probably form its own cluster.

The Texaco-Mobil-Skelly-Shell cluster does not re-emerge in Figure 3. In particular, Shell seems far from the others, especially when dimension 5, where the Shell coordinate is .62, is considered. Texaco and Mobil are still close together, but Skelly is also apart from these two brands. It appears that Skelly is as close to Phillips–D-X as it is to Texaco-Mobil.

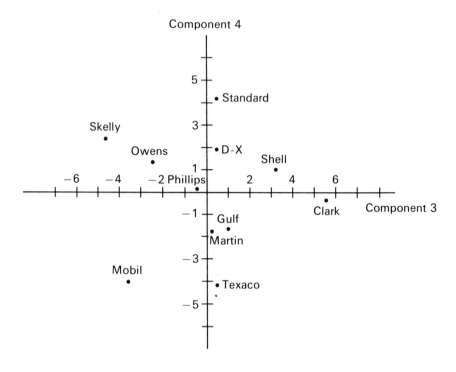

Figure 3. Components 3 and 4

Standard and Gulf are separated along dimension 4. Gulf could be placed nearly as well with the Texaco-Mobil group as with Standard. The following cluster set seems compatible with the above analysis:

1. Owens-Martin
2. Philips–D-X–(Skelly)
3. Clark
4. Texaco-Mobil (Skelly)(Gulf)
5. Shell
6. Standard (Gulf)

This analysis differs from the quick clustering conclusion in that there are six clusters instead of four and in that two objects are considered to have attachments to two clusters. More important, it provides a different and more intuitive feel for the market structure.[3]

The analysis could continue. We could present the data differently by using a three-dimensional portrayal or by plotting the objects on a space with dimensions 1 and 3 or with dimensions 2 and 4. Dimensions 5 and 6 could be introduced more formally. It would be undoubtedly possible to improve the heuristic itself. However, one reason for visual clustering (as opposed to using a formal clustering program) is to economize on the time and money of the analyst. One does not want to sacrifice this advantage without a worthwhile compensating gain.

Conclusion

There is great heterogeneity in problem situations and in the background of researchers. With this in mind it seems reasonable to suggest alternatives or complements to formal cluster programs. Visual clustering is presented in this spirit. It should provide a compromise in sophistication and cost between cluster programs and Kamen's quick clustering approach.

References

1. Frank Ronald E., and Paul E. Green. "Numerical Taxonomy in Marketing Analysis: A Review Article," *Journal of Marketing Research*, 5 (February 1968), 83–98.
2. Frost, W. A. K. "The Development of a Technique for TV Programme Assessment," *Journal of the Market Research Society*, 11 (January 1969), 25–44.
3. Gower, J. C. "Some Distance Properties of Latent Root and Vector Methods Used in Multivariate Analysis," *Biometrika*, 53 (1966), 325–337.
4. Green, Paul E., and Frank J. Carmone. "Multidimensional Scaling: An Introduction and Comparison of Nonmetric Unfolding Techniques," *Journal of Marketing Research*, 6 (August 1969), 330–341.
5. Green, Paul E., Ronald E. Frank, and Patrick J. Robinson. "Cluster Analysis in Test Market Selection," *Management Science*, 13 (April 1967), 387–400.
6. Inglis, Jim, and Douglas Johnson. "Some Observations on, and Developments in, the Analysis of Multivariate Survey Data," *Journal of the Market Research Society*, 12 (April 1970), 75–98.

---

[3] In correspondence with the author, Professor Kamen made the following comment upon this analysis: "I believe that your conclusion is fully justified by your analysis. The method you presented does make sense and overcomes a weakness in the method I presented. For example, Clark, which markets a premium grade only at a price between Majors and conventional Independents, is really in a class by itself, but quick clustering doesn't adequately take this matter into account. In Rockford, we know from other studies that Skelly is psychologically divided as you indicate, that Shell does possess uniqueness, and that Gulf, while most closely linked to Standard, also is related to brands in the two clusters you indicated."

7. Joyce, T., and C. Channon. "Classifying Market Survey Respondents," *Applied Statistics*, 15 (November 1966), 191–215.

8. Kamen, Joseph M. "Quick Clustering," *Journal of Marketing Research*, 7 (May 1970), 199–204.

9. Morrison, Donald G. "Measurement Problems in Cluster Analysis," *Management Science*, 13 (August 1967), B775–780.

10. Myers, John G., and Francesco M. Nicosia. "On the Study of Consumer Typologies," *Journal of Marketing Research*, 5 (May 1968), 182–193.

11. Neidell, Lester A. "The Use of Nonmetric Multidimensional Scaling in Marketing Analysis," *Journal of Marketing*, 33 (October 1969), 37–43.

12. Sokal, R. R., and P. H. Sneath. *Principles of Numerical Taxonomy*. San Francisco: W. H. Freeman and Company, 1963.

30

W. A. K. Frost: The Development of a Technique for TV Programme Assessment

Introduction and Background

In the past, the information concerning audience reaction that has been available to television programme planners in the independent companies has been largely limited to viewing figures. Such behavioural data is, of course, of vital importance and does contribute to major planning decisions, but it also gives rise to a host of questions concerning the reasons underlying a particular programme's success or failure in attracting an audience.

From time to time sporadic "diagnostic" research has been carried out but this has usually been qualitative and the bulk of it remains unpublished.

The Independent Television Authority, conscious of its obligations under the 1964 Television Act, asked us to consider the feasibility of systematically researching the television audience's attitudinal reactions to the whole spectrum of television programmes on an individual programme basis.

In doing so we were concerned with two broad problem area, the first of which involved the mechanics of data collection, i.e. panel recruitment, control and maintenance, whilst the second comprised questionnaire design and data processing/analysis. Whilst the two problems are not entirely unrelated it is the second area with which this paper is primarily concerned.

Abridged from W. A. K. Frost, "The Development of a Technique for TV Programme Assessment," *Journal of the Market Research Society*, Vol. XI, January 1969, pp. 25–44. Reprinted by permission.

Early Considerations and Rationale

It was decided that some attempt should be made to categorise the various TV programmes in terms of a viewer-based classificatory system and thence to develop specific attitude measuring instruments for each programme category.

A number of alternative methods of arriving at a programme classification were considered and it was decided to attempt to employ a combination of semantic differential and cluster analysis. This lacked some of the disadvantages of alternative techniques and as it was intended to construct specific semantic differentials for any programme types which we might identify there appeared to be a clear advantage in having the information that a generalized semantic differential would yield.

An overall research concept was conceived which involved:

Stage 1. The construction of a semantic differential which would be generally appropriate to all TV programmes.

Stage 2. The use of this semantic differential to collect attitude ratings (programme profiles) of all TV programmes.

Stage 3. The use of cluster analysis to group the obtained programme profiles into categories of "similar" programmes.

Stage 4. The construction of specific semantic differentials—one for each programme type revealed by the cluster analysis.

Stage 5. The use of the specific semantic differentials to obtain programme profiles.

The Research Programme

Stage 1—The Development of the General Semantic Differential

Initially a series of 20 Repertory Grid interviews were carried out and whilst it is not intended to dwell at length on the details of the basic technique or the reasons for using it as a precursor to the construction of a semantic differential as these have been described elsewhere, a few points of rationale and procedure may be worth emphasising.

1. The stimuli employed comprised virtually the whole of the then current ITV and BBC weekly schedules—61 programmes in all. These were, of course, randomly rotated between respondents, with each interview involving 18 programmes.

2. As the scales obtained from these interviews were to be factor analysed it was important that they be as linear as possible, i.e. that the universe of programmes be Normally distributed along them. To this end, and so as to ensure that each of the derived constructs was generally relevant to all TV programmes, respondents were required to divide the programmes into equal

groups at the sorting stages. If at these times, respondents found themselves unable to sort into equal groups, they were required to adjust the extremity of the adjectival phrases until equal sorting was possible.

3. After analysis the interviews yielded 58 constructs which were transposed into seven-point semantic differential scales which were felt to be:

    a.   Exhaustive.
    b.   Relevant to all TV programmes.
    c.   Meaningful to the majority of viewers.

The list of scales involved items such as those shown below.

Enjoyable ⬭ ⬭ ⬭ ⬭ ⬭ ⬭ ⬭ Unenjoyable

Simple ⬭ ⬭ ⬭ ⬭ ⬭ ⬭ ⬭ Lavish

Fictional ⬭ ⬭ ⬭ ⬭ ⬭ ⬭ ⬭ Factual

etc.

Next, a random sample of approximately 750 television viewers were asked to provide ratings via the 58 scales of two programmes each. The 61 programmes were rotated randomly between the respondents and a substitution procedure was employed so that no one was required to rate a programme with which they were unfamiliar.

In all approximately 1,500 programme ratings were obtained and this data, being found to be largely devoid of irregularities, was then subjected to a series of Principal Component Analyses, the correlation-coefficients being computed across all respondents and all programmes.

This analysis indicated the presence of nine factors and these are summarised in Table 1.

It should be noted that whilst names have been attached to these factors, this has been done simply for ease of reference and that the proper interpretation of a factor is to be found amongst the individual attitude scales which have substantial loadings upon it. Thus, for example, Factor 2 called "information" in fact describes a dimension of viewer differentiation which has at one end programmes which tend to have much scientific interest, which make the viewer think and which convey educational information and, which has at the other end programmes which contain little scientific interest which encourage the viewer to relax, being of a less informative and generally more entertaining type.

The nine factors which the analysis yielded were regarded as the basic dimensions of viewer discrimination which are generally appropriate to all TV programmes and to the majority of TV viewers. As such, they comprise generally valid bases for comparison between any TV programmes.

Table 1.   Nine General Factors Relating to All TV Programmes

Factor loading

Factor 1 " General Evaluation "

0.85	Enjoyable	Unenjoyable
0.84	Pleasing	Irritating
0.83	Absorbing	Boring
0.79	Grips the attention	Loses the attention
0.69	Well presented	Poorly presented
0.67	Fast	Slow

Factor 2 " Information "

0.89	Little scientific interest	Much scientific interest
0.80	Makes the viewer relax	Makes the viewer think
0.79	Has little information	Has much information
0.75	Pure entertainment	Has educational value
0.73	Has no effect on people	Influences people
0.63	Superficial	Deep/penetrating

Factor 3 " Romance "

0.77	Less of a woman's programme	More of a woman's programme
0.74	More of a man's programme	Less of a man's programme
0.44	Unromantic	Romantic
0.43	Tough	Tender

Factor 4 " Violence "

0.80	Involves crime	Has little to do with crime
0.68	American type	British type
0.54	Fictional	Factual
0.44	Unbelievable	Believable

Factor 5 " Conventionality "

0.73	Unconventional	Conventional
0.54	Informal	Formal
0.52	Unique type of programme	Average type of programme
0.44	Liked by youger people/teenagers	Liked by older people

Factor 6 " Scale of production "

0.69	Lavish	Simple
0.64	Big production	Small production
0.46	Spectacular	Unspectacular
0.44	Much artistic interest	Little artistic interest

Factor 7 " Noise/activity "

0.83	Noisy	Quiet
0.83	Loud	Soft
0.50	Tough	Tender
0.45	Violent	Gentle

Factor 8 " Acceptability "

0.85	Suitable for children	Unsuitable for children
0.44	Much scientific interest	Little scientific interest
0.43	Unsuitable for adults	Suitable for adults
0.38	Family entertainment	Specialist viewing

Factor 9 " Humour "

0.68	Unamusing	Funny
0.65	Little or no humour	Much humorous content
0.55	Serious	Lighthearted
0.44	Does not depend on the personality	Built around the personality

Stage 2—General Programme Profiles

Having identified the nine factors used by viewers to discriminate, in a general way, between TV programmes it was possible to compute programme attitude ratings for all of the 61 programmes covered in the survey on each of the nine factors.

There is not room in this paper to show all the results, but an extract of the data is shown in Figure 1.

In Figure 1 the "information" ratings of 14 of the 61 programmes are shown. These are not specially selected cases, but are very typical results and serve to illustrate and confirm our original interpretation of this factor as being a dimension which differentiated primarily between educational programmes and entertainment programmes. Similar results were, in fact, obtained for the other eight factors.

The general semantic differential was therefore producing meaningful results at least. As a check on its potential reliability and ability to discriminate, the differences between the mean programme ratings were tested for statistical significance and it was found that, although the sample sizes for each programme averaged in the region of 25 viewers, factors were discriminating at very satisfactory levels of statistical significance. In fact, all factors discriminated in excess of the 5% level and the majority in excess of the 1% level.

Stage 3—The Establishment of a Programme Typology by Cluster Analysis

An alternative presentation of the programme ratings to that given in Figure 1 is to examine the programme profiles, i.e., to examine the ratings obtained by a programme on all nine factors simultaneously. Some programme profiles are shown in Figure 2.

It will be seen that the profiles given in Figure 2 appear to fall into two distinct groups in which any of the members of one group are more "similar" to each other than they are to members of the other group. This pattern illustrates the type of result which we were seeking in undertaking a cluster analysis operation.

The programme clusters shown in Figure 2 were derived, along with 18 others, by means of a fairly complex computer analysis which operates on the following broad lines:

1. The frame of reference for the analysis is an n-dimensional hyperspace; in this case the hyperspace had 9 dimensions which were the 9 factors in terms of which the programme profiles were computed.

2. The computer, on being supplied with the 61 programme profiles, each of which may be represented by a point in the hyperspace, generated 20 random points within the hyperspace and allocated each programme to the nearest random point. This produced an initial set of 20 clusters of programmes.

3. Next the original random points were abandoned and the real "centres of gravity" of each of the 20 clusters were computed. Each point was then

Factor 2 'Information'

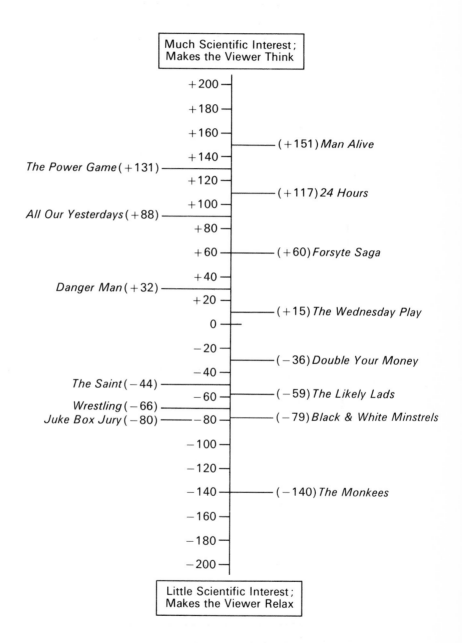

Figure 1. Programme Rating

considered in turn to see if moving the point from its original cluster to its next nearest cluster would effect a reduction in the total residual sum of squares. A point to be borne in mind here is that such a re-allocation will affect the centres of gravity of both the clusters concerned.

4. The analysis proceeded in this way, re-computing the locations of the cluster centres and re-allocating programmes to the closest one, until no

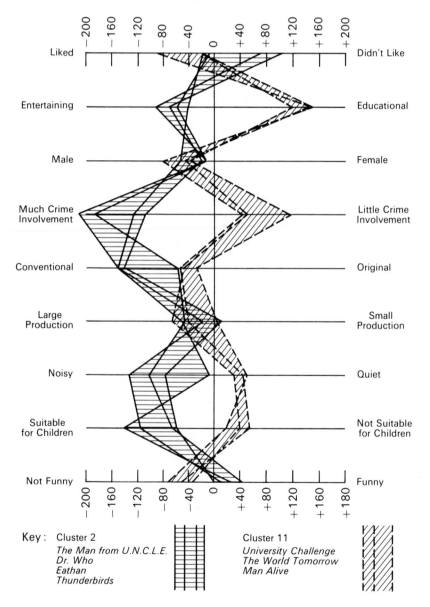

Figure 2. Profiles of Two Clusters from the 20 Cluster Level

further improvements in the clustering were obtained at which time the initial analysis was considered complete.[1]

Following the initial cluster analysis described above, further solutions were obtained by progressively "compressing" the data through 19, 18, 17 clusters and so on down to 2 clusters. At each level of clustering optimisation was achieved iteratively by re-computing cluster centres and re-allocating programmes.

The reason for requiring a range of alternative solutions from which to choose is that there is no very satisfactory way of deciding how many "real" types exist within a particular population. In fact it is important to note that we were not looking for a single "correct" answer. In a sense all of the alternatives which were produced may well have been equally correct. What was required was the identification of a reasonably small number of relatively homogeneous programme types so that any particular programme could be assessed in terms of the ways in which its ratings compared with those of similar programmes.

In examining the alternative solutions therefore and the selection of one, the main criteria employed were those of interpretability, practicality and general expediency. Of course, it was also possible to examine, in a statistical way, the homogeneity of the programme groups at various levels of clustering and this information was included in our deliberations, but it would be misleading to suggest that the typology with which we eventually proceeded with has an absolute basis in reality. In fact, the typology simply represents a convenient way of thinking about television programmes and a useful system for providing bench marks. In addition, of course, it lays the foundations for developing specialised semantic differentials which have two important advantages over a completely general semantic differential in that they cover a greater number of programme attributes and they permit more sensitive measurements.

As was intended the 20 cluster solution provided some interesting insights into the reasons underlying broader programme typologies. It may, therefore, be useful to examine the results of the 20 cluster analyses in some detail before moving on to consider the solution which was eventually adopted.

The 20 clusters that emerged are shown in Table 2. Some of the groupings that occurred are along lines that might have been anticipated. *Cluster No. 4*, for instance, groups the romantic women's programmes together. *Cluster No. 5* groups the pop music programmes together and so on. Some of the groups seem, however, particularly strange. *Cluster No. 1*, for instance, which groups *Wrestling* and *Till Death Us Do Part* seems, at first sight, to represent a curious proximity. The factors on which this clustering largely takes place are factors 6, 7, and 9. Both *Wrestling* and *Till Death Us Do Part* are seen as

---

[1] *Note:* It should be emphasized that provided there is a sufficient degree of clustering within the data, then the precise location of the original 20 random points does not affect the final outcome of the analysis.

Table 2. The 61 TV Programmes Divided into 20 Clusters

Cluster one *Wrestling* *Till Death Us Do Part*	Cluster two *The Man from UNCLE* *Dr Who* *Batman* *Thunderbirds*
Cluster three *The Walrus & the Carpenter* *On the Braden Beat* *The Frost Programme* *Points of View* *Late Night Line Up*	Cluster four *The Sunday Film* *Dr Kildare* *Peyton Place* *The Love Affair*
Cluster five *Top of the Pops* *Juke Box Jury* *The Monkees*	Cluster six *Bewitched*
Cluster seven *Emergency Ward 10* *The Wednesday Play* *Dr Findlay's Casebook* *The Newcomers*	Cluster eight *Motor Racing*
Cluster nine *World of Sport* *Sportsview* *Football*	Cluster ten *Horse Racing* *Boxing*
Cluster eleven *University Challenge* *The World Tomorrow* *Man Alive*	Cluster twelve *The Levin Interview* *The Epilogue* *The Sky at Night* *Cricket*
Cluster thirteen *The London Palladium Show* *The Morecambe & Wise Show* *The Andy Stewart Show* *The Black and White Minstrel Show* *Crackerjack*	Cluster fourteen *Coronation Street*
Cluster fifteen *Blue Peter*	Cluster sixteen *Take Your Pick* *Double Your Money* *The Likely Lads* *The Eamonn Andrews Show*
Cluster seventeen *Perry Mason* *The Saint* *Danger Man* *The Virginian*	Cluster eighteen *This Week* *All Our Yesterdays* *The News* *24 Hours* *Panorama*
Cluster nineteen *No Hiding Place* *Z Cars* *Seaway*	Cluster twenty *The Power Game* *The Forsyte Saga*

"simple," "noisy" and "funny" and both are also seen as having little scientific interest!

In *Cluster No. 2* which contains the *Man from UNCLE, Dr Who, Batman* and *Thunderbirds*, a number of exciting children's programmes seem to be grouped together. *Man from UNCLE* which is screened comparatively late in the evening would seem to be an exception to this rule; it is, however, the most typical member of the cluster and is actually seen as more suitable for children than is *Dr Who*.

Cluster No. 3 contains some serious programmes which more than anything are seen as suitable for men and also funny. The humour seems to be of a more subtle kind because the programmes are also regarded as being quiet and soft.

Cluster No. 6 contains only one programme, *Bewitched*. This is an example of a programme with extreme scores on a number of factors. It is seen as highly uninformative, highly American, unconventional, funny and suitable for children. A characteristic of this type of programme profile is that it will only cluster with other programmes at a later stage of the analysis.

Cluster No. 7 is another example of the programmes that are suitable for women. This factor seems to be a particularly important one in discriminating between programmes.

Having examined the 20 cluster solution and all the other levels of clustering the 6 cluster solution was chosen for use in the subsequent stages of the research.

In Table 3 (a)–(f) are given the identity of the programmes in each cluster together with two measurements which assist in the interpretation of the clusters. These are:

1. Distance of programme from the cluster centre.
2. Distance of programme from the centre of the next closest cluster.

In examining these tables it should be borne in mind that the closer a programme is to its cluster centre, the more typical it is of that cluster. Also programmes which are only marginally nearer to their "own" cluster than to the next cluster should really be regarded as fringe items and their current classification treated with some reserve.

Table 3 (a). The Programmes Comprising Cluster 1 at the 6 Cluster Level

Name of Programme	Distance from Centre of Own Cluster	Distance from Centre of Next Nearest Cluster
Likely Lads	0.791	2.079
Take Your Pick	0.824	1.789
Double Your Money	0.844	1.738
Newcomers	1.083	1.349
Andy Stewart Show	1.089	1.874
Eamonn Andrews Show	1.139	1.357
The Morecambe & Wise Show	1.150	2.233
London Palladium Show	1.199	2.134
Crackerjack	1.482	2.375
The Walrus & the Carpenter	1.484	2.078
Points of View	1.539	1.992
Juke Box Jury	1.672	2.121
The Black and White Minstrel Show	1.752	2.286
Coronation Street	2.005	2.428
Till Death Us Do Part	2.064	2.483
Blue Peter	2.072	2.755

The particular aspects which characterise programmes within Cluster 1 (Table 3a) and therefore the cluster as a whole, are those concerned with relaxation and entertainment (rather than being informative), little or no crime content, suitability for children and general family viewing and, finally, a fairly strong element of humour and light-heartedness. For easy reference, it would be useful to apply a composite label to each cluster, and Cluster 1 can be most conveniently labelled "Family entertainment programmes."

The peculiar characteristics of Cluster 2 (Table 3b) are that programmes within it are seen as being particularly uninformative, highly unconventional/informal, noisy and suitable for children. We feel that the most suitable general label to apply to this cluster would be "pop programmes."

Table 3 (b).   The Programmes Comprising Cluster 2 at the 6 Cluster Level

Name of Programme	Distance from Centre of Own Cluster	Distance from Centre of Next Nearest Cluster
The Monkees	1.140	2.580
Dr Who	1.156	2.446
The Man from UNCLE	1.249	2.027
Thunderbirds	1.282	2.347
Batman	1.359	3.158
Top of the Pops	1.507	1.826
Bewitched	1.935	2.509

Cluster 3 (Table 3c) is characterised by a "violence" content (as indeed was Cluster 2), but it differs markedly from our so-called "pop programmes" in being much more suitable for adult viewing. Cluster 3 may therefore best be referred to as the "Adult crime/violence" cluster.

Table 3 (c).   The Programmes Comprising Cluster 3 at the 6 Cluster Level

Name of Programme	Distance from Centre of Own Cluster	Distance from Centre of Next Nearest Cluster
Seaway	0.693	1.926
Danger Man	0.882	2.094
Z Cars	0.946	1.408
The Virginian	0.999	1.876
No Hiding Place	1.133	1.587
Perry Mason	1.215	1.843
The Saint	1.352	1.811
Wrestling	1.436	1.772
The Frost Report	1.796	1.977

Table 3 (d).   The Programmes Comprising Cluster 4 at the 6 Cluster Level

Name of Programme	Distance from Centre of Own Cluster	Distance from Centre of Next Nearest Cluster
The Sunday Film	0.869	1.448
Emergency Ward 10	0.965	1.531
Love Affair	0.993	1.938
The Wednesday Play	0.996	1.297
Dr Kildare	1.069	2.166
Dr Finlay's Casebook	1.315	1.740
Peyton Place	1.417	2.512
The Forsyte Saga	1.933	2.474

Table 3 (e).   The Programmes Comprising Cluster 5 at the 6 Cluster Level

Name of Programme	Distance from Centre of Own Cluster	Distance from Centre of Next Nearest Cluster
24 Hours	0.622	1.591
This Week	0.668	1.507
World Tomorrow	0.796	2.036
Late Night Line Up	0.836	1.585
All Our Yesterdays	0.957	1.255
Panorama	0.994	1.641
University Challenge	1.151	1.762
The Sky at Night	1.195	2.717
On the Braden Beat	1.355	1.511
Man Alive	1.376	2.196
The Levin Interview	1.696	2.894
Cricket	1.776	2 436
The Power Game	1.890	2.842
The Epilogue	1.949	2.492

Table 3 (f).   The Programmes Comprising Cluster 6 at the 6 Cluster Level

Name of Programme	Distance from Centre of Own Cluster	Distance from Centre of Next Nearest Cluster
World of Sport	0.723	2.129
Football	0.753	1.962
Sportsview	0.973	2.009
Horse Racing	1.114	2.203
Motor Racing	1.174	1.901
Boxing	1.393	2.246
News	1.500	1.680

Apart from consisting of "quiet" programmes, Cluster 4 (Table 3d) is particularly characterised by its feminine appeal and clearly justifies the title of "Women's romance" programmes.

The particular characteristics common to programmes in Cluster 5 (Table 3e) are that they are seen as being highly informative, unromantic and more suitable for men, very quiet and very much for adult viewing. It therefore seems reasonable to label this the "Intellectual" cluster of programmes.

Two programmes are conspicuous by their absence from Cluster 6 (Table 3f), *Cricket* and *Wrestling*. Subjectively, one might easily have included them under a general "sports" heading. In *viewers'* terms, however, watching cricket is more of an intellectual exercise (hence its inclusion in Cluster 5), whilst *Wrestling*, quite unlike the sports programmes, is considered to have a high humorous content as well as undertones of crime, violence and Americanism and, indeed an element of fiction and unbelievability. This places *Wrestling* firmly in Cluster 3.

In order to summarize the characteristics of the six programme clusters, mean profiles for each cluster are given in Figure 3. These profiles are very different from one another and this observation together with a statistical examination of the data supports the view that each of the clusters is dramatically more homogeneous than the parent population of all TV programmes.

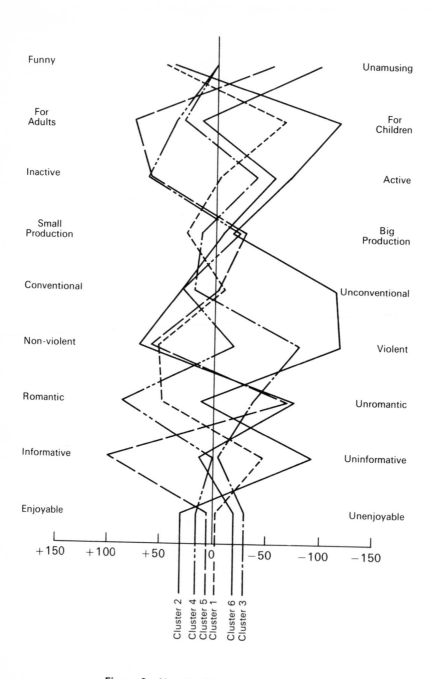

Figure 3. Mean Profiles for Each Cluster at the 6 Cluster Level

Stage 4—The Development of Specific Semantic Differentials

Having established a working programme typology it was necessary to examine each of the programme types in order to see whether there was any truth in our earlier belief that different programme types would be construed by viewers in different attitudinal frameworks and would, therefore, require measurements along different dimensions.

As a first check six separate factor analyses were carried out on the data from each of the six clusters. The factor structures which emerged were quite different and whilst some of the factors emerged relatively unchanged in other cases factors disappeared altogether and totally new factors emerged. Some of the changes were, of course, due to changes in the properties of the scales which, having been derived for the whole universe of programmes, had distributions which were severely skewed when they were applied to a single programme cluster. Despite this effect, however, there was clear evidence that the actual meanings of many of the scales were changing from context to context.

At this point the problem of developing six specific semantic differential batteries had to be faced and, as the whole project was essentially a pilot operation, it was not possible to carry out quite such a thorough-going preparation in all six areas.

In fact, an examination of the data already to hand, together with a few additional Repertory Grid interviews in each of the clusters, led to the somewhat subjective development of six separate batteries of semantic differentials scales.

A survey was then carried out in which each of these semantic differential batteries was used to collect approximately 350 ratings of appropriate TV programmes. The six sets of data so obtained were factor analyzed and the factor structures for the six programme types provided some interesting comparisons.

Table 4 shows the number of factors which emerged in each of the clusters.

Table 4

Cluster 1	15 Factors
Cluster 2	10 Factors
Cluster 3	12 Factors
Cluster 4	11 Factors
Cluster 5	12 Factors
Cluster 6	6 Factors

It will be seen from this result alone that viewers used more elaborate conceptual frameworks to construe some types of programme than they used for others.

Furthermore, a close inspection of the emergent factors showed that no factor was entirely appropriate for all programme types. Some factors appeared to express the same basic notion from cluster to cluster and might, therefore, be given the same general label in each case. However, the content of these factors (i.e. constituent scales and their loadings) usually changed quite markedly from one cluster to another. Even the General Evaluative factor which would have been expected, on theoretical grounds, to be more or less the same for all programme types showed some degree of inconsistency for, although some words such as "enjoyable" tended to load highly on the evaluative factors in all the clusters, in the case of the "pop" programmes the highest loading words were "trendy," "fast," and "much action," whilst in Cluster 5 which contained the more intellectual programmes the highest loading evaluative words were "lasting interest" and "absorbing."

The information in Table 5 is an attempt to represent, in summary, the results of the six factor analyses. As has been already mentioned no single factor was common in a precise way to all programme clusters. However, it

Table 5. The Distribution of Various Factors throughout the 6 Programme Clusters

	Cluster 1 Family enter- tainment	Cluster 2 Pop	Cluster 3 Adult Crime/ Violence	Cluster 4 Women's Romance	Cluster 5 Intellectual	Cluster 6 Sports
"Evaluation"	•	•	•	•	•	•
"Age appropriateness"	•	•	•	•	•	—
"Noise" ⎱ "Activity" "Violence" ⎰	•	{ • / • }	•	—	•	•
"Sex appropriateness"	•	—	•	•	•	—
"Suitability for children"	•	—	•	•	•	—
"Reality/credibility"	•	•	•	—	•	—
"Formality"	•	—	•	•	•	—
"Profundity" ⎱ "Information" ⎰ "Heaviness"	{ • / • }	—	•	•	•	—
"Dependence on a personality"/ ("Individualism")	•	—	•	•	•	—
"Scale of production"	•	•	—	—	•	—
"Conventionality"	•	—	—	•	•	—
"Addictiveness"	•	•	—	—	—	•
"Romance"	—	•	—	•	—	—
"Humour"	—	—	•	•	—	—
"Intelligibility"	—	•	•	—	—	—
"Star content"	—	—	•	•	—	—
"Impartiality"	—	—	—	—	•	—
"Importance of event"	—	—	—	—	—	•
"Presentation/commentary"	—	—	—	—	—	•
"Visibility"	—	—	—	—	—	•

• Indicates that a factor is operative in the cluster

was possible in a subjective way, to recognize certain basic notions which were frequently common to several of the clusters. The table shows that approximately 23 such basic notions were identified in all, and in addition it gives the distribution of these notions throughout the six programme clusters.

Stage 5—The Specific Semantic Differentials in Use

The final state of the pilot consisted of a panel operation extending over five weekly reporting periods. During this time panelists were required to rate the television programmes which they had seen on appropriate sets of semantic scales. In those cases where respondents were giving ratings of programmes which had already been classified they were directed to employ the sets of scales which were specifically relevant to the cluster of programmes concerned. In some cases, however, respondents had been exposed to television programmes which were not being screened when the programme typology was established, and in these cases they were instructed to use an abbreviated set of the general (all programmes) semantic differential, the intention being to attempt to allocate new programmes to clusters within the established typology if possible.

In examining the data obtained from the pilot panel operation we were particularly concerned with the following three questions:

1. Were the specific semantic differentials sufficiently sensitive given the sample sizes obtained?
2. To what extent was it possible to allocate new programmes to categories within the existing typology?
3. Were the results obtained meaningful to the people who were required to use them, that is to say, did the findings contribute to their understanding of viewers behavioral reactions towards the programmes?

1. The Sensitivity of the Instrument   In all, the semantic differentials were extremely successful in differentiating between programmes. Not only did they succeed in distinguishing between programmes from the same cluster but, in many cases, significant discrimination was obtained between consecutive programmes of the same series.

2. Allocating New Programmes to the Existing Typology   In all 26 new programmes were studied and of these 21 were easy to classify within the existing programme categories. For the five remaining programmes it was possible to see in each case precisely why they were difficult to classify. This result suggests that because of the continual development of new programmes and new programme concepts it is unlikely that a completely permanent and stable typology can be arrived at.

On the other hand a classificatory system which caters for the majority of programmes is likely to prove viable for a useful period of time, i.e., one or two years. It seems probable, therefore, that such a system may be used provided it is up-dated at regular intervals.

3. The Meaningfulness of the Results   The detailed results obtained have been considered in the light of programme content and whilst in many cases they appear to have been somewhat predictable, in others they do appear to have been genuinely informative.

It is, of course, extremely difficult to measure success in this area but an encouraging number of favorable reactions have been received from people within the programme companies and the Independent Television Authority.

In summary, therefore, we would conclude that the pilot panel operation has been successful and has confirmed the viability of the basic research concept. It must, however, be emphasised that the study, although fairly elaborate, was in fact only a pilot and consequently a great many questions of detail remain unanswered and much work has yet to be done.

Some Useful References

Bannister, D. (1962) "Personal construct theory: a summary and experimental paradigm." *Acta Psychol.* XX, 2.

——— (1966) *A new theory of personality—New horizons in psychology.* Penguin Books Ltd.

Emmett, B. P. (1968) "The exploration of inter-relationships in survey data," *J. Market Research Soc.*, 10, pp. 65–77.

Frost, W. A. K. and Braine, R. L. (1967) "The application of the repertory grid technique to problems in market research," *J. Market Research Soc.*, 9, pp. 161–175.

Gatty, R. (1965) *Factor analysis for market research—usefulness and limitations.* (Paper to American Marketing Association Marketing Research Group, New York City.)

——— (1966) "Multivariate analysis for marketing research: an evaluation." *Appl. Statist.*, XV, 3.

——— and Allais, C. (1961) *The semantic differential applied to image research.* New Brunswick, N. J.: Rutgers University, Technical A.E. No. 5.

——— and Heim, R. (1961) *The application of factor analysis to marketing research.* New Brunswick, N. J.: Rutgers University, Technical A.E. No. 2.

Harman, H. (1960) *Modern factor analysis.* Chicago University Press.

Joyce, T. and Channon, C. (1966) Classifying market survey respondents, *Appl. Statist.*, XV, 3.

Kelly, G. A. *Psychology of personal constructs.* Volumes I and II. New York: Norton.

Kendall, M. G. (1957) *A course in multivariate analysis.* New York: Hafner.

Osgood, C. E., Suci, G. J., and Tannenbaum, P. H. (1957) *The measurement of meaning.* University of Illinois Press.

References

Banks, Seymour. *Experimentation in Marketing.* New York: McGraw-Hill Book Company, 1965.

Campbell, Donald T., and Julian C. Stanley. *Experimental and Quasi-experimental Designs for Research.* Chicago: Rand McNally & Company, 1963.

Green, Paul E., and Donald, S. Tull. *Research for Marketing Decisions, Second Edition.* Englewood Cliffs, N.J.: Prentice-Hall, Inc., 1970.

Kendall, M. G. *A Course in Multivariate Analysis.* New York: Hafner Publishing Company, 1961.

Nunnally, Jum C. *Psychometric Theory.* New York: McGraw-Hill Book Company, Inc., 1967.

Sokal, Robert R., and P. H. Sneath. *Principles of Numerical Taxonomy.* San Francisco: W. N. Freeman and Company, 1963.

Wonnacott, Ronald J., and Thomas H. Wonnacott. *Econometrics.* New York: John Wiley & Sons, Inc., 1970.

Wonnacott, Thomas H., and Ronald J. Wonnacott. *Introductory Statistics.* New York: John Wiley & Sons, Inc., 1969.

Advanced

Anderson, T. W. *Introduction to Multivariate Statistical Analysis.* New York: John Wiley & Sons, Inc., 1958.

Christ, Carl F. *Econometric Models and Methods.* New York: John Wiley & Sons, Inc., 1966.

Harmon, Harry H. *Modern Factor Analysis, Second Edition.* Chicago: University of Chicago Press, 1967.

Johnston, J. *Econometric Methods.* New York: McGraw-Hill Book Company, Inc., 1963.

Morrison, Donald F. *Multivariate Statistical Methods.* New York: McGraw-Hill Book Company, Inc., 1967.

Scheffe, H. *The Analysis of Variance.* New York: John Wiley & Sons, Inc., 1959.

Seal, Hilary. *Multivariate Statistical Analysis for Biologists.* London: Methuen and Company, 1964.

INDEX

Aaker, D. A., 101–114, 321–334
Attribute data, 261
Attribute space (*see* Perceptual map), 275, 282
Attributes table, 12
Autocorrelation (serial correlation), 4, 28, 36, 52–53, 72, 110
  autocorrelation coefficient, 36–38
  parameter estimate, effect on, 4, 28
  serial correlation term, 52–53
  test for (Durbin-Watson statistic), 36–38, 110

Barclay, W. D., 183–188
Barnett, N. C., 282–289
Barrow, L. C., 195–204
Bass, F. M., 90–100
Beta coefficients, 115
Binary variable, 2, 4

Canonical analysis, 2, 155–173
  assumptions, 164–165
  canned programs, 165
  examples, 157–164, 166–172
  interpretation of results, 163–164, 171–172
  objectives, 156–157, 170–171
  for prediction, 163
  regression line between linear compounds, 162–163
  scatter plot of linear compounds, 161–164
  sets of canonical variates, 161
  significance test of the canonical correlation, 161, 171
Carman, J. M., viii
Carry-over effects, 4, 51–52
Clark, M. L., 251–256
Claycamp, H. J., 50–56
Clevenger, T., 251–256

Cluster analysis, 299–350
  assumptions and limitations, 314–317
  cluster profile, 337, 345–346
  different proximity measures, 303–307
  evaluation of clusters, 311–312, 341–346
  examples, 310–312, 328–333, 334–350
  examples of clustering routines, 307–308, 338–339
  hierarchical clustering, 299, 307–308, 314
  level of clustering, 299, 341–343
  limitations of specific proximity measures, 315–316
  marketing applications, 308–314
  Q factor analysis, 211, 216, 225, 243, 300, 306, 308, 316
  visual clustering, 321–334
Coefficient of multiple determination (R^2), 3–4, 37–38
Communalities, 209, 215, 224, 233
  method of estimation, 247
Confusion matrix, 115, 117, 121–123
Correction of mismatched samples, 197–201
Correlation:
  analysis, 12–15
  multiple correlation coefficient, 18–19
  partial correlation, 15–18
  partial correlation coefficient, 16–18
  simple correlation coefficient, 12–15, 22
Covariance, 13
  analysis of, 176, 195–204
    error after adjustment, 197
    example, 197–201
    limitations, 201–203
Covariance matrix, 141
Cox, K. K., 188–195
Cross-classification table, 9–11